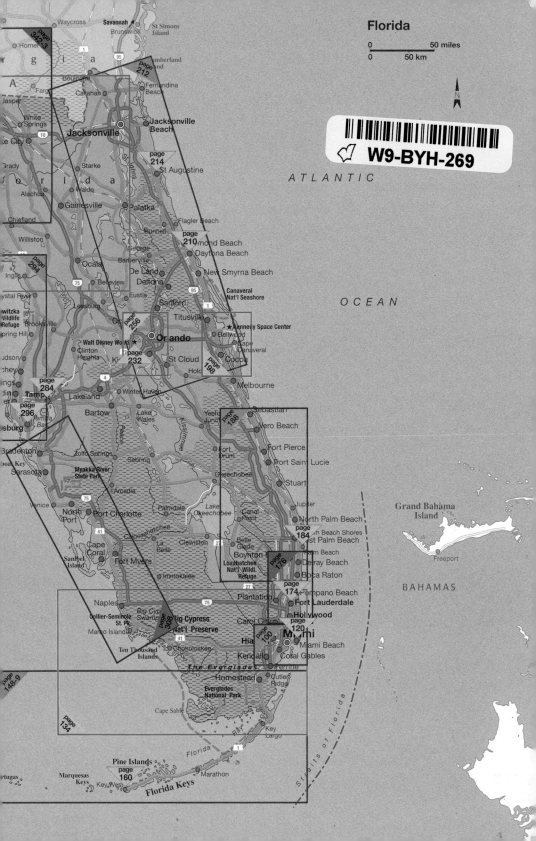

INSIGHT GUIDES

FLORIDA

APA PUBLICATIONS

Part of the Langenscheidt Publishing Group

INSIGHT GUIDE
FLORIDA

Editorial

Project Editor
Astrid deRidder
Series Manager
Rachel Lawrence
Publishing Manager
Rachel Fox
Art Director
Steven Lawrence
Senior Picture Researcher
Tom Smyth

Distribution

UK & Ireland
GeoCenter International Ltd
Meridian House, Churchill Way West
Basingstoke, Hampshire RG21 6YR
sales@geocenter.co.uk

United States
Ingram Publisher Services
1 Ingram Boulevard, PO Box 3006,
La Vergne, TN 37086-1986
customer.service@ingrampublisher
services.com

Australia
Universal Publishers
PO Box 307
St Leonards NSW 1590
sales@universalpublishers.com.au

Worldwide
**Apa Publications GmbH & Co.
Verlag KG (Singapore branch)**
7030 Ang Mo Kio Avenue 5
08-65 Northstar @ AMK
Singapore 569880
apasin@singnet.com.sg

Printing

CTPS-China

©2011 Apa Publications UK Ltd
All Rights Reserved

*First Edition 1982
Twelfth Edition 2011*

CONTACTING THE EDITORS
We would appreciate it if readers
would alert us to errors or out-
dated information by writing to:
**Insight Guides, PO Box 7910,
London SE1 1WE, England.
insight@apaguide.co.uk**

www.insightguides.com

ABOUT THIS BOOK

The first Insight Guide pioneered the use of creative full-color photography in travel guides in 1970. Since then, we have expanded our range to cater to our readers' need not only for reliable information about their chosen destination but also for a real understanding of the culture and workings of that destination. Now, when the Internet can supply inex-haustible (but not always reliable) facts, our books marry text and pictures to provide those much more elusive qualities: knowledge and discernment. A region with such a rich history and culture as Florida lends itself especially well to the approach taken by Insight Guides.

How to use this book

Insight Guide: Florida is structured to convey an understanding of the state and its people as well as to guide readers through its attractions:

♦ The **Features** section, indicated by a pink bar at the top of each page, covers the natural and cul-tural history of the region, together with illuminating essays on Florida history, culture, sports, and food, as well as an exploration of the successful theme park business.

♦ The main **Places** section, indicated by a blue bar, is a complete guide to all the sights and areas worth visiting. Places of special interest are coordi-nated by number with the maps.

♦ The **Travel Tips** listings section, with a yellow bar, provides full infor-mation on transportation, hotels, activities from culture and shopping to sports, and an A–Z section of essential practical information. An easy-to-find contents list for Travel Tips is printed on the back flap, which also serves as a bookmark.

LEFT: high-rise hotels and condos overlook the ocean at South Beach in Miami.

South Florida. Her parents still reside there, and she can't get enough of the area's beaches. Elana is a congressional political correspondent at *Greenwire* in Washington, D.C., and holds her masters' in journalism from Northwestern University. She enjoyed exploring and updating South Florida, including the bustling city of Miami and the dazzling beaches of the Keys. She also explored the Atlantic Coast, from Fort Lauderdale to Jacksonville.

Christina Tourigny used her local knowledge to update the chapters on Central Florida, including taking time to visit Walt Disney Resort and the other Orlando theme parks. She also enjoyed exploring the beaches of the Gulf Coast and the peaceful North Florida towns along the Panhandle.

This book builds on the foundations laid by writers in the previous editions, including **Nicky Leach**, whose work appears in numerous Insight Guides. Vermont-based writers **William and Kay Scheller** authored the Business of Pleasure chapter. **Joann Biondi** explored Miami and Miami Beach, while **Jason Dehart** oversaw the chapters on Tallahasee, Pensacola, and Panama City Beach. **Martha Bayne** explored Florida's northeast coast.

Most of the spectacular photography is the work of **Richard and Abraham Nowitz**, father and son, whose recent work for the Insight Guides has taken them to China, Peru, and Arizona, among other far-flung places.

Jan McCann provided a close proofread of the text, while **Helen Peters** indexed the book. The map editor was **Zoë Goodwin**.

The contributors

Nothing stands still, especially with such a fast-paced destination as the Sunshine State. For this edition of one of Insight's classic titles, the text has been thoroughly revised. We've brought together a team of expert editors, writers, and photographers who combine inside knowledge of Florida with the investigative skills of seasoned journalists to give you a true insight in the world's most popular destination.

This edition was assessed by veteran Insight Guide editor **Alyse Dar**, and commissioned and edited by **Astrid deRidder**. Together they wanted to show the many sides of Florida, from relaxing at the beach to a thrilling roller-coaster ride to an evening at the symphony.

The primary author on this fully-revised edition was **Elana Schor**, who graduated from high school in

Map Legend

— ·· —	International Boundary
— — —	State Boundary
—•—•—	National Park/Reserve
— — —	Ferry Route
⊖	Border Crossing
✈ ✈	Airport: International/Regional
🚌	Bus Station
Ⓜ	Metromover station
❶	Tourist Information
✝ ✝ ✝	Church/Ruins
✝	Monastery
∴	Archaeological Site
∩	Cave
⚊	Statue/Monument
★	Place of Interest
⚑	Beach
⛴	Lighthouse

The main places of interest in the Places section are coordinated by number with a full-color map (eg ❶), and a symbol at the top of every right-hand page tells you where to find the map.

Contents

LEFT: live oaks festooned with Spanish moss near St Augustine.

Maps

Travel Tips

THE BEST OF FLORIDA: TOP ATTRACTIONS

With 1,800 miles (2,880km) of gorgeous coast, more than 300 sunny days a year, and no fewer than nine state-of-the-art theme parks, Florida is the world's top vacation destination

△ The Conch Republic, Margaritaville, Mañanaland – call it what you like, **Key West** is always up for a party. Perched at the end of the Florida Keys, the southernmost city is a hub of colorful nonconformity where free spirits find refuge from the mainstream and the rest of us can drop in for a couple of drinks. *See page 159*

▽ Encompassing more than 1.5 million acres (607,028 hectares) of subtropical wilderness, **Everglades National Park** sustains hundreds of plant and animal species, including endangered Florida panthers and West Indian manatees. *See page 133*

△ Disney, Universal, SeaWorld, and Busch Gardens operate no less than nine **theme parks** in Florida, and each would be considered a major destination in its own right if located anywhere else in the country. At the center of the theme-park galaxy is Orlando, home of Walt Disney World Resort, which claims more than 45 million visitors each year. *See pages 231 and 255*

△ Had enough of the crowds in central Florida? The **Panhandle** has miles of undeveloped beaches and quiet seaside towns to explore at your leisure. *See page 343*

◁ History and science are brought vividly to life at the **Kennedy Space Center**, where you can explore the past, present, and future endeavors of space exploration. *See page 197*

△ The buff, bronze, and beautiful people gather at the red-hot nightclubs and glorious Art Deco hotels of Miami's **South Beach**. *See page 119*

△ White sugar sand and warm azure waters are the key ingredients of Florida's **beautiful beaches**. With miles and miles of coastline, there's a beach for every taste and occasion. *See page 304*

△ Let your imagination run wild at St Petersburg's famous **Salvador Dalí Museum**, one of the country's finest museums dedicated to a single artist. *See page 296*

◁ NASCAR's most prestigious race (and one of the country's biggest sporting events) the **Daytona 500** is a blistering, 500 mile (800km) contest of driving skill and mechanical prowess. *See page 209*

▷ A palazzo packed with priceless European art, the **John and Mable Ringling Museum of Art** is a tribute to the man known for creating the "Greatest Show on Earth." *See page 310*

THE BEST OF FLORIDA: EDITOR'S CHOICE

Sun-drenched beaches, high-tech thrill rides, romantic hideaways, historic sites, cultural attractions, and the great outdoors ... here, at a glance, are our top recommendations for a visit

BEST BEACHES

- **Bill Baggs Cape Florida State Park**
Regularly rated as one of the best in the US, this pristine beach on Key Biscayne soothes the weary soul. *See page 126*
- **Bradenton Beach**
At the south end of Anna Maria Key, Bradenton has walkable streets and beaches that attract nesting sea turtles in summer. *See page 307*

- **Caladesi Island State Park**
Florida's No. 1 white-sand beach is a boat-in-only experience with a mangrove kayak trail. *See page 293*
- **Sanibel Island**
Do the "Sanibel Stoop" to collect lovely shells washed up on the shores of this beautifully preserved island. *See page 313*

BEST HISTORIC SITES

- **Edison and Ford Winter Estates**
This popular estate offers the inside scoop on the great men of industry and their entrepreneurial work, and includes rare plants and trees, two riverfront homes, and Edison's science lab. *See page 312*

- **Castillo de San Marcos**
The 17th-century Spanish fort still guards the oldest continuously occupied city in the US. Built of *coquina*, a soft limestone made from bits of shell and coral, the fort has suvived several attacks. *See page 213*

BEST THRILL RIDES

- **SheiKra**
Busch Garden's most popular coaster, SheiKra follows its initial right-angle fall of 200ft (61 meters) with a second dive of 138ft (42 meters) at a just-as-woozy 81 degree angle. It will leave you breathless. *See page 289*

- **Kraken**
It's a gut-wrenching floorless coaster with speeds of 60mph (100kph). *See page 261*
- **Dueling Dragons**
Dual coasters careen towards each other at 60mph (96kph) – only to loop out of the way at the last moment. *See page 79*

BEST FOR YOUNG CHILDREN

- **Busch Gardens**
Conservation is job one at this top-drawer zoo and theme park, which educates as it entertains, particularly on the theme of gorillas and African animals. There are also gentle rides for the youngest children. *See page 287*

- **Florida and Mote Marine Aquariums**
Kids can dive with the sharks or swim with the fish at the Florida Aquarium, while across Tampa Bay, Mote Aquarium offers encounters with dolphins, sharks, and manatees. *See pages 286 and 309*

LEFT: Fort de Soto beach. **ABOVE:** Dueling Dragons.

BEST OF THE OUTDOORS

● **Anhinga and Gumbo Limbo Trails, Everglades National Park**
Explore the trails for a nose-to-nose encounter with a rambunctious alligator and spy the red-peeling gumbo limbo, aka the "tourist tree."
See page 139

● **J.N. "Ding" Darling National Wildlife Refuge**
Early mornings in the colder winter months bring thousands of birds to this refuge. It's a rare opportunity to see roseate spoonbills, heron, pelicans, ibis, and anhinga birds.
See page 314

● **John Pennekamp Coral Reef State Park**
The only living coral reef in the continental US reveals its riot of color to snorkelers, scuba divers, and those who take the glass-bottom boat tour.
See page 149

● **Merritt Island National Wildlife Refuge**
See manatees and sea turtles in the shadow of Kennedy Space Center.
See page 205

● **Myakka River State Park**
A former ranch, Florida's largest state park offers rustic cabins, campsites, hiking, and horseback riding. *See page 311*

ABOVE: Cà d'Zan at the Ringling Museum of Art.

MUST-SEE MUSEUMS

● **Florida Museum of Natural History**
It's a light, bright, kid-friendly museum with well-interpreted exhibits on Florida's life zones and native cultures, plus an awesome butterfly pavilion. *See page 331*

● **Salvador Dalí Museum**
The location is almost as bizarre as the large-scale psycho-drama paintings, but early Impressionist-inspired works show a more sensitive side of the surrealist master. *See page 296*

● **Norton Museum of Art**
French Impressionists, Post-Impressionists, and modern American masters put the Norton on a par with institutions many times its size.
See page 188

● **Vizcaya**
With 70 rooms of European antiques, Vizcaya is a rare example of the opulent life. *See pages 113 and 116*

BEST PLACE TO PARTY

● **CityWalk**
Universal's nightclub district caters to adult tastes with food, drink, dancing, and live entertainment designed for grown-up clientele.
See page 260

● **Key West**
A year-round party can be found at the end of the road. The "Conch Republic" is always up for a good time.
See page 159

● **South Beach**
With pulsating neon lights and scantily clad (and insanely buff) bodies, Ocean Drive is party central all night long. With its non-conformist attitude, you can find just about any vice you're looking for.
See page 119

ABOVE: dancing the night away.

RAISE A GLASS IN CELEBRATION

● **Calle Ocho**
The largest Hispanic heritage festival in the US is a sizzling, salsa-fueled street party. *See page 106*

● **Ocala Rodeo**
Forget about the long lines at the theme parks and hearken back to the good old days when the only thing treated like cattle in Florida was, well, cattle. *See page 334*

● **St George Island Mullet Toss**
This beach party gives new meaning to the term "flying fish."
See page 347

● **Sunset Celebration at Mallory Square**
Why applaud a sunset? In Key West the sun doesn't just set, it goes down in a blaze of glory.
See page 161

LET THE SUN SHINE

Florida's population has almost doubled in the past
30 years. There are plenty of reasons for the
Sunshine State's enduring popularity

rom John Steinbeck to Ernest Hemingway, some of
America's greatest artists have found a land of
refuge and adventure, whether fleeting or long-
term, along the lovely coasts and inland forests of Florida.
The image of the Sunshine State as a place where dreams
come true has lost none of its appeal, and about 1,000
newcomers arrive every day on its sunny shores. People often joke that
most of Florida's inhabitants were born elsewhere – anywhere from
upstate New York to Cuba.

Travelers regard Florida as an unbeatable vacation destination – and
with good reason. Nature has played a major role, providing everything
from the tropical Keys and wild Everglades to miles of
shimmering beaches. And when nature isn't enough,
man-made attractions fill the gap in fast-paced cities
such as Orlando, theme park capital of the world; and
Miami, where the ice-cream-colored buildings (restored
to their 1930s Art Deco glory) provide the backdrop for
posing and partying in trendy South Beach.

It is simple to get around Florida if you're comfortable behind the wheel, with rental cars easy to come
by and reasonably priced. Accommodations are also
plentiful, ranging from affordable roadside motels
to quaint bed-and-breakfasts and to lavish beachside
resorts. The weather is unlikely to disappoint, though be aware that
summers can be oppressively hot and humid with frequent rainstorms
that may interrupt outdoor pursuits.

The ethos of Florida is perhaps best embodied by Walt Disney, who
settled in similarly sunny California but had a soft spot in his heart for
the home of his eye-popping DisneyWorld. As Walt himself once put it,
"wholesome pleasure, sport, and recreation" should be as important as
work to the United States' national character. In Florida, land of expansive
vistas and heart-racing adventure, Disney found the perfect embodiment
of his vision. Visitors are unlikely to be disappointed. ❑

PRECEDING PAGES: Anna Maria Pier, Manatee County; shooting the rapids at a
Universal water ride in Orlando; a tram in Ybor City, Tampa. **LEFT:** playing in the
surf near the Naples Pier. **TOP:** flying the flag of the "Conch Republic" in Key West.
ABOVE RIGHT: the beach at Taylor State Park, Key West.

THE FLORIDIAN PEOPLE

A state with a singular identity to outsiders contains cultural multitudes, from Cuban-Americans to northern Jews to descendants of the German and Irish workers who fueled 19th-century immigration

For many Americans, even many of those who live and vacation in Florida, the state and its people have a reputation for eccentricity, a quirkiness belied by the overwhelming popularity of carbon-copy suburban housing and manicured lawns. A quote summing up the colorful characters of the Sunshine State is often attributed to *Miami Herald* journalist and best-selling author Carl Hiaasen: "There's nothing wrong with Florida that a Category 6 hurricane can't cure."

But the real Floridians carry identities much deeper than their popular caricatures. An array of ethnic and national influences have dovetailed within the boundaries of one southeast peninsula to create a thoroughly modern melting pot, where no-nonsense Manhattanites break *pan Cubano* (Cuban bread) with neighbors steeped in Greek, Caribbean, French-Canadian, and African-American cultures. Visitors may only have the time to encounter one of these many threads in the Floridian tapestry, but their intermingling is constantly driving the state's sense of itself and its unique attitude towards life.

In short, the demographics of Florida may say one thing – about 60 percent white, 22 percent Hispanic, and 16 percent black, according to the most recent US census tallies – but the state's day-to-day reality tells a much more compelling, if occasionally unsettled, saga of different peoples living together.

Drivers and shoppers

The popular image of Florida tends to resemble quintessential late 20th-century America, with

---

LEFT: children at the Southern Gardens Citrus Grove.
RIGHT: Mallory Square, Key West.

strip malls and gated communities reinforcing conformity and convenience. That stereotype manages to be at once valid and inadequate in its depiction of Floridian lifestyles; locals take to their cars for a quarter-mile trip to a chain store, but they also frequent walkable beachside boardwalks and ethnic restaurants that tend to lie hidden between the big box stores.

People come to Florida not only for vacation, but also to live. For the fourth most-populated state in the nation, Florida has a significant number of non-native residents, making the state a lively melting pot of cultures.

The economic value of tourism is embraced, with residents often taking pride in welcoming visitors as well as steering their own out-of-town friends and family to a favorite spot. Driving an hour or more to the *right* restaurant or the *best* spot to sunbathe is a common practice in a place where theme parks have made waiting in long lines less stressful than they might be elsewhere.

Floridians rarely consider their state part of the American South, despite its location, but many residents display a self-deprecating awareness of their pop-cultural role as the United States' dumb blonde. From the hanging chad scandal that held up the 2000 election to the growing popularity of weird news from the state's ample police blotters, Floridians often

hide a more complex sense of self behind their sunny weather and shiny sport-utility vehicles. Perhaps the best way to understand the local character, then, is to delve more deeply into the state's past.

A struggle for control

In the three centuries before Florida signed on as the 27th American state, three European nations jockeyed for influence over a wild region already tamed and beloved by many American Indian tribes. After the Spanish nobleman Juan Ponce de León came French Huguenots, such as Jacques Le Moyne, who put down roots in the north before battling their rivals for control over what is now the city of Jacksonville.

Florida ultimately fell to the British in the 1760s, only to be returned to Spain for about 30 years after the American colonies won their war for independence from the Crown. Today that long-ago quest for dominance plays out both in obvious and subtle ways.

The French impact on the state manifests in a long-thriving Francophone community, driven in recent years by French-Canadians and epitomized by the 27-year-old newspaper *Le Soleil de Floride*, as well as French colonial architecture still found in many cities. Spanish traditions, though subtle, were woven in to the culture through the descendants of the original Spanish settlements. Much of the state's architecture and urban design owes a debt to the Spanish colonial style.

The British role in the state's evolution is also subtle, shadowing other diverse American enclaves where ancestors from Britain have smoothly integrated into the population. The Irish have maintained a strong hold on their rituals, with several Floridian cities hosting Irish music and dance festivals, as well as theater groups and restaurant-pubs that bring a strong touch of Emerald Isle to the Sunshine State.

Hispanic heritage

Florida is one of only seven American states where more than 20 percent of residents are Hispanic, and it is also the home of more than 50 percent of Cubans living in the US. The role of immigration in shaping Floridian culture cannot be overstated. This is a place where people choose to live, not simply because they were born here. A combination of celebration and tension has greeted new arrivals over the past century.

Latin Americans have been vibrant players in Florida since its earliest days, but the influx of Cuban expatriates that came after Fidel Castro took control of the island in 1959 helped shape much of the state's current identity. South Florida, in particular, was soon dotted with Cuban-American communities that brought their own religious rituals, cuisine, and political clout to a place with a complicated background. Not only did Florida pass between French, Spanish, and British control before joining the United States, it was also a part of the Confederacy during the Civil War, and the racist attitudes of many white Floridians persisted far into the 20th century.

Although the Sunshine State has a reputation for easy living, the reality is that this is a place where many people have come together. What resulted has been a constantly changing experiment in coexistence, as Floridian newspapers indelicately referred to Cuban and Haitian "boat people" landing ashore in Miami, even as their already-arrived friends and family members were driving economic growth that benefited the state. With Nicaraguans, Venezuelans, and other Latino arrivals joining the tide by the late 1980s, the state legislature began a long debate over immigration that continues to this day.

On the lighter side, many Hispanic habits have become ingrained in Floridian culture, regardless of ethnic or cultural identity. On a lazy Sunday, you can find many locals sipping tiny cups of Cuban espresso or munching on fried plantains and guava *pastelito* pastries. At night, the hypnotic rhythms of Mexican *salsa*, Puerto Rican *reggaeton* and Dominican *bachata* music are commonly spun on both nightclub dance floors and mainstream radio stations, particularly in the southern part of the state.

Perhaps the best example of Florida's complex relationship with its Hispanic residents can be found in the bilingual signs that direct drivers

While Cubans tend to vote Republican (due to a long-standing conservative stance on cultural issues and stringent anti-communism ideals stoked by Castro), the rise of anti-immigrant sentiment among Conservatives has left Hispanic Floridians to beat back a tide of discrimination. Latino advocates and business leaders view a healthy immigrant population as an essential part of the state's culture, often butting heads with politicians who aim to crack down on undocumented arrivals by passing strong identity-verification laws.

LEFT: a portrait of John and Mable Ringling painted on the ceiling at their Sarasota mansion. **ABOVE:** fine dining at St. Armands Circle in Sarasota.

ON THE PAGE AND SCREEN

The Floridian ethos is memorably recaptured by a slew of classic books, from the 1920s drama of Zora Neale Hurston's *Their Eyes Were Watching God* to the environmental thrillers of Carl Hiaasen. For a moving take on the state, try *Key Largo*, a 1948 film noir set in the southernmost islands, or *Edward Scissorhands*, a locally shot fable that sends up the suburbanites.

Miami-set movies deserve a category of their own, particularly *The Birdcage*, a South Beach tale that helped push drag-queens into the mainstream. Or watch Will Smith's sun-drenched action flick *Bad Boys*. The quality may vary, but the imagery of the city makes a perfect introduction to its charms.

to major landmarks – despite the fact that English was named the official language of the state more than 20 years ago. Florida has joined 27 other states in declaring English the official language, although the United States as a whole has persisted in not doing so.

Native American influence

Florida's first people were tragically decimated by violence and communicable disease brought to their doorstep by European settlers. Luckily, their cultures have survived and their people play a central role in the state's story.

The Seminole Indians, also known as the Creeks before coming to Florida, maintain six reservations in Florida as well as a thriving business network that pays $3.5 million in federal taxes and directs $24 million elsewhere in the state's economy through casinos, a museum, a swamp safari, and other enterprises. The Seminole name is attached to everything from the sports team at the state's university to one of its most populous counties, and its annual powwow draws significant crowds to Tampa. As the Seminole are proud of noting, theirs was the only tribe to never sign a peace treaty with the US government.

The Miccosukee tribe, which grew out of the Seminole tradition, maintains a strong presence

in Florida. Operating everything from gas stations to a lavish country club as well as four reservations, Miccosukee members have developed their own educational curriculum to keep their traditions alive and remind locals that their history in the state predates Christopher Columbus.

Older tribes in the state include the Calusa, Ocale, and Apalachee. Over the course of several centuries, beginning with the arrival of Spanish conquistadors in the early 16th century, these tribal people intermingled and traded with the Europeans, and helped shape many of the sights currently seen in the state. It was these people who helped plant the first corn crops in Florida and carved out some of its still-vibrant recreational trails.

Retiree revival

Only in Florida could you find a city-within-a-city where children are not permitted to stay for more than three weeks at a time. But The Villages, located an hour north of Orlando and christened "Disney World for retirees" by America's National Public Radio, is only the largest of multiple planned communities in the state where senior citizens and their cultural trends are dominant.

More than 17 percent of Floridians are over age 65, making the state a popular home for senior citizens. Indeed, most Americans either have an elderly relative living in the state or know someone who does. Many restaurants are crowded with early-bird dinner patrons before 6pm, and shuffleboard and mah-jongg games are a common sight in residential developments.

Yet Florida is also an excellent example of how retirees can be participatory members of their state. Its 55-and-over residents are strong players in the AARP (American Association of Retired Persons), the advocacy outlet for older Americans, making the group's Florida chapter a major player in both local and national politics. Particularly as the baby boomer generation swells the ranks of American seniors, retired Floridians are anything but leisurely in their pursuit of financial, health-care, and Social Security reforms.

The African-American community

Florida was known for cultivating accomplished and self-sufficient majority-black communities even as other southern states struggled to put the ugly legacy of slavery behind them. One of the biggest symbols of the African-American role in Floridian development is Eatonville, the nation's first formally incorporated city led and populated by black Americans. Now an Orlando suburb, the town is the self-identified home town of writer Zora Neale Hurston, one of a handful of immortal black female writers, and remains a dearly held part of African-American history.

The same year that Eatonville was formed also saw Florida Agricultural & Mechanical University founded in Tallahassee for the express purpose of educating African-Americans. Today, A&M, as it is called, joins American Beach (on

urban blight and racial inequality still holds back the state's African-Americans, many of whom tend to be relegated by economic need to neighborhoods where education and health care are of poorer quality. Tension between African-Americans and the police remains a source of unrest, particularly in Miami's Liberty City neighborhood, where 18 people died and 800 were arrested in 1980 after racial conflict erupted into a riot.

Florida's Chosen

Of the 6.5 million Jewish-Americans in the US, nearly 10 percent of them call Florida home,

Amelia Island near Jacksonville) and other Florida sites as a reminder of the issues surrounding integration and civil rights in the state. St Augustine is also on the list of African-American landmarks, having hosted the first homestead for freed blacks in the state under the name of Fort Mose in the 1730s.

Today the state continues to rack up African-American cultural and academic achievement, sending seven black representatives to Congress and electing its first black lieutenant governor, Jennifer Carroll, in 2010. But the legacy of

LEFT: pest control officers regularly trap alligators in suburban swimming pools. **ABOVE:** the golf course at the Gasparilla Club has amazing ocean views.

VIETNAMESE IMMIGRANTS

The Vietnamese population in Florida more than doubled between 1990 and 2000. Today the cultural traditions of Southeast Asia are a particularly strong presence in the Vietnamese district of Orlando, located in the Colonialtown neighborhood, and can also be felt and tasted in popular restaurants in Miami and Tampa.

The best time to experience a taste of Saigon in central Florida is during the winter Tet holiday, which is marked by a two-day festival of food, music, dancing, and a beauty pageant. Tet celebrates the Vietnamese Lunar New Year and is held at the Central Florida Fairgrounds.

and the state has the highest density of observant residents behind California and New York. Florida's population is 3.3 percent Jewish, making the state a potent locus for Jewish cultural and spiritual development.

The Jewish influence on American arts and politics grew in leaps and bounds during the mid- to late-20th century, but the religion was alive and well in Florida nearly two centuries earlier. The state's first acknowledged Jewish settlement was begun near Pensacola in 1763, though the oldest recorded Jewish congregation did not spring up in the Jacksonville area until 1876.

AMERICAN PARADISE

Florida is the de facto vacation destination for many Americans, and there is no shortage of bold-faced names who consider it a second (or even first) home. Madonna owned a lavish Miami home and frequented the city during the 1990s, and she has been joined in her Florida favoritism at various times by Sylvester Stallone, Rosie O'Donnell, Shaquille O'Neal, P. Diddy, and Tiger Woods. In recent years, a thriving subgenre of Latin-southern fusion-style hip-hop has taken hold in Miami. Fans of that style should keep an eye out for Trina, Trick Daddy, Flo-Rida, and Rick Ross – or at least keep an ear out for their songs on the streets.

The real boom time for Floridian Jews began after World War II, when an influx drove the population from an estimated 25,000 to more than 175,000. The spike in Jewish residents also brought a notable number of unique sects within the religion to the state's sunny confines, including adherents from Cuba, Brazil, and Morocco.

Today Florida is home to an abundance of Jewish synagogues, bagel shops, and community centers where major holidays from Passover to Purim are celebrated. Jews are an active force in local politics, helping propel more than 15 of their own to the mayoralty of Miami Beach, Senator Joseph Lieberman to two runs on the national presidential ticket, and Middle Eastern relations to the top of the agenda during debating season. Meanwhile, the religion's effect on the Floridian identity has been exponentially increased by pop-cultural touchstones such as the Boca Raton retirement home where Jerry Seinfeld's parents lived in his eponymous sitcom.

The Snowbirds

Just as some types of birds fly south for the winter, so do seasonal migrants flock to Florida during the colder months. Florida is hardly the only destination for snowbirds, but it has acquired the biggest reputation for temporary residents, perhaps because of its friendliness towards retirees and its ample supply of mobile-home campgrounds, a popular vehicle of choice for middle-class permanent vacationers.

There are few reliable estimates of the current number of Floridian snowbirds, due to their constant mobility and the downturn in part-time travel brought on by the recent global financial crisis. In fact, some economic prognosticators have forecast the pending demise of the snowbird as the cost of second homes and airline travel grows ever steeper.

Far from dying out, the temporary migrant appears to be adapting, with fewer retirees and more working transients, both wealthy and working-class. The older, retired snowbird is more common in south Florida, with the Palm Beach newspaper reporting that 40 percent of local homes were considered vacant in 2011 due to seasonal residencies, but working snowbirds can be found anywhere in the state where openings exist in the service sector.

Asian-Americans

While they are far from the most visible constituency in Florida, there are more than a half-million Chinese, Japanese, Korean, Filipino, Vietnamese, and other Asian immigrants residing here. This makes the state the eighth most popular destination for Asian-American immigrants, even as the ethnic group's total population remains half of the national average. The state's native Asian population grew by more than 42 percent between 2000 and 2006 and is projected to top 1.8 million by 2050, according to the Asian-American Federation of Florida.

and the technically irrelevant but historically offensive statute remains intact.

Miami vice and spice

Florida's biggest and most famous city looms larger than life over its people, serving as the launch pad for much of its major social trends, from immigration to suburban sprawl, as well as its artistic personality. The 1980s TV show *Miami Vice* spawned a culinary festival titled Miami Spice, with both monikers channeling the city's indigenous multicultural energy into a cosmopolitan image for the rest of the state and the world.

Sadly, Asian-Americans' most vocal recent emergence in Florida society ended in defeat. A 2008 ballot initiative would have eliminated language in the state constitution that prevented "aliens ineligible for citizenship" from owning property, a measure approved in 1926 amid a cloud of racial discrimination against Japanese immigrants. But conservative political groups outgunned Asian-American groups in a public relations battle over the initiative, recasting the anti-Asian-American language as a beneficial modern move against illegal immigration,

LEFT: walking the dog on Duval Street in Key West.
ABOVE: pirates storm the city of Tampa during the annual Gasparilla Invasion.

The metropolitan area of Miami, often referred to by its county name of Miami-Dade, has a population that is largely Hispanic, with a Latino population more than three times the size of that in the rest of Florida. But the social force exerted by the largest city in the state is greater than any single group, and visitors should not think that Miami is synonymous with Latino. The city takes pride in its diversity, and while one group may speak the loudest, all are given a hearing.

As Miami modernizes and incorporates ever more diverse influences, the broader state is guaranteed to follow suit – putting the neon-lit city at the leading edge of Florida's socioeconomic evolution. Where the people of Miami lead, the state tends to follow. ❑

DECISIVE DATES

and leads to the outbreak of the First Seminole War. Andrew Jackson overcomes Seminole resistance, then sets about taking control of Florida on behalf of the US government. He becomes Florida's first governor, and later US president.

1824
The newly founded town of Tallahassee is declared the capital of the Florida Territory.

1835–42
Seminole leader Osceola launches a campaign against the US Army which ends when most Indians surrender and are deported.

1845
Florida becomes the 27th state of the Union.

1861
Florida secedes from the Union and joins the Confederate States in the Civil War.

1868
Following a revolt against Spain in Cuba, the first wave of Cubans arrives in Florida.

1883
The great railroad era begins. Settlers head south.

1898
Revolution erupts in Cuba; the US joins in to drive Spain off the island.

1912
Completion of the final section of the East Coast Railroad to Key West, prompting the first

c.8000 BC
Nomadic tribes reach the Florida peninsula and begin to settle the land a few thousand years later.

AD 300–1000
More than 10,000 Native Americans live in the Florida region when the Spanish arrive.

1513
Two decades after Columbus's voyage, Spanish conquistador

Ponce de León is the first European to set foot on the peninsula, near present-day St Augustine. He later returns to Florida with settlers, but abandons his expedition.

1562
The French arrive in Florida to challenge the Spanish, who then strengthen their hold, founding their first permanent settlement three years later.

1586
A British attack on St Augustine triggers centuries of dispute between Britain, France, and Spain, and America.

1763
The English receive Florida from Spain in exchange for Cuba. Twenty years later, the territory is returned to Spain.

1803
The Spanish cede Florida's Panhandle to Napoleon, who soon sells the region to the United States.

1817–18
Pressure from settlers results in violence with Indian tribes

1984
The influential TV series *Miami Vice* premieres, changing the public image of the city.

1992
Andrew, the biggest hurricane for decades, devastates southeast Florida.

1997
Designer Gianni Versace is shot and killed in South Beach.

property boom of the 20th century and raising the state's population to one million people.

1926–28
Two powerful hurricanes strike Miami, killing more than 2,000 people.

1930s–40s
Miami Beach's Art Deco hotels are built and tourism thrives in South Florida. During World War II Florida is used as a training ground for soldiers.

1949
A military missile test site is established at Florida's Cape Canaveral.

1959
Fidel Castro leads a communist revolution in Cuba, setting off a long-term migration of thousands of Cubans who flee his regime. More *emigrés* from Central and South America follow.

1960s
The first rockets soar from Cape Canaveral at the start of the space race; the first moonshot is launched from Florida.

1970s
An economic recession badly hurts Florida, though cheer still reigns when Walt Disney World – the state's first major theme park – opens near Orlando.

1980s
The campaign to restore the Art Deco district of Miami Beach launches the area's renaissance.

1981
The Space Shuttle *Columbia* is launched from Kennedy Space Center, the beginning of the successful shuttle program.

2000
Florida is at the center of the infamous hanging chads controversy during the presidential campaign between Al Gore and George W. Bush.

2004
Four hurricanes pummel the coastline over a 48-day period, breaking a record set in 1964.

2010
Governor Charlie Crist leaves office after announcing that $50 million of state funds would be earmarked for Everglades restoration.

2011
NASA's space shuttle program comes to an end; all five shuttles are retired to museum around the country. *Atlantis*, the last shuttle to be launched, will remain at Kennedy Space Center.

TOP LEFT: an impression of Florida Indians in 1564 by Jacques le Moyne. **BOTTOM LEFT:** a Native American woman decorated with tattoos. **ABOVE:** Art Deco buildings in Miami's South Beach. **RIGHT:** the final launch of the space shuttle *Atlantis* on July 8, 2011.

EARLY FLORIDA

Indigenous people thrived on local plenty
from both land and sea long before the European
invaders arrived and altered the course of history

Florida's first inhabitants were Paleo-Indians fleeing the frozen north during the most recent Ice Age, when the Florida peninsula was a dry desert with a landmass twice the size of what it is today. Hunters were attracted by the warm climate and abundant game, including now-extinct ground sloths, mastodons, camels, and giant bison. Paleo-era remains have been uncovered at Silver Springs and other central Florida water sources.

Ancient hunters

By 6000 BC, these first Floridians had coalesced into hunter-gatherers associated with particular territories, where they hunted otters, rats, squirrels, turtles, alligators, and opossums; they also fished in lakes, and gathered cactus fruit and other delicacies. Early Archaic people invented tools made from animal teeth and bone fastened to wooden handles. They ceremonially interred their dead wrapped in woven palmettos. The swampy land preserved the corpses so well that archeologists excavating Windover Ponder near Titusville were able to extract human brain DNA – a first on the continent.

These early people consumed oysters and conchs in coastal areas as well as mussels and snails at freshwater sites, and used large shells as tools for fashioning dugout canoes. The shell mounds were a distinguishing feature of their camps and can still be seen beside inland rivers and at the mouths of estuaries.

As early as 1500 BC, Archaic people were making the first ceramics in North America,

which they strengthened with the fibers from Spanish moss and palmetto. They grew corn and squash and traded with other tribes from Alabama and Georgia. People living along the St John's River created distinctive effigy pots, stamped with corncob patterns.

Archeologists are particularly fascinated by the more than 14,000 burial mounds, probably influenced by the Hopewell cultures of Ohio and Illinois, found throughout Florida. They occur in Matecumbe in the Keys, Bear Lake in the Everglades, Safety Harbor on the Gulf, and at dozens of sites in the Panhandle, and have yielded insight into religious rituals among these ancient people.

LEFT: an Indian leader of the upper St John's River.
RIGHT: Calusa Indians inhabited Florida's Gulf coast.

By the time Spanish conquistador Juan Ponce de León landed at Cape Canaveral in 1513, more than 150,000 Indians were living on the penin-

A sinkhole in Dade County contains evidence of human habitation dating back about 10,000 years. Found at the site were the bones of extinct Ice Age mammals as well as stone tools and human remains.

sula. The eastern Panhandle was the province of the Apalachee. Their neighbors in the western

Menendez de Aviles. Le Moyne's drawings show a tall, handsome people ruled by chiefs and nobles in villages of palm-thatched huts. Chiefs and female nobles were lavishly tattooed and wore feather capes, shell beads, and metal belts. Males wore breechcloths of deerskin, while women dressed in skirts of Spanish moss so tightly woven it shone like silk.

The Seminole

By the early 1700s, Florida's Indian population was drastically reduced by warfare and European diseases. Between 1613 and 1617, half of the 16,000 converted Indians in Spanish missions

Panhandle were the Pensacola, Apalachicola, and Chtot. The Mayaimi people lived on the shores of Lake Okeechobee. Modern-day Miami and Palm Beach were home to the Tequesta. Southwestern Florida was the territory of the fierce Calusa, whose shell-tipped arrows took Ponce de León's life in 1521. The largest group called themselves the Timucua. A related tribe called the Tocobaga lived in the Tampa Bay area.

Chiefs and nobles

The first European to document Florida's Indian culture was Frenchman Jacques Le Moyne. He made watercolors of Indians after surviving the 1565 massacre at Fort Caroline on the St John's River by Spanish conquistador Pedro

in northern Florida had died of infectious diseases. British colonists raiding from the coast of Carolina seized 1,000 Apalachee between 1702 and 1704, emptying villages in the north.

In Georgia, the Creek Indians had formed an uneasy alliance with the British, bartering animal skins and furs for guns. When that alliance collapsed, Spain seized the opportunity to invite the Creeks into depopulated areas of northern Florida. Sometime between 1716 and 1767, the Creeks began colonizing former Apalachee towns, spreading into the center of the state, where they took over former Timucuan farmlands, re-established trading networks, and lived alongside escaped slaves who had been granted sanctuary by the Spanish since 1693.

In Florida, the powerful Creek Indians transformed themselves into a new people: the Seminole. Their name was derived from the Spanish word *cimarron*, meaning "wild and unruly." Always great traders, the Seminole traveled as far as Cuba in dugout canoes and bartered with ships sailing along the Atlantic Coast. They hunted deer and other game in forested islands in the Everglades and grew corn, rice, watermelons, peaches, potatoes, and pumpkins.

In 1764, Spain gave up Florida to the British, and many Indians and black people left with the Spanish for Cuba rather than risk being forced into slavery on British plantations. The Georgia Creeks and Florida Seminole fared better. They used their alliance with the British to continue trading through the powerful Panton, Leslie & Company, owned by Scotsman William Panton, a friend of Alexander McGillivray, the half-English headman of the Creek Confederacy.

By the time Florida was returned to Spain by the American government in 1783, much of the land was settled by the Seminole and Spanish cattle ranchers and farmers. Many black people chose to live just outside Seminole villages, where they enjoyed the protection of their Indian neighbors in exchange for labor and goods.

The long war

American ire over Spain's sanctuary policy for runaway slaves led to clashes along the Florida-Georgia border between 1785 and 1821. In 1818, Andrew Jackson, who would become Florida's first territorial governor under US rule, instigated the First Seminole War in Florida. His ruthless pursuit of Indian removal and extermination led the Seminole people to call him Sharp Knife.

After spending $20 million to fight a long and difficult Second Seminole War between 1835 and 1842, the US government coerced 3,824 Seminole Indians and runaway black slaves onto reservations west of the Mississippi. They abandoned the forts they had built, leaving only citizen-soldiers to defend new settlements like Orlando and Tampa. Skirmishes between settlers and the Seminole led to the Third Seminole War, which lasted from 1855 to 1858.

At its close, the last Seminole holdouts, led by Chief Billy Bowlegs, were rounded up and sent to reservations in the Everglades and near Tampa Bay, where their descendants live today.

During this time, Florida's Seminole people proved themselves to be brave, implacable foes, well suited to guerilla warfare in the swamps. The era's best-known Indian leader, Osceola, born Billy Powell in 1804 to an English father and Creek mother in Alabama, was neither Seminole nor a chief. But after moving with his mother to Florida early in the Second Seminole War, he grew to prominence as a war leader of ruthless daring. In 1837 he was captured under

a white flag of truce by US Major General Thomas Jessup, a treacherous action that made Osceola a legend in the public's imagination.

Also legendary was Coacoochee, son of Miccosukee chief Philip and nephew of Micanopy, head of the Alachua Seminole near modern Gainesville. Coacoochee united these two main groups of Florida Indians and fought tirelessly during the Second Seminole War. But in 1842, he acknowledged defeat, telling his captors: "The white men are as thick as the leaves in the hammock; they come upon us thicker every year. They may shoot us, drive our women and children night and day; they may chain our hands and feet, but the red man's heart will always be free." ❑

LEFT: a colorful diorama at the South Florida Museum depicts a Paleo-Indian man hunting an ancient bison.
RIGHT: Osceola, a Seminole war leader.

NEW SPAIN

The first of the Iberian explorers arrived in 1513, thirsty for a taste of magical waters, before conquistadors and other treasure seekers began looking for their own place in the sun

Florida's calendar of official holidays salutes such notables as social reformers Martin Luther King Jr and Susan B. Anthony, Confederate leaders Robert E. Lee and Jefferson Davis, and of course Presidents Washington and Lincoln. And then there's Pascua Florida Day.

That occasion, known also as Florida State Day, is observed annually on April 2, and reminds us of how much of Florida's cultural and political history was built and shaped by early European explorers. The Spanish foundation was developed over three centuries of contact and conflict, adventure and achievement. The conquistadors mixed and matched their Spanish heritage with Native American and Anglo-American influences, as well as their English, French, and Dutch rivals. These interactions were rarely peaceable, and left an indelible mark that has been a part of making the state the multi-ethnic, constantly changing land it is today.

> Juan Ponce de León called the Florida Keys "Los Mártires" because the low rocky islands reminded him of a line of martyred men.

Land of flowers

The first stirrings of Spanish involvement in Florida came on March 27, 1513. On that date, crew members on the ship bearing Spanish explorer Juan Ponce de León spotted land that at first was mistaken for an island but turned out to be a peninsula, thick with vegetation. Ponce de León christened it La Florida because he

LEFT: Castillo de San Marcos in St Augustine.
RIGHT: Juan Ponce de León, European explorer.

and his men landed there during Eastertime, or Pascua Florida – the Feast of Flowers (a term still used for Easter Sunday in the Spanish-speaking world). The name stuck, and the La Florida moniker was initially applied to all Spanish holdings on the North American continent.

Some scholars believe that Ponce de León may have been preceded to Florida by earlier European pathfinders. One such explorer might have been John Cabot, who had voyaged to Labrador and northern locales years earlier, while Portuguese mariners had begun thrusting into the Atlantic nearly a full century before de León set sail. Still, credit has traditionally been given to de León.

Soldier of fortune

Who was this reputed discoverer of Florida, the state that would someday be represented by the 27th star emblazoned on the American flag? Ponce de León may have been the illegitimate son, born in 1460 of a Seville nobleman. As a young man, he fought the Moors as they made their last stand at Granada. He took part in the second of Christopher Columbus' voyages to the New World, and he became the first governor of Puerto Rico in 1509.

Said to be a frequent rival of Columbus' son, de León was given an opportunity by Spain's King Ferdinand I to become governor of a fabled island called Bimini, reputed to be a paradise flowing with waters that could perpetuate youthful vigor. The adventurer (then in his fifties) and his expedition set forth on March 3, 1513, to find what later lore labeled the Fountain of Youth. Bimini and that magically regenerative fountain would prove elusive, but Ponce de León made his fortune nonetheless.

Promised virtual ownership of the fabled island and anything else he might discover (including gold or other precious metals), the explorer and his crew poked about in the Bahamas for 25 days aboard the *Santa Maria de*

WHO'S FIRST?

Some believe that John Cabot, a Genoa-born map-maker, beat Ponce de León to Florida. Cabot made several voyages to Labrador and other northern points shortly after Columbus' voyage of 1492. He won the praise of English king Henry VII, who commissioned him to chart the newfound lands. Cabot and his son Sebastian *(right)* sailed into Spanish territory in 1498. Cabot didn't come ashore, but shortly after their voyages, maps showing Florida were circulated in Europe.

la Consolación and the *Santiago*. There was no trace of Bimini, but they did locate the Bahama Channel, a short cut to the Caribbean from the Atlantic Ocean. Ponce de León and his crew celebrated Pascua Florida aboard ship. Six days later, on April 2, an unknown shore was sighted. The expedition made landfall several days later, near the site that would become the first permanent settlement in the continental United States – St Augustine – and a river now known as the St John's.

An unfriendly people

Ponce de León's expedition ventured north to the mouth of the St John's River and south to the Florida Keys. After rounding the Keys, de León sailed up the west coast, possibly as far as Pensacola Bay. It became apparent to him that he had found more than a mythical island. He made at least one more stop at Charlotte Harbor, once called Bahía Juan Ponce, near the modern city of Fort Myers. There he encountered Florida's native inhabitants. They were tall and powerful – and intensely hostile.

Ponce de León returned to Puerto Rico to plot his conquest of La Florida, but it wasn't until 1521 that he managed to scrape together two ships, 200 men, 50 horses, and all the equipment he needed. The king commissioned him

barrage of stones and arrows. The newcomers vainly tried to lead a counterattack; the men fought pitched battles with daggers, but blood quickly stained the newly consecrated soil. By some accounts, the Spanish even set snarling dogs on their enemies.

Despite heavy losses, the Indians never retreated. An arrow hewn from swamp reed tore into Ponce de León's flesh. Six of his men, wounded, collapsed along with him. Survivors managed to get de León and the others into a boat. They reached Cuba, where de León died. Puerto Rico became the final resting place for this Spanish adventurer.

and a contingent of missionary priests to settle the "island of Florida," taking care to treat the Indians well, "seeking in every possible way to convert them to our Holy Catholic faith."

The explorer's put ashore near Charlotte Harbor, an event Catholic scholars consider the first authenticated instance of priests landing on the soil of the future United States. Unfortunately for the ill-fated entourage, their collective prayers proved fruitless. While laying foundations for the first shelters of the settlement, de León's men were surprised by a group of Calusas or Mayaimis, who attacked with a

LEFT: Jacques le Moyne's drawing depicts indigenous Indians at prayer. ABOVE: a statue of Ponce de León.

The conquistadors

Three major expeditions and several smaller ones followed Ponce de León into La Florida during the next 40 years, seeking to tame the hostile new land and its inhabitants. All failed, and about 2,000 Spaniards and an untold number of Native Americans lost their lives.

One such expedition was led by Pánfilo de Narváez, who waded ashore at Tampa Bay with about 400 men on Good Friday in 1528. A red-bearded soldier, Narváez earned his fearsome reputation when he lost an argument (and an eye) to Hernando Cortéz in Mexico. He firmly warned the Indians that if they did not obey him, and thus the king of Spain and the pope, "I will take your goods, doing you all the evil and injury that I may be able… and I declare to you that the deaths and damages that arise therefrom, will be your fault and not that of His Majesty, nor mine, nor of these cavaliers who came with me." The Indians told Narváez exactly what he wanted to hear: there existed a land to the north called Apalachee, where they would find the treasure sought by every self-respecting conquistador: gold. Pánfilo de Narváez set out for Apalachee on foot, ordering his ships to rendezvous with him there. He found tall forests of longleaf pine, vast plains of cabbage palm, and sparkling springs and rivers, but no gold.

As Narváez pushed north, Indian raids and swarms of mosquitos took their toll. His dwindling party arrived in the Panhandle land of Apalachee exhausted and starving. The ships never showed up. Narváez and his men were forced to construct six makeshift vessels in which they set off for Mexico.

Alas, the ships vanished, and Narváez was never heard from again. Years later, four survivors of the expedition turned up in Mexico with an amazing story. Led by Alvar Nuñez Cabeza de Vaca, they survived a shipwreck, and wandered in the American Southwest for eight years before finally finding their way to Mexico.

De Soto's cavaliers

Hernando de Soto, the conquistador *par excellence* of his time, led a more ambitious assault on Florida, with only slightly better results than Narváez. In an 1836 narrative *Notices of Florida and the Campaigns*, M.M. Cohen described the escapades of the adventurous 36-year-old as "poetry put in action; it was the knight errantry of the Old World carried into the depths of the American wilderness …"

De Soto landed at Tampa Bay in May 1539 with an army of 1,000 knights and fortune-hunters. They killed and enslaved Indians and penetrated the thick brush of the interior. Puzzled by the absence of gold and magnificent cities such as those he had seen in Peru and Mexico,

De Soto pushed on through the Panhandle to Georgia and North Carolina before turning west to Alabama to continue his search. Three years and thousands of miles after his arrival in North America, De Soto died of a fever. His men submerged his body in the Mississippi River. Most of his conquistadors returned to Spain empty-handed.

Unfortunately, the precise details of De Soto's historic expedition died along with him. As Garcilaso Inca de la Vega, the son of a Spanish nobleman and a Peruvian Inca princess, wrote in his 1609 *History of the Conquest of Florida*, "the Spaniards did not think so much of learning the situation of places, as of hunting for gold and silver in Florida."

One lasting legend came from De Soto's venture, however. Near Tampa Bay, the conquistadors curiously scrutinized one Indian who greeted their arrival in fluent Spanish. Under his facepaint, the man turned out to be Juan Ortiz, a soldier who had landed with Narváez and survived capture in a remarkable manner. Garcilaso described Ortiz' ordeal at the hands of a Timucuan chief – or cacique – named Harriga: "He ate and slept very little, and was tormented … he began to run at sunrise, and did not stop till night; and even during the dining of the cacique they would not suffer him to interrupt his course, so that at the end of the day he was in a pitiable condition … The wife and daughters of Harriga, touched with compassion, then threw some clothes upon him, and assisted him so opportunely that they prevented him from dying."

Ortiz finally escaped with the aid of the chief's eldest daughter. Many years later, upon reading of the adventures of Ortiz, a biographer of Captain John Smith borrowed the scenario for his own subject and an Indian girl named Pocahontas. Smith then perpetuated the plagiarism by putting it into his own history.

Tristan de Luna y Arellano, a rich Spanish nobleman, was the next man to try and conquer Florida. He was undismayed by the previous failures and undeterred by the slaying of three missionaries by Indians at Tampa Bay in 1549. Ten years later, his party of more than 1,500 tried to establish a settlement on Pensacola Bay. Devastated by a hurricane, desperate for food,

and disillusioned by Luna's quixotic leadership, the Spaniards abandoned the attempt in 1561.

A foothold in Florida

Emboldened by Spain's preoccupation with pirates and its inability to colonize La Florida, a Frenchman named Jean Ribaut captained the effort to establish a settlement on St John's River in 1562. Ribaut constructed an arrowhead-shaped fort, Caroline, near modern-day Jacksonville.

That move intensified Spain's own efforts to gain a foothold on the land, but they also wanted to expel the French trespassers. A

great armada under the command of Pedro Menéndez de Avilés established a site at a promising spot on the east coast, south of the French outpost, from which to mount its defense. The chosen day was August 28, 1565, the Feast of St Augustine. On September 8, Pedro Menéndez formally broke ground for a settlement that still bears the name of that patron saint. It was the first permanent settlement and is still the oldest continuous settlement, on United States soil, founded more than 50 years before the Pilgrims landed at Plymouth Rock in New England.

Well aware that Menéndez planned to attack, Jean Ribaut rushed back to Fort Caroline, assembled his forces, and tried to surprise the Spanish. But nature played a role in molding

FAR LEFT: a reconstruction of Spanish Mission San Luis de Apalachee, built in 1633. **LEFT:** Hernando de Soto. **ABOVE:** an engraving by Theodore DeBry.

Florida's destiny. A hurricane grounded the French ships before they reached St Augustine. Meanwhile, Menéndez marched up the coast and seized the French fort, killing all the residents except Catholics, women, and children. On the way back to St Augustine, he encountered remnants of Jean Ribaut's assault party and had all but 16 of the 150 men put to death, including Ribaut, who was beheaded. The location of that bloody meeting became known as Matanzas – in Spanish, the place of slaughter.

With the French out of the way, Menéndez tried to guarantee Spain's Florida claims by befriending various Indian tribes, aiding Jesuit mission development, and trying to colonize other parts of the peninsula. Of the settlements, only St Augustine would survive. England's Sir Francis Drake leveled the city in 1585, and another hurricane flooded the colony in 1599. Despite everything, St Augustine has survived for more than 400 years.

A portrait of the Native American

Although they were unsuccessful in their efforts to settle the land, Ribaut and his mapmaker, Jacques le Moyne, provided a meticulous word-and-picture portrait of the tribes they encountered in Florida. Ribaut wrote graphically

Saint Augustine.

Jacques le Moyne described the customs of the Indians with both pictures and words. He wrote, for example, that the east-coast groups were generally more hospitable than those on Florida's west coast. He said that they cultivated fields of beans and maize which they stored in granaries; that they worshiped the sun and scalped and mutilated their enemies. He also praised the Indians' success in hunting deer by skillfully disguising themselves in deerskins and antlers. "I do not believe," he wrote, "that any European could do it as well."

He vividly portrayed the heavily tattooed chiefs and queens, who grew their fingernails

long and sharpened them to points, and who painted the skin around their mouths blue. He said their striking attire included deer-skin capes, belts made of Spanish moss, and earrings fashioned from fish-bladders inflated and dyed red.

Describing their social institutions, Le Moyne also said that the Florida Indians practiced what could be thought of as a form of representative parliamentarianism: "The chief and his nobles are accustomed during certain days of the year to meet early every morning… If any question of importance is to be discussed, the chief calls upon his laüas (that is, his priests) and upon the elders one at a time to deliver their opinions."

in 1563: "The most parte of them cover their raynes and pryvie partes with faire hartes skins, paynted cunyngly with sondry collours, and the fore parte of there bodye and armes paynted with pretye devised workes of azure, redd, and black, so well and so properly don as the best paynter of Europe could not amend yt. The wemen have there bodies covered with a certen herbe like onto moste, whereof the cedertrees and all other trees be alwaies covered. The men for pleasure do always tryme themselves therwith, after sundry fasshions. They be of tawny colour, hawke nosed and of a pleasaunt countenaunce. The women be well favored and modest and will not suffer that

who die, and to shut up their treasures. They erect also at … these temples, in the form of a trophy, the spoils of their enemies."

Contact with Europeans nearly destroyed the Indians. Some fell victim to diseases like chickenpox, measles, and colds, while slave traders spirited away as many as 12,000 people to a life of servitude. Many of those who resisted the European invasion died defending land their tribes had occupied for 10,000 years.

Coming of the Seminole

Historians estimate that by the mid-16th century, the Indian population had dwindled

one approche them to nere, but we were not in theire howses, for we sawe none at that tyme."

Garcilaso de la Vega also provided insights into the customs and lifestyle of the Florida Indians. He noted many similarities in customs to the Incas, especially in their practice of putting their temples on artificial mounds mounted by wooden stairways: "The people of Florida are idolaters, and have the sun and moon for divinities, which they adore without offering them either prayers or sacrifices… [T]hey have temples, but they make use of them only to inter those

to less than one-fourth of its original size of about 25,000 people. Both Jesuit and Franciscan missionaries labored in Florida's humid conditions in their thick woolen robes, winning converts among the people of northern Florida with a string of about 50 missions in the 17th century. But British raiders leveled nearly everything at the turn of the 18th century, driving the few remaining Timucuans and Apalachees farther south. Spaniards took the last remaining 200 Indians to Cuba with them when they handed Florida over to the British in 1763. By that time, the Oconee Creeks had migrated into the peninsula from Georgia. In Florida, they would become known as the Seminole. ❏

FAR LEFT: 16th-century map of St Augustine.
LEFT: Sir Francis Drake. **ABOVE:** Timucua hunters used camouflage to stalk deer.

TURF WARS

Spain loses its grip, Native Americans are elbowed aside,
and the United States takes control, only to plunge
headlong into a military conflagration
that tears the nation apart

Although the Spanish presence in Florida was long in years, it was limited in scope, and was largely precarious, sporadic, and fragmented. For one thing, the peninsula lacked the precious metals (found in places like Mexico and Peru) that glittered like gold in Spanish eyes.

What mostly kept the Iberian occupiers hanging on to their peninsular possession for so long was the region's strategic location. For the conquerors of New Spain, the Straits of Florida represented a vital corridor through which their ships, laden with riches, could travel back to the homeland. For such treasures, the occupiers could put up with the persistent hostility exhibited by Native Americans, who were none too happy with the Spaniards' presence.

Britain's territorial ambitions

Despite years of occupation, Spain only managed to settle St Augustine and Pensacola, and to establish a small garrison at St Marks in the Panhandle. To the north, the British colonies cast a covetous eye on Florida, prompting Spanish authorities to build Castillo de San Marcos to defend St Augustine.

The castle's mass of earthworks and cannon repelled repeated assaults by the British, including a major attack by General James Edward Oglethorpe in 1742. As it turned out, England acquired Florida with the pen rather than the sword in 1763, via the first Treaty of Paris. Britain captured Cuba during the Seven Years War (known in America as the French and

LEFT: Billy Bowlegs, leader of the Seminole people during the Third Seminole War. RIGHT: a member of the Confederate 1st Florida Cavalry.

Indian War) and agreed to return Havana to Spanish control in exchange for Florida.

Remnants of the Spanish settlements quickly evaporated. The Creek tribes of Alabama and Georgia, who were generally on friendly terms with the British, increased their migration southward. Slicing the territory into East Florida (from the Atlantic coast to the Apalachicola River in the Panhandle) and West Florida (from the Apalachicola to the Mississippi River) made British administration easier, and the Brits virtually transformed the new territory into their 14th and 15th American colonies.

Spain had always operated from its base in Havana, but under Redcoat rule, Florida began to develop ties with the rest of the North American continent. New plantations of indigo, rice, and citrus, a subsequent increase in the slave trade from Africa and the West Indies, and a wave of new immigrants with Cork and Cockney accents marked British rule in frontier Florida.

Breaking away

The rumblings in the northern colonies that foreshadowed trouble never reached so far south. British subjects in Florida remained loyal to London when rebellion-minded American colonists turned their backs on King George III

and declared independence on July 4, 1776. Angry residents of St Augustine even strung up effigies of John Hancock and John Adams and burned them.

Capitalizing on Britain's preoccupation with fighting the American Revolution, Spain recaptured Pensacola and regained control of all West Florida. East Florida remained Tory territory, its citizens donning red woolen coats and brandishing muskets to beat back three incursions by American Whigs from the North.

Then, 20 years after acquiring Florida, the British gave it back to Spain in 1783 under the terms of the Second Treaty of Paris. That

CROSSING CULTURES

Turmoil between the various ethnic groups and political powers that inhabited Florida in the late 18th and early 19th centuries gave rise to a host of colorful characters who were adept at forging links between cultures.

Take, for example, Alexander McGillivray, the son of a Scotsman and a woman of Creek and French blood, who is remembered for his diplomatic skill. He cultivated a working relationship between Florida's Spanish governors, English traders, the US Army, and a confederation he organized among 45,000 Indians of several tribes. The alliance endured until his death in 1793.

William Augustus Bowles had no Indian blood, but he lived among the Creeks and married an Indian woman after

emigrating from England. When the Spanish returned to power, he contacted McGillivray and offered to supply the Creeks with weapons to wage war against the Georgians. His adventures included an attack on the St Marks garrison near Tallahassee before the Spaniards captured him and sent him to Havana, where he died.

Zephaniah Kingsley was a flamboyant Scot who made his fortune from the slave trade. He imported thousands of people from Africa and the West Indies in the early 1800s, trained them in the servile arts, and then resold them for a vast profit. He became a legend by defending the slave system, even marrying one of his servants and raising the children as his heirs.

the territory resisted falling into the American column was small consolation.

A cultural stew

At the time of the American Revolution, Florida sheltered a wide cross section of the world's people. There were Africans and West Indians, English and Spanish, Germans and Greeks, Sicilians and Minorcans, and Creek and Choctaw Indians. All put down roots that flourished in the bright glare of Florida's sunshine.

The second Spanish occupation of Florida fared little better than the first. British, black, and Indian refugees from the newly formed Florida instigated a movement for independence. So, in yet another twist, the British (with whom the Spanish were allied in the War of 1812) sent troops to Pensacola to reinforce Spain's claim.

This sparked concern about the return of the Redcoats. Tennessee's Andrew Jackson, nicknamed "Old Hickory" because of his stern reputation, took it upon himself to stop the British rebuilding their forces in Florida. He used a Creek Indian uprising in Alabama as a pretext for advancing toward Florida. He defeated the Indians at the Battle of Horseshoe Bend, and then marched on Pensacola and drove out the British.

United States continued to trickle southward. Georgians stirred up trouble along the northern border, forcing Spain to withdraw to the 31st parallel, the modern-day border between Florida and Georgia.

Changing hands

In 1800, Spain ceded the Louisiana Territory to France, which in turn sold the territory to the US. The US then extended its claim in 1813 to Mobile in Alabama, which, at the time, was Florida's western boundary. Americans in West

LEFT: a depiction of Fort Brooke at Tampa Bay, 1835. **ABOVE:** United States soldiers setting fire to an Indian camp. **ABOVE RIGHT:** Andrew Jackson.

A subsequent skirmish between Americans and Indians sparked the First Seminole War (1817–18). Spain accepted an offer by the US to cancel $5 million in debts to Washington in exchange for ownership of the entire peninsula. Jackson returned to Pensacola in 1821. There, on July 17, he witnessed the raising of the Stars and Stripes over the Spanish capital. Old Hickory became Florida's first American governor.

The road to conflict

Andrew Jackson remained governor for only three months before returning to Washington, where later he would exercise influence over the new territory directly from the White

House. The officials he left behind soon realized that the distance between Pensacola and St Augustine was too great to manage the territory effectively, so they consolidated the government in a village of Talasi Indians, and thus Tallahassee became the territory of Florida's capital in 1823.

Settlers pushed aside the Indians when founding Tallahassee, as so often happened when land was seized for farming. The migration of Indian tribes, who were mostly associated with the Creek nation, started in the 1700s. The Creek took over the deserted farmlands left behind by the devastated local tribes and hunted in the forests where their ancestors had pursued game. These new Indians collectively came to be known as Se-mi-no-lee, meaning wild ones. Some spoke variations of the Hitchiti language, while others spoke Nuskogee.

As white settlers and Indians trickled into the new territory, Florida's population practically doubled, from 34,370 in 1830 to 66,500 in 1845. Jackson's initial clash with the Seminoles proved to be a taste of bloodier days ahead. Pressure mounted for the government to remove Florida's native people to reservations in the West.

SHIFTING FORTUNES

The story behind the Adams-Onís Treaty of 1819 is the shifting fortunes of national power – Spain in decline, the US in flower. The treaty reconfigured the geographical dividing line in North America between the two domains, with Florida as a chief bargaining chip, and it drew on diplomatic precedents dating as far back as the papal bull of 1493 that granted Spain colonial rights in northwestern America.

For Spain, the slate was wiped clean of $5 million in debt, while the US got Florida. The treaty was ironed out in 1819 in Washington, DC, by John Quincy Adams, the American Secretary of State, and Luis de Onís, the Spanish foreign minister. It went into effect in 1821.

Removal and retaliation

In 1823, Seminole tribes massed at Moultrie Creek near St Augustine. Led by Neamathla, chief of a group called Miccosukees, the Indians agreed to a compromise with the American government. Thirty-two chiefs signed a treaty calling for them to move their people and their black slaves to a 4 million acre (1.6 million hectare) reserve in west-central Florida, in return for payment for abandoned lands and financial aid to help them live on the new lands. Neither side abided by the provisions of the agreement. The Seminole found the land unsuitable for agriculture and migrated there slowly, if at all. Drought conditions aggravated food shortages, and the US government reneged on payments.

In 1830, Congress passed a removal act requiring all Indians to be sent West.

The two sides met again at Payne's Landing on the Oklawaha River running through the rugged Green Swamp of central Florida. This time, US officials managed to coax only seven chiefs into signing a new agreement, which canceled the Moultrie Creek Treaty and required the Seminole to move to reservations in the Arkansas Territory (part of present-day Oklahoma). Most of the Seminole nation reacted angrily when the seven chiefs returned from a visit to the new reservations and reported that they had been coerced into

I will ever make is this!" With that act, Osceola became a hero. Though his great-grandfather was a Scotsman, Osceola publicly disavowed his white ancestry and fervently pursued the Creek culture. Historian Marjory Stoneman Douglas considered Osceola "unquestionably the greatest Floridian of his day."

Inspired by Osceola's act of defiance at Fort King, the Seminole rebelled. A party of warriors ambushed Major Francis Langhorne Dade while he was en route from Fort Brooke (at Tampa Bay) to Fort King. The Indians killed Dade with their first bullet and massacred all but three of his 111 men.

agreeing to the move. But President Jackson issued an edict to the Seminole in which he warned: "I tell you that you must go and that you will go."

Flanked by 10 companies of soldiers, General Duncan L. Clinch ordered Seminole chiefs at Fort King, near modern Ocala, to sign away their Florida lands. He managed to get the "X" of Micanopy, the chief of the nation, but few others. Florida tradition holds that an indignant young brave named Osceola plunged his knife into the document and cried, "The only treaty

LEFT: the Seminole attack a US blockhouse on the Withlacoochee River in 1835. **ABOVE:** dogs were used to hunt Indians during the Second Seminole War.

The capture of Osceola

The murder of Dade and his men touched off the Second Seminole War (1835–42), a bloody struggle in which the outmanned but determined Seminole fought the better-armed soldiers to a stalemate. The Indians used the wilderness of the Green Swamp to their advantage, striking at American settlements, then melting into the marshes. The war cost the US $40 million and nearly 1,500 dead. The settlers soon built defensive forts like Lauderdale, Jupiter, Myers, and Pierce.

Deception contributed to the defeat of the Seminoles. In 1837, Osceola rode into St Augustine under a white flag of truce sent to him by General Thomas S. Jessup. The general then violated his own flag by arresting Osceola. He imprisoned the now legendary warrior, his wives, children, and 116 others at Fort Moultrie in Charleston.

Suffering from malaria and a broken spirit, Osceola died just a year after his capture. The attending doctor cut off his head, supposedly in retribution for an incident in which Osceola had severed his brother-in-law's head early in the war. The doctor's great-granddaughter recalled that he hung Osceola's head on a bedpost in the room of his three little boys whenever they misbehaved. Osceola's head was passed around as a curiosity, and was even exhibited at circus sideshows. Eventually it was given to the Surgical and Pathological Museum in New York City, where it was destroyed by a fire in 1866.

Osceola's death broke the spirit of the Seminoles. Jessup continued his trickery, capturing another 400 Indians as well as Chief Alligator after promising to meet with them for truce discussions. General Zachary Taylor didn't pull any underhanded punches, however, when he defeated a party of Seminole braves on the Kissimmee River in the last major battle of the war. The army rounded up Seminole men, women, and children and

in 1842 forced 3,000 of them to march west of the Mississippi River on what has become known as the Trail of Tears.

The return of war

Some Seminole Indians managed to avoid deportation by disappearing into the Everglades. There, under Chief Billy Bowlegs, they regrouped, and in 1855 massacred a camp of surveyors whom they considered trespassers. That ignited the Third Seminole War (1855–58). Soldiers and settlers hunted the Seminole like dogs for the next three years; they offered huge rewards for the capture of Indians. Chief Bowlegs surrendered with a group of warriors in 1858 and was

OSCEOLA

Osceola, the great Indian military leader *(pictured)*, was, said an Army surgeon, diminutive and refined in appearance: "His person... was elegantly formed, with hands and feet effeminately small. He had a countenance expressive of much thought and cunning... His eyes were black and piercing; and when animated were full of dark fire, but when in repose they were softer than the soft eye of woman. His mouth, when relieved by a smile, wore an expression of great sweetness."

sent West. Others stubbornly refused to leave and were able to evade capture. The Floridians eventually gave up the search, enabling about 300 Seminole people to remain beyond the impenetrable sawgrass rivers of the Everglades and, thus, in safety.

From statehood to civil war

After two decades of politicking, Florida became an American state on March 3, 1845, but the romance ended just 16 years later. A man's wealth in Florida was measured by the number of slaves he owned. Influential planters and landowners opposed the abolition of slavery

forests of scrub and pine and linked Tallahassee to Cedar Key on the Gulf Coast.

Such progress, modest as it was, was stunted by the Civil War. Florida mustered its minuscule population and even smaller budget to join the Confederate cause. Its participation in the war was both brief and limited, but devastating nonetheless. Union forces invaded the busy northeastern port of Jacksonville four times. They seized most of Florida's forts. The town of Fernandina Beach, at one time a haven for slave-smuggling after the United States banned the practice, fell to the Union in 1861.

and convinced their legislators to secede from the Union on January 10, 1861. Florida joined forces with the Confederate States and went to war against the North.

The Civil War proved particularly disastrous for Florida. The state had only barely recovered from the Seminole Wars, which had stunted its growth for decades. Agriculture had just begun making an impact with multiplying acres of cotton, indigo, rice, sugar, and tobacco. The rugged interior of the state began to open up in 1861, when the railroad sliced through the

Florida's Confederate soldiers fought back valiantly. Their biggest battle occurred on February 20, 1864, when 5,000 soldiers wearing Confederate gray marched against 5,000 soldiers in Union blue. They clashed at Olustee, east of Lake City. The Floridians suffered nearly 100 men killed and over 800 wounded, but the survivors held their ground. They stopped the advance of the Union army, which suffered twice as many casualties.

The Cradle and Grave Company, consisting of teenagers and old men, mostly died in a Panhandle battle, but the Baby Corp, mainly schoolboys, bravely turned back Union soldiers (who were wearing hats inscribed "To Tallahassee or Hell") at a natural bridge over the St Marks

LEFT: US troops in battle.

ABOVE: Confederate soldiers successfully repelled Union troops at the Battle of Olustee in 1864.

River on March 5, 1865. Union soldiers never reached Florida's capital city, but this was a hollow triumph for the Floridians. Only a month later, General Robert E. Lee surrendered and the bloody Civil War was over.

Reconstruction

The Civil War cost Florida about 5,000 lives and $20 million in damage to its smoldering cities. The anti-slavery novel *Uncle Tom's Cabin*, published in 1852 and written by Harriet Beecher Stowe (who would spend her later years in a cottage in Mandarin on the St John's River near Jacksonville), inspired abolitionists, but hooded Ku Klux Klansmen continued to oppress the black population. Until the Civil Rights Act of 1964, black people in most of Florida and throughout the South still rode in the back of the bus and used segregated facilities.

The American flag flew over Tallahassee again on May 30, 1865. Political and economic reconstruction got off to a hesitant start. Florida remained a wild frontier where the strong and the armed prevailed. Still, the sun began to lure northerners to the warm shores in ever-larger numbers. Florida's population nearly doubled in the two decades immediately after 1860, from 140,000 to 270,000.

TOUTING THE SUNSHINE STATE

American affluence was on the rise after the Civil War, in that period generally known as the Gilded Age. Pleasure-seekers began widening their gaze beyond such standard enticements as Newport and Saratoga Springs, becoming attracted in particular in the latter part of the 19th century by Florida's natural beauty and mild climate.

Luring them on was a growing number of descriptive guides touting the charms of the Sunshine State and various of its locales. One of the earliest was by no less a literary superstar than Harriet Beecher Stowe, author of *Uncle Tom's Cabin*, the blockbuster novel that helped trigger the Civil War. Her guide, *Palmetto-Leaves*, published in Boston in 1873, glowingly evoked the sunshine springs and green

forests of the northeastern Florida region where she would spend her winters in the 1870s and 1880s. One of its chapters was entitled "Buying Land in Florida."

Singling out just two others in this early manifestation of the travelogue genre, George M. Barbour's *Florida for Tourists, Invalids, and Settlers* was first published in 1884, while the poet-critic Sidney Lanier's *Florida: Its Scenery, Climate and History* appeared even earlier, in 1875. Florida, in Lanier's florid prose, represented "an indefinite enlargement of many people's pleasures" as opposed to "that universal killing ague of modern life – the fever of the unrest of trade throbbing through the long chill of a seven-months' winter."

Among those attracted to the Sunshine State were developers, agriculturalists, and inventors. Swampland in the Caloosahatchee

> Dr John Gorrie of Apalachicola in the Panhandle changed the course of domestic life in 1848 when he invented an ice machine, the forerunner of modern refrigerators and air conditioners.

and Kissimmee valleys was drained, clearing the rivers for navigation and making the land solid enough for settlement and farming.

in the 20th century. They were Henry Morrison Flagler (1830–1913), one of the founders of Standard Oil, and Henry B. Plant (1819–99). The latter constructed the Atlantic Coastline Railroad that linked Richmond, Virginia with Tampa. At the end of the line, Plant built the luxurious Tampa Bay Hotel, complete with minarets that still dominate the skyline. Tourists arrived, and Plant then offered the option of continuing by steamer from Tampa to Cuba.

Flagler's Florida East Coast Railroad had an even bigger impact on the state's growth. Beginning in 1885, he sank about $50 million into a series of hotels at locations connected

Cubans followed Vicente Martínez Ybor to Tampa in the 1880s to roll tobacco, helping to make the name of the city synonymous with cigars. On the state's east coast, a Chinese immigrant, Lue Gim Gong, developed a frost-proof orange that began to flourish along the Indian River, laying the basis for Florida's citrus industry.

Railroads and tourists

The far-sightedness of two men of that period laid the groundwork for the boom that occurred

by his railroad line, from the posh Ponce de León Hotel in St Augustine to the Ormond north of Daytona Beach. In 1894, his line abruptly ended on a desolate slip of land by the sea. Flagler dubbed the area Palm Beach and erected the Breakers Hotel.

Mrs Julia D. Tuttle, a wealthy refugee from Cleveland, Ohio, managed to convince Flagler to extend his railroad farther south to a strip of scrub on Biscayne Bay in 1896. Thus Miami come into being. Flagler laid tracks all the way along the Florida Keys to Key West by 1912, a year before his death. Wherever Flagler went, more hotels were sure to follow. And in their wake came a flood of tourists and immigrants. Florida's boom time had finally come. ❑

LEFT: railroad and hotel baron Henry Morrison Flagler.
ABOVE: the Ponce de León was one of several hotels built to lure tourists from the North to Florida.

MODERN TIMES

They came from near and far in the 20th century,
fun-seekers and refugees seeking new lives
in a Sunshine State that was undergoing
its own form of extreme makeover

Up and down Florida's coasts, cities sprang up toward the end of the 19th century along the railroad tracks laid by entrepreneurs Plant and Flagler. The state's growth was stimulated by the Spanish-American War of 1898, a situation quite different from past occasions when conflict tended to depress economic activity.

Florida's role in the war grew out of the cigar factories and Spanish cafés of the community founded by Vicente Martínez Ybor in Tampa in the 1880s. Cuban immigrants cheered on efforts by their compatriots back home to free the island of Spanish control. Huge crowds turned out in Tampa to hear Cuban freedom fighter José Martí plead for contributions to the cause, which was so popular that a rising political star named Napoleon Bonaparte Broward achieved notoriety for surreptitiously supplying weapons and ammunition to Cuban rebels before the

> When John Ringling was first buying land around Sarasota, he managed to acquire 66,000 acres (26,700 hectares) during a game of poker.

United States officially entered the war. Soon after, Broward became one of Florida's most progressive governors.

The sinking of the battleship USS *Maine* in Havana's harbor on February 15, 1898 gave America an excuse to join the revolutionaries in the war against Spain that broke out at the

LEFT: an Art Deco building in South Beach.
RIGHT: the wreck of the USS *Maine* was raised in 1912 to clear Havana's harbor.

end of April. American troops poured into Florida, setting up tent cities while waiting to sail to Cuba.

Good times

Tampa became a command post for the military. Theodore Roosevelt stormed into town with his Rough Riders en route to glory at San Juan Hill near the Cuban city of Santiago. Red Cross founder Clara Barton established a hospital in Tampa, while a young British journalist named Winston Churchill checked into the Tampa Bay Hotel to report a bloody good story. At the very place where it began its conquest, Spain was being driven from the New World.

After the conflict, the victorious Americans returned to points north with accounts of their exploits – and glowing depictions of Tampa, Miami, Key West, and other Florida ports and their attractive ambience. Some returned home only long enough to gather up their belongings, and perhaps a few friends and intimates, before heading back to Florida. By 1920 the Sunshine State's first major boom was under way.

Many of the characters who wheeled-and-dealed in real estate were interested only in fast fortunes, and they plundered Florida much as the Spanish and British had done

districts, and alluring lots on palm-lined boulevards and canals.

Carl Fisher dredged sand from the bottom of Biscayne Bay and transformed tangles of mangroves off the coast of Miami into a beach. In 1925 alone, 481 hotels and apartment buildings rose in Miami Beach. Over on Florida's west coast, circus tycoon John Ringling created the city of Sarasota, while Dave Davis dredged up islands that became enclaves for Tampa's elite.

Onward and downward

In 1926, a cold winter slowed spiraling prices. Then a hurricane whipped across the peninsula,

earlier. Others came, made money, stayed, and became state leaders. Walter Fuller was one such man; he carved up St Petersburg, a sun-kissed Gulf Coast city founded by Russian railroad czar Peter Demens. In his book *This Was Florida's Boom*, Fuller tells how he paid $50,000 for land he resold for $270,000, a vast sum at the time.

Fast-talking salesmen sold swamp-like tracts at auction. Even the golden-tongued William Jennings Bryan (a perennial presidential wannabe) got into the act, peddling real estate at George Merrick's development in Coral Gables. That site was the nation's first planned community, replete with regal entrance gates, pools, hotels, golf courses, zoned business

killing hundreds and destroying some of the flimsy housing developments. This brought the madness to a hasty end. The Wall Street crash of 1929 and the Great Depression soon followed. Overnight, as it were, Davis and Fuller and dozens of other millionaires became paupers. Still, the groundwork was laid. When Florida's growth resumed, happy days returned.

Between 1920 and 1940, the state's population doubled to nearly two million. By the start of World War II, tourists numbering upward of 2.5 million came to visit annually – a phenomenal figure. Florida's population was also growing increasingly urban. By 1940, more than 55 percent of the people were living in towns and cities, compared to only 37 percent in 1920.

Tampa attracted industry; Miami drew the sun-worshipers. More hotel rooms were built in Greater Miami between 1945 and 1954 than in the rest of the state combined.

Pari-mutuel betting on greyhounds and horses was legalized in 1931, bringing in additional revenues for the state's coffers – and an incentive for organized-crime rings to enter the field. Members of the syndicate shuttled between profitable rackets in Miami. The notorious mobster Al "Scarface" Capone found the location so convenient that he moved into a fortified estate on Palm Island near Miami Beach.

Space Age

Florida's greatest contribution to the future began to take shape after World War II, when the War Department started testing missiles at Cape Canaveral. Florida was host to the world's first scheduled airline service – a short hop between St Petersburg and Tampa – and in 1959 the first domestic jet flights in the US were launched. By that time, Cape Canaveral was well on its way to becoming the site of Kennedy Space Center. The last steps Neil Armstrong took on Earth before his giant step on the moon in 1969 were made on the sandy soil of Florida.

Some well-known personalities brought a measure of fame to the state during the 1960s. Jackie Gleason's hit television show enhanced Miami Beach's renown, this time under the rubric of "sun and fun capital of the world." Tennessee Williams, author of such major dramatic works as *The Glass Menagerie* and *A Streetcar Named Desire*, made Key West his winter home; he died there in 1983.

The new Floridians

Florida's reputation as a haven for refugees was heightened by the Cuban revolution engineered by Fidel Castro and his socialist compatriots in 1959. It sent a wave of anti-Castro and anti-communist Cubans to Florida shores throughout the 1960s. During the 1970s a slow but steady exodus continued, and in 1980 another big influx of Cubans landed in the Key West region as part of the so-called

Mariel boatlift. Most of those 125,000 refugees eventually made their way to the Miami area where an immigrant network was in place.

The 1980s also brought to South Florida some 75,000 Nicaraguans fleeing their country and its communist regime, and about 125,000 Haitians. In addition, the 1980s saw sharp increases in population in Palm Beach County, the Orlando area, and the Gulf Coast, as many Northerners streamed into the state in search of the Sun Belt lifestyle. Many of the nation's largest companies moved their headquarters south to Florida, and the international banking industry bloomed, particularly in

BUILDING AMBITION

Architecture is indicative of a state's ability to take setbacks in its stride. After a 1935 hurricane shredded the railroad through the Keys, engineers transformed it into the Overseas Highway. Miami Beach, which sprouted Art Deco hotels in the 1930s and '40s, was one of few cities to undergo a building boom during the Depression. Construction of Florida Southern College, designed by Frank Lloyd Wright *(pictured)*, began in 1938 and is a fitting monument to Wright's originality.

LEFT: new roads and bridges, such as the Gandy Bridge across Tampa Bay, encouraged development.
ABOVE RIGHT: Cuban refugees arrive in Florida during the 1980 Mariel boatlift.

Miami, well situated for trading with Latin America and the Caribbean. For Florida, it was an invigorating period of steady growth.

Unhappily, growth came as well from opportunists dealing in extra-legal and plainly illicit pursuits. With revenue from drug sales, the so-called Cocaine Cowboys pumped billions of dollars into Florida's economy but left a trail of crime and violence.

Along with the influx of immigrants and relocated Northerners, the 1980s brought pop-culture fame to the southern regions of the state. The slick, action-packed television series *Miami Vice*, first broadcast in 1984, transformed the international image of Miami from retirement haven to sleek and sexy paradise. Syndicated in more than 130 countries, *Miami Vice* glamorized the city's crime-ridden reputation and made tropical mayhem a fashionable trend.

A flood of tourists

As the 1990s began, Florida was growing rapidly. The influx of newcomers included Europeans, South Americans, and Japanese, who saw Florida as one great sunny investment opportunity. Tourism, the golden egg for the Sunshine State's economy, continued to grow at astonishing rates. The total number of

A CHECKERED LEGACY

The Seminole influence on Floridian culture lives on in the mascot of Florida State University's American football team, named Chief Osceola after the 19th-century tribal leader. The school's use of Indian imagery and native names rankles many living Native Americans, and the issue is often debated. In 2005 the National Collegiate Athletic Association took up the case; ultimately the sporting officials decided to allow FSU to continue using the Seminole mascot, with involvement from local tribes. Today, Seminole women design and create the authentic regalia worn by the chief during football games.

annual tourists was estimated at 50 million to 80 million, with roughly one-fourth of them coming from overseas. Above all, it was the arrival of entertainment magnate Walt Disney and his theme parks, the first of which opened in 1971, that decisively transformed tourism in the state.

Theme parks and other forms of wholesome family entertainment have proliferated in Orlando and now attract far more tourists than the magnificent beaches that line much of the coast. Tourism, in all its forms, is vital to the economy of many counties. After years of development, Florida has at last learned the importance of preserving its natural heritage. The state has numerous parks and preserves, from the vast Everglades National Park to small recreation areas tucked in among the urban sprawl. And the cruise industry is booming, adding billions of dollars to the state's revenue every year.

Stormy weather

While much of Florida follows a fairly stable course, the southern half of the state continues its roller-coaster existence, especially topsy-turvy Miami. In 1992, Hurricane Andrew's four-hour devastation through southern Florida left half of Miami-Dade County in a shambles. Two years later, southern Florida received another wave of refugees. Images of Cubans arriving aboard home-made rafts made headlines around the world. Tensions inevitably resulted as the state struggled to cope with the influx.

One area to have been consistently upwardly mobile is the Art Deco district of South Beach, which has undergone a renaissance that can only be described as spectacular. Fashion models, tourists, and trendsetters elbow each other for table space at Ocean Drive's bars and cafés, while convertibles and stretch limos compete for space on the road. That opulence, however, came with a cost to the most well-heeled of Miami's modern pioneers: Gianni Versace, the virtuoso fashion designer who proudly mingled with the common people on the beach, was killed by a crazed fan who shot the 50-year-old designer on his doorstep.

Making headlines

Florida today ranks fourth in population in the Union, a number that neared 19 million in 2010. If it is not lacking in people, it is also not lacking in headline-making notoriety.

Much attention was focused in the year 2000, for example, on the plight of a Cuban boy named Elian Gonzalez. Not quite six years of age when he left Cuba, he survived a harrowing voyage in a small boat and an inner tube across the Florida Straits before being rescued; his mother and ten others perished in the attempt. Following a protracted legal tug-of-war over his custody that involved relatives, the courts, federal officials, and the Miami-based Cuban-American community, Elian returned with his father to Cuba in June.

LEFT: playing with the tigers at Busch Gardens Tampa.
ABOVE: Hurricane Andrew devastated South Florida.

There was widespread grief on February 1, 2003, when seven astronauts aboard the *Columbia* space shuttle died when it disintegrated during re-entry into the Earth's atmosphere. The cause: a piece of heat-resistant tiling had broken off during its launch from Cape Canaveral two weeks earlier.

The grandest controversy of all was the legal struggle waged to decide the victor in the 2000 presidential campaign between George W. Bush, the Republican governor of Texas, and Al Gore, the Democratic vice president. The tally in the contest for Florida's 25 electoral votes was exceedingly close, and the legal jockeying by

cadres of high-powered attorneys that resulted over the issue of a recount was unprecedented. A 5–4 decision of the US Supreme Court decided the election in Bush's favor. The ruling remains highly contentious.

The battle over offshore oil drilling is argued throughout Florida, where concerns over the threats posted by coastal rigs to tourism and the environment were exacerbated by the 2010 oil spill in the Gulf waters of nearby Louisiana. Floridians can be bitterly divided on the question of whether the state should chase the economic benefits of oil exploration despite the risk of an environmental and economic calamity, but for now the inland waters remain as pristine as ever. ❏

THE CULTURAL LANDSCAPE

Florida is sometimes comically dismissed as the "land of the newlyweds and the nearly dead," but the influx of newcomers has created a lively market for both the visual and the performing arts

Like its history, the development of Florida's cultural character unfolded in a distinctly different pattern than the rest of the American South. During its initial period of Spanish rule, Florida was held primarily for strategic reasons and was sparsely colonized, with only a few Spanish residents. Consequently, the long colonial period left a scant legacy of Hispanic culture.

During the British occupation, an influx of other European emigrants flowed in, primarily from Italy and Greece. A Greek Orthodox shrine in St Augustine serves as a vivid reminder of the religion and culture of these early arrivals.

Although most American Indians in Florida were either killed by war or disease, or forced to march West on the Trail of Tears, a few hardy souls remained hidden in the Everglades.

The top American states feeding Florida's population boom are New York, New Jersey, Ohio, Michigan, and Illinois. Some might say that Yankees have remade South Florida in the image of the Northeast.

These Seminole Indians, with their sub-tribe the Miccosukee, continue to practice their traditional crafts and rituals, as evidenced at the Miccosukee Cultural Center in the Everglades, along the Tamiami Trail, and at the annual Seminole tribal fair in Hollywood.

PRECEDING PAGES: bar dancers in South Beach.
LEFT: a replica of Michelangelo's *David* at the Ringling Museum of Art in Sarasota. **RIGHT:** *Young Shepherdess* by William Bouguereau at the Appleton Museum of Art.

Slow start

When Florida became a state in 1845, nearly half of its population of 60,000 were black slaves working on cotton and sugar plantations, and maintained a culture steeped in West African traditions of music and storytelling. Among white settlers – most of whom came to Florida from Georgia and the Carolinas – a folk culture akin to that of the southern Appalachians predominated. There were only 140,000 Floridians (nearly half of them slaves) at the time of the Civil War. Any cultural awakening in the state would clearly have to wait for a significant increase in population, and for the growth of cities.

The population increase began with the discovery of Florida as a winter retreat for northerners, beginning with the arrival of railroads along the state's east coast in the 1880s. The 1920s saw the state's year-round numbers begin to climb; wealthy winter sojourners (known as snowbirds) such as circus king John Ringling gave a tremendous boost to the Florida arts scene. Ringling, who built his Venetian-inspired fantasy home, Cà d'Zan, in Sarasota, opened the John and Mable Ringling Museum of Art in the west-coast city in 1931. Another overwintering businessman, James Deering, created Miami's lavish Vizcaya estate.

Sudden shift

In the first half of the 20th century, Florida's cultural atmosphere reflected a mix of white, Southern farmers and black, former slaves. Also in the mix were émigrés from the North, and local island populations. The political sea change that overtook Cuba in 1959 following the socialist revolution led by Fidel Castro, brought the arts and traditions of Florida's island neighbor into the mainstream. The great migration of Cubans – abetted by a smaller influx of Haitians, Dominicans, and people from other Caribbean nations – made a Latin American capital of Miami and transformed the cultural flavor of all but the northernmost portions of the peninsula.

For a sample of the Cuban performing-arts scene, take in one of the programs offered by IFÉ-ILÉ Afro-Cuban Dance and Music, a Miami-based organization that presents traditional and contemporary dances, concerts, and poetry readings (in Spanish), and sponsors a dance and music festival each July. There's also a Cuban-American Heritage Festival in Key West each June.

You don't have to visit Florida in the warmer months to enjoy the biggest of all Cuban celebrations: Miami's Calle Ocho (Eighth Street) Festival, held in March, draws 1 million visitors to a bash that concludes with a massive block party featuring 30 music stages. If March is too far off, head to Calle Ocho on the last Friday of each month, when the Viernes Culturales street party rollicks with music, dancing, and street performers. Miami's Haitian community, too, highlights its music and dance traditions with the annual Compas Festival, held in Bayfront Park each May.

Visual arts

The visual and performing-arts scene in Florida revolves around various venues, museums, and festivals scattered among a half-dozen or so important population centers. In metropolitan Miami, the Bass Museum of Art supplements its post-Renaissance European painting and sculpture with a strong Caribbean and Latin American presence, and Wolfsonian-Florida International University showcases decorative arts. But the biggest fine arts presence in the area is the ever-changing canvas of the Art Basel festival, an exhibition held every December that draws some of the

CHORAL CAPITAL

Residents of Palm Beach have a special love for choral music. Six fine choral groups flourish near the city, including the Master Chorale of South Florida; the Masterworks Chorus; the Choral Society of the Palm Beaches; the Boca Raton Singers; and Voices of Pride, a gay chorus. Performing at venues throughout Florida's east coast, these polished vocalists – most local residents – offer a repertory ranging from classical oratorios to Gilbert and Sullivan, and from spirituals to show tunes. Among favorite performances is the Masterworks Chorus's annual rendition of Handel's *Messiah*. The concert is held in December at the Royal Poinciana Chapel in Palm Beach.

world's finest galleries and dealers to chic shows and sleek parties.

Fort Lauderdale has a more low-key arts scene, with several up-and-coming contemporary galleries in the Las Olas neighborhood and a more traditional, European focus at the city's Museum of Art. Jacksonville has a thriving arts culture of its own, shaped by students at the local University of North Florida, as well as Art Walk and First Friday events in a core crop of downtown studios.

Orlando boasts several respectable art museums, showcasing everything from pre-Columbian American art to the American

of funky downtown spots, the ARTpool Gallery and Vintage Boutique offers upstart creatives a chance to showcase their fine and decorative artwork. The Chihuly Collection transports locals and tourists to the colorful, madcap oeuvre of glass artist Dale Chihuly.

Sarasota has more of a quietly creative energy, thanks to the largesse of museum-endowing snowbird John Ringling, whose Ringling Museum of Art and Ringling College spawned no fewer than nine promising academic galleries for emerging contemporary art, led by the Selby. Off campus, the Art Uptown is the only formal co-operative

Hudson River School of landscape painting to the entire Louis Comfort Tiffany chapel designed for the 1893 Chicago World Columbian Exposition. The town best known for Mickey Mouse also showcases more refined modern art at three publicly owned galleries, two of which are inside City Hall.

Over on the west coast, St Petersburg has built a thriving local community around its world-famous museum dedicated to Spanish surrealist Salvador Dalí, which received a much-anticipated makeover in 2011. Among a slew

---

Left: the Cummer Museum of Art in Jacksonville.
Above: works of modern masters are the highlight of the collection at the Boca Raton Museum of Art.

gallery in Florida, giving artists a chance to share the spotlight.

Performing arts

For classical music, the most important Miami area institutions are the Miami Symphony Orchestra, which performs at the University of Miami's Gusman Hall and at Miami Beach's Lincoln Theater; Florida Grand Opera, based at the Carnival Center for the Performing Arts (also with performances in Fort Lauderdale); the Miami Lyric Opera, offering performances at the Colony Theater in Miami Beach as well as outdoors at Flamingo Park once a year; and Michael Tilson Thomas' New World Symphony, which bills itself as the "only full-time orchestral academy" in America. New World also makes its home at Lincoln Theater, but is in the midst of building a stately new campus at downtown Miami's redeveloped City Center, to be designed by renowned architect Frank Gehry.

The Miami City Ballet makes its local home in the state's biggest metropolis, but also takes its ultra-modern twists on Twyla Tharp and other master choreographers north to Broward and Palm Beach counties, and the International Ballet Festival of Miami takes to the road in late summer. For an edgier take on moving bodies, the Miami Contemporary Dance Company can be found partnering with international cohorts while the Dance Now! Ensemble stages frequent classics along with works influenced by its residence at the Little Haiti Cultural Center.

Further north on the "Cultural Coast," the Sarasota Ballet of Florida stages a sampling of classics every season while the non-professional West Coast Civic Ballet offers its own spring dance festival and classes. Also in Sarasota, the Florida West Coast Symphony often plays selections from popular Broadway shows and movies. The Sarasota Opera performs traditional selections such as *La*

SOUTHERN SYMPHONY

The Key West Symphony Orchestra was founded by Sebrina Maria Alfonso, a fifth-generation "Conch" of Cuban ancestry, who serves as its conductor and music director. Each year, she assembles a group of up to 70 musicians who can commit to perform-ing in Key West during the orchestra's four-concert winter series, which is supplemented by free out-door concerts, children's programs, master classes, and a popular annual Christmas season revival of Menotti's *Amahl and the Night Visitors*. The Key West Symphony players all have careers with other orchestras, but enjoy bringing classical music to this arts-loving town in the Keys.

bohéme, and modern tales such as *The Crucible*. Visiting groups perform at Sarasota's Van Wezel Performing Arts Hall.

In the Fort Lauderdale and Palm Beach areas, the Symphony of the Americas focuses on diversity in its concert selections while the Palm Beach Symphony takes a more classical approach. Fort Lauderdale's Broward Center for the Performing Arts, anchoring the city's Riverwalk Arts and Entertainment District, hosts the first of those two orchestras in addition to an array of hot-ticket Broadway-style theatrical performances at its four affiliated venues.

Northeastern Florida's classical music scene revolves around the Jacksonville Symphony Orchestra. The 60-year-old ensemble, and its affiliated Youth Orchestra, perform in an acoustic gem, the Robert E. Jacoby Symphony Hall at the Times-Union Center for the Performing Arts.

The Tampa Bay Performing Arts Center, the largest center of its kind south of Washington, DC's Kennedy Center, is a complex of five theaters that serve as home to the Tampa Bay Symphony and Opera Tampa. Also on the state's west coast, the Naples Philharmonic Orchestra performs at the city's Philharmonic Center for the Arts. The nearby Orlando Ballet stages a sampling of classics every season, at least two of which are also performed in Tampa. The Orlando Philharmonic Orchestra, meanwhile, does its fare share of traditional numbers but gave a nod to its home town by performing live at the opening of the Universal Studios theme park's Harry Potter ride with famed film composer John Williams.

Stage to screen

Miami is the live theater capital of Florida, with dozens of stages large and small, as well as several locally based drama companies. Among them are the Actors' Playhouse at the Miracle Theater in Coral Gables, offering professionally staged theater for children and adults, and City Theater, specializing in new, shorter drama. Plays bound for Broadway often stop at the Coconut Grove Playhouse. For Spanish-language performances, try the Teatro de Bellas Artes, in Miami's Little Havana neighborhood, where drama, comedy, and musical performances fit the bill. Foreign movie buffs shouldn't miss the Miami International Film Festival every March, not to mention the dozen-plus smaller retrospectives that often bring new flicks from overseas.

Further south, the intimate Red Barn Theatre on Key West's lively Duval Street puts on a half-dozen shows between December and March, while the Tennessee Williams Theatre takes in more mainstream, crowd-pleasing productions. The Keys also host their own opera theater, which plays host to musical shows and the Key West Symphony Orchestra (*see box on opposite page*).

The unquestioned star of Sarasota's theater scene is the Asolo Repertory Theatre, where new standards such as the musical *Boeing Boeing*

are paired with risky reboots of *Bonnie and Clyde* and *Antigone*. Other local theater venues include The Players of Sarasota, a community group staging comedy acts and dramas; and the Venice Little Theater, 20 miles (32km) south of Sarasota in Venice, with a varied and ambitious schedule of comedy, drama, and musicals. The Sarasota Film Festival is a draw in its own right for top-drawer independent titles, such as the Oscar-nominated documentary *Gasland*.

In the Palm Beach area, the Dramaworks company mingles historically inspired dramas with established comedies, a template followed at Boca Raton's Caldwell Theatre Company

with the added bonus of an acclaimed Adult Storytelling Series. Widely hailed film festivals also draw behind-the-camera talent to Palm Beach in spring and Fort Lauderdale in the fall.

Orlando and environs are richly endowed with live theater organizations. The Orlando Repertory Theatre presents an ambitious program of family-friendly plays; the Orlando Shakespeare Theater mounts 10 productions each year, including several of the Bard's works. The downtown Mad Cow Theatre presents stagings of classic and modern dramas in addition to a cabaret festival in May. The Orlando Film Festival, usually held in November, distinguishes itself by helping cultivate live comic talent as well as screen whizzes. ❏

LEFT: the sculpture garden at the Ringling Museum.
RIGHT: alternative transportation in Key West.

EXTREME WEATHER

Florida does nothing by halves. Famously, it boasts more sun than most corners of the United States, but it also has more than its fair share of rain and thunderstorms

In her book *Cross Creek*, Marjorie Kinnan Rawlings says that in Florida the seasons "move in and out like nuns in soft clothing, making no rustle in their passing." It is hard to tell spring from summer, and fall slips into winter almost without notice. Temperatures drop in winter but rarely approach freezing; the coldest temperature ever recorded was a frosty –2°F (–19°C) in Tallahassee in 1899. It is rare, but not unheard of, for snow to fall in Florida, typically in the northern or Panhandle regions. Accumulation of more than a few inches is unusual.

Florida has the advantage of being sunny all year round. The Sunshine State isn't merely a catchy slogan dreamed up to lure tourists, but an official name that demonstrates the importance of the sun in raising billions of dollars for Florida by attracting tourists, baseball squads, and fashion photographers, who revel in the fact that in winter their models can pose in next to nothing against a blue sky while most of the nation is bundled up in sweaters. Many crops, including vegetables and fruit from oranges to mangoes, thrive in the warm and wet climate. Since more than 70 percent of the country's orange crop is grown in Florida, farmers anxiously monitor the weather throughout the growing season.

Although Florida is known for sunshine, the state is also a place of extremes. Florida is wetter than anywhere else in the US. More than half the average total rainfall is recorded from June to September, when the state can be subjected to as much rainfall as some European cities get in a whole year. Key West is the driest city in the state and it still gets 40 inches (100cm) of rain annually.

ABOVE: a hurricane can lift boats out of the water, flatten houses and rip the facades off buildings. Hurricane Andrew, which buffeted Florida in 1992, left 250,000 people temporarily homeless.

BELOW: Florida is the lightning capital of the US, and ranks fourth in the world in the frequency of lightning strikes, which have killed 425 and injured more than 2,000 people in the state since 1960 – more than all other risky weather events combined. The lightning belt extends from Jacksonville to Fort Myers, with Fort Myers averaging 100 lightning-packed days a year.

LEFT: seven of the 10 hottest US cities are in Florida. Key West ranks first, then Miami, with a year-round average of 75.6°F (24.2°C). In the sultry summer months, Miami Beach's famous Art Deco thermometer simply cannot cope.

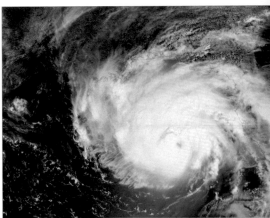

THE DEVELOPMENT OF A HURRICANE

A tropical storm is called a hurricane when its wind speed exceeds 74 miles (119km) per hour. The hurricane is then classified from 1 to 5 according to the Saffir-Simpson Scale, which measures the wind speed and expected flooding. Category 5 is the worst, with winds of more than 155 miles (249km) per hour.

Many of the hurricanes that hit Florida develop off the coast of Africa and move across the Atlantic. Several factors contribute to the formation of a hurricane, above all heat and wind. The key ingredient is the heat of the summer sun, which warms the surface of the ocean enough for water to evaporate. As the warm air rises, it condenses into thunderclouds, which are sent spinning by the rotation of the Earth. The hurricane moves forward at 7–30 miles (11–48km) per hour and can measure hundreds of miles across.

The National Hurricane Center in Miami tracks a hurricane's progress using radar and satellites. Pilots, known as Hurricane Hunters, also fly in and out of the storm in order to gather data. Warning of the severity of a hurricane can greatly reduce the damage done if the storm eventually makes landfall. While the winds can be devastating, most damage and deaths are caused by flooding from the storm surge – a wall of water that can reach a height of 20ft (6 meters).

RIGHT: snow is so rare that merely a touch of it can cripple Florida. The highest recorded snowfall in the state was on March 6, 1954, when 4 inches (10cm) of the white stuff fell in Santa Rosa County near Pensacola. Frost and flurries are more common than actual flakes.

BELOW: the Gulf Coast between St Pete Beach and Clearwater Beach enjoys an average of 363 sunny days a year. From 1967 to 1969 an amazing 768 consecutive days of sunshine were recorded here, so be sure to pack a hat and sun screen.

RIGHT: all along the Gulf Coast, official evacuation routes head north and west, while on the Atlantic coast, the routes head inland to the west. In case of a mass evacuation, follow the blue road signs with the large directional arrow to safety.

FLORIDA CUISINE

It's not all shrimp, alligator tail steak, and Key lime pie; the state's multi-ethnic population is reflected in its cuisine, and the strong Caribbean influence can add a tangy flavor when least expected

For centuries, Florida cooks have charted a varied culinary course, drawing upon a bounty of local ingredients and a broad range of regional and international influences. There's no single Florida cuisine, but rather a panoply of Southern, Anglo, Caribbean, and Latin American trends that enliven an ever-changing food culture, one of the most exciting in the US.

In the beginning, Floridians – Indians and Europeans alike – dined off the peninsula's abundance drawn from land and sea. One passionate chronicler of old Floridian cuisine was the late Marjorie Kinnan Rawlings, Pulitzer-Prize-winning author of *The Yearling*, whose books *Cross Creek* and *Cross Creek Cookery* documented her life and kitchen adventures in her adopted home of Cross Creek, a tiny village in the northern part of the state where she lived in the 1930s and '40s. In *Cross Creek Cookery*, Rawlings set down her recipes for old-time dishes such as hush

Florida's early explorers dined on boar, venison, and even bear, which the native people sometimes bartered with the settlers. The Indians also simmered turtle, duck eggs, frog legs, eels, and alligator in herbs.

puppies, pecan pie, cream of peanut soup, and the more exotic coot surprise and alligator tail steak. One of Rawlings' favorite dishes

LEFT: Columbia Restaurant in Ybor City, Tampa.
RIGHT: a taste of lobster from Caretta on the Gulf at the Sandpearl Resort in Clearwater Beach.

was turtle eggs (not from sea turtles), whose "fine and distinct flavor" she praised, noting that "a dozen turtle eggs, with plain bread and butter and a glass of ale, make all I ask of a light luncheon or supper."

Hotel fare

Many of these dishes are representative of the coastal South. Before it was discovered by winter-weary northerners, Florida was much more a typical Southern state than it is today, and Southern culinary folkways were predominant. When the outsiders did arrive, their tastes ran to the conventionally substantial hotel menus of the era. The table d'hôte offerings at the big Atlantic coast hotels might have been perked up with fresh local orange juice and locally caught seafood, but they were essentially what a traveler might expect at chic hostelries from Philadelphia to Boston.

When Miami began to attract vacationers and retirees from the North, one of the greatest culinary influences became the Jewish delicatessen found in New York. In Miami Beach, you'll never look far for a bagel with cream cheese and lox. In Florida's cities and resorts, as in any cosmopolitan environment, Italian, French, Chinese, Thai, and a host of other international dining choices are always available.

Florida oranges

Despite rivers, lakes, and offshore waters that teemed with fish and shellfish, the food that first drew the attention of the outside world to Florida was the orange. Oranges are not native to Florida; they were first brought to the peninsula by the Spanish explorers Ponce de León and Hernando de Soto and soon grew wild.

The orange industry in Florida got its start as early as the 1770s. A century later, thousands of acres of groves had been planted, and Florida oranges were heading north by train just as the tourists were traveling south.

OYSTER BAR

Apalachicola Bay, one of the world's richest estuarine systems, is famous for its oysters, providing Florida with 90 percent of its annual oyster harvest. Oyster farmers in the bay, poised on their small boats, use tongs fashioned from two giant rakes to pincer their crop, which is cultivated in carefully selected water (neither too salty nor too fresh) in nurseries known as oyster bars. They can be harvested year-round, but the catch tends to be smaller during summer.

The region around the Indian River (which is not a river but a saltwater lagoon 120 miles [190km] long and seldom more than 2 miles [3km] wide) became a prime growing area. Indian River is also famous for its grapefruit, a citrus family member that originated in the West Indies and was first planted in Florida in 1823. Shipments of grapefruit didn't reach the northeastern US until the 1880s, when Americans began to develop a taste for their tart, juicy flesh.

Key lime and conch

One Florida crop that is indelibly linked with one of the state's most distinctive regions is, ironically, no longer grown commercially here:

the Key lime. This small, yellowish lime is known to most visitors as the main ingredient in Key lime pie. Even in the Keys, when you order a slice of Key lime pie you'll be savoring fruit grown in Mexico – unless you've lucked into a mom-and-pop bakery or coffee shop that has a Key lime tree or two in the back yard. Like the Keys' pygmy deer (which are emphatically not on any menus), Key limes are far more famous than they are abundant.

Any mention of Keys cuisine brings to mind another of the island's iconic dishes: conch (pronounced *konk*). Conch is so indelibly linked with the culinary traditions of Key West that its

have been tenderized by pounding and lightly breaded or battered and fried; and in conch fritters, the best of which have a high ratio of conch to batter and have been fried at just the right temperature to avoid greasiness. There are some terrific conch fritters served by street vendors in Mallory Square, Key West, around the time when the inevitable tourist throng applauds the sunset.

Fresh seafood

Florida waters still yield a delicious array of seafood. Key West pink shrimp are a succulent alternative to the farm-raised supermarket

native-born residents call themselves conchs, but the mollusk itself, at least as far as local tables go, is a native no longer. Restrictions on harvesting the now-depleted shellfish in Florida waters mean that all conch served in the state are imported from the Bahamas. When you do order conch, it's the queen conch that you will be served. Its flesh, which is similar to that of calamari, is most frequently prepared in one of four ways: as conch salad, sort of a *ceviche* with a hot pepper kick; in a chowder, either tomato or cream-based; as cracked conch, strips that

---

FAR LEFT: Key lime pie is a classic tropical dessert.
ABOVE LEFT AND ABOVE: fresh local shrimp and stone crab are Florida specialties.

variety, especially when tossed with pasta or fried and tucked into that New Orleans import, the po'boy sandwich. Stone crabs (there's a famous and eponymous restaurant in Miami Beach that built its reputation on them) are unique among sustainable shellfish resources in that their big, sweet claws (where all the meat is) grow back after they are removed and the crab is returned to the sea. Claws, however, don't figure at all as part of the lobsters harvested in South Florida waters. These are a different species from the cold-water specimens in New England. More properly called spiny lobster or langouste, they aren't armed with fat pincers but instead are nearly all tail meat. They're most often served broiled; just make sure they don't spend too much time under the flame, which can make the flesh dry.

Finned fish commonly found on Florida menus include members of the snapper clan – yellowtail, hog, and mutton snapper are predominant – as well as mahi-mahi, the name given to the fish once commonly known as dolphin but rechristened to avoid confusion with the beloved mammal. Grouper turns up on quite a few Florida restaurant tables as well. Like conch, it's a versatile and delectable ocean denizen that's a dietary mainstay of the nearby Bahamas, but fishing pressure on grouper has caused a worrisome decline

in stocks, so it's best to save this fish for the occasional meal.

A taste of the islands

By far the biggest news on the Florida food scene over the past few decades has been the impact made by the variegated cuisines of Latin America. Given the close proximity of Floridian the peninsula to the West Indies (Grand Bahama Island is a scant 60 miles [95km] from Florida, Cuba only 90 miles [140km]), it would seem to have been natural for Bahamian and Caribbean influences to have shown up earlier. But for centuries,

SUSTAINABLE SEAFOOD

Given the extensive variety of seafood on Florida menus, it's a good idea to be aware of which species are relatively abundant and which have been negatively affected by fishing pressure. Grouper is a long-lived species that is particularly vulnerable to overfishing, and management of the fishery has been spotty. Orange roughy is another species with a long reproductive cycle – they don't mature until 20 years old – and their stocks have been significantly depleted by trawler fishing, which also damages their deep-water spawning habitat. Sharks, too, are slow-growing and do not reproduce prolifically and are heavily overfished in international waters.

Among the least threatened commercially caught fish is mahi-mahi, which reproduces quickly and can sustain high

fishing pressure – especially when the method used is trolling, as opposed to longline fishing. Albacore, yellowfin, and skipjack tuna stocks also stand up to commercial harvest, as long as pole and troll methods are used, although longline and purse-seine fishing for tuna takes a heavy toll and causes the collateral destruction of sharks.

Among sustainable shellfish species, Florida hard clams are a particular standout. The clams, which are farmed commercially off Brevard County on the Atlantic and along the Gulf Coast, grow to maturity in suspended nets, which eliminates the need for harmful dredging, and do not require feeding with fishmeal or other potential pollutants, as the mollusks filter nutrients from seawater.

mainland American tastes prevailed, and foreign flavors intruded mainly in Key West. One very old neighborhood in that city has long been imbued with the tastes of its Bahamian-descended inhabitants and their way with conch, grouper, pork, chicken, and the ubiquitous side dish of pigeon peas with rice.

During the late 19th century Cuban cigar makers began migrating to Key West, and they brought with them the harbingers of the cuisine that has since become part of the cultural signature of all of South Florida, especially Miami and its Little Havana neighborhood. The recipes the Cubans brought with them included *ropa vieja* (old clothes), a long-simmered stew of shredded beef; the slow-roasted pork called *lechon*; plantains fried in butter until they caramelize; and *picadillo*, a mélange of ground meat and potatoes seasoned with onions, tomatoes, pimientos, green olives, and capers. Black beans and rice are a universal accompaniment, and a mainstay throughout the day is strong Cuban coffee, usually well sweetened and served in the morning with hot milk as *café con leche*. The one Cuban dish nearly every visitor can find, even without seeking out a Cuban restaurant, is the sandwich Cubano, stuffed with ham, roast pork, cheese, and pickles, served hot from a press. The *medianoche* version (named for its popularity as a midnight snack) is usually made with a sweeter variety of the thin-crusted Cuban bread that has a soft, flaky inside.

Island flavors

Other kinds of Caribbean cuisine have followed the waves of immigrants that have come to Florida. A sizable Dominican community brought *pastelitos*, turnovers filled with meat or cheese; the hearty stew called *sancocho*, made with chicken or beef melded with the flavors of green plantains and any combination of cassava (yucca), the similar but creamier yautia, and potatoes, and invariably served with rice; and fish poached in coconut milk. *Buñuelos*, sweet donuts, are a popular accompaniment to coffee.

From Jamaica come spicy meat pasties (sometimes called turnovers) and jerk chicken and pork, the time-honored street foods of Kingston and Montego Bay, along with curried goat, chicken, and shrimp. The tamarind and ginger native to the island season many Jamaican dishes, and cassava bread is always a favorite.

Haitians, one of the most recent émigré groups, carried with them their fondness for fish boiled with lime juice, onion and garlic, and hot pepper. Highly seasoned beef patties and corn fritters are also reminders of the creole cuisine of their homeland.

Florida's chefs experiment with all of these traditions, adding local produce and seafood to create a fusion all their own. The wonderful thing about the dishes of Florida is that they haven't supplanted each other either through the passing of time or the arrival of ethnic newcomers. The flavors of Florida exist side by side, admittedly more traditionally Southern in the north and Latin in the South, but always in close enough proximity so that a single sojourn in the state can supply a visitor with savory memories of Dixie barbecue, luminously fresh shellfish, a hefty *medianoche* sandwich consumed in the wee hours … and that sack of oranges, so juicy that they should have been sold with a roll of paper towels. ❑

LEFT: pasta with shrimp and mussels at the Naples Tomato. **ABOVE RIGHT:** the hearty Dominican stew called *sancocho* includes chicken, beef, plantains, yucca, and *naranja agria* (very sour oranges).

THE BUSINESS OF PLEASURE

It takes a heap of manpower and a lot of logistics
to keep Florida's theme parks up and running
and ahead of the competition

Each evening, after approximately 117,000 guests exit through the turnstiles at Walt Disney World, the park's night crew swings into action. Almost 25,000 people work until morning to refresh the cobwebs and "antique" grime in the Magic Kingdom's Haunted Mansion, mowing more than 2,000 acres (810 hectares) of grass, distributing three tons of food to more than 1,000 animals at Animal Kingdom, even refilling the toilet tissue holders that will dispense 19,000 miles (31,000km) of paper in a year. This crew is about half of the "cast" of 62,000 people hired by America's largest single-site employer to help keep Disney World "the happiest place on earth" – and perhaps the best maintained, as well.

For the Disney Company, Mickey and the gang are big business: the estimated more than 30 million people (that's nearly equivalent to the population of Canada) who pass through the gates every year will spend more than

> Every day an average of 100 pairs of sunglasses are turned into the Lost and Found at the Magic Kingdom. That's more than 1.2 million pairs since the park opened in 1971.

$100 each on tickets, meals, refreshments, and souvenirs. It's no wonder so much hard work goes into ensuring that everyone has fun.

The folks at Disney produce and package pleasure. They provide a controlled, safe, and

LEFT: riding the Shamu Express at SeaWorld.
RIGHT: a friendly Busch Gardens staff member.

clean environment staffed by cast members (the Disney term for employees) who are always neat and well-groomed, and who never sport beards, long nails, tattoos, or visible body piercings. They buff and polish a place where youngsters can frolic and parents can relive their childhood fantasies alongside Cinderella, Peter Pan, and a host of cartoon characters that by now seem part of the American family. The cast does all these tasks well: Walt Disney World is the most visited vacation destination on earth.

Day-to-day Disney

Disney World functions well because it was planned that way from the beginning. When

Walt and his brother Roy began scouting sites for an East Coast theme park, they wanted to avoid the mistakes they'd made in building Disneyland in California. One mistake was not purchasing a piece of land large enough to accommodate a self-contained vacation resort that could offer visitors everything they would want or need, so that they wouldn't have to go off-property to spend their money. Under a blind trust, Disney purchased 27,300 acres (11,000 hectares) of rural central Florida for an average of $200 an acre. Although it was mostly swamp, the 43 square mile (111 sq km) parcel – a piece of land twice the size of Manhattan

From the outset, Disney's plan was to retain complete control of the environment. With an initial investment of $400 million, the company built a plant that generates approximately 35 percent of the electricity needed to operate the park. (Each year, Disney World uses about half as many kilowatt hours as the entire state of Maine.)

Disney also set up its own waste disposal system, which now handles a daily load of up to 50 tons of trash – much of it generated at the park's restaurants. The heart of the disposal system is a giant underground vacuum that sucks refuse from points scattered

– would allow Disney to create a buffer large enough to keep competition at bay.

A home of its own

Equally important was having the authority to develop and manage the property as Disney saw fit. The Florida legislature knew that the park would be profitable for the state, and thus approved a bill granting Disney permission to establish the Reedy Creek Improvement District, an area some have dubbed the Florida Vatican. The legislation gave Disney the authority to develop and manage every aspect of its property, including decisions about zoning, taxes, and even building an airport or nuclear power plant (should the need arise).

throughout the park and moves it at 60 miles per hour (97kph) through tubes leading to a central repository, where it is compacted and transported to a landfill. Enormous amounts of material, including 6,500 pounds (3,000kg) of aluminum cans, are processed each day at the park's recycling center.

When the Magic Kingdom was in its planning stage, designers came up with an elegant way to hide from guests the day-to-day operations necessary to run the park. They built a 2.8 mile (4.5km) utility corridor, or "utilidor," with 15ft (5 meter) -high tunnels at ground level, covered it with 8 million cubic yards (6 million cubic meters) of soil dug to create the Seven Seas Lagoon, and built the park over it. The utilidor houses the park's computer operations, offices, make-up operations, and costuming rooms. Color-coded connecting corridors permit Mickey and the gang a quick and easy way to suit up and scoot to different parts of the park.

Vying for dollars

The Orlando Convention and Visitors Bureau estimates that more than 45 million people visit the city annually. The hundreds of area hotels (with a combined total of more than 110,000 rooms), restaurants, stores, and attractions all want a share of the money these visitors will spend, and most of them pool a portion of their advertising budgets to get it. Theme parks, including Universal Orlando, SeaWorld, and Gatorland, offer discounts in a myriad of free coupon books and through programs including the Convention and Visitors Bureau's MagiCard and the Orlando Flexticket.

Disney managers have taken a different route. Not only do they decline to advertise cooperatively with other businesses, they've pursued a policy of building attractions in an attempt to monopolize tourist dollars: hence the additions in recent years of Typhoon Lagoon (to compete with Wet 'n' Wild), Hollywood Studios (to combat Universal Studios), and Animal Kingdom (to draw clientele from Busch Gardens and SeaWorld). The building of Downtown Disney to compete with Universal's CityWalk and downtown Orlando's Church Street Station was so effective that the latter closed its doors in 2002.

Disney does offer a few discounts – generally on multiday packages and through its own Disney Club, as well as in cooperation with the American Automobile Association (AAA). In an unusual move for a company that retains ironfisted control over its marketing, the company has entered a distribution agreement with Travelocity.com, giving the travel website the authority to book theme park tickets, onsite hotels, and cruises for its customers.

Disney World, here I come

The Travelocity deal may well be an acknowledgment of the fact that there is more

competition than ever for tourist dollars, and Disney is aggressively protective of its market share. Competition may also be the reason that Orlando theme parks, and Disney in particular, have stepped up their advertising campaigns.

Few sloganeering efforts have been as effective as the two-decade project that finds celebrity athletes gazing into a TV camera at the moment of their greatest victories and uttering the five words that confirm their status as superstars: "I'm going to Disney World." The catchphrase is the foundation of the successful "What's Next" campaign, designed to present Disney World as the place for people to go

when they're celebrating. After all, what did quarterback Alex Rodriguez say after leading the Green Bay Packers to victory in the 2011 Super Bowl? "I'm going to Disney World."

Staying on top

Despite the growth of competing attractions, Disney World remains the 800-pound gorilla of Orlando theme parks, outdistancing its nearest competitor by more than four times. In 2009, 47.5 million people paid admission to Disney World's four major theme parks, 5.5 million went to Universal Orlando, and 5.8 million flocked to SeaWorld. But management knows that to stay on top, the park has to continue to meet – better yet, to exceed

– the expectations of its guests, approximately 70 percent of whom are repeat customers. So in a business climate in which fuel costs are prohibitively high, the US economy is in a funk, and tourists are rethinking the whole idea of a family vacation, quality must be maintained and image burnished even more aggressively.

There's grumbling among some Disney aficionados that new entries such as Epcot's Mission: SPACE don't measure up to the latest generation of high-tech rides that are being developed at other theme parks. Indeed, that's what the folks at Universal and SeaWorld might well be counting on to boost their attendance figures. Universal's East Coast working studio has evolved into an entertainment empire, with two distinct theme parks, a water park, the CityWalk entertainment complex, and three huge theme hotels.

On the edge

The words most often used to compare Universal with Disney are "hipper," "edgier"... and "newer." It's hard to imagine two more different experiences than listening to a calm, carefully scripted presentation at the Magic Kingdom's Jungle Cruise (ad-libbing by cast

MOB MANAGEMENT: FOLLOW THE WIENIE

Crowd control designed to keep guests docile, mannerly, and patient in lengthy queues starts at Walt Disney World before visitors even enter the park. It begins as cars funnel into lanes at parking toll booths and drivers thread their way through the cones to assigned spaces. It continues as visitors listen to a barrage of instructions on the tram ride to the ticket booth, then wait in line to buy an admission ticket, pass through security, and, finally, clear a park turnstile.

Inside, guests are moved along with what the Disney people call wienies: lures like Cinderella's Castle and Big Thunder Mountain that draw them from one spot to another. As Walt said, "you've got to have a wienie at the end of every street." Other controls include peppy music to keep guests moving and a flow-through ride protocol, whereby passengers enter on one side and leave on another, reducing loading time.

Many attractions have hidden lines: no one is waiting outside, but once inside, guests are channeled into winding corridors and wend slowly toward the loading zone. Because the scenery changes as they move, they sense progress. A variation is the pre-show – usually presented on video screens – that keeps guests entertained and fills them in on the ride's story line. In essence, the line becomes an extension of the ride – yet another Disney innovation.

members is forbidden on all Disney properties) and hearing a sweating, frantic "guide" at Universal's Poseidon's Fury scream in terror, "open the friggin' door." And there's no Disney equivalent to Universal's Horror Make-Up Show, a raucous, pun-filled comedy whose hosts aren't above taking a potshot at the Mouse next door.

Because it's so much newer than much of Disney and is not as concerned with overall family image, Universal's rides and attractions tend to be much more state-of-the-art and hair-raising. Even a fairly mild ride like Men in Black: Alien Invasion, a ride-through,

Magical thrills

Universal's Islands of Adventure park lays to rest any debate as to which Orlando park offers the best thrill rides. In addition to gut-twisting roller-coasters like the Incredible Hulk, Dueling Dragons, and the Revenge of the Mummy, there are innovative 3-D and simulator rides like the Amazing Adventures of Spider-Man and the Simpsons Ride.

Perhaps the brightest jewel in Universal's crown, however, is the new Wizarding World of Harry Potter, a re-creation of the famous young fictional hero's magical domain. Kids can pop into the same shops where Harry and

interactive shooting gallery, makes its Disney equivalent, Buzz Lightyear, feel almost quaint by comparison. Terminator 2: 3-D, which combines live action with a 3-D movie, is a wild and violent extravaganza that assaults the senses with explosions, gunfire, billowing smoke, and ear-splitting volume. This is emphatically not the sort of show you want a young child to experience, especially those who may not fully understand the difference between playacting and real life.

LEFT: an evening show at SeaWorld keeps the crowds present after dark. **ABOVE:** the Blue Man Group plays at Universal Studios. **ABOVE RIGHT:** park maps are available at the gate to help you find your way.

his magic-loving friends bought their brooms, wands, and other gear (a canny merchandising crossover) while chowing down on food themed to J.K. Rowling's popular books and riding two types of Potter roller-coasters.

Although SeaWorld has been rated the world's best marine life park, management realized that it would have to introduce several thrill rides to keep attendance figures up. Its response to the challenge was Kraken, the tallest, fastest, and steepest roller-coaster in the South. Also in SeaWorld is Journey to Atlantis, described as part water ride, part roller-coaster – a white-knuckle combination that includes two of the steepest, wettest, and fastest drops of any ride in the world.

SeaWorld also offers a very un-Disney-like attraction: free beer. The drink that is banned in the Magic Kingdom flows at the marine park's Hospitality House, where customers can sample the wares of its parent company, Anheuser-Busch.

Alcohol was forbidden at Disney World until 1984 because Walt didn't feel that it was appropriate in a family environment. (This policy almost sank Disneyland Paris when it first opened: Parisians, incredulous that they couldn't have a glass of wine, boycotted the park until management gave in.) Alcohol is also available at Universal Orlando – for a price, of course – and

acts, opened Discovery Cove, where visitors can swim with dolphins and snorkel through a coral reef. SeaWorld's water park, Aquatica, puts a spin on the traditional panoply of flumes and slides by introducing dolphins and other sea creatures into the mix.

Universal and Disney are also locked in a battle to keep tourists from leaving their properties. Guests who stay at one of Universal's resort hotels enjoy a variety of special privileges, including complimentary on-site transportation, priority restaurant seating, and, most important at a park where lines for major attractions can be up to 90

it's not unusual to see visitors strolling the park with a tall glass of beer in hand.

The war of more

Every attraction in the Orlando area wages a daily battle for tourist dollars, but the big three are engaged in a "war of more." Universal's answer to Downtown Disney, an entertainment complex anchored by DisneyQuest (a center for virtual-reality amusements), Cirque du Soleil, and Planet Hollywood, is CityWalk, a similar complex occupied by theme restaurants and hip nightclubs as well as high-profile live shows such as Blue Man Group.

SeaWorld, vying with Disney's Animal Kingdom to be the No. 1 park for live animal

minutes long, express access on most rides. Not to be outdone, Disney offers similar perks to guests at its hotels, most notably its Extra Magic Hours program, which allows resort guests to enter a designated park an hour before the offical opening time and stay as long as three hours after closing.

Each year the parks raise their admission fees: as of 2011, the average cost for a one-day visit to the big three parks was $70. So it's important for each of them to continue to make their customers believe they are the biggest and the best. That's only good business. ❏

ABOVE: the Wizarding World of Harry Potter replicates many features found in the popular books.

Thrill Machines

The coasters at Florida's biggest theme parks are faster, wilder, and more imaginative than ever before

When you get right down to it, we don't really visit theme parks for the themes. Walt Disney World's animated characters are appealing, but many of us much prefer the feeling of flying through space and plummeting earthwards with harrowing abandon. When we surrender ourselves to the untender mercies of the best thrill rides, we are craving a taste of real-life mortal danger, while knowing that the brakes will work just in the nick of time.

The marquee thrill rides at the big Florida parks are high-tech cousins to the wooden roller-coasters that marked many early 20th-century amusement parks, and they use the same tricks of physics and physiology to induce delightful terror.

G-force and air time

The most exciting sensations on a roller-coaster are the result of shifting G-forces, which lessen and magnify the force of gravity upon the riders.

A force of 1G, at which a 170-pound (77kg) man feels like he weighs 170 pounds, is what we feel under normal circumstances. Double the G-force and gravity's apparent effect is doubled: in other words, our 170-pounder feels like he's packing 340 pounds (154kg). Most American coasters exert forces under 3Gs. A scant few pin riders back into their seats with 5Gs.

The initial descent from the top of the lift hill lessens G-force. Whipping back uphill increases it, while sharp turns exert G-force in a lateral direction.

These external effects focus on the inner ear, a tiny but crucial component of our anatomies that contributes not only to exhilaration but to the disorientation that makes rapid, twisting rides unappealing for many theme-park patrons. The inner ear is our gyroscope, enabling us to walk upright, but it cannot keep up when circumstances are manipulated as quickly and unnaturally as they are on a coaster ride. The result is dizziness, compounded by the sloshing and squeezing of the stomach.

RIGHT: Kumba is among the wildest rides at Busch Gardens, a park famous for fast coasters.

The steel age

Coaster design was revolutionized by the 1959 introduction of the tubular steel track. Steel liberated coaster cars from having to remain right side up and made possible rides with corkscrews, helixes, and other gravity-defying effects. Later came suspended coasters, in which seats hang from the tracks.

On inverted coasters, seats are suspended without hinges to allow passengers to turn upside down. Universal Orlando's Dueling Dragons adds a new wrinkle, as dual coasters careen towards each other at 60mph (96kph) – only to loop out of the way at the very last moment. Conventional

coasters with their wheels on the bottom can also turn upside down, as they do on Universal's Incredible Hulk.

Kick start

Explosive, high-speed new propulsion systems are replacing the old chain-lift approach to launching a coaster. Among the new methods are blasts of compressed air and a tire-driven launch.

The latest in hair-raising adventure is Busch Garden's Cheetah Hunt coaster, which has three separate launches at a brisk 60mph (96kph). Even more thrilling, the coaster dangles you dangerously close to the cheetah enclosure, prompting the question: who is the hunter and who is the hunted? ❏

SPORTS AND OUTDOOR ACTIVITIES

In addition to baseball, football, and basketball,
Florida hosts a variety of outdoor activities,
including the rush of surfing and diving

Florida can be a very dangerous place for sports-junkie gamblers. But once you see that the rush of a twenty-yard fall into cool blue water and a speeding ball across the net is just as thrilling, you won't need to pay much to have a good time.

Speed demons

On a crisp February day in 1959, a race was held at Daytona International Speedway, and the world of stock car racing changed forever. Since then, headlines in newspapers the world over have chronicled car racing in Florida, but no story has ever approached that first race at Daytona in significance. It was the race that took Florida stock car racing out of the proverbial backwoods and brought with it a following that had previously been reserved for classic American race cities like Indianapolis.

Not that stock car racing in Florida was new. William H.G. "Bill" France, seeking his fortune in the South years before, transformed

The sport of jai alai originated in the Basque country and reached the US in the early 20th century. It came via Cuba, so it is no surprise that Florida has more jai alai arenas than anywhere else in the country.

a group of grease-covered speed demons into the National Association for Stock Car Auto Racing, now better known as NASCAR. If the popular open-wheel cars could have a show-place like the Indianapolis Speedway, France speculated, why couldn't stock cars have a similar showplace?

The Daytona International Speedway made its debut on that February day in 1959. Its "D"-shaped speedway and ultra-high banking turns were designed for blazing speeds, and first-day fans were left enthralled – stock car racing, born in the north Florida hill country decades before, came of age in Daytona.

Today, spectators are still enthralled by the course and even more enthralled by the speeds. The patch of land in suburban Daytona Beach has since become the second most famous race-course in the United States, next to Indianapolis. Names like Richard Petty and Mario Andretti have established Daytona as one of the greatest fuel-guzzling, engine-blasting, high-excitement speedways in the world. It is estimated that between 150,000 and 200,000 fans jam the speedway each February for the Daytona 500, its premier race.

Shortly after Daytona is the famous 12 Hours of Sebring endurance race at Sebring International Speedway about 80 miles (130km) south of Orlando. Sebring is known for its less-than-smooth track, but drivers seem to relish the rough and rugged conditions. For the 35,000 or so spectators who converge on this small Florida town each March, the 12 Hours – like the Daytona 500 – is a good excuse to throw a party. The land surrounding the course turns into a huge campground; during the race it looks like a giant cookout.

Taking a gamble

If the incessant roar of engines isn't enough to sate a craving for a sports-induced high, Florida offers the intoxicating thrill of legalized gambling. More than 15 million people a year wage at least $1.6 billion on jai alai and on greyhound and horse racing in Florida. Generally, pari-mutuel sports attract two distinct types of fans: the serious player who approaches his or her wager of choice with a steadfast dedication and desire to win, and the casual gambler betting for fun rather than profit.

Florida is one of the few states in the US where you can wager on human beings – as long as they are playing jai alai. Florida has numerous jai alai arenas (known as frontons), including those in Miami, West Palm Beach, Tampa, and Daytona Beach. The wagers common to other pari-mutuel sports hold for jai alai: win, place, show, quinela, perfecta, and trifecta. All apply to the athletes who play this (currently male-only) version of handball.

And they're off!

Thoroughbred racing is a major force in the state's gambling industry, though legalized gambling on Indian reservations has certainly cut into the sport's revenue stream. Horse racing's high-society tradition is known throughout the world and earned it the sobriquet the "Sport of Kings." The Miami area has been a winter destination for the nation's best horses and jockeys for years; in a routine

winter season, every important thoroughbred in training east of the Mississippi River is likely to be stabled somewhere in South Florida.

Years ago, prominent sports, entertainment, and political figures made South Florida's horse tracks a place to see and be seen. These days, those memories still have a hold over some of the more elaborate tracks, but for the most part the crowds are more pedestrian than genteel. Gulfstream Park, north of Miami Beach and once one of the state's premier racing venues, is now more urban and sits in the middle of a high-rise condo community. Tracks are situated in Pompano Beach and Tampa as well.

Between October and April, South Florida is also the focal point of the nation's harness racing. The opening of Pompano Park in Pompano Beach about 30 years ago served as the catalyst for what has become an annual southern migration of big-name harness horsemen to Florida. Virtually all of the sport's superstars ship their stables to Pompano for winter racing. They also prepare young horses being developed for the next summer's races in the North.

Dog races

Along with horses, Florida's greyhound racing industry is without peer. The state is by far the most important greyhound area in the nation if for no other reason than sheer volume. Annual paid attendance statewide is about 8 million people who wager, with zeal, some $900 million per year. All major metropolitan areas have at least one track nearby, where the sleek canines can be watched as they are lured by an artificial rabbit around the track to the cheers of the crowd. The modern version of greyhound racing is believed to have evolved from a coursing meet held in 1904 in North Dakota. Anthropologists claim that Cleopatra kept greyhounds, a trait she shared with most Egyptian royalty. In England, the sport reached its great popularity during the Tudor period, in the reign of Queen Elizabeth I, who inspired the slogan "Sport of Queens".

Into the deep

For those craving the intense thrills of scuba diving, companies such as Force E, with centers in Boca Raton and Fort Lauderdale, and Diving Tampa in the Tampa-Orlando area, are the best pathways to a safe and memorable undersea experience. You can expect to pay a premium for a single scuba run without certification, which requires the accompaniment of a trained diver, which makes investment in a training course a

PADDLING PARADISE

Florida's coastline is known for its underwater vistas, from coral reefs to schools of angelfish, but above the waterline the scenery is just as thrilling. Kayakers flock to the state's islands and inland trails, with the Everglades' Wilderness Waterway and Cape Romano, located off Marco Island near Naples on the Gulf Coast, ranking near the top. Canoes are also available at many parks in the south, where mangroves are popular for exploring, but not advisable for sea adventuring. To find a rental company or compelling trip in a specific area, try the Kayak Online directory at www.kayakonline.com/florida.html or the Florida guide at www.visitflorida.com/kayaking.

tempting choice for those planning on taking the plunge.

Snorkeling, scuba's less challenging cousin, is another popular sport along the state's long sapphire coasts. The Florida Keys offer an official shipwreck trail of sunken wrecks, dating back to the early 18th century and fully available to navigate. On the Gulf Coast, fossilized shark teeth draw hordes of treasure-seekers to the waters off Venice Beach. The only prerequisite for snorkeling is a reliable boat captain, for which prices can vary depending on the city and season, and a sturdy mask to keep your view clear. Avoid paying to snorkel in Miami Beach, where the crowds leaves little to gape at beneath the surface.

If staying dry sounds more appealing, Florida offers plenty of other sports to divert the athletic tourist. Parasailing, where a speeding boat pulls harnessed cruisers until they soar high in the air to dip and dive, can be tried on almost every large beach, but is particularly popular on Cocoa Beach, near Orlando, and Bradenton Beach, in the Sarasota Area. Beach volleyball is the pick-up game of choice along Miami Beach, and jet skis are commonly seen zipping across the horizon on sunny days, and can usually be rented for about $50 per hour.

Teeing off

The spectacular weather in Florida makes it a destination for golfers. Many fans of the sport consider it a must to play the greens of famous courses such as the TPC Sawgrass in Ponte Vedra Beach, home of the PGA tour's Players Championship.

Beyond the daunting challenges of world-class runs such as the Blue Monster course at Miami's Doral resort, nearly every city in the Sunshine State beckons to casual golfers with affordable and reservable tee times. Not every course is open to the public, but most hotel concierges can provide a recommendation to a nearby 18-hole jaunt. For the more dedicated golfer, sprawling resorts such as Arnold Palmer's Bay Hill offer a resort atmosphere, complete with salons and spas for partners who may be coaxed along for the ride.

Prices for a golfing excursion can vary widely, from less than $40 for a garden-variety afternoon to more than $400 per night for a full-service experience.

Casting a line

Visitors to the Sunshine State may not realize how all those tasty cuts of fish make it to their plates, but those with the yen to bait a hook can experience the satisfaction of catching their own dinner – for the species that the state does not subject to strict catch-and-release require-ments, of course. Fishing must be done with a license, making a trustworthy captain just as important for this sport as it is for snorkeling or scuba diving.

LEFT: the Daytona 500 Experience, an interactive motorsports attraction, captures the thrill of auto racing. RIGHT: a close finish at a Florida racetrack.

Many of the state's prized saltwater gamefish, such as bonefish and red snapper, are subject to per-day limits that licensed fishermen know how to monitor. Freshwater gamefish, such as the striped bass and bluegill, are less strictly curtailed. The biggest charter fishing hotspots are Destin in the northern Pandhandle, the Gulf Coast waters off Fort Myers, and the Keys, where fishermen exert an immutable pull on the culture.

Game, set, match

Even before superstar coach Nick Bollettieri opened his famous tennis academy in the town

of Bradenton, between Tampa and Sarasota on the Gulf Coast, Florida was a top destination for tennis. Thousands of fans and enthusiasts follow in the professionals' footsteps every day by taking to hotel and public courts with nothing but a racket and a will to win.

Today the US Tennis Association helps foster new talent in the state with copious tournaments, and the Bollettieri academy has become a destination in its own right for ama-teurs looking to take the leap to pro at the same spot where Monica Seles and Andre Agassi cut their teeth. For the tennis aficionados seeking only a fun afternoon in the sun, courts are even more common than golf courses, both at hotels and in city centers. ❑

PLACES

A detailed guide to the entire state, arranged
by region, with all the main sites clearly
cross-referenced by number to the maps

Florida-based balladeer Jimmy Buffett put his guitar-pickin' finger on a fundamental reason for Florida's popularity as a retreat for routine-weary travelers with his 1977 album, *Changes in Latitudes, Changes in Attitudes*. In fact, no other place in the continental United States lies on a latitude further south. Some folks have become so addicted to the tranquilizing effects of Florida's balmy climes, they return year after year for another dose.

Nature laid the groundwork for this annual people invasion by providing the beaches and forests. Then entrepreneurs added hotels and theme parks. Now, it's a rare corner of Florida that doesn't have a gator farm or an orange grove – or at least a place to try deep-fried gator meat and freshly squeezed juice.

Florida is much too big and diverse to swallow in one gulp. The following sections are designed to help you find your way around the state in smaller sips:

- **South Florida** is anchored by Metropolitan Miami and Miami Beach, with its famous Art Deco District. It extends west to take in the wild expanse of the Everglades and Big Cypress Swamp, then south to the Florida Keys.
- **The Atlantic Coast** stretches from Fort Lauderdale, within easy reach of Miami, right up to Jacksonville in the far north – taking in en route Palm Beach, the Space Coast, Daytona Beach, and historic St Augustine.
- **Central Florida** revolves around Orlando and crowd-pulling attractions such as Walt Disney World Resort.
- **The Gulf Coast** has Tampa-St Petersburg as its nucleus, with Marco Island at its southern end and Cedar Key at its northern tip. Sarasota and Fort Myers are the other major cities in this region.
- **North Florida** encompasses the Panhandle region – anchored by Tallahassee, the state capital, in the east, and Pensacola in the far west. It also takes in the "Forgotten Coast" of Florida's Big Bend region. ❑

PRECEDING PAGES: Miami Beach; kayaking in Everglades National Park; Gulf Islands National Seashore near Pensacola in the Florida Panhandle.
LEFT: a relaxing afternoon at the Don CeSar Beach Resort in St Pete Beach.
TOP: the Florida Aquarium, Tampa. **ABOVE RIGHT:** fishing on Amelia Island.

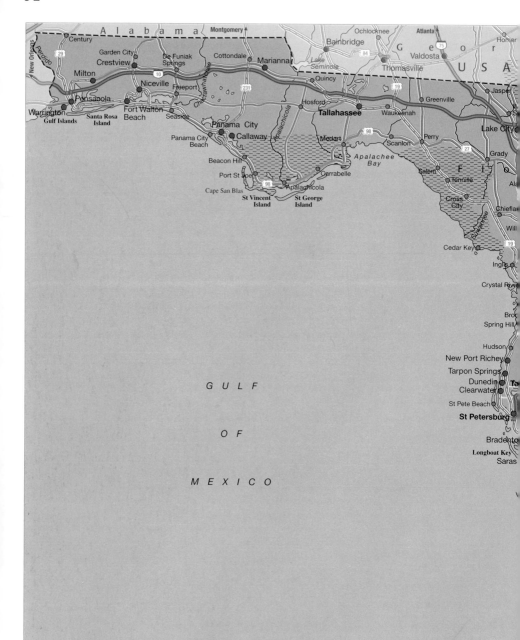

Florida

0   50 miles
0   50 km

N

Savannah
Cumberland
Island
a
Fernandina
Beach
ahan
Jacksonville
Beach
ksonville

starke
St Augustine
d   a
aldo
sville
Palatka
Flagler Beach
Bunnell
George
Ormond Beach
Daytona Beach
Barberville
Ocala
De Land
New Smyrna Beach
Belleview
Deltona
Eustis
sburg
Sanford
Pine
Hills
Titusville
Olono
★ Kennedy Space Center
Walt Disney World ★
Orlando
Bellwood
nton
ights
Kissimmee
St Cloud
Cape
Canaveral
27
Holopaw
Cocoa
4
Winter Haven
Melbourne
land
Bartow
Lake
Wales
Sebastian
Yeehaw
Junction
95
Vero Beach
o Springs
Sebring
Fort
Drum
Fort Pierce
Port Saint Lucie
Okeechobee
Stuart
Arcadia
75
Palmdale
Lake
Okeechobee
Canal
Point
Jupiter
o Port Charlotte
41
Caloosahatchee
La
Belle
Clewiston
27
Belle
Glade
North Palm Beach
Palm Beach Shores
West Palm Beach
Cape
Coral
Fort Myers
Immokalee
Boynton Beach
Delray Beach
Boca Raton
Naples
Big Cypress
Swamp
75
Plantation
27
Pompano Beach
Fort Lauderdale
Hollywood
Carol City
Marco Island
41
Ten Thousand
Islands
Chokoloskee
The Everglades
Miami
Hialeah
Kendall
Perrine
Miami Beach
Coral Gables
Homestead
Cutler
Ridge
Everglades
National Park
Cape Sable
sas
Pine Island
Florida
Bay
Key Largo
Key West
Florida
Keys
Marathon
1

ATLANTIC

OCEAN

Little Abaco
Island
Grand Bahama Island
Great Abaco
Island
Freeport

BAHAMAS

New
Providence
Island

Straits of Florida

Andros
Island

SOUTHBEACH

⬆ Post Office
⬅ Española Way
⬅ Police Station
⬅ Old City Hall
⬅ Flamingo Park
↗ Collins Avenue Shopping District
↗ Ocean Drive

MIAMIBEACH

246
CH

HIGHT
MIAMI B
CYTNE
HT 5BM
SKYLAR

SOUTH FLORIDA

Miami offers urban thrills, with the Everglades
just a short drive away and, to the south,
the alluring, tropical Florida Keys

South Florida is a region of extremes. In Miami you will find a great metropolis with a distinctly Caribbean flavor. In South Beach, the Art Deco architecture, chic shops, sizzling nightlife, and throngs of beautiful people (including quite a few actors and models) are the very height of celebrity chic. But equally compelling are the city's up-and-coming neighborhoods, such as the Design District, home to popular shops and bistros.

Beyond the skyscrapers of Miami are the swamps of the Everglades – an alligator-inhabited area of 1.4 million acres (565,000 hectares). This "river of grass" encompasses a fascinating blend of tropical and temperate environments, a laboratory where nature experiments with the ever-changing cycles of life and death.

Emblematic of Florida's physical and cultural connection to the Caribbean, the state's southern boundary doesn't come to an abrupt end, but trickles gently away in a necklace of coral and limestone islands known as the Keys. The archipelago stretches 180 miles (290km) from Miami's Biscayne Bay to the Dry Tortugas, just 86 miles (140km) north of Havana. The islands are sewn together by 113 mile (182km) -long US Highway 1, the Overseas Highway, stretching across 43 bridges from Key Largo to Key West.

From the scuba culture of the Upper Keys to the bohemian counterculture of Key West, each island maintains its own identity. Even the people differ from one key to the next: disillusioned Gold Coasters populate the upper islands, while people of the lower keys proudly call themselves Conchs and have removed themselves from the 9-to-5 hustle. Mañanaland, Margaritaville, the American Riviera – the Keys have been called many things. Whatever the appellation, they are a place to take off your watch and kick back. ❏

LEFT: a favorite of celebrities, models, and the beautiful people, South Beach is a hub of sizzling nightlife and stylish shops. **TOP:** lounging on Smathers Beach in Key West. **ABOVE RIGHT:** the sunset reddens the horizon at Key Largo.

METROPOLITAN MIAMI

South Florida's urban hub is a crossroads of Latin
American, Caribbean, and Yankee cultures with
a vibrant arts scene, great restaurants,
and a distinctly tropical ambience

Miami is the big dot on the Florida map. Brash, beautiful, exotic, and vibrant, it is the state's most complex and multifaceted city, large in size as well as personality. Made up of over 30 municipalities, Greater Miami is situated within Miami-Dade County and encompasses more than 500 sq miles (1,300 sq km) that contain a rich and diverse ethnic stew. About 60 percent of the area's population is foreign born, which means the city speaks with many accents – Spanish, French, Hebrew, Portuguese, Russian, Creole, and Jamaican, to name just a few.

With a population of more than 2.4 million, Greater Miami has its share of big-city problems, but it also has a stunningly beautiful natural landscape, a cutting-edge art community, the best Latin music this side of the Gulf Stream, and a restaurant scene that has finally come of age. Throughout its many incarnations of the past 20 years – from Paradise Lost to the New Riviera – it has always fascinated visitors, and for good reason. It is full of energy yet laid-back and casual. It embraces all things shiny and new but remains a few steps behind other major American cities. It boasts of a world-class sophistication but is riddled with insecurities.

None of this is more apparent than in downtown Miami, where new skyscrapers sit empty or unfinished. The building boom at the turn of the millennium was phenomenal, fueled by get-rich-quick speculators and foreign investors. But it also created an urban core that's jam-packed with construction sites and road detours that will likely be around for a long time. This congested mess, however, has in no way dampened the excitement and enthusiasm that permeates the neighborhood.

Main attractions
BAYSIDE MARKETPLACE
ARSHT CENTER FOR THE
  PERFORMING ARTS
RUBELL FAMILY COLLECTION
MUSEUM OF CONTEMPORARY ART
ANCIENT SPANISH MONASTERY
CALLE OCHO
BILTMORE HOTEL
MIRACLE MILE
ZOO MIAMI
MIAMI MUSEUM OF SCIENCE
  AND PLANETARIUM
VIZCAYA MUSEUM AND GARDENS

PRECEDING PAGES: Miami Beach.
LEFT: colorful art is displayed on the street.
RIGHT: palm trees ring the water's edge.

Waterfront dining and shopping at Bayside Marketplace.

Downtown

As it curves northward along Biscayne Bay, Brickell Avenue eases into downtown Miami and is studded with futuristic buildings, many of which sparkle at night with colorful neon lights. Brickell crosses over the Miami River and becomes the major thoroughfare of **Biscayne Boulevard**. On the south bank of the Miami River and the east side of Brickell Avenue sits a controversial piece of land. Here, in 1989, construction workers unexpectedly uncovered a circle of stones that turned out to be the remnants of a Tequesta Indian settlement dating back more than a thousand years. After years of

battles between historians and the developers who owned the land, the site – now deemed the Miami Circle – is slated to be turned into an urban park that will preserve the stones and contain an interpretive center placing them in their historic context.

By the bay

Anchoring much of the downtown tourist traffic on Biscayne Boulevard is **Bayside Marketplace ❶** (401 Biscayne Blvd; tel: 305-577-3344; Mon–Thur 10am–10pm, Fri–Sat 10am–11pm, Sun 11am–9pm; free), a 16 acre (6 hectare) waterfront extravaganza of more than 100 shops, restaurants, and attractions

Metropolitan Miami

that often hosts free live concerts. Within walking distance of Bayside to the south is **Bayfront Park**, a verdant and peaceful waterfront public space.

At the southern end of the park is a memorial designed by the late Japanese sculptor Isamu Noguchi; it is dedicated to the crew who lost their lives aboard the space shuttle *Challenger* when it exploded over Florida in 1986. At night, Bayfront Park often puts on laser-light shows that throw beams of bright colors into the Miami night sky.

A few steps to the north of Bayside is the **American Airlines Arena**, home to the Miami Heat basketball team and a venue for major music events. Just beyond it is **Bicentennial Park**, a lush greenway that often hosts outdoor concerts. Nearby is the entrance to the **Port of Miami**, a major marine commerce hub as well as the busiest port for cruise ships in the world, funneling over 3 million passengers a year to all points in the Caribbean.

Across the street is the **Freedom Tower ❷**, one of the more significant historic buildings in the downtown area. Built in 1925, the peach-colored Mediterranean Revival building was the home of the now defunct *Miami News* and served as a processing center in the 1960s for Cuban immigrants who fled the communist takeover of their country, hence the name. Today, the perfectly preserved 17-story building occasionally hosts art shows and cultural events.

Art and culture

Behind the Tower is a series of dense streets filled with electronic and jewelry shops, and the downtown campus of **Miami-Dade College**, site of the **Miami Book Fair International** held every November. Nearby on Flagler Street is the **Gusman Center for the Performing Arts**, a glorious Baroque-style theater that hosts the **Miami International Film Festival** each winter. Named for railroad magnate Henry Flagler, Flagler Street is one of

the busiest thoroughfares in downtown, packed with small stores catering to shoppers who arrive in Miami with large empty suitcases.

At 101 W. Flagler is the **Metro-Dade Cultural Plaza ❸**. A popular lunch site for downtown lawyers and office workers, the Plaza has an expansive tiled courtyard graced with flowing pools of water. It is also home to the **Miami-Dade Main Library**; the **Historical Museum of Southern Florida** (tel: 305-375-1492; Tue–Fri 10am–5pm, Sat–Sun noon–5pm; charge), which maintains a permanent exhibit depicting 10,000 years of South Florida history; and the **Miami Art Museum** (tel: 305-375-3000; Tue–Fri 10am–5pm, Sat–Sun noon–5pm; charge), where rotating exhibits range from American modern to European classical art.

Downtown's cultural hub, and a major element in the city's revitalization plan, centers around the **Arsht Center for the Performing Arts ❹** (1350 Biscayne Blvd; tel: 305-949-6722; www.arshtcenter.com). The $461 million César Pelli-designed center was intended to elevate Miami's ranking

Many Miami addresses are given according to their location relative to Miami Avenue and Flagler Street: for example, 1200 NW 26th Street is 12 blocks west of Miami Avenue and 26 blocks north of Flagler Street.

BELOW: the County Courthouse near the Metro-Dade Cultural Plaza.

Florida Grand Opera opened the 2010-2011 season with a production of Puccini's Turandot.

BELOW: the Wynwood Walls build on Miami's dramatic traditions of street art.

among the world's great cities. Spectacularly beautiful, the venue includes a state-of-the-art concert hall and a separate ballet house that host major cultural events, including those of four resident companies – the **Concert Association of Florida**, **Florida Grand Opera**, **Miami City Ballet**, and **New World Symphony**. The smaller Black Box Theater is where more offbeat and intimate productions are held. On weekends, the center has free events on the plaza, such as flamenco dance classes, Caribbean steel bands, and Latin jazz ensembles.

The Upper East Side

Continuing north on Biscayne Boulevard, the urban atmosphere becomes more gritty but also more interesting and artsy. In recent years this area has been tagged the Upper East Side by hip young developers (many from New York) who see the neighborhood as an evolving work of art.

Also known as the **Biscayne Corridor**, this bustling area includes the neighborhood of **Buena Vista**, the **Wynwood Art District**, and the

Miami Design District. A bohemian frontier, it's where many enterprising artistic types have settled after fleeing the mainstreaming of South Beach in the last few years. Some are hard at work breathing new life into old MiMo (Miami Modern architecture) motels built in the 1950s or transforming shabby bungalows and small apartment buildings into hipster enclaves where emerging young artists in worn-out jeans mingle with interior decorators in designer clothes. With dozens of sleek Greenwich Village-like lofts popping up all over, it's a thriving area quickly rising in prominence in the international art world where intrepid visitors can view impressive private art collections during the day or dodge the lingering drug dealers late at night.

Wynwood

From 19th to 37th streets is the neighborhood of Wynwood, where funky galleries are sandwiched between auto repair shops that also share the streets with two private collections: the **Rubell Family Collection** ❺ (95 NW 29th St; tel: 305-573-6090;

Wed–Sat 10am–6pm, closed late Aug; charge) and the **Margulies Collection** ❻ (591 NW 27th St; tel: 305-576-1051; Wed–Sat 11am–4pm, closed summer; charge). Housed in enormous warehouses, both collections contain a broad representation of contemporary art, sculpture, and photography.

The Rubell site is owned by New Yorkers Don and Mera Rubell, relatives of the late Steve Rubell, who owned the famous Studio 54 nightclub. Other respected art venues include the **Cisneros Fontanals Arts Foundation** and the **Frederic Snitzer**, **Diana Lowenstein**, **Spinello**, **Gary Nader**, and **World Class Boxing** galleries. On the second Saturday of every month, Wynwood – in conjunction with the Design District – hosts a Gallery Walk when art lovers stroll from gallery to gallery and enjoy complimentary wine, champagne, and hors d'œuvres.

Design District

Although the Wynwood Art District is the sassy new kid on the block, it would not have been possible if it weren't for the more dignified **Design**

District (www.miamidesigndistrict.net) a few blocks to the north. About 16 square blocks that run from NE 36th to NE 41st streets between NE 2nd and N. Miami avenues, the Design District is a dense cluster of all things divine in the design world. In the 1920s the area was called Decorator's Row and has since gone through various periods of boom and bust. These days represent another boom period, and the compact village is once again an example of tropical splendor.

Easily explored in a few hours, it's full of high-end furniture importers, interior design showrooms, art galleries, and kitchen and garden boutiques. Anchoring the cluster is the historic **Moore Building** ❼ (4040 NE 2nd Ave), a gleaming white four-story gem that has an outdoor bamboo garden lounge and a nonprofit art gallery that consistently exhibits internationally acclaimed artists. The Moore serves as home base for **Design Miami**, the design offshoot of the phenomenally successful Art Basel Miami Beach, held each December. During the event, the Moore Building and other venues in

An installation piece at the Rubell Family Collection.

BELOW: a show opening at the Rubell Family Collection.

the Upper East Side have satellite art and design shows, parties, films, and seminars that compliment the main schedule of events at the Miami Beach Convention Center.

Most shops in the Design District are open to the public Monday through Saturday from 11am to 5pm. As the area has grown in popularity, a few clever restaurants have shown up as well. Among them are **Fratelli Lyon**, an intellectual and inspiring Italian kitchen; **Grass**, a sophisticated alfresco dining space; and **Michael's Genuine Food and Drink**, an unpretentious but highly rated bistro (*see page 115*).

Little Haiti

One of the great things about Miami is its ethnic enclaves, and Little Haiti is no doubt among the more fascinating. Beginning a few blocks north of the Design District, it lies within the boundaries of 79th Street to the north, 46th Street to the south, Biscayne Boulevard to the east, and I-95 to the west.

Little Haiti is a juxtaposition of immigrant optimism and inner-city decay, and it offers an intimate encounter with a rich Caribbean culture. Although perhaps not as economically successful as its Cuban-immigrant counterpart, Miami's Haitian community has prospered in the local arts scene and now plays an active roll in city politics. Many Miami Haitians have moved into the middle-class suburbs, but the heart of the community is still in Little Haiti.

Here mom-and-pop grocery stores and small restaurants thrive as they cater to the community with heaping servings of *griot* (fried pork), *lambi* (stewed conch), and spicy oxtail stew. There are several small botanicas in the neighborhood, and they welcome visitors who want to sample or just look. Shops that specialize in religious paraphernalia and medicinal herbs for practitioners of the Afro-Caribbean religions of voodoo and Santeria, botanicas can be found in many other areas of Miami as well.

The **Haitian Catholic Center** and **Church of Notre Dame d'Haiti** ❽ (130 NE 62nd St; tel: 305-751-6289) has long been an advocate of Haitian

A mural adorns a brick building in Little Haiti.

BELOW: ceramic saints and other figurines at a Little Haiti botanica.

immigrant rights in Miami. It is also a great venue to meet local Haitians, especially on Sunday mornings when thousands come out for a Mass that blends traditional Catholicism with rhythmic Haitian music.

A few blocks away is **Libreri Mapou** (5919 NE 2nd Ave; tel: 305-757-9922), one of the few bookstores in Florida that specializes in Haitian Creole books and music. Owned by Haitian writer Jan Mapou, the bookstore also stocks Haitian arts and crafts and is a popular gathering place for Haitian writers and musicians.

North Miami

About 2 miles (3km) to the north of Little Haiti is the city of North Miami, which for a few years had a Haitian-American mayor. A very diverse middle-class neighborhood, the city is also one of the area's up-and-coming arts districts. Most of the action here is around 125th Street, where there are several cafés, restaurants, and galleries that put on poetry readings and world music concerts. The big draw, however, is the **Museum of**

Contemporary Art ❾ (770 NE 125th St; tel: 305-893-6211; www.mocanomi. org; Tue and Thur–Sat 11am–5pm, Wed 1–9pm, Sun noon–5pm; charge). Known for fresh contemporary art with lots of attitude, MoCA features rotating exhibits of local and internationally recognized artists. Its permanent collection includes works by Julian Schnabel, Louise Nevelson, and Yoko Ono. On the last Friday of each month is a free outdoor concert; the audience gathers on the grass with coolers full of wine and takes in the sounds of jazz, Latin, and folk music.

The other attraction in North Miami is the **Ancient Spanish Monastery** ❿ (16711 W. Dixie Hwy; tel: 305-945-1461; www.spanishmonastery. com; Mon–Sat 10am–4pm, Sun 11am–4pm; charge). Built in Segovia, Spain, in the 12th century, then dismantled and shipped to Florida in 1925, the monastery was rebuilt in 1952. Tucked behind stone walls with meandering tropical gardens, it's now a peaceful oasis within a busy neighborhood that is welcoming to visitors from all walks of life.

The Museum of Contemporary Art is host to changing exhibits as well as films, musical performances, and artist workshops.

BELOW:
the Museum of Contemporary Art.

Miami-Dade County is bilingual. Signs are often in both English and Spanish, and the Miami Herald (the state's most widely read daily) has a Spanish edition, El Nuevo Herald.

BELOW: Jamie Foxx and Colin Farrell star in a new version of *Miami Vice*.
BELOW RIGHT: a reconstructed cloister at the Ancient Spanish Monastery.

Little Havana

Another ethnic enclave that offers an authentic experience is Little Havana, located in the south part of Miami-Dade County just to the west of downtown. It is here that the first wave of Cuban immigrants settled in the early 1960s; the cultural infusion is still apparent. While the Cuban population of Greater Miami – approximately a million people – has spread throughout every corner of the city, it is in Little Havana that the scent of Cuban coffee and the blare of salsa trumpets permeate the air, and heated arguments about a post-Castro Cuba can be overheard on almost every corner.

Although it is still a scruffy, lower-income neighborhood, Little Havana has gone upscale in some places with the addition of new art galleries, nightclubs, and restaurants that serve as the symbolic heart of the exile community. On the last Friday of the month, the place pulsates with **Viernes Culturales** (Cultural Fridays), a street party of concerts, gallery openings, and historic walking tours of the neighborhood.

Most of the action takes place on **Calle Ocho** ⓫ (SW 8th St) between 14th and 27th avenues. This is also where the wildly flamboyant Latin street festival takes place each March.

But you don't need a festival to enjoy Calle Ocho, since the street bustles with action both day and night. At **Versailles Restaurant** *(see listing, page 115)* the Cuban food is hearty and plentiful, and the clientele ranges from power brokers and politicians to poets and musicians. Always loud and very busy, it's perhaps the most famous Cuban restaurant in the US. Directly across the street is **La Carreta** *(see listing, page 115)*, another popular Cuban eatery, open 24 hours.

Heading eastward toward the Miami River, in the 1600 block of 8th Street, there are a few good finds, including **Alfaro's**, a cozy wine and tapas lounge; **Art District Cigars**, where visitors can watch artisans hand-roll stogies while taking in live Latin music; and **Molina Fine Art**, a gallery featuring vibrant paintings that reflect tales from Afro-Cuban folklore. Around the corner is the

Miami on Screen

With its exotic ambience and endless sun, it's no surprise that Miami has served as the setting for so many movies and TV shows. It started in 1941 with *Moon Over Miami*, starring the woman with the great legs, Betty Grable. Frank Sinatra came to town in 1959 to film *Hole in the Head*, followed the next year by Jerry Lewis starring in *The Bellboy*. The swinging sixties was the decade of Jackie Gleason, who shot his weekly TV show in the "sun and fun capital of the world." It was also when American TV viewers fell in love with a friendly bottlenose dolphin named Flipper.

The 1980s brought grit and lots of it – *Scarface*, starring Al Pacino as a Cuban drug dealer, and the violent yet glamorous *Miami Vice* television series. The 1990s brought a series of comedies in *Ace Ventura Pet Detective* (1994), *The Birdcage* (1996), *Something About Mary* (1998), and, of course, the resurrection of *Miami Vice* as a feature film (2006). Contemporary movies include *Marley and Me* (2008), *New in Town* (2009), and *Up in the Air* (2009).

small **Bay of Pigs Museum** (1821 SW 9th St; tel: 305-649-4719; Mon–Sat 9am–4pm; charge), a crowded collection of artifacts and memorabilia honoring those who died in the failed 1961 US invasion of Cuba.

Just like home

On the corner of 8th Street and 15th Avenue is **Domino Park** ⑫, also known as Máximo Gómez Park, a fenced-in courtyard where Cuban men gather for lively games of dominoes and talk about the good old days in Havana. Park officials enforce a custom that restricts admittance to men over the age of 55, but tourists are welcome.

Next door to the park is **Little Havana To Go**, a playful souvenir shop where visitors are treated to a complimentary *cafecito* and the shelves are brimming with all things Cuban – music, art, domino sets, cigars, and guayabera shirts. Across the street from the shop is the beautiful **Tower Theater**. Built as a movie palace in 1926, this perfectly restored Art Deco building is owned by the City of Miami and is host to film festivals, lec-

tures, book signings, dance, and theatrical performances.

About two blocks away is **La Casa de los Trucos** (1343 8th St), a business originally founded in Cuba. Also known as House of Tricks, this neighborhood institution sells costumes, funny hats, masks, maracas, and magic tricks. On the corner of SW 12th Street is **La Esquina de Tejas**, a family-style Cuban restaurant that still boasts about the day that President Ronald Reagan stopped in for lunch while on the campaign trail. On the same street is **Casino Records**, a famed Latin music shop that sells an enormous selection of material, including early 20th-century Cuban danzons, Latin jazz, Afro-Cuban drumming, mambo, salsa, meringue, tango, and samba.

At 1106 8th Street is **El Credito Cigar Factory** ⑬ (tel: 305-858-4162; Mon–Fri 8.30am–5pm, Sat 9am–4pm), the oldest and largest cigar factory in Miami and the producer of four distinct brands, including the famous La Gloria Cubana. Founded in 1907 in Cuba, the shop moved to Miami after the Cuban revolution, and the interior

Cuban men often engage in spirited games of dominoes at Domino Park.

BELOW LEFT: Calle Ocho festival.
BELOW: a Little Havana cigar shop.

Smells of Havana can be found at the El Credito Cigar Factory.

feels, smells, and looks like Havana circa 1950. Dozens of workers chop heaps of tobacco on antique tables and load them into vintage wooden presses as Spanish-language radio programs blare in the background.

Coral Gables

To the south of Little Havana is a city where many affluent Cuban exiles moved after climbing the socio-economic ladder in Miami. Designed by developer George Merrick in the 1920s, Coral Gables is an enchanting city of Mediterranean-style architecture, ornate limestone arches, and a vibrant art and culture scene. With avenues named after cities in Spain and street signs on tiny white stones, it is not easy to navigate. But it has several landmark properties that are worth seeking out.

Surrounded by palatial mansions, the old **Biltmore Hotel ⓭** (1200 Anastasia Ave; tel: 305-445-1926) was the grand dame of South Florida hotels in the Roaring Twenties. Its swimming pool – billed as the largest in the US, was once the setting for elegant water ballets, and Johnny Weissmuller, star of

BELOW: the Biltmore Hotel.

Tarzan movies, set a world swimming record here in the 1930s. Today it is a playground for the international jet set and is often used for fashion shoots. The hotel offers free walking tours of the property on Sunday afternoons.

Within the hotel, the modern theater company **GableStage** (tel: 305-445-1119; performances Thur–Sun evenings and Sun afternoons) is a rising player in the local arts scene. Its seasons are dominated by the type of witty, intellectual plays more commonly found in New York City, while tickets cost less than half of those on Broadway.

Another stunning swimming hole in Coral Gables is the **Venetian Pool ⓮** (2701 DeSoto Blvd; tel: 305-460-5306; Mon–Fri 11am–5.30pm, Sat–Sun 10am–4.30pm May–Sept, closed Mon Oct–April; charge), a freshwater coral rock lagoon with caves and waterfalls amid lush tropical gardens. The pool is drained nightly and refilled in the morning with artesian well water. Its Venetian-style architecture and soft sandy beach provide a fine setting for an afternoon swim.

Making the Miracle

Coral Gables' Miracle Mile is now known as a shopping destination, but its origins lie down a different path. It was the urban planning movement that first motivated George Merrick to craft one of the first planned communities during the booming 1920s. Long before the rise of the suburbs and the establishment of the interstate road system forced Americans into their cars, Merrick took pride in his vision of a district where every business was no further than a "two-block walk" away.

Today the rise of crippling gridlock has made the Miracle Mile's pedestrian-friendly flavor a modern asset. Even the free circular trolley service is a throwback to Merrick's day, when electric trolleys roamed the Vizcaya-inspired streets of his city beautiful.

Miracle Mile

The commercial center of the Gables lies along and parallel to **Miracle Mile** ⓰, a visitor-friendly street filled with upscale boutiques, cafés, and restaurants. From several points on Miracle Mile, the **Coral Gables Trolley** offers free transportation throughout the business hub of the city every day to 10pm.

The Trolley is also a convenient way to take in the **Gables Gallery Night** held on the first Friday of every month. Mostly specializing in fine Latin American art, there are many respected galleries in downtown Coral Gables such as **Virginia Miller Galleries**, **Americas Collection**, **La Boheme Fine Art**, and **Cernuda Arte**. There are several modern luxury hotels in the downtown area, including the Hyatt Regency and Omni Colonnade, but they can't compete with the charming Old World ambience of the historic **Hotel Place St Michel** (162 Alcazar Ave), which was built during the 1920s and includes an intimate French restaurant.

Within walking distance is Miami's literary epicenter, **Books & Books** (265 Aragon Ave; tel: 305-442-4408; www. booksandbooks.com; Sun–Thur 9am–11pm, Fri–Sat 9am–noon). Housed in a stark white Mediterranean building with an inner courtyard, this is more than a bookstore. It's a full-service restaurant and bar that also offers live music and foreign films at night. Every night the store hosts readings by some of the world's most famous authors – Nobel laureates, Pulitzer Prize winners, politicians, presidents, talk-show hosts, movie stars, and the like. It also presents many local authors and readings in both English and Spanish.

Art, history, nature

Toward the southeast of Coral Gables is the **University of Miami**, home of the **Lowe Art Museum** ⓱ (1301 Stanford Dr; tel: 305-284-3535; www.lowemuseum. org; Tue–Sat 10am–4pm, Sun noon–4pm; charge). One of Miami's finest museums, the Lowe has a permanent collection that includes Renaissance and Baroque art; 19th- and 20th-century art; Egyptian, Greek, and Roman antiquities; Latin American and Asian collections; and Native American art and artifacts.

Avid readers gather for books, author events, drinking, and dining at Books & Books.

BELOW: the historic Venetian Pool is open to the public.

A classical sculpture at the Lowe Museum.

BELOW: schoolchildren take a tour of the Lowe Museum.

Continuing east, near Biscayne Bay, the attractions feature the handiwork of nature instead of people. **Matheson Hammock Park** ⑱ (9610 Old Cutler Road; daily sunrise–sunset; charge) is a 100 acre (40 hectare) park with a marina, saltwater atoll pool, and small beach. Along with beautiful walkways and cycling trails through dense mangroves, Matheson Hammock has a restaurant, picnic facilities, barbecues, and sailboat and kite-surfing rentals.

A little farther down the road is **Fairchild Tropical Garden** (10901 Old Cutler Rd; tel: 305-667-1651; daily 9am–4.30pm; charge), the largest garden of its type in the continental US. Named for famed botanist David Fairchild, it has an outstanding collection of tropical flowering trees and more than 5,000 species of palms, ferns, and orchids. Many species in the park are rare and endangered; others are used for medicinal purposes and some for the making of perfume (the ylang-ylang tree blossoms are the primary ingredient of Chanel No. 5). Tram tours include a 40-minute narrated ride that is informative and fun. A vir-tual oasis in the middle of a big city, Fairchild also has several lakes that are a delight to the senses.

Coconut Grove

Next door to Coral Gables is the Miami neighborhood of **Coconut Grove**. Formerly an art colony and hippie hangout, the Grove (as locals call it) is one of Miami's oldest and most interesting neighborhoods. Built by Bahamian laborers about a century ago, it still has much of their laid-back attitude. At various times in its history it has claimed famous American writers, musicians, and artists as residents. Each June it hosts the **Goombay Festival**, a weekend street party that pays tribute to its Bahamian roots with live Junkanoo bands, conch fritter vendors, and dancing in the streets.

Under a dense canopy of green, the houses in the Grove run the gamut from palatial pink mansions to funky old Florida cottages. There is still a Saturday morning **farmers' market** (Grand Ave and McDonald St), where locals gather to buy organic fruits and vegetables as well as famous pies and

fresh-squeezed juices. The main commercial activities center around Main Highway and Commodore Plaza, where on weekend nights the pedestrian traffic is heavy. Here, restaurants such as **Greenstreets** *(see listing, page 114)* and **Cefalo's Wine Corner** are busy both day and night. Nearby is the old **Coconut Grove Playhouse**, a Mediterranean-style venue built in 1926 but currently out of commission due to financial woes.

Across the street is the **Barnacle State Historic Site ⓳** (3485 Main Hwy; tel: 305-442-6866; Fri–Mon 9am–4pm; charge), home of the Miami pioneer Commodore Ralph Munroe (1851–1933), a boat-builder, mariner, botanist, and photographer. Built in 1891, the home overlooks Biscayne Bay and is filled with family heirlooms and antiques. It is totally secluded from traffic and other buildings. It's possible to sit on the home's wrap-around porch and imagine what life was like in South Florida before tourism took hold of the economy. Tours of the home and grounds are given about every two hours throughout the day.

Shop and dine

A few blocks away is **CocoWalk ⓴** (3015 Grand Ave; www.cocowalk.net; Sun–Thur 10am–10pm, Fri–Sat 10am–11pm, bars and restaurants open later), a multistory shopping center and entertainment complex and the Grove's busiest attraction. Popular with college students on weekends, it has an eight-screen movie theater and numerous bars.

Next door is the **Streets of Mayfair** (2911 Grand Ave; tel: 305-448-1700; Mon–Fri 11am–7pm, Thur until 8pm, Sun noon–5pm), another shopping venue, but this one anchored by the **Mayfair Hotel and Spa**, a tranquil and plush property with a soaring atrium, copper sculptures, and gushing fountains.

Near the entrance of CocoWalk, Grand Avenue connects with McFarlane Road, and this leads to S. Bayshore Drive. At McFarlane and Bayshore is **Peacock Park ㉑**, a large green playground that once contained South Florida's first hotel, the Peacock Inn, built in 1882. Today the waterfront park is popular with Frisbee players

Fairchild Tropical Garden is filled with flowering plants.

BELOW: Florida is home to some of the most colorful flowers in the United States.

Coconut Grove has a reputation for being an artsy, eclectic community.

and sunbathers, and it occasionally hosts outdoor concerts.

Continuing north on Bayshore Drive is **Miami City Hall** ㉒, a beautifully preserved Art Deco building originally built to be a passenger terminal for Pan American Airways' seaplanes in 1934. Nearby is **Dinner Key Marina**, a popular mooring site filled with sailboats and yachts, as well as several landmark restaurants, including **Monty's Stone Crab**, **Chart House**, and **Scotty's Landing** (*see listing, page 114*). Arriving by boat at these waterfront seafood spots is a popular and offbeat way for visitors to see the night skyline while making the most out of a day-long charter rental.

Animal kingdom

About 3 miles (5km) west of the Grove is the sprawling **Zoo Miami** ㉓ (12400 SW 152nd St; tel: 305-251-0400; www.miamimetrozoo.com; daily 9.30am–5.30pm), where more than 2,000 animals roam among the thousands of plant and orchid species nurtured on the 740 acre (296 hectare) grounds. This is the only tropical zoo in the US,

and is one of only two zoos to display a pair of black-necked storks. The zoo is laid out in four zones: Asia, Africa, Australia, and Amazon and Beyond; each displays plants and animals from these regions of the world. Visitors can travel back and forth between zones on a comfortable and air-conditioned monorail.

The zoo's current cast of characters – including a locally beloved baby koala and river-otter pups bred successfully on the continent for only the second time in history – is more than enough to hold wildlife-lovers of all ages in thrall.

Science museum

Heading northward from the waterfront, Bayshore Drive becomes Miami Avenue, where you'll find the **Miami Museum of Science and Planetarium** ㉔ (3280 S. Miami Ave; tel: 305-646-4200; www.miamisci.org; daily 10am–6pm; charge). Dedicated to science exploration and the mysteries of outer space, this hands-on museum contains over 150 exhibits, natural specimens, and interactive games.

The planetarium offers astronomy shows on Friday and Saturday evenings guided by Jack Horkheimer, well-known public television astronomer. Also part of the complex is a wildlife center, where ailing birds of prey and reptiles are nursed back to health and allowed to mingle with wide-eyed guests during scheduled encounter sessions.

Ever looking forward, museum planners are preparing to redesign and move closer to the beach, to a $275 million waterfront park anchored by the planetarium and a new Miami Art Museum. The building is scheduled to open in 2014, and the remixed MiaSci is already buzzed about in the community.

Vizcaya

Tucked behind coral rock walls across the street from the science museum is Miami's grandest residence – **Vizcaya Museum and Gardens** ㉕ (3251 S. Miami Ave; tel: 305-250-9133; www. vizcayamuseum.org; daily 9.30am–4.30pm; charge; *see pages 116–7*). Built between 1914 and 1916 for industrialist James Deering and intended to resemble an Italian Renaissance villa, Vizcaya required 10,000 laborers to complete. During its heyday it occupied 180 acres (70 hectares) and was a totally self-sufficient enclave with its own livestock and vegetable gardens.

Today, the opulent 70-room palace is a museum filled with European antiques, oriental carpets, tapestries, and fine art. Its Baroque and rococo interiors look exactly as they did when it was a private home. A few of the more dramatic rooms are the Tea House, inspired by French architecture; the Music Room, which contains an 18th-century harpsichord; and the Dining Room, which has the air of a Renaissance-era banqueting hall.

Docent-guided tours are offered all day long, and a special "Vizcaya by Moonlight" tour is offered one evening a month during the full moon from January to April. Surrounded by gardens and islands connected by footbridges, the mansion also has a coral rock grotto and swimming pool, dozens of outdoor sculptures, an orchid house, and a coral rock dock on Biscayne Bay complete with a vintage gondola. ❏

miami science museum

The Miami Science Museum is reached easily by public transportation. Take Miami MetroRail to the Vizcaya station.

BELOW: the Vizcaya Museum and Gardens.

RESTAURANTS AND BARS

Restaurants

Prices for a three-course dinner per person, excluding tax, tip, and beverages:
$ = under $20
$$ = $20–45
$$$ = $45–60
$$$$ = over $60

Coconut Grove

Berrie's
2884 SW 27th Ave
Tel: 305-448-2111
http://berriesinthegrove.com
$$
A popular hangout with knowledgeable locals, this little juice bar has grown into a full-fledged restaurant with salads, sandwiches, wraps, and handmade pastas as well as fresh blackened mahi-mahi. The setting, with wooden tables, brick

flooring, and market umbrellas, is charming and the daily happy hour is the best in town.

Bizcaya Grill at The Ritz Carlton Coconut Grove
3300 SW 27th Ave
Tel: 305-644-4675
www.ritzcarlton.com $$$$
This Mediterranean stunner is perfect for an elegant meal in the otherwise very casual Grove. Set against a cascading waterfall with accents of wood and marble, the food and service are top-notch to match.

Greenstreet Café
3110 Commodore Plaza
Tel: 305-567-0662
http://greenstreetcafe.net $$
This child- and dog-friendly café has great views of colorful characters gliding by one of Coconut Grove's busiest corners. The French-Med fare includes a snapper in white-wine sauce, vegetable lasagne, lamb burger with goat cheese on brioche, and divine desserts.

The Original Daily Bread
2400 SW 27th St
Tel: 305-856-5893
www.dailybreadmarketplace.com $
This Middle Eastern market and cafeteria-style eatery serves Miami's best hummus and baklava. There are seats inside among the racks of dried beans and bins of olives as well as outdoor tables.

Scotty's Landing
3381 Pan American Dr
Tel: 305-854-2626
www.sailmiami.com/scottys $$
A salty shack with million-dollar views, this old-time Miami hangout on the marina offers grilled fish sandwiches, coleslaw, and tasty burgers.

Coral Gables

Fleming's Prime Steakhouse
2525 Ponce de León Blvd
Tel: 305-569-7995
www.flemingssteakhouse.com $$$
It may be a chain, but this value-priced chophouse gives nearby steak spots a run for their money. The exceptional wine list features more than 100 labels by the glass.

Miss Saigon Bistro
148 Giralda Ave
Tel: 305-446-8006
www.misssaigonbistro.com $$$
Waiters in Vietnamese garb sing and sometimes dance, but they aren't the only attractions at this Restaurant Row veteran. The Vietnamese fare is fresh and tasty.

Palm d'Or at the Biltmore
1200 Anastasia Ave
Tel: 305-445-1926
www.biltmorehotel.com
$$$$
Small plates of exquisite French cuisine are served in one of Miami's most romantic settings. Deft wine pairings and a professional staff add to the experience.

Pascal's on Ponce
2611 Ponce de León Blvd
Tel: 305-444-2024
www.pascalmiami.com
$$$
Magnificent French fare draws Francophiles to this pocket-size hideaway. Leave space for a dessert soufflé.

Downtown Miami

Acqua at the Four Seasons Miami
1435 Brickell Ave SE
Tel: 305-358-3535
www.fourseasons.com $$$$
This international restaurant in the Four Seasons Hotel offers elegance unmatched in Miami. The food is excellent and the European-trained servers pamper their guests. The restaurant is reason enough to book a room.

Caribbean Delight
236 NE 1st Ave
Tel: 305-381-9254 $
Serving what may be the best Jamaican food this side of Kingston, this cheery little dive offers jerk chicken, curry goat, and much more. Note that they close at 6pm most nights, so dine early.

Garcia's Seafood Grille
398 NW North River Dr
Tel: 305-375-0765
www.garciasseafoodgrill.
com $$
This seafood shack on
the Miami River is great
for grilled mahi-mahi,
fried fish sandwiches,
and stone crabs.

Blue Sky Food by the Pound
3803 W. Flagler St
Tel: 305-642-4388
www.blueskyfood.biz $
Locals love the hearty
Cuban food, and they
feast on it here or take it
out to enjoy as a picnic.

La Carreta
3632 SW 8th St
Tel: 305-444-7501
www.lacarreta.com $
With outlets all over the
city, this rustic fast-food
chain offers cheap Cuban
fare, especially welcome
after a night on the town.

Islas Canarias
285 NW 27th Ave
Tel: 305-649-0440
www.islascanariasrestau-
rant.com $$
Fast service and some of
the best Cuban cooking in
the neighborhood.

Versailles
3555 SW 8th St
Tel: 305-444-0240
www.versaillescuban.com
$$
Feel the pulse of the
Cuban community and
enjoy traditional, hearty
Cuban fare.

Canela Café
5132 Biscayne Blvd
Tel: 305-756-3930
www.canelamiami.com $$
Excellent tapas are
served at night at this
Latin café. The paella is
the best in town, and the

lunch menu includes
Cuban sandwiches, ropa
vieja, and grilled meats.
Great sangria, too.

Dogma
7030 Biscayne Blvd
Tel: 305-759-3433
www.dogmagrill.com $
A real gourmet wiener
stand, this busy outlet
also offers Greek salads,
chicken sandwiches,
thick-cut fries, and
shakes.

Grass
28 NE 40th St
Tel: 305-573-3355
http://grasslounge.com
$$-$$$
Dine alfresco at this cool,
sophisticated restaurant
and bar, with a well-
deserved reputation for
fresh, innovative cuisine
with an Asian and Medi-
terranean flare.

Michael's Genuine Food and Drink
130 NE 40th St
Tel: 305-573-5550
www.michaelsgenuine.com
$$-$$$
Try fish, chicken, pizza,
and other dishes pre-
pared in the wood-fired
oven at this collegial bistro and bar with seating
indoors and out.

Michy's
6927 Biscayne Blvd
Tel: 305-759-2001
http://michysmiami.com $$$
Book in advance for this
charming 50-seat bistro.
Celebrity chef Michelle
Bernstein, with husband
David running the front of
the house, ensures a
delicious meal.

Fratelli Lyon
4141 NE 2nd Ave
Tel: 305-572-2901
www.fratellilyon.com $$$
Fresh Italian fare, served
in the slow food tradi-
tion... inside a furniture
store? It's true, you can
browse the funky chairs

at Driade while waiting for
a table at this in-house
restaurant.

Soyka
5556 E. 4th Court
Tel: 305-759-3117
www.the55thstreetstation.
com/soyka $$
Large portions and rea-
sonable prices keep
patrons coming back to
this industrial-chic spot.
Offerings include grilled
salmon, big burgers, and
hummus and pita.

Bars

Café TuTu Tango
3015 Grand Ave
Tel: 305-529-2222
www.cafetututango.com
With a swinging singles
scene fueled by imagina-
tive drinks and eclectic
small dishes, this is a
perennial favorite in
CocoWalk. All this is
coupled with a killer
sangria and an abun-
dance of art, tango, belly
dancing, and tarot
readings.

Mai Tardi
163 NE 39th St
Tel: 305-572-1400
www.maitardimiami.com
Sipping a mojito at sun-
set, lounging on the plush
couches in this Italian
kitchen's airy outdoor bar
while a DJ spins mellow
beats, is the epitome of
Miami style.

The Pawn Shop
1222 NE 2nd Ave
Tel: 305-373-3511
www.thepawnshoplounge.
com
An especially happening
scene erupts here on Sat-
urday nights with '80s
music. The all-round
good-time atmosphere
starts late and continues
until the wee hours.

XXI Amendment
190 NE 46th St
Tel: 305-571-7200
With a liquor license and
a bordello-like setting,
this space hosts live
music and other cool per-
formances. A tapas menu
sates the palates of the
hip young crowd.

LEFT: an artistic presentation of dinner.
RIGHT: a caipirinha will cool down the day.

VIZCAYA

A bayfront villa set in formal gardens offers an evocative glimpse of bygone days and moonlit nights

Inspired by the opulent country estates of the Veneto region of northern Italy, James Deering – a member of one of the wealthiest families in the US – set out to build a winter retreat in Miami. Constructed in 1916 on 180 acres (73 hectares) of spectacular bayfront, the house was designed to resemble an Italian Renaissance villa but also has Baroque, rococo, and Neoclassical features. The estate's name is from the Basque word for "elevated place" and is also the name of a Basque province on the Bay of Biscay, which itself inspired the name of Miami's Biscayne Bay.

Deering, architect Burrall Hoffman Jr, and painter Paul Chafin inspired themselves by traveling to Italy to study architectural details. Along with imported doors, ceilings, and fireplaces, Florida limestone and native plants were employed to maintain a local ambience.

The house has 70 rooms and needed a staff of 30 during the four months the Deerings were in residence. Today, half of the rooms are open to public view. Every detail is exquisite, from the black-and-white marble tub to the gold-leaf cornices. Especially stunning is the swimming pool, extending from the sun-lit exterior to a grotto beneath the house, its ceiling adorned with shells and carved stone.

Sadly, Deering was able to enjoy the estate for less than a decade; he died in 1925. The family sold the estate to Dade County in 1952. In 1994 the Vizcaya estate was declared a National Historic Landmark.

ABOVE: the villa's south side faces the Italian Renaissance-style formal gardens, featuring elaborate stonework, pools, and greenery.

RIGHT: the 17th-century statuary adorning the gardens includes mythological figures such as Neptune, Minerva, and Apollo.

ABOVE: the Entrance Loggia's shaded vaults and marble surfaces invite visitors into the cool rooms within.

VIZCAYA BY MOONLIGHT

"Miami by Moonlight" has long been a romantic angle for poets and songwriters to explore. Now visitors can enjoy "Vizcaya by Moonlight" on an evening spent wandering among the sweetly scented gardens, guided by a knowledgable docent.

The tours are held once a month, on the night of the full moon, and only in the more temperate season (January to April), weather permitting. The visit begins inside the palazzo itself, with a short talk on the gardens and statuary, including tips on the sights that are to be found throughout the moonlit grounds and what views to look out for along the way.

Programs begin at about 6.30pm and last around 90 minutes. The tour takes in Vizcaya's subtropical forest, proceeds toward the main house along a lit walkway lined with fountains and foliage, and includes live music, views of Biscayne Bay, and the gorgeous orchids in the David A. Klein Orchidarium on the north side of the main house. Vizcaya's café and gift shop remain open on these evenings.

BOVE: Deering named each guest room for the style in which it is corated. The Cathay Bedroom is decorated with chinoiserie, pular in the 18th century.
ELOW: Colombian landscape designer Diego Suarez spent seven ars working on the grounds at Vizcaya.

Vizcaya is open every day (except Tuesday) from 9.30am to 4.30pm, and closes for Christmas and Thanksgiving. For information on tours, visit www.vizcaya museum.org or tel: 305-250-9133.

RIGHT: the inlaid marble flooring in the Entrance Loggia catches the eye. The Loggia was originally open to the exterior.

MIAMI BEACH

Art Deco treasures; sizzling nightlife; a sun-kissed beach; and an endless parade of the rich, famous, and beautiful have transformed this once troubled strip into the American Riviera

Miami Beach is a barrier island barely 15 miles (24km) long and a mile (1.7km) wide. Physically (and psychologically) distinct from its mainland big sister, it is a man-made paradise dedicated to the pursuit of pleasure.

Since it was incorporated as a city in 1917, countless people have come to its shores. They come to play, work, drink, dance, and run away from humdrum lives elsewhere. Although it has gone through several incarnations in its short lifetime – from elite playground of the rich in the 1940s and 1950s to the urban decay and rampant crime of the 1970s and then the hip New Riviera of the 1990s – Miami Beach continues to seduce visitors with its unique charms and glorious beach.

Today Miami Beach is a vibrant village filled with colorful characters who include American celebrities, vanguard artists, real-estate investors, wealthy South Americans, Caribbean immigrants, nouveau-riche Russians, fashion models, gays and lesbians, and world-weary New Yorkers. Spanish is the dominant cultural language of South Florida, making a basic phrasebook a helpful tool for chatting up locals, but those not conversationally fluent will find shopkeepers and locals more than willing to switch from their usual tongue to English.

SoBe and Art Deco

At the southern tip of Miami Beach is the neighborhood of **South Beach**, or SoBe. When the Swinging Sixties came to an end, Miami Beach slipped into a period of decline that lasted for almost two decades. But then a few forward-thinking preservationists came to the rescue and spread the word that this thing called Art Deco was something worth saving. In 1979, the Miami Beach Art Deco National Historic District was founded, and things have been looking up ever since.

Main attractions
SOUTH BEACH
JEWISH MUSEUM OF FLORIDA
OCEAN DRIVE
WORLD EROTIC ART MUSEUM
ESPANOLA WAY
LINCOLN ROAD
FILLMORE MIAMI BEACH
HOLOCAUST MEMORIAL
BASS MUSEUM OF ART
BAL HARBOUR

LEFT: Miami Beach from above.
RIGHT: socializing on Ocean Drive.

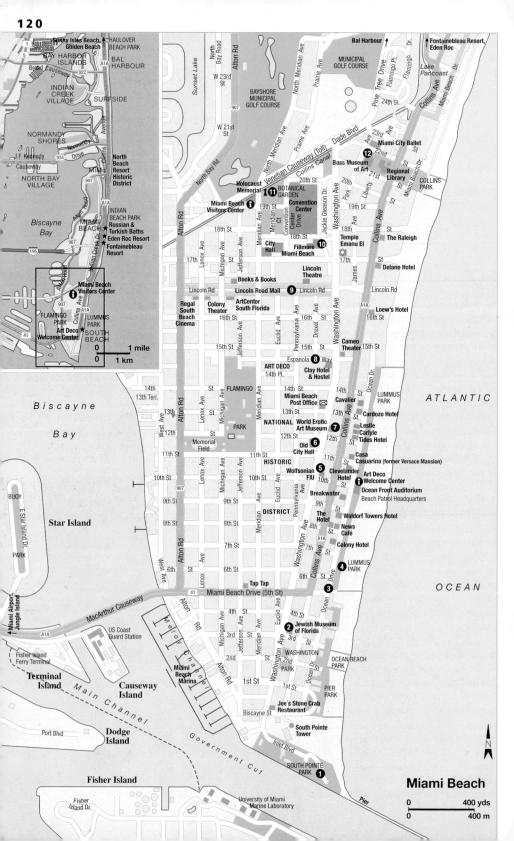

Miami Beach

Containing more than 500 Art Deco buildings constructed in the 1930s and 1940s, the Deco District is the youngest historic district in America. It has grown and prospered and served as the cornerstone of a new wave of preservation pride that has swept the entire island. Encompassing about 1 sq mile (2.5 sq km), it runs roughly from 6th to 23rd streets and Ocean Drive to Alton Road.

After driving across the MacArthur Causeway, the main thoroughfare to SoBe, the highway becomes 5th Street. Between Jefferson and Meridian on 5th is **Tap Tap** *(see page 129)*, Miami Beach's only Haitian restaurant. Tap Tap also hosts live bands, author signings, and screenings of film documentaries with a socially conscious slant.

To the south of 5th Street is **South Pointe Park ❶**, a verdant 17 acre (7 hectare) playground with meandering walkways and great views of the Port of Miami that was given a $22 million makeover in 2009. It is also one of the few vacant pieces of land on the island. A few blocks away is the **Jewish Museum of Florida ❷** (301 Washington Ave; tel: 305-672-5044; www.jewishmuseum.com; Tue–Sun 10am–5pm; charge). Housed in a beautifully restored 1936 synagogue, the museum is full of artifacts that document the history of Jews throughout the state of Florida.

A few blocks away is the oldest restaurant on Miami Beach, **Joe's Stone Crab** *(see page 128)*, which has been serving the succulent crustaceans since 1913 and lists as a former customer gangster Al Capone. Families visiting the beach may be diverted before exiting the Causeway, however, by the lush expanses of **Jungle Island** (1111 Parrot Jungle Trail; tel: 305-400-7000). Formerly known as the Parrot Jungle and first launched in the mid-1930s, this interactive zoological park lets visitors mingle with colorful monkeys and tropical birds. There is even a liger (a lion-tiger hybrid) named Hercules who calls the island home.

Ocean Drive

Fifth Street ends at **Ocean Drive ❸**, the world-famous see-and-be-seen street where curvaceous Latin beauties and handsome bronzed hunks strut their stuff. Always busy, Ocean Drive is one of the prettiest streets in Miami Beach, filled with restored Art Deco hotels and dozens of outdoor bistros. One of the most popular is the **Pelican Café** between 8th and 9th streets. Located in a perennially hot hotel run by the Diesel clothing empire, it combines stellar people-watching with reliable but creative American fare.

Across the street is **Lummus Park ❹**, a hub of beach activity with a tree-lined promenade ideal for roller-bladers, a children's playground, and volleyball nets. Several unique lifeguard stands mark this part of the beach, each in a pseudo-Deco style. In the next few blocks are some of the beach's great Art Deco darlings – the **Waldorf Towers**, **Breakwater**, and **Clevelander** hotels, all preserved architectural gems.

On the beach at 10th Street is the **Miami Beach Ocean Front Auditorium**, a public venue that hosts

A bar dancer at Mango's Tropical Café in South Beach.

BELOW: Tap Tap restaurant is covered with colorful murals.

The World Erotic Art Museum.

BELOW: an exhibit at the Jewish Museum celebrates Jewish comic book artists and writers.

concerts and events. Next door in a tiny blue building is the **Art Deco Welcome Center** (daily 10am–7pm), a nucleus of information on local architecture and history run by the Miami Design Preservation League, founded more than 35 years ago to help preserve the region's built legacy.

At 1114 Ocean Drive is **Casa Casuarina**, a strikingly beautiful Mediterranean Revival mansion surrounded by pine trees. Like Miami Beach itself, the property has undergone many metamorphoses. Designed to resemble Christopher Columbus's home in the Dominican Republic, it was originally built as an apartment house called Amsterdam Palace. In 1992 Gianni Versace bought the building and transformed it into a private Italian-style villa. Following Versace's death it was sold and now functions as a private club with VIP clientele.

A block away is the **Tides Hotel**, once owned by Island Records founder Chris Blackwell. Billed as the Diva of Ocean Drive, the Tides is a tower of luxury with a soothingly neutral palette that blends historic ambience with modern service – every guest is assigned a "personal assistant." In the next few blocks is a group of historic properties that were among the first to be restored in the late 1980s – the **Carlyle**, **Leslie**, **Cavalier**, and **Cardozo**, which is owned by singer Gloria Estefan.

Washington Avenue

Two blocks to the west and running parallel to Ocean Drive is Washington Avenue, a less glamorous but more interesting street. While many great restaurants can be found here, there are also lots of tiny cafeterias, mom-and-pop grocery stores, tattoo parlors, and clothing boutiques selling garments that leave little to the imagination. Plenty of tourists can be found on Washington, but it is also where locals come for late-night snacks.

At 10th and Washington is the most impressive building on the street, the **Wolfsonian-Florida International University ❺** (1001 Washington Ave; tel: 305-531-1001; www.wolfsonian.org; Mon–Tue and Sat–Sun noon–6pm, Thur–Fri noon–9pm; charge). Housed in a 1920s Spanish Baroque structure that once served as a storage facility, the offbeat Wolfsonian-FIU museum was founded by Mitchell Wolfson Jr, heir to the Wometco movie theater chain, and contains a collection of decorative and propaganda arts from 1895 to 1945. Focusing on the social, political, and esthetic significance of design, the eccentric collection includes bronze busts of Mussolini, Hitler posters, textiles, comic books, and furniture designed by Frank Lloyd Wright.

One block to the north is **Old City Hall ❻**, a beautiful Mediterranean Revival structure built to help the city revive from a devastating 1926 hurricane. It later became the first building in Miami Beach to be granted an historic designation. Behind City Hall is the **Miami Beach Police Station**, where officers gear up on bicycles for their daily patrols.

Nearby is the **World Erotic Art Museum ❼** (1205 Washington Ave;

tel: 305-532-9336; www.weam.com; daily 11am–midnight; charge). Founded by Naomi Wilzig, a Jewish grandmother who amassed a 4,000-piece erotica collection, the museum holds a smoldering and informative display of sculptures, prints, and paintings.

Between 14th and 15th Streets on Washington Avenue is the block-long **Espanola Way** ❽. A charming assortment of Spanish Mediterranean buildings, all painted bright pink and white, Espanola is one of the last bohemian sections of South Beach. Originally built to be an artist colony in the 1920s, it became a red-light district soon after and still retains a nonconformist spirit. It was here in the late 1930s that Desi Arnaz, Cuban singer and future husband of Lucille Ball, first performed in the US. With wrought-iron balconies and lots of outdoor tables, Espanola often hosts belly-dancing shows, Cuban jazz bands, and Haitian drummers. It is also home to the **Clay Hotel and International Youth Hostel** (tel: 305-534-2988), the only real bargain accommodation left on the beach, and a favorite hangout for backpackers.

Lincoln Road

Once called the Fifth Avenue of the South, **Lincoln Road** ❾ (between 16th and 17th Streets) is the prime artery for local street life in South Beach. Unlike the frenetic energy of Ocean Drive, Lincoln Road is more mellow and much easier to navigate. With roots that go back to the late 1920s, it is a storied place that was transformed into a pedestrian-only thoroughfare in the 1960s by modernist architect Morris Lapidus. Today it bustles with bars, restaurants, boutiques, galleries, coffee houses, jazz clubs, and theaters. Families with strollers, beautiful women walking their toy terriers, trendy artist types, and flamboyant drag queens all mingle here as one.

Much of Lincoln Road's revival goes back to 1984, when **ArtCenter South Florida** (924 Lincoln Rd; tel: 305-674-8278; www.artcentersf.org; call for hours) first opened its doors. A nonprofit gallery with several working studios, it features three exhibition areas and regularly hosts cocktail parties and special arts events.

BELOW LEFT: the Wolfsonian-Florida International University Museum. **BELOW:** the Art Deco District encompasses hundreds of notable buildings.

Art Deco Walking Tours

Covering the spectrum from flamingo pink to cool turquoise, with sculpted mermaids and neon lights thrown in for fun, tropical Art Deco architecture is a whimsical sight to behold. With its small scale and many nooks and crannies, the Art Deco District is best explored on foot because there are so many details to take in.

The Miami Design Preservation League offers some of the best walking tours in all of Florida. Hosted by historians and architects, the 90-minute tours tell the story behind the style. Tours depart from the **Art Deco Welcome Center** (1001 Ocean Drive) at 10.30am Wednesday, Friday, Saturday, and Sunday, and at 6.30pm Thursday. Tours focus on Art Deco as well as Mediterranean Revival structures and include fascinating tidbits of local lore. In-depth explanations are given about the buildings' design and history as well as their decline and restoration.

Reservations are not required, but a hat and comfy shoes are suggested. Self-guided audio tours in five languages are also available daily from 10am to 4pm. For information, call 305-531-3484 or go to www.mdpl.org.

A barista awaits the morning's customers at A La Folie Café on Espanola Way.

BELOW: biking past shops and restaurants on Espanola Way.

About two blocks away is the **Colony Theater** (1040 Lincoln Rd; tel: 305-674-1026), an Art Deco jewel that was once a movie theater and is now a city-owned performing-arts venue. At 541 Lincoln Road is the **Lincoln Theatre** (tel: 305-673-3330), home to the New World Symphony, America's only national orchestral training company for musicians aged 21 to 30. The New World Symphony recently moved to a new home designed by renowned architect Frank Gehry and acoustician Yasuhisa Toyota.

At the western edge of Lincoln Road is the **Regal South Beach Cinema**, a modern multiscreen movie theater that hosts many of the foreign films featured during the **Miami International Film Festival** each winter. Local residents regard the cinema as a much-needed addition but are less sanguine about nearby chain stores that lack the quirky character the beach prides itself on. One place that clings to the neighborhood's independent spirit is **Books & Books** (933 Lincoln Rd; tel: 305-532-3222; daily 10am–11pm). Like its sister store in Coral Gables, Books

& Books on the beach is more than a bookstore; it's a restaurant, café, and meeting place for local literati that often hosts readings by award-wining authors and special events supported by the arts community.

An ample stretch of Lincoln is transformed every Sunday into a popular farmers' market, where fresh organic fruit and home-made jellies can be purchased for an impromptu streetside picnic.

17th Street

To the north of Lincoln Road is **17th Street**, also known as Hank Meyer Boulevard – named for the publicist who convinced Jackie Gleason to move his show to Miami Beach in 1964. On the north side of the street is the **Fillmore Miami Beach ❿** (1700 Washington Ave; tel: 305-673-7300), formerly the Jackie Gleason Theater. After the Arscht Center opened in downtown Miami, the old Gleason Theater underwent a renovation and now stages major rock, comedy, and pop performances. On the sidewalk along the south side of the theater is Miami Beach's version of

the Walk of Stars, where handprints of famous inductees include Muhammad Ali and Ann-Margret.

On the west side of the theater is the **Miami Beach Convention Center**, home to the December art extravaganza known as **Art Basel Miami Beach** as well as dozens of other trade shows and events. Nearby is the new **Miami Beach City Hall**, and a much welcomed patch of green, the **Miami Beach Botanical Garden** (2000 Convention Center Dr; tel: 305-673-7256; www.mbgarden.org; Tue–Sun 9am–5pm; free). Full of native plants and exotic orchids, this 4 acre (1.6 hectare) tropical garden offers classes and lectures and serves as the main environmental entity that encourages the densely built city of Miami Beach to "go green."

Holocaust Memorial

Until about a decade ago, Miami Beach had one of the largest populations of Holocaust survivors in the US, so it made sense that the island would want to commission a testament to the tragedies of World War II. Designed by Kenneth Treister, the **Holocaust Memorial** ⓫ (1933–45 Meridian Ave; tel: 305-538-1663; daily 9am–9pm; free) is a somber reminder of those who lost their lives in the Nazi death camps. The 42ft (13 meter) bronze sculpture is that of an outstretched hand reaching toward the heavens, with nearly 100 life-size statues of tormented people grasping for help. The memorial also has a peaceful garden and plaza, a pictorial history of the Holocaust, and a granite wall inscribed with the names of thousands of victims.

Collins Park

In an effort to reduce some of South Beach's congestion and move the arts-and-culture scene a little northward, the city created the **Collins Park Cultural Center** between 17th and 25th Streets. Part of a project that plans on bringing affordable housing to resident artists – many of whom can no

longer afford to live in Miami Beach – the Collins Park "campus" runs along Collins Avenue and is made of three components: headquarters of the **Miami City Ballet**; the **Miami Beach Regional Library**, a state-of-the-art facility and repository for books and artifacts on Miami Beach history; and the **Bass Museum of Art** ⓬ (2121 Park Ave; tel: 305-673-7530; www.bassmuseum.org; Tue–Sat 10am–5pm, Sun 11am–5pm; charge).

Built in 1930 as the city library, the Art Deco building has been a museum since the 1960s when philanthropist John Bass donated his own art collection. The Bass hosts visiting exhibits but is most noted for its extensive European collection, including Renaissance works, 16th-century Flemish tapestries, paintings by Peter Paul Rubens, ecclesiastical artifacts, and lithographs by Henri Toulouse-Lautrec.

Middle Beach and MiMo

North of the Bass Museum, the beach takes on a different tone and the buildings become taller, less Deco, and

A bit mellower than Ocean Drive, Lincoln Road is nonetheless a colorful and lively place for shopping, dining, and strolling.

BELOW: jazzy art at an Ocean Drive gift shop.

Key Biscayne

Just minutes from the hustle of Miami is an island getaway with golden beaches, secluded coves, plush resorts, and water sports

A tiny barrier island just a few minutes from downtown Miami, Key Biscayne is an oasis of tranquility (famously, President Richard Nixon used it as a winter escape from his Washington woes in the 1970s). Although it has a sizable residential community, the island is also an exclusive tropical getaway that offers a serene alternative to Miami Beach with water sports, lovely beaches, a world-famous tennis center, and plush resorts.

After crossing the Rickenbacker Causeway Bridge over Biscayne Bay, the atmosphere quickly mellows. The first stop is **Virginia Key** where several outlets offer windsurfing and kiteboarding rentals on the calm bay waters. On the left side of the highway is a turn-off to **Virginia Key Beach Park**, a 2 mile (3km) stretch of sand that during segregation served as Miami's only "black beach." A dirt road nearby meanders down to **Jimbo's**, a quirky Old Florida eatery that has been serving smoked fish and cold beer since the 1950s.

Aquatic theme park

On the opposite side of the highway is the **Miami Seaquarium** (4400 Rickenbacker Causeway; tel: 305-361-5705; daily 9.30am–6pm; charge). Founded in 1955, the Seaquarium is a stellar marine research center as well as an aquatic theme park that features enormous tanks full of sharks, manatees, stingrays, alligators, and dolphins; exotic birds and wildlife; and spectacular water shows starring killer whales and sea lions. For an extra fee, the Seaquarium offers two-hour tours of the facilities that include a magical half-hour of swimming and playing with the resident dolphins.

Farther down the spine of the island is **Crandon Park Beach**, a public park complete with a soccer field and 18-hole public golf course. Considered one of Miami's most popular "party beaches," Crandon tends to be very busy on weekends. On the bay side nearby is the **Crandon Park Tennis Center** (tel: 305-446-2200), where top-ranked tennis pros compete each spring for prizes worth millions during the Sony Ericsson Open. Over 200,000 spectators turn out to watch such top-ranked players as Venus Williams and Roger Federer compete in the week-long event, and then partake in the after-hours parties.

Past the tennis center is the **Village of Key Biscayne**. With a population of about 10,000, the village is definitely for the well-heeled, and the tempo is slow and casual. Several bicycle rental shops make it easy for tourists to tour the island by bike.

At the far end of the island is **Bill Baggs Cape Florida State Park** (daily sunrise to sunset; charge). Regularly rated as one of the best beaches in the US, Bill Baggs is a unique experience for a Miami-area beach – there are no lifeguards and no buildings within site of the sand. Dotted with endangered sea oats and towering Australian pine trees, the beach is broad and soft, and the water is deep close to shore. At the park's southern end is the **Cape Florida Lighthouse**. Built in 1825, it is one of the oldest structures in South Florida and the only lighthouse in the country to have been attacked by American Indians (Seminoles). Park rangers offer tours Thursday through Monday at 10am and 1pm. A few steps away is a restaurant with good seafood and frosty drinks. In the distance offshore are the few remaining stilt houses that comprised a once-vibrant community known as **Stiltsville**. ❑

LEFT: strolling on the boardwalk.

more futuristic in design. Stretching from 23rd to 47th Streets is an area known as **Middle Beach**, which includes a few landmark properties. Built in 1954, the **Fontainebleau Resort** (4441 Collins Ave) was where the Kings of Cool – Frank Sinatra, Sammy Davis Jr, and Dean Martin – serenaded the crowds in the 1950s and 1960s. Ostentatious to the core, it was designed by the late Morris Lapidus, who today is considered the father of MiMo (Miami Modern) architecture.

Lapidus also designed its neighbor, the **Eden Roc** (4525 Collins Ave), the other grande dame of MiMo. Both are perfect examples of the over-the-top resort vernacular that came about during the unbridled American optimism of the 1950s. Both have also been renovated and expanded. For years MiMo buildings were considered tacky, an embarrassment to the esthetically inclined, but after the millennium they were elevated to historic status and praised for their naive playfulness.

Common throughout Miami and Miami Beach, MiMo buildings are characterized by flamboyant angles and lines, accordion walls, cheese-hole masonry, massive columns, anodized aluminum, and terrazzo floors.

For visitors seeking an unusual afternoon, the **Russian and Turkish Baths** (5445 Collins Ave; tel: 305-867-8313) should get the blood going. Gender mingling is encouraged at this cavernous old-school steam and spa complex, located in the decidedly un-modern Castle Beach Condominiums building. The "shvitz" room is a particular favorite, with buckets of cold water that provide relief from rocks that emit radiant, furnace-like heat.

NoBe

Once Collins Avenue passes north of 47th Street, the neighborhood becomes NoBe, **North Beach**, one of the more desirable residential areas. Formerly the realm of northern retirees, NoBe is now a hip and happening neighborhood full of young Brazilians, savvy

Europeans, and other trendy newcomers. Full of MiMo architecture and a diverse group of good restaurants, it also has great beach access and an easy-going attitude.

To the west are the upscale resident islands of **Normandy Shores** and **Indian Creek**; to the north are the towns of **Surfside**, **Sunny Isles**, **Golden Beach**, and **Bal Harbour**, home of a famous upscale shopping center. At **Bal Harbour Shops** (9700 Collins Ave; tel: 305-866-0311), which cites a Women's Wear Daily report that ranks its business per square foot as highest in the nation, there are only luxury shops, from Bulgari and Gucci to Armani and Prada.

For a less expensive afternoon in the area, while away an hour at the **Old Spanish Monastery** (16711 West Dixie Hwy; tel: 305-945-1461), technically the "oldest building in the Western Hemisphere." This beautiful chapel was first built in the 12th century before being carefully deconstructed and shipped to Florida in the 1920s by William Randolph Hearst, the news baron who inspired the movie *Citizen Kane*. ❏

TIP

Gay and lesbian travelers can get information about accommodations, dining, events, and other services from the Miami-Dade Gay and Lesbian Chamber of Commerce (tel: 305-573-4000; www.gogay miami.com).

BELOW: shopping in Bal Harbour.

RESTAURANTS, BARS, AND CAFÉS

Restaurants

Prices for a three-course dinner per person, excluding tax, tip, and beverages:
$ = under $20
$$ = $20–45
$$$ = $45–60
$$$$ = over $60

A La Folie
516 Espanola Way
Tel: 305-538-4484
www.alafoliecafe.com **$$**
A romantic outdoor setting with the atmosphere of a Left Bank café, where handsome young waiters serve French crêpes with good-value wine.

Arnie & Richie's
525 41st St
Tel: 305-531-7691
B & L daily **$**
Still Miami Beach's best deli after six decades, this

is a temple to New York-style bagels, pastrami, and corned beef on rye. A recent revamp has not detracted from the authentic fare or the brusque service.

Café at Books & Books
933 Lincoln Rd
Tel: 305-695-8898
www.booksandbooks.com **$$**
Fresh, well-composed lunches and dinners make this bookstore's New American café one of the best on Lincoln Road. Outdoor seating and sassy servers add to the literary allure.

Café Ragazzi
9500 Harding Ave
Tel: 305-866-4495
www.caferagazzi.com **$$**
You'll feel like one of the *famiglia* at this crowded but charming Italian ris-

torante. Waits are common but compensated for by a glass of great wine.

Carpaccio
Shops of Bal Harbour,
9700 Collins Ave
Tel: 305-867-7777
www.carpacciobalharbour.com **$$$**
Armani, Fendi, and Gucci are on parade in this posh Italian restaurant for ladies who lunch. The signature carpaccio is recommended, as are the delicate, handmade pastas, the fresh salads, and the extensive wine list.

Eleventh Street Diner
1065 Washington Ave
Tel: 305-534-6373
www.eleventhstreetdiner.com **$$**
This classic diner in an aluminum trailer smack dab in the middle of South Beach clubland is a perfect spot for the "morning after" cure. Greasy grill fare, with a full bar. Best of all, the diner is open 24/7.

Emeril's Miami Beach
The Loews Resort,
1601 Collins Ave
Tel: 305-695-4550
www.emerils.com **$$$**
Effusive TV chef Emeril Lagasse may not actually be here, but his specialties like blackened pecan redfish and gumbo have a big presence. Quality can vary, but the star power is definitely in abundance. Make a reservation and ask for an outdoor table.

Escopazzo
1311 Washington Ave
Tel: 305-674-9450
www.escopazzo.com **$$$$**
Northern Italian dishes are made with lots of local produce, accompanied by a fine, all-Italian

wine list and served by knowledgable, helpful staff. A better choice than many of the flashy South Beach eateries.

The Forge
432 41st St
Tel: 305-538-8533
www.theforge.com **$$$$**
An institution in Miami Beach for four decades, this gilded icon is a magnet for celebrities and celeb-spotters. Tuxedoed servers give tours of the historic and well-stocked wine cellar.

Joe's Stone Crab
11 Washington Ave
Tel: 305-673-0365
www.joesstonecrab.com **$$$$**
The oldest and most talked about restaurant on the beach – some might even call it a tourist trap. But Joe's is still great if you can nab a table (reservations are not accepted). Service is brusque but worth it for the stone crabs, which are in season from mid-Oct through mid-May. The restaurant is closed from Aug through Sept.

La Provence French Bakery
1629 Collins Avenue
Tel: 305 538-2406
www.laprovencemiami.com **$**
The beach's finest French bakery has a constant carb-hungry line for baguettes and croissants. Big salads are on offer, as are yummy sandwiches with prosciutto or mozzarella, quiches, and temptingly pretty pastries.

Shoji
100 Collins Ave
Tel: 305-532-4245 **$$$**
Sushi like you won't find

elsewhere. Shoji impresses even Japanese expats with huge slabs of jewel-like fish and shellfish, as well as cooked dishes like oyster miso and grilled skirt steak with enoki mushrooms.

Spris
731 Lincoln Rd
Tel: 305-673-2020
www.spris.cc **$**
Roman-style pizza with paper-thin crusts charred on the edges and nearly see-through in the middle are all the rage at this busy pizzeria. You can also order from the menus of the eateries on either side of Spris, so try the mussels from Le Bon or the pasta from Tiramisu; all are owned by restaurateur Graziano Sbroggi.

Talula
210 23rd St
Tel: 305-672-0778
www.talulaonline.com **$$$**
Frank and Andrea Randazzo delight their regulars with impressive tartare of ahi tuna dotted with serrano chiles, cucumber, and crisped rice and conch ceviche. The rustic brick interior is romantic and cozy, while the enchanting courtyard is a dream in the cool months.

Tamarind
946 Normandy Dr
Tel: 305-861-6222
http://tamarindthai.us **$$**
A little-known Thai delight, almost lost in an area dominated by Argentinian eateries, this authentic, good-looking and moderately priced spot is well worth a detour. Specialty dishes include tamarind duck, shrimp, and sweet corn cake, or you could opt for the fantastic pad Thai.

Tap Tap
819 5th St
Tel: 305-672-2898
www.taptaprestaurant.com **$$**
The beach's only Haitian eatery, this Caribbean restaurant is decorated with brightly colored murals. The food, including fried pork tidbits and curried goat stew, recalls the taste of the islands. Live music on weekends completes the scene.

Taverna Opa
36 Ocean Drive
Tel: 305-673-6730
www.tavernaoparestaurant. com **$$**
Opa is like a souped-up Greek frat party, replete with raucous plate-smashing. The lamb, squid, and moussaka make the inevitable wait worthwhile.

Toni's Sushi Bar
1208 Washington Ave
Tel: 305-673-9368
www.tonisushi.com **$$$**
This Japanese pearl pleases lovers of raw fish with pristine sushi served in cozy curtained booths. It's usually crowded with regulars on weekends, but always worth the wait.

Wish at the Hotel
801 Collins Ave
Tel: 305-674-9474
www.wishrestaurant.com **$$$$**
Delightful and totally tropical, the romantic setting is enchanting in this Todd Oldham-designed restaurant. The inner garden is exotic, but the outside tables among palms and twinkling lights are truly magical, while the classic American and contemporary Asian cuisine is a perfect match for the setting. Be sure to enjoy a pre-dinner drink at the upstairs terrace bar.

Bars and Cafés

Buck 15
707 Lincoln Lane
Tel: 305-534-5488
www.buck15.net
A hip hideaway where you can find the coolest kids gathering for drinks before hitting the South Beach scene. It's also a good after-hours haunt.

Clarke's
840 1st St
http://clarkesmiamibeach.com
An Irish pub and bar that serves remarkably good food way beyond shepherd's pie and fish and chips. There's a killer wine list and a great range of beers and ales on tap.

Kafka's
1464 Washington Ave
Tel: 305-672-4526
www.kafkas-cafe.com
A bookstore and cyber café, this corner spot appeals to the literary crowd as well as to their smart friends.

Mac's Club Deuce
222 14th St
Tel: 305-531-6200

An all-day and all-night institution on South Beach, this hard-drinking Deco bar is a place not to be missed. Everyone from bikers to bankers is made to feel welcome.

Segafreddo Café
1040 Lincoln Rd
Tel: 305-673-0047
www.segafredo-cafes.com
Luxurious sofas with lounging Europeans come here for cocktails and even better coffees, carpaccio, and sandwiches, served at all hours.

VIX and VUE at the Hotel Victor
1144 Ocean Dr
Tel: 305-779-8888
The Victor plays host to one of the hottest scenes on the beach. On offer is not only the unbeatable view over South Beach's sexy oceanfront, but also the gathering of pretty young things who lounge under the stars on canopied orbit beds – all the while nibbling on tasty tapas and sipping the latest luscious libations.

LEFT: an artfully prepared dish at Emeril's.
RIGHT: the neon lights of the Hotel Victor.

ART DECO: SOUTH BEACH STYLE

The exotic and colorful buildings on Ocean Drive are the product of Miami's unique interpretation of Art Deco style

The splendid Art Deco buildings in Miami Beach were built to raise the spirits of Americans during the Great Depression. Many decades later, preservationists say that they are among the most architecturally significant structures in the US.

The roots of Art Deco go back to 1901, when the Société des Artistes Décorateurs was formed in Paris with the goal of merging the mass production of industrial technology with the decorative arts. It was proudly introduced to the world in 1925 at the Paris Exposition Internationale des Arts Décoratifs et Industriels Modernes. The nickname "Art Deco" gained currency only in 1966, when it was dreamed up for a retrospective of the 1925 Paris show. The Art Deco style was evocative of the new Machine Age, and was inspired by the aerodynamic designs of airplanes and cars; but it combined all kinds of influences, from the swirls of Art Nouveau to the hard lines of Cubism.

In the 1930s and '40s, hundreds of Deco structures were built in South Beach. Art Deco's stark, white exteriors were already well suited to Florida's hot climate, but architects in Miami soon developed their own style, later dubbed Tropical Deco. Many features, from window design to color choice, were inspired by South Florida's balmy weather and its seaside location. The more futuristic Art Deco style known as Streamline Moderne, which replaced some of the detail characteristic of traditional Art Deco with smoother lines and sweeping curves, was particularly popular in Miami.

LEFT: several elements of Art Deco, such as tube railings and porthole windows, were borrowed from the design of ocean liners.

ABOVE: the Marlin Hotel on Collins Avenue is a classic Streamline Moderne building, and represents the design style that evolved from Deco. Notice the rounded corners and "eyebrows" – canopies which shade the windows against the sun. The long horizontal lines emphasize the aerodynamic design elements. The floral designs popular in Art Deco have been eliminated, leaving the lines of the building lean and sleek. Both Deco and Moderne roofs were typically flat, but often broken by a raised central parapet or pointed finial.

THE FIGHT TO SAVE MIAMI DECO

The Art Deco hotels of South Beach provided a welcome refuge for visitors from all over the world, but by the 1960s the buildings had begun to decay. Several of the area's once-glamorous hotels became low-rent housing for the elderly, and much of the district became run-down.

In 1976, Barbara Capitman (*above*) set up the Miami Design Preservation League to stop the demolition of the Art Deco buildings and to encourage their restoration. In 1979, 1 sq mile (2.5 sq km) of South Beach was listed in the National Registry of Historic Places. It was the first 20th-century district to receive such recognition.

In the 1980s, designer Leonard Horowitz endowed South Beach with a new color scheme, nicknamed Deco Dazzle, by painting many of the older buildings in bright and lively colors; originally most would have been painted white with color trim. Media interest in Miami's Art Deco enclave skyrocketed after South Beach became a favorite backdrop in the hit TV series *Miami Vice*. Fashion photographers such as Bruce Weber were drawn south to Florida for the gorgeous and colorful scenes.

ABOVE: the Colony Hotel graces Ocean Drive, in the heart of Miami's Art Deco district. More than 800 buildings in either Art Deco or Streamline Moderne style can be found in close proximity.

BELOW: the Raleigh Hotel is considered an Art Deco masterpiece. The stones along the pool's edge emphasize its luxurious curls and curves, and complement the lush garden and ritzy bar nearby.

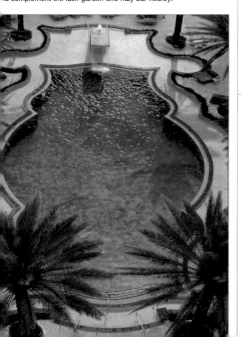

RIGHT: the Art Deco architects in Miami tried out all kinds of new materials, including chrome, glass blocks, and terrazzo (a cheap, imitation marble). Stainless steel became a popular material, as did more exotic fabrics for furnishing coverings such as zebra and shark skin. Neon lighting was used for the first time in 1926, and is one of the most distinctive features of South Beach. While only a few colors were available when neon signage first became popular, nearly two dozen colors were available by the 1960s, and today there are more than 100 shades to choose from.

THE EVERGLADES

A two-hour drive from Miami takes visitors to
Florida's untamed heart – an ecological treasure
rich in subtropical plants and animals

I t's an unseasonably warm, humid
February morning in **Everglades
City ❶**, the fishing village that
serves as the gateway to the Ten
Thousand Islands unit of **Everglades
National Park** on the Gulf of Mexico.
The sun is already glinting off the
sapphire waters in front of the park's
Gulf Coast Visitor Center (tel: 239-
695-2945). At the dock, a narrated
boat tour of scenic Chokoloskee Bay
is just pulling out, while a seasonal
park ranger gets ready to guide a paddling tour to Sandfly Island, a shell-
mound island that was once home to
Calusa Indians.

Water world

About a mile away, another kayaking
trip is loading outside Ivey House, a
popular eco-lodge. On the screened
porch, a group of kayakers dressed in
roll-down pants and shirts, closed-toe
sneakers, and broad-brimmed hats
lathers on sunscreen and insect repellent while listening to an orientation
from the tour leader. They will drive
by van north to the intersection of SR
29 and US 41, then another 6 miles
(10km) east through Big Cypress
National Preserve to the Turner River
highway bridge. From this put-in, it's
a leisurely southward paddle through
the largest mangrove ecosystem in the
US, a boggy place of tangled branch

tunnels, estuary waters, and intimate
wildlife viewing.

Day trips like these offer an enjoyable and safe introduction to the
watery beauty of the **Ten Thousand
Islands**, the Wild West frontier of
the Everglades. The park's signature
kayaking route, the 99 mile (160km)
-long **Wilderness Waterway**, passes
through the **Marjorie Stoneman
Douglas Wilderness**, the largest
wilderness east of the Mississippi,
linking Ten Thousand Islands with
Cape Sable and Florida Bay, the

Main attractions
EVERGLADES CITY
FLAMINGO
ERNEST COE VISITOR CENTER
SHARK VALLEY VISITOR CENTER
MICCOSUKEE CULTURAL CENTER
AH-TAH-THI-KI MUSEUM
PA-HAY-OKEE OVERLOOK
CHOKOLOSKEE ISLAND
BIG CYPRESS NATIONAL PRESERVE
FAKAHATCHEE STRAND PRESERVE
    STATE PARK

LEFT: kayakers near Everglades City.
RIGHT: an alligator waits in the water.

Mosquitoes are abundant during the rainy season, from roughly June through October.

southernmost tip of the main park. You can do the challenging eight-day trip in either direction, beginning or ending at the old fishing village of **Flamingo ❷** in Florida Bay.

The visitor center and marina at Florida Bay are relatively small; only basic facilities are available. Self-sufficient visitors may still enjoy outdoor activities like kayaking, boat tours, birding, ranger walks, and camping in the large, semideveloped beachfront campground (reservations strongly advised in high season; tel: 800-365-CAMP). Those unprepared for roughing it will want to base themselves elsewhere.

Orientation

Hurricanes are a fact of life in South Florida. In the 1900s, killer hurricanes devastated Ten Thousand Islands, Lake Okeechobee, Homestead, and Flamingo. Overall, the loss of services at its major visitor hub has been a blessing in disguise for Everglades National Park. Many of the park's million annual visitors – most of whom arrive in Miami and devote a

single day to the park before heading to the Florida Keys – explore farther afield and learn that the Everglades is much more than bogs, birds, and bugs. It's actually a complex mosaic of nine ecosystems, comprising ponds, sloughs, sawgrass marshes, hardwood hammocks, and forested uplands essential to native wildlife, and covers all of South Florida from Biscayne Bay to the Gulf of Mexico.

The main part of the park is an hour south of Miami, off US 1. Hotels and restaurants are modest. One good choice for adventurous travelers is funky Everglades Hostel in Florida City. It has dorms and private rooms, self-catering facilities, Internet, and, like Ivey House in Everglades City, specializes in kayak tours of the park.

Park headquarters is next to **Ernest Coe Visitor Center ❸** (tel: 305-242-7700; www.nps.gov/ever; daily 9am–5pm), just inside the park entrance. The visitor center is named for feisty landscape architect Ernest Coe who, starting in 1928, spearheaded the effort to get Everglades National Park authorized by Congress. It has exhibits, a film, a

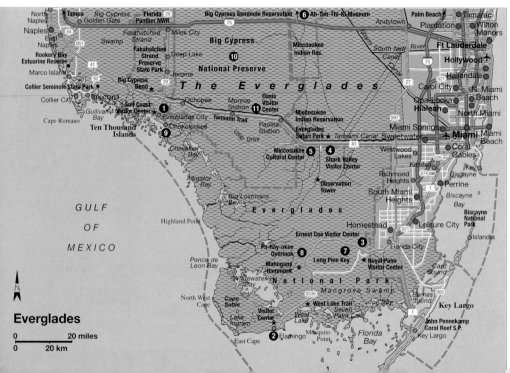

Everglades

0   20 miles

0   20 km

bookstore, and two campgrounds and trails at nearby Long Pine Key. The two most popular trails in the park are 4 miles (6km) away at **Royal Palm Visitor Center** (exhibits, gift shop, ranger-led activities), the former state park that was the first piece of land acquired for the national park. The road to Flamingo is a 38 mile (61km) scenic drive that winds through the peaceful landscape.

The main entry to Everglades National Park along historic **Tamiami Trail** (US 41) is 30 miles (48km) west of Miami at **Shark Valley**. Biologically rich, Shark Valley is one of the three vital drainage areas for the Everglades and was added to the park in 1989. The unit's chief attractions are its proximity to US 41 and the accessible 15 mile (24km) loop road and side trails adjoining Shark River Slough. **Shark Valley Visitor Center** ❹ (tel: 305-221-8776) is open daily and has ranger-led activities. You can walk or ride a bicycle or open-air tram on the paved loop year-round, although the wet season inundates many areas, making it hard to see the dispersed wildlife.

Close encounters with alligators and wading birds are guaranteed in the dry season, when animals concentrate in major sloughs. Alligators have an important role to play in the functioning of this ecosystem. Their thrashing creates wallows that fill with water used by other wildlife. A 50ft (15 meter) observation tower overlooks the River of Grass to give you great views.

A photographer gets a close-up of the local birdlife.

Miccosukee heritage

Here you are in Florida's Indian Country. Airboat rides are available on

BELOW: Miccosukee children on an airboat, the fastest way to travel in the backcountry.

Tribute in Rock

The Coral Castle (28655 S. Dixie Hwy; tel: 305-248-6345; www.coralcastle.com; Mon–Fri 8am–6pm, Sat–Sun 8am–8pm; charge) is not usually considered an Everglades tourist attraction, but this mind-boggling limestone palace in the nearby town of Homestead lures many visitors a half-hour south from downtown Miami.

The castle area, which features a sundial, rocking chairs, barbecue, and fountain all made of megalithic limestone (formed from coral) and held together solely by their own weight, is said to have been built by one man: a Latvian immigrant named Edward Leedskalnin, who spent 28 years designing and moving materials for a romantic tribute to Agnes Scuffs, the 16-year-old fiancée who broke his heart.

A park ranger offers advice to visitors at the Ernest Coe Visitor Center.

BELOW: tourists snap photos on the Anhinga Trail.

the large reservation belonging to the Miccosukee Tribe (tel: 305-223-8380), whose private chickee-hut village compounds and tourist-oriented **Miccosukee Cultural Center** ❺ adjoin Shark Valley on US 41. There are about 369 enrolled tribal members living on the reservation. Information is available at the tribal offices on the north side of US 41. The Miccosukee Tribe also runs a casino-hotel at the junction of US 41 and Krome Avenue (SR 997), the closest hotel to this part of the park, and has lands near the Big Cypress Seminole.

The **Big Cypress Seminole Reservation** is a quiet, pastoral landscape reached from Exit 49 of I-75 (Alligator Alley) near Miami. The Seminole are renowned for cattle ranching and maintain a big operation, along with a rodeo stadium. There are several tourist facilities, including a casino, gas station, convenience store, restaurant, and guided outdoor activities.

By far the best interpretation of Seminole culture in Florida is available at the tribe's excellent **Ah-Tah-Thi-Ki Museum** ❻ (tel: 863-902-1113; www.ahtahthiki.com; daily 9am–5pm; charge), an affiliate of the Smithsonian Institution. The museum has a film about Seminole history and interesting dioramas showing their distinctive chickee-hut architecture, distinctive colorful patchwork clothes, canoes, traditional foods, and seasonal ceremonies like the Green Corn Ceremony. Out back is a boardwalk trail with interpretive plaques about plants used for food and medicine. It ends at a replica Seminole Village.

River of grass

Exhibits at its three visitor centers tell the story of Everglades National Park. It's a long, complex, cautionary tale of what happens when a unique ecosystem is misunderstood, misappropriated, and misused by humans intent on their own agenda. The designation of the park was just the beginning; the ending is still to be decided (probably in court, if past battles are any indication).

Authorized in 1934 but only dedicated in 1947 after funds to purchase the land were approved, Everglades National Park is now recognized worldwide for its unique habitat. It protects the only subtropical preserve in North America and is a major edge place, where northern and southern flora and fauna species mingle. A large, flat prairie whose highest point is 8ft (2.5 meters) above sea level, at Chokoloskee Island, the park is, contrary to rumor, not a large, impenetrable swamp. It is, as author, conservationist, and park champion Marjorie Stoneman Douglas famously observed, a "River of Grass" – at 50 miles (80km) wide, the largest continuous stand of seasonally inundated sawgrass prairie in North America.

Jeopardized by the rampant development surrounding it, today the Everglades is on life support. Its subtle beauty inspires visitors who take the time to get to know it, but the Everglades is most important as a sanctuary for wildlife. Living here are more than 400 species of birds, 125 species of fish, 60 species of reptiles and amphibians, 25 species of mammals, more than 120 species of trees, 1,000 species of seed-bearing plants, and 24 species of orchids, including the rare ghost orchid. The Everglades is the only place in the US where you'll find both crocodiles and alligators living side by side. Crocodiles (distinguished from alligators by a spade-shaped snout and two visible sets of teeth rather than one) are one of 14 endangered species protected here. Others are Florida panthers, West Indian manatees, Cable Sable sea sparrows, and wood storks.

Troubled waters

The headwaters of the Everglades are 80 miles (129km) to the north in the Kissimmee River Basin, now protected in the Nature Conservancy's Disney Wilderness. Disastrously channelized for ranching and agriculture, the Kissimmee River was once a wide, shallow river whose waters used to wend slowly south to Lake Okeechobee.

Surrounded by the massive 1930 Hoover Dike, which controls flooding and provides irrigation for agriculture,

BELOW: thick vegetation grows in the Big Cypress Preserve.

TIP

If time permits, stop at Clyde Butcher's Big Cypress Gallery (52388 Tamiami Trail, Ochopee; tel: 239-695-2428). Butcher's gorgeous, large-format, black-and-white images of Big Cypress and the rest of the Everglades will haunt your dreams. Look for them on the walls of many hotels and other businesses throughout southwest Florida.

BELOW: sunset over Chokoloskee Bay.

Lake Okeechobee, Florida's largest lake, is a dying ecosystem. The lake's historic role in the Everglades system was pivotal. Up to 60 inches (150cm) of summer rainfall caused it to seasonally overspill its margins, allowing flood-waters to slowly move south across the sawgrass prairie. This water nourished the wetlands and percolated through limestone into the Biscayne Aquifer, the main source of drinking water for South Florida. It then exited the main-land via the huge mangrove swamps at the salty edge of the estuaries into Biscayne and Florida Bays and the Ten Thousand Islands region of the Gulf.

Fully 50 percent of the Everglades has been lost since the 1930s, along with 93 percent of its 2 million birds. Encroaching urban settlements, pollution by nitrate fertilizers from subsidized sugar-cane agriculture around Lake Okeechobee, subsequent invasion by exotic species, and habitat loss have been an ecological disaster.

Recently, one of the world's largest environmental efforts, the Comprehensive Everglades Restoration Plan, was authorized by Congress. It is designed to return water to more natural patterns of quantity, timing, and distribution throughout the South Florida ecosystem. The South Florida Water Management District, together with the US Army Corps of Engineers, is working to mimic nature with seasonal water releases south of Lake Okeechobee's agricultural areas. The effort will be given a huge boost thanks to the state's purchase of land back from the US Sugar Corporation.

The Main Park

The collision of urban environment and natural ecosystem is easy to appre-ciate when you visit the main park. Agricultural fields and tropical plant nurseries surround homely Homestead and Florida City, continuing all the way to the park entrance where, magically, human development disappears and the huge vistas of sawgrass prairie and tree hammocks take center stage all the way to Flamingo.

For many visitors, the highlights of a visit to the main park are the two easy trails at historic Royal Palm, east of the scenic drive. Nothing seems

to perturb the lively shenanigans of alligators and anhingas and the silent predations of blue herons, snowy egrets, and other wildlife going about their lives in the Taylor Slough. The short **Anhinga Trail** lets you get astonishingly close to wildlife. The **Gumbo Limbo Trail**, named for the tree with the red peeling bark known as "the tourist tree," loops through a hardwood hammock forest reshaped by Hurricane Andrew in 1992.

Heading south, the **Pineland Trail** leads through some of the most diverse pinelands in south Florida, ending at the campground at **Long Pine Key 7**. The **Pa-hay-okee Overlook 8** is a boardwalk trail that offers the best place in this part of the park to experience the more than 20 different grasses that compose the sawgrass prairie at the heart of the Everglades.

If you continue to Flamingo, you'll be rewarded by views of white and brown pelicans and other birds massing offshore on white sandbars in the turquoise waters of Florida Bay. Meander along the beach trail to get a closer look, or stand on the concrete breezeway at

the **Flamingo Visitor Center** (tel: 239-695-2945; daily 9am–4.30pm Nov–May), binoculars in hand, and enjoy the tranquil beauty. Part of the Florida Keys is in the park, along with the Intracoastal Waterway. For more information, contact the Key Largo Ranger Station (tel: 305-852-0304).

Ten Thousand Islands

Like Flamingo, Everglades City and **Chokoloskee Island 9** are former fishing villages. Chokoloskee Island was settled by Europeans in the 1870s, although it had long been home to

A survivor of several hurricanes, historic Everglades City Hall remains a handsome local landmark.

BELOW: the Gumbo Limbo Trail leads through a hammock of strangler figs, gumbo limbo trees, and royal palms.

The Chokoloskee Murders

The most notorious outlaw of Ten Thousand Islands was Ed Watson, who moved to Chokoloskee in the early 1880s. Watson was suspected of murder in Florida and in the Oklahoma Territory. His luck ran out in Chokoloskee. First, he got into a fight with town patriarch Adolphus Santini and tried to slit his throat. Then two squatters turned up dead on his land. Three more corpses were found on his property, ostensibly murdered by a man named Cox. Watson threatened to kill the man, but the locals had had enough. A mob grabbed Watson and killed him. After this, the murders stopped, leading to the inevitable conclusion that Watson had been behind them all. The critically acclaimed book *Killing Mr. Watson*, by Peter Matthiessen, fictionalizes the tale.

An airboat operator guides visitors on a tour of the Everglades.

BELOW: several companies offer eco-tours, with an emphasis on low-impact modes of travel like canoes and kayaks that are excellent for spotting wildlife.

Calusa Indians. Smallwood Store, a stilted building with its own quay, is now a dusty family-run museum, open daily for a small fee. It belonged to Charles Smallwood, who ran a trading post in the Ten Thousand Islands region. Supplies were shipped from Key West, Fort Myers, or Tampa by boat; local sugar-cane syrup, fish, and produce were shipped in return.

In Everglades City, the Stone Crab Capital of Florida, early 20th-century homesteader George Storter was a merchant, as well as postmaster and a hotel owner. Hurricanes devastated Everglades City and Chokoloskee in 1909 and 1910, leveling all but the highest ground of the old Calusa shell mound, salting farm fields, and forcing many homesteaders to leave.

Tragedy gave entrepreneur Barron Collier an opening to buy southwest Florida on the cheap. Collier initially used Everglades City as his base for building the 1928 Tamiami Trail, later moving the county seat to Naples. The lodge that adjoins the bed-and-breakfast inn at Ivey House is Everglades City's oldest structure: a former boarding house for trail workers. Collier bought Storter's waterfront hotel to use as a hunting and fishing retreat. These activities, popular with residents and visitors, are still a draw at the Rod and Gun Club, although the hotel has seen better days.

Big Cypress

Early in the history of Everglades National Park, it was clear that Big Cypress Basin, which receives much of the water flowing southwestward from Lake Okeechobee, warranted protection as a key element of the hydrologic system. The calls for action became urgent in the 1960s, when burgeoning land development and speculation schemes led to extensive logging and the partial draining of Big Cypress Swamp. In 1968 a proposed jetport on the swamp's eastern edge created a land rush and provoked massive opposition to development.

In 1974, a compromise between pro-development and pro-conservation groups was reached, when Congress authorized 720,000 acre (290,000 hectare) **Big Cypress National Preserve**

❿. It was one of the first preserves to be managed by the National Park Service for multiple uses that include hunting, fishing, and off-road vehicles and airboats in addition to wildlife protection and low-impact activities like birding, hiking, and camping.

Oasis Visitor Center ⓫ (33100 Tamiami Trail East, Ochopee; tel: 239-695-1201; www.nps.gov/bicy; daily 9am–4.30pm) is exactly halfway between Naples and Miami, 5 miles (8km) east of SR 29, and has exhibits to help you plan a visit. All attractions are accessed off the Tamiami Trail. There are four scenic drives (The Loop, Turner River Road, Wagonwheel Road, and Birdon Road) and developed **Monument Lake** and **Midway campgrounds** along US 41.

The 27 mile (43km) **Loop Drive**, beginning opposite the visitor center, is your best introduction to the beauty of Big Cypress. A gravel road travels among the glades (a term first used to describe the Everglades by an English surveyor in the 1700s). There are numerous openings in the forest that offer a peek at dwarf cypress trees (there are no "big cypress" – the name refers to the size of the forests) reflected in mirror-smooth brackish waters. Look for alligators, snowy egrets, and other bird rookeries. There are four small campgrounds, available on a first-come, first-served basis, with no water or usage fee.

A 6.5 mile (10km) one-way portion of the **Florida National Scenic Trail** begins near the entrance to the Loop. Passing through **Roberts Lake Strand**, it's a wonderful way to find solitude among the haunting cypress. Remember: Outdoor activities are really only tolerable in the winter dry season, when temperatures average 75°F (25°C), humidity is generally low, and bugs are less pesky.

West Tamiami Trail

All along the Tamiami Trail are places to pull off and watch egrets, herons, ibis, anhingas, cormorants, and other birds fishing in the Tamiami Canal. West of Big Cypress are several enjoyable trails and campgrounds. **Kirby Storter Roadside Park** has a pleasant boardwalk trail among the dwarf cypress. **H.P. Williams Roadside Park**, on the north

> They are, they have always been, one of the unique regions of the earth, remote, never wholly known.
>
> Marjory Stoneman Douglas

BELOW: The Ochopee Post Office is reputed to be the smallest in the US.

Saving the Glades

About 30 percent of the Everglades has been lost due to human interference. Roads, canals, and dikes impede the water's normal flow, and much land has been drained for farming. The use by industrial agriculture of chemical fertilizers has taken a heavy toll as well.

The campaign to save the Everglades took a step forward in 2010 when Governor Charlie Crist finalized the purchase of more than 70,000 acres (28,000 hectares) of land from the US Sugar Corporation before leaving office. The deal was originally expected to be at least double that size before political and bureaucratic pressures cut it down, but Crist's plan for the state to begin active conservation work still holds the promise of restoring the natural flow of water from Lake Okeechobee south across the Everglades.

Birdwatching on the Big Cypress Bend boardwalk.

BELOW: elevated boardwalks allow hikers to view the watery sections of the park.

side of the road, adjoins the Turner River highway bridge and has picnic tables. The tiny roadside hamlet of **Ochopee** is famous for having the smallest post office in the country. Ochopee is one of the few places on US 41 with a restaurant, actually a roadside shack serving seafood on paper plates.

Just past the turn-off for SR 29 is **Big Cypress Bend**, a delightful boardwalk trail that offers a glimpse of **Fakahatchee Strand Preserve State Park** (tel: 239-695-4593), dubbed the Amazon of North America. If you only have time to hike one trail on US

41, this is a great choice. Fakahatchee Strand is a productive bird rookery. It's also the only spot where you'll see stately royal palms growing alongside dwarf cypress in strands.

Fakahatchee Strand is most famous as the orchid and bromeliad capital of the US, with 44 native orchid species and 14 native bromeliad species, many epiphytes, or air plants, that grow on tree branches. Fakahatchee's orchids gained notoriety in the 1998 bestseller *The Orchid Thief*, author Susan Orlean's evocative account of the $10-billion illegal orchid trade. The exposé focused on orchid collector John Laroche, a horticulture consultant arrested for stealing rare ghost orchids in Fakahatchee Strand and propagating them for profit. The book was the source material for the 2002 movie *Adaptation*.

Wildlife and wilderness

If you have time, consider driving the **Jaynes Scenic Drive** north into the park, which takes you through open prairie that is home to Florida panthers and raptors like red-tailed hawks and vultures. Endangered panthers, which require several hundred square miles of habitat each, are almost never seen, although you may see their preferred prey, white-tailed deer. Naples Zoo, which has an excellent panther exhibit, works closely with Panther National Wildlife Refuge and Everglades National Park staff to radio-collar and track panther activity in the Everglades.

From Fakahatchee it's only 25 miles (40km) to Naples, a wonderful base for day trips. As you drive north you'll see the sparkling Gulf of Mexico. Ten Thousand Islands National Wildlife Refuge protects wildlife and is also a good place for kayaking. Another state park, Collier-Seminole State Park, sits at the turn-off for Marco Island across from Rookery Bay Estuarine Preserve. It has excellent camping, hiking, and picnicking. One of the walking dredgers used to drain the Tamiami Trail route is on display. ❑

RESTAURANTS

Restaurants

Prices for a three-course dinner per person, excluding tax, tip, and beverages:
$ = under $20
$$ = $20–45
$$$ = $45–60
$$$$ = over $60

Chokoloskee

Big House Coffee
238 Mamie St
Tel: 239-695-3633 **$$**
This fusian restaurant is housed in the old 1890 McKinney Store on Chokoloskee Island. The menu includes hot pressed Cuban sand-wiches, crab cakes and mango salsa, an organic Florida citrus salad, and a vegetarian special of portobello mushrooms broiled with goat's cheese over linguine with pan-fried yams, apples, and scallions.

Everglades City

Ghost Orchid Grill at the Ivey House Bed and Breakfast
107 Camellia St
Tel: 239-695-3299 **$**
Mingle with kayakers and other eco-adventurers while you enjoy a basic but satisfactory buffet breakfast at this small and historic lodge.

Oyster House
901 Copeland Ave E.
Tel: 239-695-2073
$$–$$$
With sunset views over Chokoloskee Bay and a choice of fresh seafood and meats (the owner is a passionate hunter),

Oyster House is one of the area's best dining experiences. The grilled grouper seems to have swum to your plate it's so fresh, and the stone crab can't be beat.

Rod and Gun Club
205 Broadway
Tel: 239-695-2101
$$$$
If only the dark paneled walls of this historic landmark could talk. A celebrity hideaway for a century, the club is a little long in the tooth, but you can still have them cook whatever you caught that day in the bay or enjoy their stone crab, mullet, grouper, and other local seafood served with traditional hush puppies and corn on the cob.

Homestead

Farmers' Market Restaurant
300 N. Krome Ave
Tel: 305-242-0008 **$**
The plain appearance of this small family-run restaurant next to a farmers' market can be deceiving. But you should always trust the locals, who flock here for egg breakfasts and the super-fresh seafood and home-made pies. It's a great place to rub shoulders with those who call the town home, who, under-standably, like to keep this particular treasure to themselves.

Main Street Café
28 N. Krome Ave
Tel: 305-245-7575 **$–$$**
Main Street Café serves deli sandwiches, soups,

vegan sandwiches, and Caribbean specialties right on the main drag in Homestead. The café is popular for its excellent home-made soups, which are ladled from a soup bar at the rear of the restaurant. You'll also find conch salad, chicken potpie, smoked mahi-mahi, and pizza.

Robert Is Here
9200 SW 344th St
Tel: 305-246-1592 **$**
This fruit stand is way out in the country at the turn-off from US 1 to the national park. But it's worth the trip, because tropical fruit shakes are made in front of your eyes. Try the key lime shake or the refreshing mango. Florida fruit, veg-gies, salsa, and other goodies are available as

well. Robert – a larger-than-life character who has been in business here since 1960 – is on hand to answer all your questions.

Ochopee

Joannie's Blue Crab Café
39395 Tamiami Trail
Tel: 239-695-2682 **$**
A real Everglades experience, this highway café is on the Tamiami Trail in blink-and-you'll-miss-it Ochopee. It's classic backwoods cuisine: alligator fritters, Indian fry bread and salsa, and home-made sangria. You'll also find blue crab soup, fruit smoothies, and a salad that combines fresh grilled veggies, bananas, and salsa.

RIGHT: the Ivey House offers tasty food and comfortable lodging in Everglades City.

EVERGLADES ECOLOGY

The "River of Grass" sustains a combination of tropical and temperate species found nowhere else in the United States

The Everglades ecosystem is entirely dependent on the subtropical cycle of dry winters and wet summers. The fauna and flora of the region have adapted to these alternating seasons, often moving from one part of the Everglades to another according to the fluctuations in water level – the lifeblood of this vast and mysterious wilderness.

The larger Everglades ecology consists of a variety of smaller systems, each vital to the health of the overall ecosystem. The various habitats that make up the Everglades ecosystem include:

- **hardwood hammocks**: tree islands that stand above the high-water level and support mahogany, cabbage palms, and other trees, and also provide a refuge for mammals such as raccoons in the wet season.
- **bayheads**: small, shallow islands dominated by bay trees growing on rich, organic soil.
- **willows**: wispy vegetation that grows in the deep water near hammocks – generally in the shape of a donut with a gator hole at the center.
- **sawgrass prairie**: covering much of the Everglades, sawgrass grows on a thin layer of soil formed by decaying vegetation on the region's limestone base.
- **freshwater sloughs**: channels of freshwater that help plants and animals survive the harsh conditions of the dry season.
- **cypress swamps**: areas where the water is deepest and the layer of soil extremely thin. Cypress trees are among the few species that tolerate such water-logged conditions.
- **coastal prairie**: areas that contain salt-tolerant plants like cactus or saltwort.

ABOVE: alligators are vital to the ecology of the Everglades. During the wet season, they use their feet and snout to dig holes that store water during the dry months and serve as an oasis for many animals, including turtles and birds.

RIGHT: epiphytes, also known as air plants, are nonparasitic plants that grow on trees but get water and nutrients that run down the bark and gather in crooks and hollows. Among the most distinct epiphytes found in the Everglades are Spanish moss and orchids.

LEFT: the cats get the right of way.

LEFT: the Florida panther is subspecies of the cougar tha has adapted to a subtropical climate. This shy cat lives in the most remote areas of the Everglades, particularly in Bi Cypress Swamp. The panther is endangered: only 30 to 50 survive in the wild.

EVERGLADE NATIVES

A long list of animals call the Everglades home, among them several iconic types of American wildlife:

- birds of prey: colorful and talkative red-shouldered hawks favor the sawgrass, while ospreys like to dive for their dinner in the mangroves and a small group of bald eagles, the iconic American bird, nest at their leisure.
- reptiles: more than 50 of these cold-blooded water-lovers dwell in the park, with the alligator and crocodile getting much of the spotlight; but lizards and snakes, from the endangered Eastern indigo to the invasive boa constrictor, also lurk in the dark.
- carnivorous mammals: harder to spot at times, these include the tree-climbing gray fox, the majestic bobcat, the playful river otter, and the Everglades mink, a semi-aquatic predator that is a skilled and athletic hunter.
- water-loving mammals: the pilot whale and the well-known bottlenose dolphin are the leaders of this pack, according to the US National Park Service.
- amphibians: jumping in and out of the water, this tiny, often camouflaged group includes the Florida chorus frog and the spadefoot toad.

OVE AND RIGHT: the Suncoast
a Bird Sanctuary in Indian
ores is the largest non-
ofit wild bird hospital in
e US. Many birds are
ught here to recover
m illness or accident,
d then returned to
e wild.

LEFT: a great expanse of sawgrass, punctuated by tree islands known as "hammocks," is the classic Everglades landscape. Because hammocks are slightly elevated, the ground rarely floods and remains dry, while the air remains moist because it is protected from the sun by the tall, leafy trees that grow in the dry earth.

FLORIDA KEYS

A string of islands off the state's southern tip beckons travelers with beautiful beaches, crystal-clear waters, and some of Florida's best snorkeling and scuba diving

The Florida Keys are a ragged skein of some 800 islands formed of ancient coral reefs transformed into limestone bedrock. Only about 80 of them have names. The 20-plus islands that lie in a direct line were strung together first by an improbable railroad. Later the islands were connected by the southernmost portion of US 1, dubbed the **Overseas Highway**, a 125 mile (200km), 43 bridge exercise in forced linear travel, passing through each Keys community in unalterable sequence. The entire coastline – 2,800 sq nautical miles (9,603 sq km) – is a designated National Marine Sanctuary.

The road through the Keys may appear to be a tacky strip lined with seedy storefronts, billboards, and gas stations. In many places, that's exactly what it is – but stifle your disappointment. Like the Everglades, the Keys do not dazzle the casual tourist who stays behind the windshield. Park the car. Get on a bicycle or boat. Suck in the sweet, clean air. Gape at the immense canopy of sky and the mounds of whipped clouds. Can you see the curve of the earth in the distance, where the sea turns from aqua to azure? Put on a mask, snorkel, and fins, or rent a rod and reel. However you experience this amazing place, you'll soon be overcome by Keys Disease.

Biscayne National Park

Although not officially on the Keys, **Biscayne National Park ❶** (tel: 305-230-7275; www.nps.gov/bisc), a few miles east of **Homestead**, encompasses the northernmost portion of the region. Most of the park's 173,000 acres (70,000 hectares) are inaccessible by car. It's a watery world of coral reefs, mangrove shoreline, and tropical lagoons, inhabited by an astoundingly varied array of creatures ranging from manatees and parrotfish to pelicans. At the **Dante Fascell Visitor Center** on Convoy

Main attractions
BISCAYNE NATIONAL PARK
KEY LARGO
JOHN PENNEKAMP CORAL REEF STATE PARK
WINDLEY KEY
ISLAMORADA
PIGEON KEY
BAHIA HONDA STATE PARK
BIG PINE KEY

LEFT: Pennekamp State Park.
RIGHT: a patient at the Turtle Hospital.

Feeding an ailing dolphin at the Dolphin Cove Research & Education Center.

Point, visitors can opt for glass-bottom boat tours, scuba and snorkeling excursions, and boat rentals. The center also offers films, interactive exhibits, and an art gallery aimed at introducing visitors to the sights and sounds of the world underwater.

On to the Keys

There are two ways to drive to the Keys from the mainland. The slower but more scenic route is US 1 south to Route 997 just beyond Florida City. A column of tall Australian pines graces the path to the Card Sound toll bridge. On either side of the bridge, clumps of red and black mangroves impersonate solid islands. The bridge ends on North Key Largo. A right on SR 905 leads through hammocks of Jamaica dogwood, loblolly, feathery lysiloma, and mahogany until the road runs directly back into US 1, the Overseas Highway.

The toll bridge and scenic detour can be avoided by continuing south on US 1 over Jewfish Creek and a sliver of road once known as Death Alley until it was widened. Signs still advise drivers to be patient, because a passing zone is

only minutes ahead – such signs are a recurrent feature throughout the Keys, as are frequent roadside memorials to accident victims testifying to the folly of impatience. When US 1 eventually runs out, you've entered Key West.

Key Largo

Humphrey Bogart, Lauren Bacall, and Edward G. Robinson confronted a killer hurricane on **Key Largo ②** in the movie of the same name. All that remains of those nostalgic Bogie days is the Caribbean Club Bar (MM 104), where a few scenes are rumored to have been filmed, and the original *African Queen*, cradled on davits and looking quite forlorn just down the road.

The conch is queen of the Keys. Inside its shell – a familiar coffee-table ornament – the stalk-eyed blob is not among Earth's handsomest creatures. But if you can put the conch's looks out of your mind, conch fritters, chowder, or salad make a tasty meal with a spicy kick (although today most of the conch eaten in the US comes from the Bahamas). For a close-up look at queen or horseshoe conchs in their natural

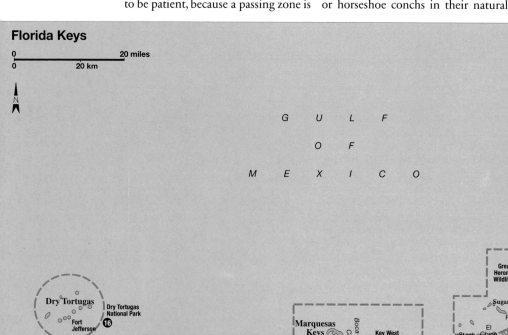

Florida Keys

0 ————————— 20 miles
0 ——— 20 km

N

GULF

OF

MEXICO

Dry Tortugas

Dry Tortugas National Park

Fort Jefferson **16**

Marquesas Keys

Boca Grande Channel

Key West National Wildlife Refuge

Great Heron N Wildlife

Sugar

El Stock Chico

Key Island

Key West **15**

Saddl

14 Boca Ch Key

Pe

habitat, visit **John Pennekamp Coral Reef State Park** ❸ (MM 102.5; tel: 305-451-1202; www.pennekamppark.com; daily), the country's first undersea park. Here, a 78 sq mile (200 sq km) coral reef extends 3 miles (5km) into the ocean, providing a home for a diverse community that includes nearly 600 species of fish. The park offers glass-bottom boat rides, sailing and snorkeling tours aboard a 38ft (12 meter) catamaran, and kayak rentals. It also conducts scuba tours, ranging from a brief lesson followed by a non-certified dive that afternoon to four-day classes earning PADI open water certification. One of the highlights of a dive trip is a visit to **Key Largo Dry Rocks**, where the *Christ of the Deep*, a replica of Guido Galletti's statue *Christ of the Abyss* (in the Mediterranean Sea off Genoa, Italy) lies submerged in a natural valley surrounded by a coral reef in 21ft (7 meters) of water.

Swim with dolphins

Two facilities within a few miles of each other provide an opportunity to learn about and swim with dolphins. **Dolphin Cove Research & Education Center** (MM 102; tel: 305-451-4060; www.dolphinscove.com; advance reservations; charge) offers bottlenose dolphin swims and encounters as well as eco-tours, sunset cruises, and flamingo trips. The friendly mammals can join visitors for a natural snorkel session, where any touching not instigated by the dolphin is prohibited, or a structured experience that includes a brief crash course in the species' anatomy and behavior. Dedicated dolphin-heads with $630 to spend can immerse themselves in the Trainer for a Day program, where students help with the less romantic jobs of cleaning and preparing for meal times in addition to taking private time with the animals.

Dolphins Plus (MM 100; tel: 305-451-1993; www.dolphinsplus.com; daily; charge), where disabled people participate in a five-day dolphin therapy program and visiting scientists apply to conduct their own on-site research, also provides the opportunity to swim and interact with dolphins in structured or unstructured swims. A special dolphin swim day is available for those fighting

TIP

Addresses on the Keys are given as mile markers (MM). The markers begin just south of Florida City at MM 126 and end in Key West at MM 0. The Keys are divided into four sections: upper, MM 106–65; middle, MM 65–40; lower, MM 40–9; and Key West, MM 9–0. The designations B/S and O/S refer to bayside or oceanside locations.

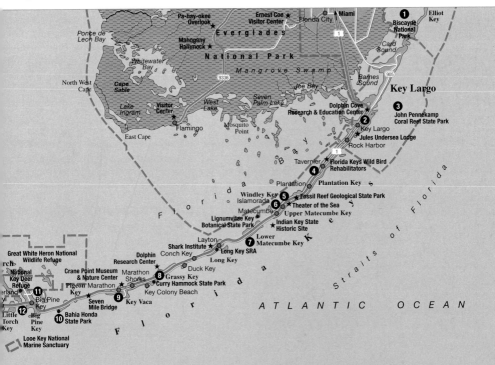

Sunbathing in Marathon.

BELOW: a Florida wrecker in 1858.

popular activity comes at 3.30pm – pelican feeding time.

cancer, and the center's California sea lion even has an encounter day of his own that lets children high-five their new whiskered friend.

US 1 continues through Rock Harbor to Tavernier ❹, once the site of a huge wrecking fleet that cruised the reefs claiming salvage from grounded ships. Today the nonprofit Florida Keys Wild Bird Rehabilitators (MM 93.6; tel: 305-852-4486; www.fkwbc.org; daily) salvage and rehabilitate wild birds that have been injured by fish hooks, cars, and other human-related causes. Their outdoor facility is a wonderful place to learn about the birds of the Keys, and offers a different culture than many of the state's more stage-managed and glossy wildlife centers. Visitors are free to take self-guided tours, but the most

Wrecking Crew

It's difficult to imagine that abandoned and overgrown Indian Key was once a bustling settlement. It was the home port of Jacob Housman, one of the Keys' most notorious "wreckers," who bought the property in 1831 for $5,000. In an age before lighthouses, he was one of a hearty breed of seagoing salvagers who sailed out to distressed ships that had foundered on coral reefs to rescue passengers, and then strip the vessels of anything valuable. Wrecking was an honorable, legal, and profitable enterprise.

It was indeed profitable for Housman, who brought slaves to Indian Key to build him a mansion. There's speculation, however, about a dark side to his reputation: some wreckers were known to move navigation warning lights to assure they kept busy. It is known that Housman left the Keys under a cloud of suspicion.

Indian Key was devastated in the Second Seminole War, and it is believed that Housman died while working on a wrecker. Others of his profession fared better: In Key West, John H. Geiger's handsome home is now the Audubon House, and Asa Tift built the residence that Ernest Hemingway later made famous.

South to the Purple Isles

Watch on the bay side for the **Rain Barrel Art & Craft Gallery** (MM 86.7; tel: 305-852-3084; daily 9am–5pm), a unique artisans' village where sculptors and glassblowers sell their wares. On **Windley Key ❺** at the 125,000-year-old **Windley Key Fossil Reef Geological State Park** (MM 85; tel: 305-664-2540; visitor center: Thur–Mon 8am–5pm; charge) visitors are offered a rare opportunity to view fossilized specimens of coral animals.

The 50-year-old landmark **Theater of the Sea** (MM 84.5; tel: 305-664-2431; www.theaterofthesea.com; reservation desk: daily 10am–5pm; charge) is host to sea lion and dolphin shows, glass-bottom boat rides, and a shark pit. Reserve well in advance for the Dolphin Adventure package, which includes a swim with the dolphins, and the similar sea lion and stingray swims. Younger children and those less comfortable in deep water can wade with the animals for a lower price.

The realization that vast seas completely surround these small tufts of land sinks in as you cross the bridge over Whale Harbor to **Upper Matecumbe Key**. Polished fishing vessels lining the harbor trumpet the area's focus on sport fishing. The action revolves around **Islamorada ❻** (pronounced *EYE-la-mo-RA-da*), which bills itself as the world's sport fishing capital. At the southern end of town, the **Hurricane Monument** (MM 81.6) commemorates the 600 people who died in the Labor Day hurricane of 1935.

Tarpons, spiders, dolphins

Robbie's Marina (MM 77.5; tel: 877-664-8498) on **Lower Matecumbe Key ❼** is the embarkation point for a visit to **Lignumvitae Key Botanical State Park**, accessible only by privately owned or charter boats (for reservations, tel: 305-664-9814; park: Thur–Mon, one-hour tours at 10am and 2pm). The tour includes a visit to the 1919 Matheson House and a stroll through a tropical forest. Rent a glass-bottom kayak at Robbie's and paddle out to **Indian Key**, an early wreckers' settlement.

From the Matecumbes, US 1 winds its way across increasingly breathtaking waterscapes to **Long Key State Recreation Area**, with a beach, observation tower, boardwalk, and the Golden Orb Weaver Nature Trail – named after the large but harmless spiders that spin sturdy, ornate webs in the trees.

On **Grassy Key** ❽, Flipper is the most famous graduate of the **Dolphin Research Center** (MM 59; tel: 305-289-1121; www.dolphins.org; daily 9am–4.30pm; charge), the oldest and most respected wildlife nonprofit organization in the region and a source of public education about the endangered local manatee population. This teaching and research facility offers tours and swims with the dolphins, but reservations must be made months in advance.

The center has no shortage of more frequently available shorter programming for those fascinated by its mission. Everything from T-shirts hand-painted by dolphin noses to photographic embraces with sea lions is on hand, with prices varying depending on the service. Kids with dreams of a future career can enroll in a Trainer for a Day or a Researcher for a Day program.

Marathon

On the outskirts of **Marathon** ❾, the 1,000 acre (400 hectare) **Curry Hammock State Park** (MM 56; tel: 305-289-2690; www.floridastateparks. org/curryhammock; daily 8am–sunset; charge) encompasses five islands and the world's largest concentration of Florida thatch palms. The park also offers cabins for rent, a rare local alternative to beachside tent camping.

Crane Point Museum and Nature Center (MM 50.5; tel: 305-743-3900; www.cranepoint.net; Mon–Sat 9am–5pm, Sun noon–5pm; charge) offers a comprehensive overview of the Keys' history, wildlife, and ecology. Highlights include a wild bird center, a "creature feature" where snakes and hermit crabs roam, and a simulated coral reef.

The **Turtle Hospital** (MM 48.5; tel: 305-743-2552; www.turtlehospital.org; by

TIP

Some people refer to the Keys as a 126 mile (203km) traffic jam, which is at its worst on weekends. Try to plan your arrival and departure on a weekday.

BELOW: sunset provides a spectacular backdrop to an evening meal.

TIP

There are chamber of Commerce information centers along US 1 that offer numerous money-saving coupons for many popular Keys attractions.

reservation; charge) in the center of town has an ambulance to transport sea turtles during rescues and releases. The facility – the only state-certified veterinary hospital in the world for sea turtles – has been looking after its patients for more than 20 years.

Guests who stay overnight at the adjacent Hidden Harbor Motel get a free tour of the hospital, but others interested in watching the vets work up close can make reservations any day of the week. The hospital, which has tended and released more than 1,000 sea turtles since its 1986 opening, is largely donor-funded.

Pigeon Key

Henry Flagler built housing on **Pigeon Key** to shelter the workers he brought to Florida to work on his Overseas Railroad (the nearby town earned its name when one of the workers referred to the project as a marathon). Several of the structures survive and are part of a tour that departs from the **Pigeon Key Visitors Center** (MM 48; tel: 305-743-5999; www.pigeonkey.net; departures at 10am, 11.30am, 1pm, 2.30pm; charge).

A film tells the fascinating story of Mr. Flagler and Flagler's Folly, the railroad he built from Miami to Key West in spite of huge obstacles, and guided ferry tours are billed as a brief trip back to the early 20th century.

Seven Mile Bridge

The part of the highway that hops from Marathon to Big Pine Key is called **Seven Mile Bridge** and spans the longest between-island stretch you can drive in the Keys. Actually just a shade under 7 miles (11km) and built between 1979 and 1982, it runs over a channel between the Gulf of Mexico and the Straits of Florida. Paralleling it is the original bridge built for Flagler's railroad. The trains ran until the hurricane of 1935 ruined the roadbed and the Great Depression ruined the economy, making an automobile route the more practical alternative.

Just over the bridge, Big Pine Key is second in size only to Key Largo. **Bahia Honda State Park** ⑩ (MM 37; tel: 305-872-2353; www.bahiahondapark.com; daily 8am–sunset; charge) has one of the best beaches on the Keys. You can rent a beach chair for the afternoon, camp out for a night, or explore the waters with rented dive equipment or a kayak. The highlight of a visit is a snorkeling tour out to **Looe Key National Marine Sanctuary**, whose 5 mile (8km) stretch of reef is one of the world's most sensational aquatic showcases.

Big island, little deer

Big Pine Key ⑪ is home to the **National Key Deer Refuge** (visitor center at MM 30.5; Big Pine Shopping Center, 28950 Watson Blvd; tel: 305-872-0774; http://fws.gov/nationalkey deer; park: daily sunrise–sunset). The diminutive deer, a subspecies of the Virginia whitetail, grow to about 30 inches (75cm) tall and 38 inches (95cm) in length. In earlier days, hunters, developers, and automobiles reduced the population to less than 50, but efforts at the refuge – including strictly enforced speed limits – have

BELOW: personal watercraft are available to rent throughout the Keys.

boosted their numbers into the hundreds. Turn right near MM 30 onto Key Deer Boulevard to the **Blue Hole**, a flooded quarry that attracts both deer and alligators.

The final keys

Farther down US 1, the **Torch Keys** ⓬ are named after their flammable trees. A short distance off **Little Torch Key** is a private island that houses the secluded and exclusive **Little Palm Island Resort and Spa**. Accessible by a ferry from Little Torch Key, the resort's villas cater to an elite clientele. The restaurant, however, is open to the public.

Summerland Key offers scenic side roads, and **Cudjoe Key** has modern campsites for large trailers. On **Sugar Loaf Key** ⓭, named for an Indian midden that looked like loaves of old-fashioned sugar, turn right just past MM 17 to view **Perky's bat tower**, built in 1929 as a boarding house for bats. The local businessman imported them in the hope they would swallow the island's mosquito problem, but once released from the tower, they never returned.

The **Saddlebunch Keys** are little more than a series of mangrove outcroppings. Big Coppit, Rockland, and East Rockland house the servicemen of the US Naval Air Station on **Boca Chica Key** ⓮. Stock Island serves as a suburb of Key West and is the home of the **Tennessee Williams Performing Arts Center** (tel: 305-295-7676; www.twstages.com).

Before crossing the next bridge, prepare yourself for a very different world. You have literally reached the end of the road. This is Key West. ❏

A two-man band keeps patrons entertained at a waterfront bar.

BELOW: Bahia Honda State Park.

RESTAURANTS AND BARS

Restaurants

Prices for a three-course dinner per person, excluding tax, tip, and beverages:
$ = under $20
$$ = $20–45
$$$ = $45–60
$$$$ = over $60

Big Pine Key

Rob's Island Grill
31251 Avenue A (MM 31)
Tel: 305-872-3022 **$**
With wall-to-wall TVs and two high-definition big screens, Rob's Island Grill is the place for sports fans during college and professional games. Rob's offers American pub fare as well as a raw bar and more ambitious entrées such as prime rib on Friday and Saturday nights.

Islamorada

Chanticleer South
81671 Overseas Hwy (MM 81.5)
Tel: 305-664-0640 **$$$**
Chef Jean-Charles Berruet, for 35 years one of the premier restaurateurs of Nantucket, Massachusetts, has brought his considerable skill and creativity to the Keys. The contemporary French menu has a heavy emphasis on seafood, and because there are just 16 tables – 12 inside and 4 outside – he cooks almost all entrées by himself. Desserts, such as chocolate soufflé and apple tart with calvados, range from $14 to $17.

Islamorada Fish Company
81532 Overseas Hwy (MM 81.5)
Tel: 800-258-2559 **$**
Dine on the waterfront patio or in the original Island Conch House eatery, where stone crab and dynamite fish sandwiches get top billing. The historic and handsomely furnished Zane Grey Lounge hosts live music on weekends.

Lazy Days Oceanfront Bar & Grill
Overseas Hwy (MM 79.9)
Tel: 305-664-5256 **$–$$**
Chef Lupe whips up tasty home-made soups, terrific fish sandwiches, and sublime coconut fried jumbo shrimp. And if you bring in your own fresh-caught seafood, she'll cook it to order. The outside patio overlooks the water. Happy hour from 4–6pm brings three-for-$1 appetizers.

Marker 88
88000 Overseas Hwy (MM 88)
Tel: 305-852-9315
$$$–$$$$
Sit back with a key lime Martini and an appetizer of blackened tuna sashimi and enjoy the fabulous sunset over Florida Bay. All the fish on the menu is fresh from local waters; for the undecided, there's a seafood platter served over pasta.

Key Largo

Ballyhoo's Island Grille
97860 Overseas Hwy (MM 97.8 Median)
Tel: 305-852-0822 **$**
Although it's right on Route 1, this venerable restaurant in a 1930s conch house was once part of a fishing camp and evokes a feeling of stepping back in time. The all-you-can-eat fish and stone crab claw specials can't be beat, and there's a very cheerful happy hour from 4 to 7pm.

The Fish House
102401 Overseas Hwy (MM 102.4)
Tel: 305-451-4665
$–$$
Fresh fish is delivered right to the kitchen door and filleted on the spot at this Conch-style eatery which specializes in… fish. Next door, the Fish House Encore has a sushi bar, all-you-can-eat specials, and piano music weekend evenings.

Key Largo Conch Restaurant & Coffee Bar
100211 Overseas Hwy (MM 100.2), Oceanside Key
Tel: 305-453-4844 **$**
There's a full roster of home-made treats, including terrific lobster bisque and freshly prepared seafood. Patrons can access Wi-fi, and pets are welcome as well.

Mrs Mac's Kitchen
99336 Overseas Hwy (MM 99.5)
Tel: 305-451-3722 **$**
Terrific Keys fare is served in a funky diner atmosphere. All the standard American favorites are here, along with more ambitious offerings prepared with a Caribbean flair. House specialties include conch salad and chowder, crab cakes, and fish of the day with home-made Tijuana sauce. Wine and beer are served, and there's a kids' menu.

Snook's Bayside Restaurant

99470 Overseas Hwy (MM 99.9)
Tel: 305-453-3799 **$$$**
Overlooking the Gulf of Mexico, this informal spot with an outdoor tiki bar offers a creative menu featuring mahi-mahi tacos and pistachio-crusted yellowtail snapper. Tapas, served from 3pm, range in price from $7 to $14. There's nightly entertainment, a Thursday-night pig roast with dancing, and a Sunday brunch buffet.

Little Palm Key

Dining Room at Little Palm Island

28500 Overseas Hwy
Tel: 305-872-2551 **$$$$**
Reserve well in advance for the Dining Room at this island resort, which serves sophisticated French and pan-Latin cuisine. Patrons (who must be a minimum of 16 years of age, please) can opt for the elegant candlelit waterfront dining room or a table on the beachfront terrace.

Little Torch Key

Parrotdise Waterfront Bar and Grille

83 Barry Ave (MM 28.5)
Tel: 305-872-9989 **$–$$**
"You hook it, we cook it" is the motto at Parrotdise. For the fishing-challenged, there are tasty treats such as lobster macaroni and cheese, smoked dolphin dip, and cashew grouper. Happy hour is 3–7pm daily, and the mellow sounds from solo acoustic guitar music entertain patrons Thursday, Friday, and Sunday.

Marathon

Farella's Village Café

Overseas Hwy (MM 50.5)
Tel: 305-743-9090 **$–$$**
For 20 years this has been Marathon's favorite destination for Italian food. Pizza, pasta, home-made soups, and a salad bar share the menu with fish specialties, including shrimp scampi and bouillabaisse. On Sunday there are breakfast and dinner buffets. There's live music and dancing on weekends, and Wednesday is Latin night.

Island Fish Company

12648 Overseas Hwy (MM 54)
Tel: 305-743-4191 **$–$$**
She-crab chowder, freshly shucked oysters, and stone crab claws are among the house specialties. Tex-Mex choices include seafood quesadillas and grilled shrimp tacos. And for dessert – fried key lime pie.

Keys Fisheries Market & Marina

3502 Gulf View Ave (MM 49 at the end of 35th St)
Tel: 305-743-4353 **$**
It's flopping-fresh seafood all the way at this dockside fish market, marina, and restaurant. House favorites include blackened mahi-mahi and Cajun snapper, but the lobster Reuben tops the charts. Music at the tiki bar begins at 3pm.

7 Mile Grill

1240 Overseas Hwy (MM 47.5)
Tel: 305-743-4481 **$**
For 50 years a Keys favorite for freshly prepared, moderately priced American fare. Many items on the menu are priced under $10, including the fried oyster sandwich and stuffed crabs.

Bars

Big Pine Key

No Name Pub

N. Watson Blvd
Tel: 305-872-9115 **$**
Since 1936 tourists have been getting lost trying to find their way here, and they keep on looking. Perhaps it's because this is one of the Keys' few remaining untarted-up restaurants, a place where locals come to quaff a beer or down a tasty burger or cheesesteak sub. It's right next to the No Name Bridge… ask a local for directions.

Grassy Key

The Wreck & Galley Grill

58835 Overseas Hwy (MM 59)
Tel: 305-743-8282 **$**
A lively sports bar with indoor and outdoor tiki dining and daily all-you-can-eat specials including Monday frogs' legs, Thursday BBQ pork ribs, Friday prime rib, and Saturday crab.

Islamorada

Whistlestop

Overseas Hwy (MM 82.5)
Tel: 305-664-2623 **$**
This popular and mellow sports bar offers a wide range of pub and comfort fare, including meatloaf and brick-oven pizza. At happy hour (4–6pm) the game room is a boisterous and clubby spot.

Stock Island

Hogfish Bar/Grill

6810 Front St
Tel: 305-293-4041 **$**
A bustling but laid-back spot on the waterfront adjacent to the marina that served as headquarters for the Bay of Pigs operation. House specialties include a "Killer" hogfish sandwich on Cuban bread and BLTs. Live weekend entertainment and a mellow atmosphere make this a favorite local hang-out.

LEFT: both kids and adults enjoy Mrs Mac's Kitchen.
RIGHT: fresh seafood is a staple of Keys cuisine.

FLORIDA'S CORAL REEF

Coral reefs have been described as underwater tropical forests. They teem with wildlife, from sea slugs to shoals of brilliantly colored fish

The Florida Keys are fringed by the only true living coral reef in the continental US, stretching for more than 200 miles (320km) all the way from Miami to the Dry Tortugas. The reef is particularly rich in the Upper Keys, where it harbors around 500 species of fish and 50 types of coral.

A coral reef is an efficient and diverse habitat. Every source of nutrients is used and recycled through a variety of food chains. Each chain starts with algae, which is either loose in the water or living inside corals. Small fish graze on corals, and in turn they are preyed upon by large fish.

Inner or patch reefs develop in shallow waters and feature delicate corals and colorful residents such as angelfish, tang, and spiny lobster. Farther out is the main barrier reef, with larger stands of hardier coral, where predatory fish such as barracudas and sharks cruise around and moray eels lurk in caves.

ABOVE: many types of fish like to hide in the nooks and crannies created by the coral, which also provides shaded areas for predator to lurk and wait for lunch to swim by.

Coral might look rock hard, but is fragile, and sensitive to the changes in conditions. Coral grows in shallow and clean salt water, where the temperature is at least 68°F (19°C). The water must also be low in nutrients; an excess of nutrients causes algae to flourish until it eventually smothers the coral.

LEFT: the bigeye squirrelfish has a large eye and distinctively downturned mouth.

Florida's reef has been under intense ecological pressure. The main threats are pollution (from agricultural run-off, oil, and sewage), overfishing, and tourism (the reef is damaged by clumsily driven boats and by careless divers who touch or step on it). A reef takes thousands of years to form, and new growth of coral cannot keep pace with rapid destruction.

RIGHT: the lionfish, with its distinctive stripey spines, is an invasive species that is harming much of the underwater ecology of Florida. The most unusual method of population control is the newly created Lionfish Derby, where teams compete to catch the most lionfish, and then eat them for dinner.

How Coral is Formed

Every coral is a colony of hundreds of soft-bodied animals called polyps, each of which usually measures about a quarter of an inch (5mm) across.

By extracting calcium from the sea water, each polyp constructs a skeleton of limestone that forms a protective casing; together these skeletons make up a coral. Most of the reef consists of the casings of dead polyps, which build up on top of one another over many thousands of years. Only the top surface of the reef is alive.

Until around 200 years ago, people commonly believed that polyps were plants. They are, in fact, related to jellyfish and sea anemones, and have tentacles, a mouth, and a stomach. During the daytime, the polyp extends its stinging tentacles around the mouth in order to catch phytoplankton in the surrounding sea water; they close again at night.

Most coral grows in partnership with algae, which exist inside them. Polyps get oxygen and nutrients from the algae and, in return, the algae extract carbon dioxide for photosynthesis. Algae also give coral its stunning array of colors.

The manner and rate at which a coral grows depends on the individual species and the health of the local water conditions.

OVE: a school of
sotremus virginicus, also
wn by the common name
porkfish or paragrate
nt. The porkfish can
duce a grunting sound by
bing its teeth together.

LEFT: coral comes in many shapes and sizes, from the minute and pale to the large and colorful, like this brilliant pink specimen. Scientists have predicted that nearly 50 percent of the world's coral will be extinct by the year 2030.

KEY WEST

At the state's southernmost tip is the Conch
Republic, a place that draws freethinkers with a
laid-back attitude and a penchant for good times

Orlando

Florida

Miami

Key West

The gateway to **Key West** 🅑 – the
southernmost point in the continental United States – is as prosaic
as any in Florida. US 1 on the outskirts
of town is littered with the detritus of
modern life – an unbroken chain of
shopping centers, hotels, car dealers,
and fast-food restaurants. However,
as you proceed south into the town
center, the character changes: the
American flavor of fast-food chains and
strip malls evaporates into an ambience
that's not quite Bahamian, not quite
Cuban, and not quite nautical – just
very Key West.

Here homes and businesses – some
restored, some crumbling – meld in a
collage of discordant color. The people
who blend into this bizarre landscape
are as incongruous as the palette: long-
haired survivors of the hippie era, gay
couples, leather-faced fishermen, jet-
setters and yachters, and, of course, an
enormous number of tourists. Only
in Key West could so much that is so
different seem so right.

The early days

The character of Key West derives from
its history as a haven for transients. Its
proximity to the American mainland
and the West Indies has introduced
many different influences, but the city
has transformed those influences into
something totally its own.

The Calusa Indians managed to
get to this speck 100 miles (160km)
from the Florida peninsula, 90 miles
(145km) from Cuba, and 66 miles
(106km) north of the Tropic of Cancer.
The Spanish were the first Europeans
to explore the waters and build settlements here, but Indians and pirates
made life dangerous. In fact, a young
Spanish cavalryman, granted Key
West by his governor in 1815, gladly
sold it six years later for just $2,000 to
Alabama businessman John Simonton.
The settlement became part of the

Main attractions

FORT ZACHARY TAYLOR
LITTLE WHITE HOUSE
MALLORY SQUARE
PIRATE SOUL MUSEUM
AUDUBON HOUSE AND
  TROPICAL GARDENS
DUVAL STREET
WRECKER'S MUSEUM
SLOPPY JOE'S
HEMINGWAY HOME AND MUSEUM
SOUTHERNMOST POINT
KEY WEST CEMETERY

LEFT: a classic Conch house.
RIGHT: at the Key West Aquarium.

The 2,000 to 3,000 free-range chickens that peck their way through Key West descend from the mid-1800s when residents kept the birds for cock fights and food. Many townspeople extend their "live free" philosophy to the birds. Others consider them a pestilence. The Chicken Store, at 1229 Duval Street, is dedicated to keeping the flock safe, often sending out the Rooster Rescue Team to aid orphaned and injured birds.

US in 1821 when Florida was ceded by Spain. In 1845 the government began constructing a Naval Base (now called **Truman Annex**) and in 1866 completed **Fort Zachary Taylor Ⓐ** (Southard St; tel: 305-292-6713; www.floridastateparks.org; daily 8am–sunset; charge), now a museum of Civil War artifacts, to defend the coastline. The **East Martello Museum and Gallery** (3501 S. Roosevelt Blvd; tel: 305-296-3913; www.kwahs.com; daily 9am–5pm; charge) was one of two towers that were begun – but never completed – and was meant to help defend the fort. Today it houses local-history exhibits.

Mixed fortunes

For many years the business of wrecking – the salvaging of ships that foundered on treacherous offshore reefs – was a boon to the economy. By 1888 Key West was the largest city in Florida and had become the richest city per capita in the US, a distinction that lasted into the early 1900s. Towards the end of the 19th century, lighthouses reduced the need for wreckers, Cuban migrants had imported cigar-making along with

their rich culture, and sponge fishermen also prospered.

Completion of the Overseas Railroad in 1912 added another dimension to the booming economy: tourism. Yet by 1930 Key West faced collapse. The stock market crash of 1929, coupled with the closing of the US naval station, disease in the sponge beds, and labor troubles that forced cigar makers to Tampa, began a decline that reached rock bottom with the destruction of the railroad in the 1935 hurricane.

World War II provided a catalyst when the Navy reclaimed their island facilities and President Harry S. Truman established his **Little White House Ⓑ** (111 Front St; tel: 305-294-9911; www.trumanlittlewhitehouse.com; daily 9am–4.30pm, tours every 20 minutes; charge) on the base. The disastrous Bay of Pigs invasion followed by the Cuban Missile Crisis during John F. Kennedy's presidency brought another brief wave of military money. While not as visible as in the past, the Navy is still present in Key West, though tourism, shrimping, and restoration are major businesses.

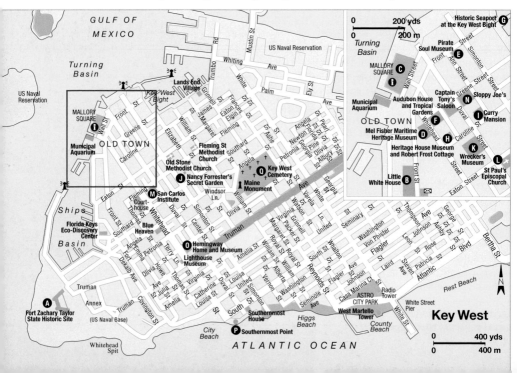

Getting oriented

Old Town, the original part of the city, encompasses approximately 3,000 historic buildings, as well as Mallory Square and the Historic Seaport. There are two ways to get an overview of the island: the venerable **Conch Train** (tel: 305-294-5161; www.conchtourtrain. com) and its newer clone, the **Old Town Trolley** (tel: 305-296-6688; www. historictours.com). The trolley allows riders to hop-on and hop-off at several spots along the route. Both leave every 30 minutes from different locations around town.

If Old Town is the heart of Key West, **Mallory Square** ◗ is its commercial soul. Throngs of visitors gather here every evening for the famous **Sunset Celebration**, because the sun doesn't just set here. On the contrary, the shiny orange orb gets an extraordinary send-off from an astonishing assortment of jugglers, fire-eaters, acrobats, and peddlers. The sunset teases the sky with a pink streak before torching it aflame in reds and oranges, eliciting standing ovations from the assembled crowd.

A word to the wise: Watch for the mega-cruise ships docking in the morning at Mallory Square, because-tourist hordes will bum-rush the downtown area for the remainder of the day. It's best to avoid it if possible.

The East Martello Museum is housed in a structure built – but never used – as a defensive tower.

Of pirates and painters

Many of the main attractions are within walking distance of Mallory Square, and most of them tell a story about the area's rich history. The **Mel**

BELOW LEFT: music man in Mallory Square. **BELOW:** Little White House.

Harry's Hideaway

There was once a famous part-time resident who loved this town even though he was the last person anyone would have diagnosed with Keys Disease. "I've a notion," he once remarked, "to move the capital to Key West and just stay."

Harry S. Truman used to duck out of Washington whenever he could and settle in, loud Hawaiian shirts and all, at the former commandant's quarters at the Key West naval station. He brought plenty of work with him, but there was always time for fun. One of the highlights of a tour of the Little White House Museum is a poker table on the downstairs veranda, where Truman would stay up late with naval officers and civilian aides, playing hand after hand in a mellow matrix of bourbon, conversation, and cigar smoke. For lunch he would walk over to Pepe's on Caroline Street.

Other presidents have also found Key West to be a salubrious and sometimes strategic spot. President Kennedy set up his command post here during the Bay of Pigs Invasion in 1961, and many of the 125,000 Cubans who arrived in the 1980 Mariel boatlift landed here.

Colorful shops and cottages line Duval Street.

Fisher Maritime Heritage Museum **D** (200 Greene St; tel: 305-294-2633; www.melfisher.org; Mon–Fri 8.30am–5pm, Sat–Sun 9am–5pm; charge) displays treasures from the Spanish ships *Nuestra Señora de Atocha* and *Santa Margarita*, which sank in the waters west of Key West during a fierce hurricane in 1622, as well as accounts of the hunt and dramatic salvage operation.

Pirate lore, Ernest Hemingway's bloodstained World War I uniform, and fanciful paintings by folk artist Mario Sanchez are among the permanent exhibits at the **Museum of Art & History** (281 Front St; tel: 305-295-6616; www.kwahs.com; daily 9.30am–4.30pm; charge) in the 1891 Custom House.

Pat Croce's **Pirate Soul Museum** **E** (524 Front St; tel: 305-292-1113; www.piratesoul.com; daily 9am–7pm; charge) re-creates piracy's golden age from 1690 to 1730; displays include the world's only authenticated pirate treasure chest.

John James Audubon (1785–1851) usually heads the lists of painters associated with Key West. In fact, the naturalist-artist spent only a short time here while sketching Florida's birds, but that tenuous connection with the city didn't stop entrepreneurs from renovating and reopening the 1830 house where he stayed. The **Audubon House and Tropical Gardens** **F** (205 Whitehead St; tel: 305-294-2116; www.audubonhouse.com; daily 9.30am–4.30pm; charge) showcases the artist's original of *Birds of America*.

Historic seaport

Once home to the island's shrimping fleet, the **Historic Seaport at**

the **Key West Bight** Ⓖ is now home port of most of the island's charter and touring boats, as well as the **Harborwalk** that connects a number of popular restaurants and bars, including **Turtle Kraals** and **Half Shell Raw Bar**. A visit to the city isn't complete without a voyage on its waters, and schooners such as the 80ft (24 meter) *Liberty* (tel: 305-292-0332; www.libertyfleet.com) offer a magnificent opportunity.

The **Key West Express** (tel: 888-539-2628; www.seakeywestexpress.com) to Fort Myers Beach, Marco Island, and Miami also sails from here.

Old Town ramble

Key Westers have long indulged an infatuation with restoring their homes, a hobby that has transformed the island into a live-in architectural museum, and the best way to savor Old Town is on foot.

Start on Caroline Street, with several fine old mansions. The **Heritage House Museum and Robert Frost Cottage** Ⓗ (410 Caroline St; tel: 305-296-3573; www.heritagehousemuseum. org; Mon–Sat 10am–4pm; charge) at No. 410 is typical of Bahamian styles. The **George A.T. Roberts House** at No. 313, with its spacious veranda and gingerbread trim, exemplifies Conch architecture. The **Curry Mansion** Ⓘ at No. 511, which admits visitors (tel: 305-294-5349; charge), is also a guest house, as is the 1887 **Conch-style Cypress House** at No. 601.

Other highlights include **Nancy Forrester's Secret Garden** Ⓙ (Free School Lane, just past 521 Simonton; tel: 305-294-0015; www.nancyforrester. com; daily 10am–5pm; charge), a lush rainforest with orchids, palms, and tropical birds; writer Shel Silverstein's Greek Revival home and studio on the 600 block of William Street; the Octagon House at 712 Eaton Street was once owned by famous clothing designer Calvin Klein; and poet Elizabeth Bishop's home at No. 624 White Street.

The Duval crawl

Duval Street, which stretches from the Gulf to the Atlantic, has an iconic status in Key West. It's where the bars are – not all of them, but enough for a slow promenade down this bright, boisterous avenue where the music begins in the afternoon and continues into the wee hours at places like **Jimmy Buffett's Margaritaville** and the **Hog's Breath Saloon**.

The lower end of Duval, toward Mallory Square, has a slew of souvenir shops selling lewd T-shirts and shot glasses. Wade past them to No. 322, the Oldest House Museum, also known as the **Wrecker's Museum** Ⓚ (tel: 305-294-9501; www.oirf.org; Thur–Sat 10am–2pm; charge), the 1829 home of a sea captain who made his money from wrecking.

St Paul's Episcopal Church Ⓛ at No. 401 offers free organ and piano concerts on weekdays at noon. At No. 516 the **San Carlos Institute** Ⓜ (tel: 305-294-3887; Fri–Sun noon–6pm), a theater, museum, and cultural center, caters to the Cuban emigrant community.

TIP

One of Key West's most edifying attractions is the $6 million Florida Keys Eco-Discovery Center (accessed through the Truman Annex at the end of Southard St, closed Sun and Mon; tel: 305-809-4750). The facility showcases the Keys' habitats.

BELOW: Audubon House.

The Hemingway Home is decorated with hunting trophies and other objects from the author's many adventures.

BELOW: Southernmost House.

Papa's place

At the corner of Greene and Duval streets is one of Key West's most famous bars, **Sloppy Joe's** . Touted as one of Ernest Hemingway's favorite watering holes when he lived here from 1931 to 1940 with his wife Pauline, Joe's also plays host to the popular Hemingway Days, a July celebration of the author's persona. Purists will want to visit **Captain Tony's Saloon** (428 Greene St), the oldest licensed saloon in Florida. The interior, wallpapered in business cards and newspapers, will take you back to the time when Hemingway relaxed with a drink after a hard day at the typewriter.

Hemingway would stroll down to the saloon from his home, now preserved as the **Hemingway Home and Museum** (907 Whitehead St; tel: 305-294-1136; www.hemingwayhome.com; daily 9am–5pm; charge). His writing studio appears as it did when he worked there on such novels as *To Have and Have Not*. Descendants of his six-toed cats still have the run of the place and drink from a fountain that once served as the urinal at Captain Tony's.

The southern tip

Across the road from Hemingway's house is the **Key West Lighthouse and Keeper's Quarters Museum** (938 Whitehead St; tel: 305-294-0012; www.kwahs.com; daily 9.30am–4.30pm; charge). Built in 1847 and decommissioned in 1969, the lighthouse has been restored and visitors can climb the 88 steps for incredible views of the surrounding town.

A rather smaller beacon is the **Southernmost Point** , at the corner of Whitehead and South streets. While the town has lost its title as southernmost point in the US to a spot on the Big Island of Hawaii, this landmark is still 755 miles (1,215km) south of Los Angeles.

Nearby is the 1896 **Southernmost House** (1400 Duval St; tel: 305-296-3141; www.southernmosthouse.com; daily; charge), which exhibits documents, including autographs of George Washington and Thomas Jefferson, and memorabilia from former Key West residents Hemingway and Tennessee Williams (who lived at 1431 Duncan St).

Bahama Village

In **Bahama Village** on the western edge of Old Town, the city's Caribbean atmosphere is at its strongest, with modest, colorfully painted wooden houses, restaurants, and shops. On Thomas Street, Ernest Hemingway sometimes boxed at the **Blue Heaven** restaurant, back when it was a saloon with a reputation for roughness. If you like your historical sights with a bit of swing, Jazz trumpet legend Theodore "Fats" Navarro lived at No. 828.

Key West Cemetery

Even the 20 acre (8 hectare) **Key West Cemetery Q**, established in 1847, has fascinating sights. Among them is a statue of a lone sailor that commemorates the 252 men who died aboard the battleship USS *Maine*, which sank in Havana in 1898. Other famous epitaphs read "I told you I was sick" and "Devoted fan of singer Julio Iglesias." The unique nature of Key West's residents is apparent even after death. The cemetery has been the center of a controversy because of the local custom of recycling graves, although space is at a premium, since at least 100,000 people are buried here, when only 30,000 live on the island.

Off key

Key West isn't the last of the Florida Keys. To reach the westernmost of the islands, you have to travel by boat or seaplane to the Dry Tortugas, 68 miles (109km) beyond Duval Street's last bar.

Romantic as it sounds today, the name merely told 16th-century mariners that the island was "dry," meaning there was no fresh water; *tortugas*, Spanish for turtles, meant there was no fresh meat. There wasn't much on the island until 1846. That was when the US government started laying bricks on the Tortugas' Garden Key to create the hexagonal Fort Jefferson – the "Gibraltar of the Gulf" – and provide a safe haven for American vessels pausing near the entrance to the Gulf of Mexico. Never

completed, and abandoned by the Army in 1874, in 1992 the fort became **Dry Tortugas National Park ⑯** (for ferry information, tel: 305-292-6100; www.fortjefferson.com; departures daily at 8am, return at 5pm; charge). Today, the appropriate line for the place might be "ye shall beat your swords into snorkels." The waters beneath the fort's walls are ideal for exploring the coral reefs that are one of the Keys' most famous attractions. ❏

Sloppy Joe's, one of Ernest Hemingway's favorite bars, has been in business for more than four decades.

BELOW: Key West Lighthouse and Keeper's Quarters Museum.

RESTAURANTS AND BARS

Restaurants

Prices for a three-course dinner per person, excluding tax, tip, and beverages:
$ = under $20
$$ = $20–45
$$$ = $45–60
$$$$ = over $60

A&B Lobster House
700 Front St
Tel: 305-294-5880
$$$–$$$$
The caviar is delivered fresh daily, and lobsters are flown in from Maine. House specialties include grouper Oscar, Brazil nut snapper, and farm-raised baby conch sautéed in rum butter sauce. But the beef here also measures up, with offerings such as filet mignon Béarnaise. The waterfront view is spectacular from the wrap-around balcony, and a stop at the property's Berlin's Cocktail & Cigar Bar for a nightcap rounds out a perfect evening.

Alice's Restaurant
1114 Duval St
Tel: 305-292-5733
$$$
Chef Alice Weingarten, "the queen of Key West cuisine," describes her food as "New World fusion confusion." But don't let her fool you; she knows exactly what she's cooking up – dishes like crispy lacquered duck, macadamia coconut crusted shrimp, and spicy pink vodka conch bisque. Small and large plates are available. Start off with a pomegranate cosmopolitan cocktail, and finish up with Alice's terrific cappuccino bread pudding or tropical fruit shortcake.

Blue Heaven
729 Thomas St
Tel: 305-296-8666
$–$$
Journalist Charles Kuralt said of the scallop sauce here: "[it] would make cardboard taste good." The breakfasts, including shrimp and grits and made-from-scratch pancakes, are delicious. The lunch and dinner menu relies heavily on Caribbean influences, with specialties including Caribbean barbecue shrimp and yellowtail snapper. There's a lovely outdoor patio.

B.O.'s Fish Wagon
801 Caroline St
Tel: 305-294-9272 **$**
Many consider this rustic, open-air spot to be a defining Key West dining experience. Get in line for delicious, if somewhat pricy, fish sandwiches, chili, conch fritters, and home-made fries. Live entertainment makes the evenings a pleasure. No credit cards are accepted, so bring some cash.

Café Marquesa
Marquesa Hotel,
600 Fleming St
Tel: 305-292-1244
$$$–$$$$
This is a popular spot for an elegant and romantic meal. The sophisticated New American menu emphasizes seafood and includes macadamia-crusted yellowtail snapper or Nantucket scallop lasagnetta with blue crab and porcini sauce.

Café Solé
1029 Southard St
Tel: 305-294-0230
$$$
Chef John Correa combines his extensive knowledge of French sauces with local seafood to create a unique menu that might include bouillabaisse or conch carpaccio – Bahamian conch sliced thin and served with virgin olive oil and lime juice. But his signature dish – hog snapper with a red pepper zabaglione – is a culinary standout.

Commodore Waterfront Restaurant
700 Front St,
Historic Seaport
Tel: 305-294-9191
$$$–$$$$
When you're tired of grouper and snapper and looking to sink your teeth into a succulent hunk of prime rib or a New York sirloin with melted Roquefort cheese and cream, head over to this bustling, open-air waterfront spot. There are, however, loads of fresh fish items on the menu, including Florida lobster tails, if you still haven't had enough seafood. Three-course prix fixe menus are offered.

El Siboney Restaurant
900 Catherine St
Tel: 305-296-4184 **$**
Here's a Key West treasure: a Cuban restaurant with great ambience and ample portions of well-prepared, reasonably priced food. Order a sangria and perhaps the daily special, which might be grilled grouper fillet, *masas de*

puerco fritas (fried pork chunks), or bistec de Palomilla. All entrées are served with rice, black beans, sweet plantains, and Cuban bread.

Martin's Fine European Dining
917 Duval St
Tel: 305-295-0111
$$$–$$$$
Expect fine European dining with an accent on German cuisine served in elegant, contemporary surroundings at Martin's. House specials include marlad confit, wiener schnitzel, and jager schnitzel with homemade spaetzle. Brunch selections include a handsomely prepared seafood crêpe and lobster Benedict.

Paradise Café
1000 Eaton St
Tel: 305-296-5001 $
As advertised, the "home of the monster sandwich" serves up terrific and huge sandwiches on Cuban bread toasted on a press, along with half-pound burgers, homemade soups, Cuban cooked pork, breakfast sandwiches, and terrific key lime pie. Indoor and outdoor seating is limited, but the waterfront is just a short walk away.

Pepés Café and Steak House
806 Caroline St
Tel: 305-294-7192
$$–$$$
The oldest restaurant in the Keys (established in 1909) isn't resting on its laurels: the food is excellent and still served in the outdoor enclosed courtyard where Harry Truman loved to dine. Hand-cut steaks are a house specialty, as are fresh oysters and key lime pie.

Sunday-night BBQ packs in the crowds.

Pisces Seafood Restaurant
1007 Simonton St
Tel: 305-294-7100
$$$–$$$$
For 25 years now this intimate, candlelit restaurant has been one of the most popular destinations for award-winning seafood. In their signature dish, "tango mango," shelled Maine lobster medallions and shrimp are flambéed in cognac. Original artworks by Andy Warhol are on display, which add a nice touch to the ambience.

Turtle Kraals Restaurant & Bar
Margaret St and Historic Seaport
Tel: 305-294-2640
$–$$
The large and diverse menu at this waterfront eatery features classic fried seafood platters, chowders, and dishes prepared with a Southwestern flair. It opens at 7am for breakfast and stays open until the wee hours, perfect for those late-night munchie attacks.

Bars

Aqua Nightclub
711 Duval St
Tel: 305-294-0555
Gays and straights turn out to party at this club that has one of the island's largest dance floors and best sound systems. Tuesday to Sunday nights at 9pm the popular drag performers, the Aquanettes, take the stage. Monday is karaoke night, and on other nights DJs and/or live performers entertain a

crowd looking for a fun night.

Bull & Whistle Bar
224 Duval St
Tel: 305-296-4565
A three-tiered establishment, the Bull & Whistle has something for almost everyone: The Bull, an open-air bar with live entertainment; The Whistle, with a wraparound balcony overlooking Duval Street action below; and the Garden of Eden, a clothing-optional rooftop bar.

Fogarty's Flying Monkey's Saloon
227 Duval St
Tel: 305-294-7525
A favorite watering hole for Key West 20--somethings attracted by the 22-ounce key lime margaritas, $1 Jell-O shots, and "Howlers" – a lethal potion of grain alcohol, vodka, and lemonade. Bring a designated driver. The food here is surprisingly good, too.

Green Parrot
601 Whitehead St
Tel: 305-294-6133
The first and last bar on US 1 has been a popular watering hole since 1890. Tourists and locals pack the house to listen to blues, whether it's a weeknight and on the legendary jukebox or the famous live weekend entertainment.

Hog's Breath Saloon
Duval and Front sts
Tel: 305-296-4222
A Key West institution, Hog's Breath features live entertainment; happy hour daily 5–7pm; a raw bar; and Coney Island hot dogs.

Virgilio's
524 Duval St
Tel: 305-296-8118
A classic cocktail lounge with live music, dancing, Monday-night $5 Martinis, and a varied clientele dressed in everything from Carhartts to Chanel. La Trattoria, in front of the bar, provides a late-night dining menu.

LEFT AND RIGHT: a cool drink and a tasty bite on the patio at the Blue Heaven.

ATLANTIC COAST

The sunshine and beaches are a big attraction, but
there are also fascinating historic sites, including
the oldest continuously occupied city in the US

Driving Florida's Atlantic coast retraces the route
that funneled early tourists toward the seaside
playgrounds of Miami and Fort Lauderdale. Strung
along the coast are dozens of towns, each with a distinct
personality and its own slice of the tourism market.

Fort Lauderdale, on the southern end of the Gold Coast
(which starts just north of Miami), was once known for
hard-partying college students, but has worked hard to
refashion itself into a family-friendly and less fast-paced
sightseeing alternative. Palm Beach and Boca Raton, on
the other hand, are favored by the upper crust, who inhabit
lavish waterfront mansions and
exclusive country clubs.

To the north is the Space Coast, site of
the Kennedy Space Center. Nearby are the
brackish lagoons and pristine beaches of
Merritt Island National Wildlife Refuge and
the old-time, seaside town of Cocoa Beach.

The pace quickens dramatically at Daytona
Beach, which is notable as a spring break
destination and as the home of the Daytona
500 and other auto races. Historic St Augustine,
the oldest continuously inhabited city in the
US, operates at a decidedly slower pace and
contrasts sharply with Jacksonville, Florida's
largest city, with a revitalized downtown,
numerous museums, and an active port.

Motorists on the Atlantic coast have a choice of routes. A1A is slow
and narrow but usually within tantalizing sight of the ocean; US 1 is
somewhat speedier but tends to be clogged with local traffic; and I-95 is,
predictably, the fastest and least scenic but is still a sensible choice if you
need to cover the greatest distance in the least time. ❏

PRECEDING PAGES: a quiet inlet on Amelia Island.
LEFT: nightly entertainment at the Trade Winds Lounge in St Augustine.
TOP: kitschy architectural detail at the Magic Beach Motel in Vilano Beach.
ABOVE RIGHT: the Apollo/Saturn V Center at the Kennedy Space Center.

FORT LAUDERDALE

The party scene has mellowed and the town is cultivating a family-friendly image, but the Strip remains a popular destination for those in search of sun, surf, and sand

It seems almost inconceivable that the beautiful beaches of **Fort Lauderdale ❶** were a dismal swamp less than a century ago. A wooden fort built here during the Seminole Wars rotted for two decades after troops left in 1857. The only significant development during this period was the construction of a House of Refuge for shipwrecked sailors. For the most part, it remained a waterlogged hideaway for escaped slaves and army deserters.

Henry Flagler's railroad changed everything. In 1911, the city was incorporated. The swampy coast kept construction off the beach, and, as a result, the sands were kept open to the public, and hotels and businesses were situated on the far side of Route A1A.

Beach party

Known as the **Strip**, the city's palm-lined, 2 mile (3km) beachfront was romanticized as a spring-break destination in the 1960 movie and song *Where the Boys Are*. For much of the 1970s, the Strip was the site of what seemed like one big drunken beach party. A crackdown in the 1980s put an end to the brawls and other disruptions. New bars that were not part of hotels were banned, as was public consumption of liquor. Arrests for violations were common. By 1990, many spring-break revelers decamped to Daytona Beach.

Kids still come for a glimpse of the Strip, but their numbers are smaller and their behavior has been tempered; you'll find many more families these days. The once-notorious **Elbo Room** bar ❷, made famous in the movie, is still open, but even the bartenders admit that it's not what it used to be. Although toned down, Fort Lauderdale still has a lively bar scene, with much of the action along Commercial and Las Olas boulevards and the banks of the Intracoastal Waterway.

Main attractions
THE STRIP
BONNET HOUSE MUSEUM AND GARDENS
RIVERWALK ARTS AND ENTERTAINMENT DISTRICT
MUSEUM OF ART FORT LAUDERDALE
MUSEUM OF DISCOVERY AND SCIENCE
FLAMINGO GARDENS
SEMINOLE INDIAN NATIVE VILLAGE
BOCA RATON
LOXAHATCHEE NATIONAL WILDLIFE REFUGE

LEFT: the beach at Las Olas Boulevard.
RIGHT: tropical blossom at Butterfly World.

TIP

The hop-on, hop-off Sun Trolley (tel: 954-761-3543; www.suntrolley. com) links downtown Fort Lauderdale with the beach and most major sights. Just wave to the driver and the tram will stop to pick you up. The fare for most destinations is just 50 cents.

The waterfront

Fort Lauderdale is heralded as the Yachting Capital of the World; more than 44,000 yachts are registered here. Many tie up at **Bahia Mar Yacht Basin B** at the southern end of town. Fans of John D. MacDonald's Travis McGee novels may recognize the marina as home of the fictional detective's houseboat, *The Busted Flush*.

Just to the north, the **International Swimming Hall of Fame C** (1 Hall of Fame Dr; tel: 954-462-6536; www. ishof.org; daily 9am–5pm; charge), a showplace for water sports, houses two pools, a diving well, and a swimming flume, as well as Olympic memorabilia.

The Strip's northern end

At the northern end of the beach, hidden behind seagrape trees, **Bonnet House Museum and Gardens D** (900 N. Birch Rd; tel: 954-563-5393; www.bonnethouse.org; guided tours Tue–Sat 10am–4pm, Sun noon–4pm; charge) is perhaps the city's most curious sight. Built in 1920 by the late Evelyn and Frederick Bartletts, it is

a lyrical mansion of artistic whimsy, decorated with unusual antiques and an odd collection of knick-knacks. Descendants of Mrs. Bartlett's beloved Brazilian monkeys still inhabit the manicured grounds of the 35 acre (14 hectare) estate, now listed in the National Register of Historic Places.

Across the way, at the 180 acre (70 hectare) **Hugh Taylor Birch State Recreation Area E** (3109 E. Sunrise Blvd; tel: 954-564-4521; daily 8am–sunset; charge), visitors can swim, hike, and rent canoes to explore the watery lagoons.

The Venice of America

When developer Charles Rodes was faced with transforming acres of mangrove swamp into real estate in the 1920s, he resorted to "finger-islanding" – dredging up a series of parallel canals and using the fill to create long peninsulas between them. Rodes dubbed his creation **The Isles F**, and Fort Lauderdale earned the nickname "Venice of America." The Isles have more than 300 miles (484km) of canals and inlets, and along their frontage

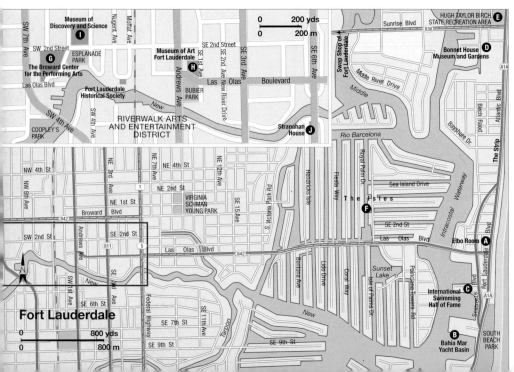

Fort Lauderdale

ornate mansions sit cheek-by-jowl with tiny boxes awaiting the wrecking ball.

Numerous companies offer narrated tours of The Isles' "millionaire's row." The somewhat worn but serviceable *Jungle Queen* (tel: 954-462-5596; www.junglequeen.com), an old-fashioned riverboat, sails from a dock just off Seabreeze Boulevard, next to Bahia Mar. The *Carrie B* (Las Olas Blvd at SE 5th Ave; tel: 954-768-9920; www.carriebcruises.com), a replica 19th-century paddle-wheeler, offers 90-minute narrated cruises. Riders pay a one-time fare for unlimited trips aboard the **Water Bus** (tel: 954-467-6677; www.watertaxi.com), which cruises the waterways and includes stops at many downtown attractions.

Riverwalk

Gas-lit Las Olas Boulevard, peppered with shops, restaurants, and galleries, is the major thoroughfare from the beach to downtown's **Riverwalk Arts and Entertainment District** (tel: 954-462-0222, 800-249-ARTS; www.stay4stars.com). Many of the city's top attractions are here, linked by a

promenade along the New River. Close by is the **Las Olas Riverfront** (tel: 954-522-6556), where local restaurateurs are happy to serve docked boats at the marina and a Sunday jazz series brings harmonious horns to match the tropical breezes.

On the western end, **The Broward Center for the Performing Arts** Ⓖ (201 SW 5th Ave; tel: 954-462-0222; www.browardcenter.org) hosts a full roster of concerts, dance, opera, and ballet.

At the **Museum of Art Fort Lauderdale** Ⓗ (1 E. Las Olas Blvd; tel: 954-525-5500; www.moafl.org;

Fort Lauderdale's party scene isn't as wild as it used to be, but it's still a popular destination for college-age beachgoers.

BELOW: a Riverwalk restaurant.

Wed–Mon 11am–7pm; charge) is an impressive collection that includes works by Picasso, Calder, Dalí, Warhol, and William Glackens. There's also an extensive exhibit of European Expressionists from the late 1940s and '50s, the so-called CoBrA works by artists from Copenhagen, Brussels, and Amsterdam.

Nearby, the **Museum of Discovery and Science** ❶ (401 SW 2nd St; tel: 954-467-6637; www.mods.org; Mon–Sat 10am–5pm, Sun noon–6pm; charge), South Florida's largest science museum, has more than 200 hands-on educational exhibits and the region's only IMAX 3D/PSE theater.

The **Fort Lauderdale Historical Society** (219 SW 2nd St; tel: 954-463-4431; www.oldfortlauderdale.org; Tue–Sat 10am–5pm, Sun noon–5pm; charge), housed in the New River Inn, oversees several historic properties. At the promenade's eastern end is **Stranahan House** ❶ (Las Olas Blvd at 335 SE 6th Ave; tel: 954-524-4736; www.stranahanhouse.org; tours daily 1pm, 2pm, and 3pm; charge), the restored turn-of-the-19th-century home of Fort Lauderdale pioneer Frank Stranahan, and Broward County's oldest structure. Try the quaintly thrilling River Ghost and Sixth Sense tours on Friday and Sunday nights.

A sea of slots

Numerous cruise ships with onboard casinos set sail from **Port Everglades** ❷ in the southern part of the city. **SeaEscapes Cruises** (tel: 877-SEA-ESCAPE; www.seaescape.com) specializes in day and evening cruises; **Imperial Majesty Cruise Line** (tel: 954-453-4625; www.imperialmajesty.com) is host to two-night cruises to Nassau.

Around Fort Lauderdale map:

Loxahatchee National Wildlife Refuge ❶
The Everglades
Hillsboro Canal
West Dixie Bend
CORAL SPRINGS
Festival Flea Market Mall
Butterfly World ★
MARGATE
NORTH LAUDERDALE
TAMARAC
Oakland Park Blvd
SUNRISE
Sunrise Blvd
African American Research Library ★ & Cultural Center
Broward Blvd
PLANTATION
Pine Island Ridge ●
Flamingo Gardens ❺ DAVIE
Cooper City
PEMBROKE PINES
Seminole Indian Native Village ❼
Pines Blvd
Miami ♦

Palm Beach ♦
BOYNTON BEACH ● Ocean Ridge
Florida's Turnpike
Jog Rd
Military Turnpike
DELRAY BEACH ❿
Morikami Museum & Japanese Gardens ★
Royal Palm Polo Sports Club ★
Linton Blvd
Highland Beach
Yamato Rd
A1A
Glades Rd
Palmetto Park Rd
Gumbo Limbo Nature Center ★
Boca Raton Museum of Art ★
Boca Raton Resort ★
BOCA RATON ❾
DEERFIELD BEACH
COCONUT CREEK
Sample Rd
Copans Rd
Lighthouse Point
Hillsboro Beach
POMPANO BEACH ❽
Cypress Cr Rd
Lauderdale-by-the-Sea
LAUDERDALE LAKES
Wilton Manors ●
LAUDERHILL
OAKLAND PARK
ATLANTIC OCEAN
The Strip
Fort Lauderdale ❶
Port Everglades ❷
John U. Lloyd Beach State Recreation Area
Dania Jai-Alai ★
Dania ❸
HOLLYWOOD ⊙ ❻ Anne Kolb Nature Center
Sawgrass Expressway
Everglades Expressway
Naples

Around Fort Lauderdale

0 — 5 miles
0 — 5 km

N

Jai-alai, fishing, butterflies

Five miles (8km) south of Fort Lauderdale, in **Dania ❸**, is the **John U. Lloyd Beach State Recreation Area ❹** (tel: 954-923-2833; daily 8am–sunset; charge), with 244 acres (99 hectares) of barrier island and a stunning beach where boats of all sizes, as well as volleyballs and grills, can be rented for a small fee. It is also home to the **International Fishing Hall of Fame and Museum** (300 Gulf Stream Way; tel: 954-927-2628; www.igfa.org; Mon–Sat 10am–6pm, Sun noon–6pm; charge), which calls itself the world's largest resource for sport fishing history. But most folks visit to catch the live sports action at **Dania Jai-Alai** (301 E. Dania Beach Blvd; tel: 954-920-1511; www.betdania. com; games Tue–Sat at 7pm; Tue, Sat, and Sun matinees; charge). A blend of lacrosse and racquetball, played with a scooping basket called the *cesta*, jai-alai is a fast-paced treat.

Just to the west, in **Davie**, **Flamingo Gardens ❺** (3750 S. Flamingo Rd; tel: 954-473-2955; www.flamingogardens. org; daily 9.30am–5.30pm; closed Mon June–Sept; charge) encompasses an historic home, 60 acres (24 hectares) of rare plants, and a wildlife sanctuary with an expansive free-flying aviary of wading birds. The grounds are home to more than just feathered friends, with otters, panthers, and alligators.

Hollywood

Continue south to **Hollywood ❻**, which was founded by a Californian but bears no resemblance to its West Coast namesake. The major draw is the 2 mile (3km) oceanfront board-walk – dubbed a "broadwalk" for its roomy width – and its entertainment complex of restaurants, bars, shops, and cinemas.

A stone's throw from the beach, **West Lake Park** and its **Anne Kolb Nature Center** (751 Sheridan St; tel: 954-926-2480) offers a rare chance to hike or kayak through a preserved system of mangroves, imposing tropical

trees that gather fresh water from the salty sea. Even paddling beginners will enjoy a trip through its secluded 3 miles (4.8km) of byways, but a $5 guided boat tour is available for those who prefer narration by an expert.

Just inland, on SR7, attractions at the **Seminole Indian Native Village ❼** (tel: 954-961-4519) include alligator wrestling shows, a poker casino and bingo hall, and a history museum. The nearby **Seminole Hard Rock Hotel**

The Museum of Discovery and Science features interactive exhibits designed to educate and entertain.

LEFT: a game of jai-alai.
BELOW: a peacock at Flamingo Gardens.

The Seminole Hard Rock Hotel and Casino.

BELOW AND OPPOSITE: kids learn about birds, bugs, and tropical plants at Butterfly World.

and Casino (tel: 954-327-7625; www. seminolehardrockhollywood.com; 24 hrs) is a modern gambling halls.

Up the coast

The beach drive north from Fort Lauderdale is particularly rewarding. The oceanfront strip of A1A through Lauderdale-by-the Sea is lined with small, moderately priced motels and inexpensive restaurants. From here the road brushes the shoreline Intracoastal Waterway.

Although it has grown rapidly as a resort, **Pompano Beach ❽** is still a major agricultural center. The area's fruits and vegetables – along with pickles from New York, bagels, and fresh-baked treats – are sold at the farmers' market at the **Festival Flea Market Mall** (2900 W. Sample Rd; tel: 954-979-4555; www.festival.com; Mon–Fri 9.30am–5pm, Sat–Sun 9.30am–6pm), which has more than 500 vendors selling trinkets of all shapes, sizes, and colors.

At Coconut Creek's **Butterfly World** (3600 W. Sample Rd; tel: 954-977-4400, www.butterflyworld.com; Mon–Sat 9am–5pm, Sun 11am–5pm; charge), visitors can view more than 5,000 butterflies representing some 50 species that fly freely in aviaries at the world's largest facility of its kind.

Boca Raton

When architect Addison Mizner built the Cloister Inn in 1926 on 356 prime acres (144 hectares) in **Boca Raton ❾**, he envisioned the entire area becoming a resort, with a fleet of gondolas romantically plying a canal through town. The waterway was never completed;

instead, the filled-in ditch became the Camino Real, where tall palms grace the route to his inn, now the **Boca Raton Resort** (tel: 561-447-3000). The **Boca Raton Historical Society** (tel: 561-395-6766; www.bocahistory.org) offers regular guided tours as well as special jaunts on trolleys and antique trains.

The **Boca Raton Museum of Art** (501 Plaza Real, Mizner Park; tel: 561-392-2500; www.bocamuseum.org; Tue–Fri 10am–5pm, Wed to 9pm, Sat–Sun noon–5pm; charge) exhibits works by artists ranging from Matisse and Modigliani to Warhol, as well as pre-Columbian and African art.

Also in Mizner Park is the **Centre for the Arts** (433 Plaza Real, Mizner Park; tel: 561-368-8445; www.centre4arts-boca.com), where sopranos share the stage with lecturers at the annual Festival of the Arts every March. When rain makes indoor browsing preferable, many locals flock to the sprawling **Town Center** (600 Glades Rd, Boca Raton; tel: 561-368-6001).

Boca doesn't neglect nature; at one end of **Red Reef Park** lies the **Gumbo Limbo Nature Center** (1801 North Ocean Boulevard, Boca Raton; tel: 561-338-1473; www.gumbolimbo.org), where injured sea turtles are nursed back to health and butterflies fly freely.

Delray Beach

Delray Beach ❿ is an inexpensive alternative to the resorts to the north and south. The nearby **Morikami Museum and Japanese Gardens** (4000 Morikami Park Rd; tel: 561-495-0233; www.morikami.org; Tue–Sun 10am–5pm; charge) is a tribute to the culture of a colony of Japanese immigrants. With lush Zen gardens and rotating exhibits of sumptuous visual arts from the Japanese imperial era, the space has something for everyone.

It is well worth making the trip 10 miles (16km) inland to the **Loxahatchee National Wildlife Refuge** ⓫ (tel: 561-734-8303; www.fws.gov/loxahatchee; refuge: daily sunrise–sunset, visitor center: Wed–Fri 9am–4pm, Sat–Sun 9am–4.30pm; charge), which contains the most northerly part of the Everglades. Wildlife ranges from alligators to a great variety of birds. ❑

The Morikami Museum is a Japanese cultural center, with exhibits of fine art, gardens, and festivals.

BELOW: civil rights protestors, 1963.

African-American History

Fort Lauderdale's $14-million African American Research Library and Cultural Center (2650 Sistrunk Blvd; tel: 954-625-2800; Mon–Thur 10am–9pm, Fri–Sat 10am–6pm, Sun 1–5pm) is one of the country's three such public research facilities, and the only one that includes Caribbean as well as African cultures. Today the local black population is growing rapidly, largely due to the arrival of Caribbean immigrants. But the area was not always so welcoming; segregation was a way of life well into the 1960s. Many citizens remember the days when they could swim only on holidays at John Lloyd State Park and had to attend segregated schools. The Old Dillard School (1009 NW 4th St; tel: 754-322-8828) was built in 1924 to serve as the first school for black children in Broward County. The 10-classroom building is now a museum and education center.

Today Fort Lauderdale is a melting pot: immigrants from a host of other nations are settling here, and the ethnic diversity is creating a cosmopolitan atmosphere unusual for a city of its size.

RESTAURANTS AND BARS

Restaurants

Prices for a three-course dinner per person, excluding tax, tip, and beverages:
$ = under $20
$$ = $20–45
$$$ = $45–60
$$$$ = over $60

Boca Raton

Henry's
16850 Jog Road
Tel: 561-638-1949 **$$**
Care for a glass of champagne with your meatloaf? This "country club row" restaurant's impressive wine list accompanies a menu of gourmet comfort food. Diner aficionados will be happy to see standard classics along with more upscale offerings for discriminating palates.

Jake's Stone Crab Restaurant
514 Via De Palmas
Tel: 561-347-1055
$$$–$$$$
King crab is given the royal treatment, as is the stone crab and a huge selection of fish delivered daily. House specialties include Bahamian conch chowder and she-crab soup.

Mark's Mizner Park
344 Plaza Real, Mizner Park
Tel: 561-395-0770 **$$**
Chef Mark continues his award-winning contemporary American formula in a spacious, ultra-chic spot with an alfresco patio. In addition to pizza and handcrafted pasta, signature dishes include black spaghetti with clams, mussels, shrimp, and scallops, and oak-grilled veal chop.

Dania

Le Petit Café de Dania
3308 Griffin Rd
Tel: 954-967-9912 **$$–$$$**
French-born chef Christian le Padellac combines some of Brittany's tastiest treats with contemporary American touches. Luncheon crêpes with fillings such as Swiss cheese, shrimp, and garlic butter are ethereal. Dinner entrées range from frogs' legs with garlic and herbs to veal cordon bleu.

Fort Lauderdale

Aruba Beach Café
1 E. Commercial Blvd
Tel: 954-776-0001 **$–$$**
A diverse menu and live entertainment keep this waterfront spot hopping. The broiled seafood platter tops $30, but burgers, salads, and conch fritters are always on the menu.

Canyon
1818 E. Sunrise Blvd
Tel: 954-765-1950 **$$$**
Reservations for this popular, intimate Southwestern bistro? "No way – forget about it," warns the website. But patrons stoically wait in line for an opportunity to relax in one of the intimate, draped booths, sip prickly-pear margaritas, and graze on specialties such as masala-dusted bison skewers and jalapeño panko-crusted jumbo shrimp.

Capital Grille
Galleria Mall, 2430 E. Sunrise Blvd
Tel: 954-462-0000 **$$$$**
The steakhouse chain that originated in Washington, D.C., specializes in dry aged beef, with specialties such as Kona-crusted sirloin and porcini-rubbed Delmonico steak. The atmosphere is akin to a gentlemen's club, with dark wood and stuffed animal heads.

Casablanca Café
3049 Alhambra St
Tel: 954-764-3500 **$$**
Although it bills itself as an American piano bar and restaurant, the menu at this romantic beachside spot ranges from spanakopita to fettuccine con pollo. Live entertainment Wednesday, Friday, and Saturday evenings features jazz and contemporary pop.

Chima Brazilian Steakhouse
2400 E. Las Olas Blvd
Tel: 954-712-0580 **$$$$**
Bring a big appetite to this fixed-price, all-you-can-eat Brazilian barbecue, where gaucho-costumed waiters dart about the elegantly decorated room with huge skewers of more than 15 different cuts of meat. A large and diverse salad bar is included.

Eduardo de San Angel
2822 E. Commercial Blvd
Tel: 954-772-4731 **$$$**
Gourmet magazine has rated Eduardo Pria's restaurant one of the best in the US, and indeed the Mexican-born chef has put together a menu that may be unique north – and south – of the border. Fresh flowers and crisp linen tablecloths set the mood for elegantly prepared dishes such as slow-roasted crispy duck with spicy guava syrup and ancho chile-flavored

crêpe with *cuitlacoche*, serrano chiles, and onions.

Grille 66 and Bar
Hyatt Regency Pier 66, 2301 SE 17th St
Tel: 954-728-3500
$$$–$$$$
You've got to respect a place that features "The Baked Potato," sea-salted, with Vermont butter, smoked bacon bits, and chive sour cream. It works because it's delicious, as is the 24-ounce porterhouse with truffle butter and the veal Milanese with arugula salad. And somehow it all tastes better because your table overlooks the intracoastal waterway. The wine list features more than 400 vintages.

Quarterdeck
2933 E. Las Olas Blvd
Tel: 954-525-2010 **$–$$**
This is a Florida chain decorated in nautical paraphernalia and serving burgers, seafood, sandwiches, and other hearty staples. The bar attracts a young, lively crowd.

River House
301 SW 3rd Ave
Tel: 954-525-7661 **$$–$$$**
Housed in three historic buildings along the scenic Riverwalk, the specialty here is "day boat" fish – freshly caught and delivered to the kitchen door. Many of the dishes reflect a fusion of Caribbean, Asian, Mexican, Mediterranean, and American influences. Sunday brunch includes a raw bar and carving stations.

Thai Spice
1514 E. Commercial Blvd
Tel: 954-771-4535 **$$**
Traditional and original Asian dishes, with an emphasis on fresh seafood, in three intimate

dining rooms. There's a fine wine list and an unusually lengthy dessert menu.

Lake Worth

Bizaare Avenue Café
921 Lake Ave
Tel: 561-588-4488 **$$$**
There are two floors in this renovated 1926 building. Patrons dine upstairs on a traditional American bistro menu while watching "beautiful and bizarre images" on a 6ft (2 meter) screen. Downstairs they lounge in easy chairs and order tapas, wraps, and light fare.

Oakland Park

Catfish Dewey's
4003 N. Andrews Ave
Tel: 954-566-5333 **$–$$**
The ambience – complete with sea horse chandelier and stuffed fish – is old-time Florida, as are the reasonable prices. Nightly all-you-can-eat specials feature farm-raised catfish, fried sea scallops, barbecue ribs, and stone crabs in season.

Pompano Beach

Darrel & Oliver's Café Maxx
2601 E. Atlantic Blvd
Tel: 954-782-0606
$$$–$$$$
For more than 20 years Darrel & Oliver's has been one of the area's most highly regarded restaurants, and has been serving its own version of eclectic New American dishes, creating treats such as blue cheese and pine nut-crusted rack of lamb and mango jerk-glazed pork tenderloin. There's a superb wine list as well as a full bar.

Bars

Boca Raton

Gatsby's
Shoppes at Village Point, 5970 SW 18th St
Tel: 561-393-3900
The place to watch a Gators game, play some pool, and chow down on classic pub grub.

Delray Beach

Blue Anchor
804 Atlantic Ave
Tel: 561-272-7272
There's Guinness on draft (served ice cold, Florida style) and a menu of authentic dishes such as steak-and-kidney pie and roast beef with Yorkshire pudding at this beachfront British pub. Live entertainment Thur–Sat.

City Limits
19 NE 3rd Ave
Tel: 561-279-8222
Don't look for bar snacks and pizza. This place is all about the music. The club's sound system pumps out some of the area's best live entertainment, from blues to funk to Latin Thur–Sat night.

Fort Lauderdale

O'Hara's Music Café
722 E. Las Olas Blvd
Tel: 954-524-1764
A favorite for weekday happy hour and live music ranging from jazz and R&B to classic rock. The patio is a prime spot for people-watching.

Village Pump Bar
4404 El Mar Dr
Tel: 954-776-5840
One of Fort Lauderdale's oldest bars is always hopping. But when Boston's favorite baseball team is playing, the "home of Red Sox Nation" really rocks.

Waxy O'Connor's Irish Pub & Eatery
1093 SE 17th St
Tel: 954-525-9299
Huge digital screens are tuned into current sports matches at this Irish pub. Patrons begin to pack the outdoor patio beginning at happy hour at 4pm and stay into the wee hours as live bands rock.

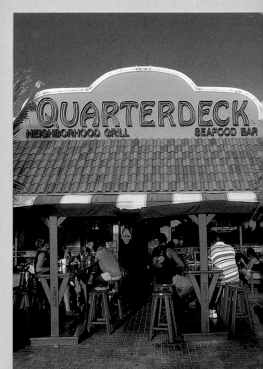

LEFT: Riverwalk has more than a dozen eateries.
RIGHT: the Quarterdeck is good for a casual meal.

PALM BEACH

There are Mediterranean-style mansions, classy shops and restaurants, pristine nature preserves, and several fine cultural venues in and around this sanctuary for the super-rich

The joke has it that Mother Nature would have built **Palm Beach ❶** if she had enough money. Indeed, the sweet aroma of dollars permeates the entire length of the 4.5 mile (7km) island, a living tableau of over-the-top opulence. Fortunately, plans floated by locals over the years (including one requiring residents to have ID cards to enter) sank, and the roads into – and out of – one of the country's wealthiest towns are open to all.

You can leave plebian Florida – and enter Palm Beach – by proceeding north on Route A1A. You can't miss it. The garish shopping centers and neon hotel signs vanish. Clean, uncluttered streets take over. The structures behind the high walls of concrete and ficus hedges aren't museums; they're the trophy homes of the ultra-rich.

Palm Beach takes root

There seem to be various stories as to the origins of the city's signature palm trees. The most popular relates how a boatload of Spanish sailors transporting 100 cases of wine stumbled upon the barren strand in 1878. They sold their cargo, including 20,000 coconuts, to a shrewd islander for $20. The islander sold two coconuts for a nickel to his neighbors. They planted them in the sand and, voilà, the beach got its palms.

In the 1890s, Henry Flagler visited the area. He liked it, built a winter home (Whitehall), and transformed Palm Beach into a personal playground for his wealthy, fun-loving friends. Astors and Vanderbilts and assorted dukes and duchesses followed Flagler into town. They stayed at Flagler's Royal Poinciana Hotel, one of the largest wooden buildings ever constructed and the largest resort hotel of its time. With more than a touch of the era's characteristic racism, black men once

Main attractions
THE BREAKERS
WORTH AVENUE
THE SOCIETY OF THE FOUR ARTS
FLAGLER MUSEUM
CITYPLACE
NORTON MUSEUM OF ART
LION COUNTRY SAFARI
SAVANNAS PRESERVE STATE PARK
VERO BEACH
SEBASTIAN INLET STATE PARK

LEFT: downtown Palm Beach.
RIGHT: relaxing in the sun.

pedaled guests around the grounds aboard "Afromobiles," and a feature attraction was Cakewalk Night, when black dancers competed for a big white cake, then entertained richly dressed guests with spirituals.

The hotel burned down several times and eventually was reborn as **The Breakers Ⓐ** (1 S. County Rd; tel: 561-655-6611; www.thebreakers.com), but its spirit carries on – fortunately, minus the Afromobiles and tasteless entertainment. Two world-class golf courses and 10 tennis courts, in addition to a litany of high-end shops and a kids' camp program, make the resort a perennial favorite with visitors.

Palm Beach's transformation began when New York architect Addison Mizner came to visit in 1918. He stayed on, adding his ostentatious flourishes to existing Spanish structures, creating a fanciful yet functional self-contained world of spires, courtyards, plazas, and arcades that contribute greatly to the town's present-day charm and distinctive appearance. Visitors can see his designs along many of the manicured avenues.

The season

Unless you prefer to gape at empty mansions undergoing beauty treatments and garden manicures, visit during the social season – an indeterminate period of time that falls between Thanksgiving and Easter. That's when you'll glimpse the beautiful people who actually live in these palatial dwellings. The annual migration of the moneyed class ignites a round of galas, charity balls, and cocktail parties. People willing to pay $1,000 or more per plate can get invited to some of the prestigious balls.

Touring the town

The centerpiece of downtown Palm Beach is **Worth Avenue Ⓑ**. It has been likened to London's Bond Street, Paris' Faubourg St Honoré, and Rome's Via Condotti. Here a multitude of art galleries, boutiques, antique shops and jewelry stores – many housed in buildings designed by Mizner – open onto courtyards and winding vistas. Mizner's 1920s Town Hall and Casa de Leoni (450 Worth Ave), which hints at a Venetian Gothic influence, also

Palm Beach

exemplify his style. For those less eager to give the credit card a workout, offical Palm Beach historian James Ponce gives an appealing historical walking tour; he can be contacted through the Worth Avenue Association (tel: 561-659-6909; www. worth-avenue.com).

The cultural hub of Palm Beach is **The Society of the Four Arts**  (2 Four Arts Plaza; tel: 561-655-7226; www.fourarts.org; gallery: Mon–Sat 10am–5pm and Sun 2–5pm, gardens: daily 10am–5pm; charge), a nonprofit cultural organization founded in 1936. The campus, on the Intracoastal Waterway, encompasses an art gallery, auditorium, two libraries, and botanical garden.

Continue down Coconut Row to Whitehall, built in 1902 and now open to the public as the **Flagler Museum** ❶ (1 Whitehall Way; tel: 561-655-2833; www.flaglermuseum.us; Sun noon–5pm, Tue–Sat 10am–5pm; charge), the top attraction in Palm Beach. Flagler and his third wife lived in this great Beaux Arts mansion, dubbed the Taj Mahal of North America, for only four years. The rooms and most original furnishings have been restored, and one of Flagler's railroad cars is on display in the garden. Highlights inside include the Marble Hall, with its painted ceiling and elegant staircase, and the master bathroom, with a wonderful onyx washstand. Nearby is the Royal Poinciana Chapel and Sea Gull Cottage, which were built by Flagler in 1886 to be his first winter home.

The Breakers has weathered booms, busts, and even two fires, but it remains one of the nation's first-class resorts. Stately Venetian arches lead into the lobby, comfortable sofas and

Worth Avenue is the centerpiece of Palm Beach's up-market shopping district.

BELOW: Bethesda-by-the-Sea Episcopal Church was built in 1925.

CityPlace has more than 65 shops and restaurants, plus nightclubs and a movie theater.

BELOW: the Cuillo Centre for the Arts on Clematis Street is a performing-arts venue.

Persian carpets line the rambling hallways, and the Circle Dining Room has a skylight, cathedral windows, and a bronze chandelier. The Flagler Steak House is one of the town's power restaurants.

Show up at least a half-hour before noon to get a courtyard table at the elegant **Café Boulud** (*see listing page 194*) in the Brazilian Court Hotel. Younger heirs gravitate to **Ta-boo** (*see listing page 194*), right on the Avenue, and the cigar room at the **Leopard Lounge** (*see listing page 195*). The Esplanade, at the eastern end, is a two-story clutch

of shops surrounding a courtyard with another popular lunch spot, **Café L'Europe**.

Mansion Row

Known as Mansion Row, South Ocean Boulevard runs past the Moorish estate of late cereal heiress Marjorie Merriweather Post. It's now **Mar-A-Lago ❸**, a National Historic Landmark owned by entrepreneur Donald Trump, who bought the 17 acre (7 hectare) property in 1985, turned it into a spa and country club, and opened membership to anyone who could afford the $150,000 initiation fee. It was here, in 2004, that Trump married supermodel Melania Knauss.

At No. 126 is the estate Addison Mizner built in 1919 for cosmetics mogul Estée Lauder. Nearby is El Mirasol, a home built by Mizner and formerly owned by John Lennon. Next door stands a house that once belonged to Woolworth Donahue, heir to the dime-store fortune.

On North Ocean Boulevard is the former estate of the Kennedys. It became known as the "Winter White

House" in the 1960s when John F. Kennedy first wintered here, but John Ney wrote of a local prejudice against this neighboring "royal family." It was here, in 1992, that Kennedy's nephew, William Kennedy Smith, was charged with raping a young woman he had met in a Palm Beach bar. After a televised trial, Smith was found not guilty.

If you keep driving north on Ocean Boulevard you will eventually run out of road. Park in a metered space and take the short hike to the wooden clock on the **Palm Beach Inlet**. For those seeking a less motorized look at all the hoopla, the 9 mile (14.5km) **Lake Trail**, nicknamed the "Trail of Conspicuous Consumption", offers stellar people- and mansion-watching.

The sport of kings

With champagne and canapés hawked from a canopied cart instead of hot dogs and beer, it's obvious that polo is not like a Sunday-afternoon baseball game. Palm Beach's pet sport is played at the nearby **Palm Beach Polo and Country Club** (11199 Polo Club Rd, West Palm Beach) and Boca Raton's **Royal Palm**

Polo Sports Club. You must either be rich or have a wealthy sponsor to participate. But it costs little to watch from your car. More than 20 area polo fields host matches from October to July. In the spring, the **International Polo Club Palm Beach** (3667 120th Ave S, Wellington) brings out a crowd of young swells for its popular Sunday brunch-and-polo events.

The other Palm Beach

Across Lake Worth, the city of **West Palm Beach ❼** was conceived as a satellite by its rich patron, Flagler. It was

Formerly a church, the Harriet Himmel Theater for Cultural and Performing Arts is the centerpiece of CityPlace.

BELOW:
with a staff of 1,800, the Breakers is kept tidy.

reserved for servants, gardeners, and other workers who toiled to keep Palm Beach from crumbling while their employers partied, shopped, and played polo. In fact, parts of the city are still in need of major repairs. But **CityPlace**, an upscale shopping, dining, and entertainment complex, has changed the face of downtown. Centennial Square, at the top of Clematis Street, has a new, $2-million interactive fountain, and is host to a free concert series – Clematis By Night – every Thursday.

One good reason to come to West Palm Beach is to visit the **Norton Museum of Art** (1451 S. Olive Ave; tel: 561-832-5196; www.norton.org; Tue–Sat 10am–5pm, Sun 1–5pm; charge), which has an outstanding collection. Among its most vaunted possessions are works from Cézanne to Picasso, as well some by Georgia O'Keeffe, Edward Hopper, and Andy Warhol.

The **Raymond F. Kravis Center for the Performing Arts** (701 Okeechobee Blvd; tel: 561-832-7469; www.kravis.org) is a major venue for a wide variety of performing artists and groups, ranging from the Monterey Jazz Festival to Gregorian Masters to the doo-wop standards of the *Forever Plaid* touring company.

Palm Beach Gardens

Much of Palm Beach County around Lake Okeechobee is given over to sugar cane; construction, real estate, and banking are other big industries. **Palm Beach Gardens** , a burgeoning upscale suburb north of Palm Beach, is headquarters of the Professional Golfers Association (PGA), which has given its initials to one of that town's main thoroughfares. The PGA operates numerous championship golf courses and a Hall of Fame.

Twenty miles (32km) west of downtown West Palm Beach in the town of **Loxahatchee** is **Lion Country Safari** (2003 Olion County Safari Rd; tel: 561-793-1084; www.lioncountrysafari.com; daily 9.30am–5.30pm; charge), the area's top family attraction, where you can drive along 4 miles (6km) of jungle trails past nearly 1,000 roaming animals. The well-fed lions seem to have grown rather lazy, but it's thrilling to watch one lead a parade of cars

BELOW: patio dining at the elegant Café Boulud.

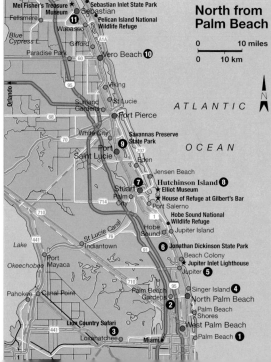

North from Palm Beach

or see a giraffe peering back at you; keep your windows closed. There are also safari boat rides, a petting and feeding area for small animals, and a reptile and dinosaur park.

Jupiter and Singer Island

Route A1A curves back to the beach over Blue Heron Boulevard. You can follow it through the high-rises of **Singer Island** ❹ (home of John D. MacArthur Beach, one of the state's best) all the way to **Jupiter** ❺. This town once was a terminal for the Celestial Railroad, which took its name from the stations it served – Juno, Neptune, Mars, and Venus, as well as Jupiter. Flagler's railroad bypassed this peninsula, so it remains less developed.

Just off Route A1A, visitors can climb the 105 steps of the restored 1860 brick **Jupiter Inlet Lighthouse and Museum** (tel: 561-747-8380; www.jupiterlighthouse.org; Tue–Sun 10am–5pm; charge). The reward is a fabulous view of the Gulf Stream – a veritable river in the Atlantic Ocean. Cross the bridge to tour the museum's

Dubois Pioneer Home, the oldest in Palm Beach County, then quench your thirst at **The Crab House**, just up the road and part of a popular Florida franchise that replicates the feel of an old-fashioned lighthouse.

Jupiter is perhaps most famous as the home town of actor Burt Reynolds, whose dad once served as the town sheriff. The **Burt Reynolds and Friends Museum** (100 N. US Hwy 1; tel: 561-743-9955; http://burtreynoldsmuseum.org; Fri–Sun 10am–4pm; charge) houses his collection of film

The Kravis Center encompasses a 2,200-seat concert hall, a playhouse, and an outdoor amphitheater.

BELOW: the Norton Museum includes works by 19th and 20th century European and American artists.

Lake Okeechobee

Water-management schemes and agriculture have taken a heavy toll on the lake, though restoration plans offer a glimmer of hope

It was once a mythical lake, unknown to European settlers until 1837, when Colonel Zachary Taylor stumbled upon it during the Second Seminole War. People of the Mayaimi and Tequesta cultures, and later the Seminole, lived on its margins, paddling out on the lake to fish. At 730 sq miles (1,890 sq km), Lake Okeechobee (from the Seminole *oki chubi*, or "big water") is the largest lake in Florida. For 6,000 years it has been the canary in the coal mine for the ecological health of the Everglades.

The Kissimmee River fed the lake, flushing the central Florida prairie country through a broad, winding floodplain to the limestone basin that impounds the lake. During the wet season, the 20ft (3 meter) -deep lake self-regulated by spilling its banks, sending a sheet flow trickling into the sawgrass wetlands of the Everglades. During the dry season, the lake shrank, exposing littoral bulrush marshes that supported apple snails, the principal diet of birds called snail kites. Nature's

polarities – large and small, fast and slow, wet and dry – were all embraced by the complex ecosystem. It was a marvel of natural engineering, unique in the world.

Starting with Howard Disston in 1881 and Governor Napoleon Broward in 1905, irrigation schemes designed to stoke new agricultural development began to drain the Everglades and tame Lake Okeechobee. Hurricanes in 1926 and 1928, which killed more than 2,500 people when a wall of water from Lake Okeechobee flooded towns, led to the creation of the 20ft (18 meter) -high Herbert Hoover Dike, part of the popular 1,400 mile (2,250km) Florida National Scenic Trail.

In 1948, Congress authorized the Central and South Florida Project, creating 1,800 miles (2,900km) of roads, canals, and levees designed to provide flood protection for urban and agricultural lands and preservation of fish and wildlife habitat. In 1971, the US Army Corps of Engineers channelized the Kissimmee River, opening up lands for ranching. On the south, sugar plantations pumped runoff into the lake to keep cane beds dry. Lake levels dropped to 12ft (4 meters).

For the Everglades, it's been an ecological disaster. Fifty percent of the original wetlands are gone. Wading bird populations have been reduced by 90 percent. Fourteen animal species are listed as endangered. Lake Okeechobee has become a dumping ground, its bottom sediments overloaded with phosphates from agricultural runoff, arsenic, and pesticides that must be disposed of as hazardous waste. There has been an outcry on the tourist-dependent Gulf and Atlantic coasts as polluted freshwater releases into the Caloosahatchee and St Lucie estuaries have created red tides and disturbed the delicate ecosystem of oyster and crab hatcheries.

A $7.8-million rescue plan offers a glimmer of hope. Work has begun on a new reservoir and stormwater treatment areas, and the Kissimmee River has been returned to its original floodplain. The trimming of the state's once-grand plan to purchase land from US Sugar Corporation, the country's largest sugar producer, to restore the southward flow of water from the lake through the Everglades has renewed some alarm over the area's future. But a 2010 wildlife refuge plan unveiled by the Interior Department could help things along by reducing the amount of waste sent into Okeechobee. ❑

LEFT: crop dusting near Lake Okeechobee.

and sports memorabilia, including quirky autographed copies of books he helped adapt, and letters from Frank Sinatra and Elizabeth Taylor.

The mansions of Jupiter Island house millionaires who aren't fond of Palm Beach, and the owners are equally wary of tourists. You will find no hotels, convenience stores, or gas stations here. Police tend to pull over any vehicles that stray off public roads into the private drives. Still, it's worth a look. Turn off US 1 to SR 707 through an archway of overhanging trees.

Into the wild

Just north of Jupiter off US 1 in **Hobe Sound**, **Jonathan Dickinson State Park ❻** (tel: 772-546-2771; www.floridastateparks.org; daily 8am–sunset; charge) preserves the last wild river in southeast Florida. You can rent a canoe or kayak and paddle along the upper Loxahatchee River past alligators and rarities like bald eagles. The park rolls through tall sand dunes that peak at Hobe Mountain, an 86ft (26 meter) sand pile with an observation deck. It is the highest point in South Florida.

The park encompasses the restored homestead of Trapper Nelson, a folk hero who opened a zoo where he wrestled alligators and devoured raw possum. After health officials closed the zoo, he retreated into isolation. When police found him dead, some suspected foul play because he had been holding up a multimillion-dollar land deal. The Trapper Nelson Interpretive Site is accessible only by boat with park staff.

Farther north, you cross the St Lucie Canal, which, together with

John D. MacArthur Beach State Park on Singer Island is a favorite destination for swimming, kayaking, fishing, and nature walks.

BELOW: Savannas Preserve State Park.

TIP

The 56 acre (23 hectare) Florida Oceanographic Coastal Center (Hutchinson Island; tel: 772-225-0505; www.florida oceanographic.org), between the ocean and Indian River lagoon, offers guided nature walks along a 1 mile (1.6km) trail from Mon–Sat at 11am and Sun at 2pm, immediately after the stingray feeding.

the Caloosahatchee River, forms the Okeechobee Waterway linking the east and west coasts. It is used by thousands of craft annually. In **Stuart ❼**, naturalist Nancy Beaver offers two-hour trips into the Indian River Lagoon on **Sunshine Wildlife Tours** (her boat leaves from Finn's Waterfront Grill; tel: 800-517-7207; www.sunshinewildlifetours.com; charge). Bottlenose dolphins and manatees are often spotted from aboard the cruise, which includes a visit to Bird Island, one of the state's top bird rookeries.

On the beach

East of Stuart is **Jensen Beach**, where turtles are a big attraction. In May of each year, large loggerheads and green sea turtles crawl out of the ocean at night to lay eggs in the sand. Nearby, on the rocky shores of **Hutchinson Island ❽**, you'll find two fascinating properties owned by the Historical Society of Martin County (825 NE Ocean Blvd; tel: 772-225-1961; www.elliottmuseumfl.org; Mon–Sat 10am–4pm, Sun 1–4pm; charge). **The House of Refuge at Gilbert's Bar** is the

last of 10 houses built more than a century ago for shipwrecked sailors and travelers, its ambience haunting enough to draw an honest-to-goodness paranormal investigation by the non-profit Florida Ghost Team. **The Elliot Museum**, named for inventor Harmon Elliot, contains all manner of wonderful things, from Elliot's inventions to a mini-circus.

Savannas Preserve State Park ❾ (tel: 772-398-2779; www.floridastateparks.org; daily 8am–sunset; charge), a freshwater marsh that stretches for 10 miles (16km) to Fort Pierce, has habitats similar to those of the Everglades. The park's education center is in Port St Lucie. The drive up Route A1A to **Fort Pierce**, home to an experimental preserve for the imperiled ivory bush coral, is particularly scenic.

Driftwood and Disney

Vero Beach ❿ has miles of lovely beaches, plus the Indian River Island Sanctuary, which can be reached by a footbridge at the end of Dahlia Lane. Another chief landmark is the rickety-looking **Driftwood Resort** (www.thedriftwood.com) on Ocean Drive. Eccentric entrepreneur Waldo Sexton fashioned it from just that. Visitors can snack in the dining room or stroll through this architectural jumble perched like a shipwreck at the tide line. So improbable is the construction, it looks as if a simple tug might bring the whole thing down. Yet it has withstood high waves and fierce hurricanes ever since the 1930s.

The **Ocean Grill** (lunch Mon–Fri, dinner nightly), also created by Sexton, is a short stroll up the beach. Its bar extends over the water, where windows mist with sea spray. There are several similarly named spots in the Palm Beach vicinity, but only Vero's version was built by Sexton and converted into an officer's club during World War II.

Another major presence here is **Disney's Vero Beach Resort** (www.dvc.disney.go.com), a sprawling, elegant

BELOW: outdoor dining at Vero Beach.

complex with several restaurants and a lavish new spa.

Pelican Island National Wildlife Refuge is the oldest wildlife sanctuary in the US, established in 1905 by President Theodore Roosevelt to protect all manner of birds. Charter a boat for a close look, particularly if you are a knowledgable birdwatcher, but obey signs warning you to "Stay off the island."

Sebastian Inlet

Thirteen miles (21km) north is **Sebastian ⑪**. **Sebastian Inlet State Park** (tel: 321-984-4852; www.floridastateparks.org; charge), on the ocean, is excellent for fishing and swimming. At the southern end of the park, the **McLarty Treasure Museum** (daily 10am–4.30pm; charge) is on the site of an old Spanish salvage camp. It deals mainly with the loss of a Spanish Plate Fleet during a hurricane in 1715. The displays include coins and jewelry. Archeologists believe an Indian mound nearby may contain the skeletal remains of some of Florida's first European settlers.

Some claim that shipwreck survivors may have lived with the Ais tribe even before the founding of St Augustine in 1565.

Sebastian Inlet is unique on this side of the state becuase it offers decent surfing. Most non-wind enthusiasts hang out in the regions between Sebastian Inlet and Daytona Beach.

On Route 1, **Mel Fisher's Treasure Museum** (1322 US Hwy 1; tel: 772-589-9875; www.melfisher.com; Tue–Sat 10am–5pm, Sun noon–5pm; charge), a northern franchise of a Key West staple, exhibits the astounding finds that "The World's Greatest Treasure Hunter" and his crews salvaged from numerous sunken ships. ❏

Hobe Sound provides habitat for 30 threatened and endangered species as well as sea turtle nesting sites.

BELOW:
Juno Beach.

RESTAURANTS AND BARS

Restaurants

Prices for a three-course dinner per person, excluding tax, tip, and beverages:
$ = under $20
$$ = $20–45
$$$ = $45–60
$$$$ = over $60

Fort Pierce

Mangrove Mattie's
1640 Seaway Dr
Tel: 772-466-1044
$
A prime location overlooking the Fort Pierce inlet plus all-you-can-eat specials (summer only) and terrific seafood make Mangrove Mattie's one of the area's most popular dining choices. The outdoor patio is delightful when there's a breeze, and the wine list is surprisingly thoughtful for a casual spot.

North Palm Beach

Ruth's Chris Steak House
700 S Rosemary Ave, City Place
Tel: 561-514-3544
$$$$
Prime Midwestern corn-fed beefsteak is seared at 1800°F (982°C) and served on plates heated to 500°F (260°C). Some argue that this is the best of the premium beef chains. Heretics can opt for seafood, lamb, or pork. There are additional locations in Fort Lauderdale, Coral Gables, and Boca Raton.

Palm Beach

Café Boulud
Brazilian Court Hotel,
301 Australian Ave
Tel: 561-655-6060
$$$$
Renowned French chef Daniel Boulud re-creates his New York City success at this "secret garden of elegance, charm, and comfort" just a few steps from Worth Avenue. The three-course prix fixe luncheon bistro menu, which changes daily, is an excellent way to test the waters. Jackets required at dinner.

Flagler Steakhouse
The Breakers, 313 Worth Ave
Tel: 561-835-1600
$$$$
Only 5 percent of all beef is awarded the distinction of prime, and we're pretty sure that much of that is consumed in this elegant dining room overlooking The Breakers' golf course. The meat is aged, hand cut, and served in the restaurant's signature colossal prime rib chop, steak au poivre, or a myriad of other dishes that may include broiled twin lobster tails.

Hamburger Heaven
314 S. County Road
Tel: 561-655-5277 $
Here's proof that even the rich and beautiful people like a good burger, a thick and creamy milkshake, and a wedge of freshly baked chocolate cake. Despite the area's pretension, the quality of these staples makes Hamburger Heaven worth a visit. And it all seems to taste better at the counter of this simple, old-fashioned spot just a few steps from tony Worth Street.

Ta-Boo
221 Worth Ave
Tel: 561-835-3500
$$–$$$
How many restaurants can claim to have served such diverse clientele as the Duke and Duchess of Windsor, Jimmy Buffet, and Donald Trump? More than 60 years old, this institution is where people come to be seen and overheard – a chic American bistro with the ambience of a British gentlemen's club. Surprisingly, much of the food is unpretentious – pizza and cheeseburgers can be found on the menu, alongside veal Milanese. Bloody Marys and espresso Martinis are specialties at the weekend piano bar.

Palm Beach Gardens

Seasons 52
11611 Ellison Wilson Road
Tel: 561-625-5852
$$
Seasons 52 offers new American food served up with a guarantee: every dish weighs in at less than 475 calories and contains no butter or transfats. Many menu options are grilled over an open fire, which works particularly well with dishes such as Thai lemongrass grilled chicken skewers. Patrons with a sweet tooth may want to order a couple of the famous desserts – tasty treats such as tiramisu and key lime pie are served in shot glasses at $2.25 each. There's also live entertainment at the sophisticated wine bar.

West Palm Beach

Havana
6801 S. Dixie Hwy
Tel: 561-547-9799
$–$$
A casual spot with ample portions of some of the area's best Cuban fare. The mojitos are frosty, the bistec especial Havana with chichuri sauce spicy, and the hospitality warm and inviting. The coffee – best with a creamy flan – is not to be missed. For more than a decade the 24-hour walk-up window has been one of the busiest spots in town during the wee small hours.

Marcello's La Sirena
6316 S. Dixie Hwy
Tel: 561-585-3128
$$$–$$$$
Marcello Fiorentino's parents opened this intimate, 60-seat Italian restaurant in 1986, and he's ably carried on their tradition of serving deftly prepared classic treats such as vongole al forno and saltimbocca alla Romana. The restaurant serves only wine, but its list – heavy on Italian vintages – is excellent.

Mark's City Place
700 S. Rosemary Ave
Tel: 561-514-0770
$$$
Mark Militello's fourth South Florida location offers the same innovative contemporary American fare that has won him a host of national awards. Although the menu changes daily, favorites include duck leg confit, pan-seared pork loin, and Australian kobe short ribs.

Sushi Jo
319 Belvedere Rd
Tel: 561-868-7893

$$
American-born Jo Clark has been working in restaurants since the age of 13 and trained under some of this country's finest sushi chefs. He combines his knowledge and passion for the cuisine to turn out terrific sushi in one of the area's trendiest restaurants, just across from the Biba Bar (see below). There are outposts in Palm Beach Gardens and Manalapan.

Spoto's Oyster Bar
125 Datura St
Tel: 561-835-1828 $$
Seafood-lovers will have a field day at this cool, contemporary restaurant and lounge. Start with a platter from the raw bar or a bowl of oyster stew, then dig into a selection of grilled specialties. The patio is pleasant on a warm, breezy evening.

Bars
Palm Beach

The Leopard Lounge
Chesterfield Hotel,
363 Cocoanut Row
Tel: 561-659-5800
Everything is spotted, from the carpets and the waiters' vests to the occasional celebrity. Don't expect much of the local wildlife to show up, however. The nightly entertainment ranges from classical guitar to show tunes.

West Palm Beach

Biba Bar
Hotel Biba,
320 Belvedere Road
Tel: 561-832-0094
One of the country's first motor lodges has been retrofitted with vibrantly colored eclectic furnishings and now

boasts an Asian-inspired outdoor garden where the young and chic gather to sip vintage wine and champagne and listen to house music.

Blue Martini
Okeechobee Blvd, City Place
Tel: 561-835-8601
James Bond might not recognize his beloved libation in one of its many new guises: a "sex in the city" or "mango madness." But this popular spot with outposts throughout the state offers more than 20 variations, along with sophisticated bar snacks and live entertainment nightly.

E.R. Bradley's Saloon
104 Clematis St
Tel: 561-833-3520
This is a waterfront restaurant by day, but by night it is one of the town's liveliest venues, where DJs and live bands crank up the music. It is said that a Bradley bloody Mary works wonders on those who

overimbibed the night before.

Respectable Street
518 Clematis St
Tel: 561-832-9999
This is one of the area's major live music venues. Wednesday to Sunday nights, local folks mix with tourists to dance the night away to tunes by DJs and performances by regional and touring bands.

Palm Beach Gardens

Club Safari
4000 RCA Blvd
Tel: 561-622-8888
The rumble in the jungle is at the hotel on the highway. It's as if Walt Disney had been commissioned to overdesign a nightclub, and the customers – drawn heavily from Marriott guests – love the video wall where videos from the 1970s and 1980s are broadcast. The hits of the 1950s–1980s are spun by local DJs Thur–Sun.

LEFT: Café Boulud at the Brazilian Court.
RIGHT: Ta-Boo is a favorite of Palm Beach socialites.

THE SPACE COAST

Kennedy Space Center, at the heart of NASA's launch pad to the heavens, tells the story of America's adventures in space

Orlando
Florida
Miami

The National Aeronautics and Space Administration (NASA) launch center is at the heart of the Space Coast, a 40 mile (65km) swath of land that stretches from its northern end in Titusville through Cocoa Beach and south to the Melbourne–Palm Bay area.

Center of operations

Cape Canaveral has long been the name of the peninsula that extends south from Merritt Island and east of the Banana River. (Its name was changed to Cape Kennedy after the president's 1963 assassination but was changed back to Canaveral in 1973.) It's the site of the Cape Canaveral Air Force Station, where the earliest experimental American military rockets were launched. **Kennedy Space Center ❶** (NASA Pkwy; tel: 321-449-4444; www. ksc.nasa.gov; daily 9am–6pm, center may be partially or completely closed on launch days), including launch pads for the space shuttles, is on Merritt Island. It lies within Merritt Island National Wildlife Refuge.

Although the space center is a government facility, the **Visitor Complex** is operated by a private company without the benefit of taxpayer funds. The complex sprawls across a landscaped campus, incorporating nearly a dozen buildings and several outdoor exhibits. Begin by getting oriented at **Information Central**, where a multimedia presentation introduces the themes and attractions within the facility. Use the schedule for films, live events, and tours posted here to plan your day.

The red planet and beyond

Robot Scouts, located in a wing of the main building, is a walk-through exhibit that takes a whimsical look at the role of robot probes in interplanetary exploration. At the opposite

Main attractions
KENNEDY SPACE CENTER
ASTRONAUT HALL OF FAME
MERRITT ISLAND NATIONAL WILDLIFE REFUGE
BLACK POINT WILDLIFE DRIVE
CANAVERAL NATIONAL SEASHORE
COCOA BEACH

LEFT: the shuttle *Endeavour* is launched.
RIGHT: a Hubble photo of the Carina Nebula.

TIP

The International Space Station travels around the Earth at 17,500mph (28,200kph), which is 10 times faster than a speeding bullet.

end of the main building is the venue for **Astronaut Encounter**. Here guests get the chance to discuss space travel with NASA astronauts. Representing the fewer than 500 men and women who have flown in space, the astronauts answer questions, narrate videos, and invite a young audience member onto the stage to become part of the presentation.

Mad Mission to Mars is the title of a live-action stage show using theme-park techniques and 3-D computer animation to teach an audience of "astronaut trainees" essential facts about physics, rocketry, and living in space. The show is aimed at kids, but adults come away with a better understanding of what will be involved in the first interplanetary journey.

At the **Nature and Technology** exhibit, visitors are introduced to the diverse environment in which the space center is located. Some 5,000 alligators make their home in Merritt Island National Wildlife Refuge – they've been known to loll alongside the 15,000ft (4,600 meter) runway where space shuttles land – and this

exhibit explains how an almost pristine environment co-exists alongside the realm of advanced technology.

To get up close and personal with one of the space-traveling elite, make a reservation to have **Lunch with an Astronaut**. Offered at 1pm Monday through Friday, this extra-cost option (about $23 for adults, $16 for children) is exactly what it says it is: an opportunity to join a crew member for a multicourse lunch, complete with a briefing, conversation, and photo-and-autograph session. (It's advisable to make reservations in advance.)

The end of the shuttle program in 2011 may make astronauts less available to visitors, but Kennedy has filled the void with a new **Star Trek Live** program that whisks you into the future with Captain Kirk and Spock for a 30-minute interactive adventure. The cost of participation is included with every ticket.

Space exploration, though only a recent development, has a remarkably rich and vivid history. At the **Early Space Exploration** exhibit, visitors can watch a re-creation of a Project

BELOW: Mad Mission to Mars has a stage show that takes the audience on a voyage through the cosmos.

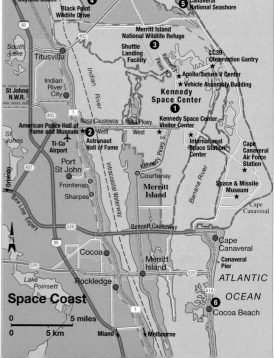

Mercury launch, see the mission control-room consoles used by ground crews during Mercury and Gemini missions, and even examine the interiors of the tiny capsules from those pioneering days.

Heavy lifting

Just outside the main building is the **Rocket Garden**, resembling nothing so much as a display of stark modern sculpture. Eight rockets, all but one mounted vertically as if ready to soar skyward, trace the evolution of the technology that made manned space flight possible. Here are the Redstone, Atlas, and Titan models, including an example of the Mercury-Atlas engine that blasted John Glenn into orbit in 1962. The one horizontal specimen is a Saturn 1B, an enormous vehicle designed by NASA (the others were adapted from military rockets) and originally built as a rescue vehicle

Space Camp gives kids the opportunity to experience what life is like on the International Space Station.

BELOW LEFT: the Rocket Garden.
BELOW: a space suit.

Kennedy Space Center – Tours and Tickets

The standard admission charge to the Kennedy Space Center Visitor Complex includes entry into the Astronaut Hall of Fame *(see page 204)*; the standard KSC bus tour, which stops at the LC39 Observation Gantry, the Apollo/Saturn V Center, and the Space Station Facility; and admission to all the attractions at the Visitor Complex, including Mad Mission to Mars and the outdoor exhibits.

For those who want to see more of the Kennedy Space Center, there are two other visitor tours. NASA Up Close (2 hours) stops at the A/B Camera Stop, the closest you can get to the shuttle launch pads; the Shuttle Landing Facility; and the enormous Vehicle Assembly Building. Cape Canaveral Then and Now (2.5 hours) tours the base's first launch sites, which were used in the early Mercury and Apollo moon-landing programs, and includes a visit to the Air Force Space and Missile Museum. Both tours cost $21 and must be booked in advance.

Audiovisual displays, interactive exhibits, and numerous artifacts chronicle the development of the US space program.

BELOW: visitors can view a mock-up of mission control.

combines archival footage of the first lunar explorers with 3-D IMAX technology to amazing effect, giving the audience an opportunity to share in the awesome experience of walking on the moon and highlighting the dangers these brave astronauts faced.

Exploration in the New Millennium takes a more serious approach to the next phase of space exploration. The presentation starts with terrestrial voyages of discovery such as the Vikings' adventures in Greenland and Iceland a thousand years ago, then speculates on the logistics of travel to Mars. A small chunk of the red planet is on the premises: this is the only place in the world where it's possible to touch an actual piece of the Mars, which fell to Earth as a meteorite. Afterwards, you can send a bit of your own identity Mars-ward, by creating an electronic signature to be stored on a microchip that will one day make the interplanetary journey.

rocket for Skylab astronauts in the 1970s; it later served as a backup for the Apollo–Soyuz project. If you're still around the Visitor Complex at dusk, head over to the Rocket Garden for a look at the dramatic lighting display.

The space center is home to the only back-to-back **IMAX theaters** in the world. Two films are shown throughout the day: *Space Station* is a remarkable 3-D look at the shape, character, and challenges of life on the international space station. *Walking on the Moon 3D*

Shuttle mission central

Another impressive outdoor display dominates the opposite corner of the

campus. This is **Explorer**, a full-size replica of a space shuttle that includes an accurate mockup of the flight deck. Climbing aboard is as close as most space enthusiasts will come to sitting inside a real shuttle. Near the shuttle are the orange fuel tanks and twin solid rocket boosters used in the early stages of launch. The boosters are recovered after being jettisoned; boats dedicated to this function are moored in the Banana River nearby.

If clambering through Explorer whets your appetite for information on the shuttle, head next door to the **Launch Status Center**, which offers live briefings on past launches and missions in progress.

From the Launch Status Center, it's a short walk to the **Astronaut Memorial**, dedicated in 1991 to honor Americans who lost their lives in service to the space program. Elegant in conception, the memorial consists of a highly polished, 50ft (15 meter) granite space mirror in which the astronauts' names are engraved. The granite surface reflects passing clouds, so names appear to float in the heavens.

The **Shuttle Launch Experience** (minimum height: 48in/122cm) was created shortly after Epcot's Mission: SPACE *(see page 239)*. This is a much tamer ride, but the concept is the same: to let you feel just what the astronauts feel when a space shuttle is launched. The biggest difference between the two rides is that you do not feel heavy G-forces as there is no spinning involved. The pre-show also pays more attention to the science of what actually happens in a real shuttle launch, explaining the physics of getting into outer space in one piece. Compared to Orlando's motion simulators, this ride is rather mild, allowing visitors who are not fans of thrill rides to get a taste of what it takes to travel into space.

On your way to the bus tours, have a quick look at the floating 9-ton granite sphere in **Constellation Square**. Water pressure keeps this ball afloat, allowing you to find your favorite constellation by spinning it around.

Restricted area tour

After touring the Visitor Complex, board a bus for a tour of outlying space

The space shuttle has played a key role in the construction of the International Space Station. The first pieces of this international venture were launched in 1988, and formal completion of the structure is scheduled for 2012. The space station is expected to remain operable until 2020, with a potential extension until 2028.

BELOW LEFT: Apollo/Saturn V Center. **BELOW:** Apollo 14 command module.

TIP

The day-long Astronaut Training Experience (ATX) is a hands-on program that gives visitors a sample of space flight. After a mission briefing, you go through a series of realistic simulator training exercises before participating in a mock shuttle mission. Numbers are limited, so book ahead. The minimum age is 14 and the cost is $250.

BELOW: *Endeavour* is seen after the rotating service structure is rolled back in preparation for the shuttle's final launch.

center facilities that play a vital part in NASA operations. (Itineraries may be altered or tours suspended, depending on mission schedules.)

The route passes the **Orbiter Processing Facility**, where (before their retirement) shuttles spent several months for maintenance and repair. This is one of the few places, outside of space itself, where shuttle cargo doors could be opened and closed. The spacecraft were then transported to the 525ft (160 meter) -tall, 8 acre (3 hectare) **Vehicle Assembly Building**, the largest building by volume in the world. This is where shuttles were outfitted with twin solid rocket boosters and an external fuel tank. Nearby is the **Launch Control Center**, familiar from television coverage.

Equally impressive, if only for their sheer size, are the **Crawler Transporters**, two 6 million pound (2.7 million kg) tracked vehicles built to carry assembled shuttles along the 3.5 mile (5.5km) route to the launch pads, but now retired along with the shuttles. In service for more than 30 years, the Crawlers traveled at 1mph

(1.6kph) when carrying a shuttle, boosters, and a fuel tank.

The first stop is at the **LC 39 Observation Gantry**, a 60ft (18 meter) platform that affords a sweeping view of the launch pads, Vehicle Assembly Buildings, and the surrounding area. On display is a 7,000lb (3,200kg) shuttle main engine, and a model re-creation of a launch countdown. A 6 minute film presents a briefing by astronaut Marsha Ivins on how a space shuttle was prepared for launch.

Launch Pads 39A and **39B** are historic structures – they were used for the Apollo moon launches. With their service structures towering alongside, the massive concrete pads are rivaled only by the spacecraft themselves as emblems of modern space exploration.

The tour continues to the **Apollo–Saturn V Center**, dedicated to the men and machines whose work culminated in the moon landings of 1969 and 1971. A video presentation reviews the early phases of the Apollo program, prior to a re-creation of an

Apollo launch in the firing room. Still the main attraction here is a re-creation of the July, 1969, Apollo 11 landing presented in the **Lunar Theater**. The Center houses the original **Lunar Module** and **Command Service Module** and one of only three Saturn V rockets still in existence.When the first of the rockets was fired in 1967, it created the loudest noise ever made by human beings.

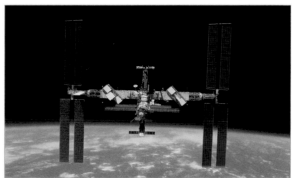

Viewing a launch

The high point of visiting the Space Coast is viewing an actual launch. Although the iconic shuttles have retired, NASA will continue to use the launch facilities at Cape Canaveral for the foreseeable future to launch satellites and other objects destined for orbit. Don't worry, you can still experience the excitement of a launch.

As the countdown clock ticks off the remaining minutes before a new craft launches, the anticipation becomes almost unbearable until its final seconds draw near. The cheers of the crowd are soon drowned out as the roar of the craft's engines reaches you

while the magnificent flying machine heads for space.

A place to watch

How can you experience this cosmic departure? Like thousands of others, you can simply find a spot along US 1 in Titusville or Route A1A in Cape Canaveral or Cocoa Beach. Or, if you're going to be at the Kennedy Space Center on launch day, purchase a Launch Viewing ticket (first-come, first-served), which allows you to ride a bus to a viewing site about 6 miles (10km) from the launch pad. Don't forget to bring a pair of binoculars.

The International Space Station.

BELOW LEFT: Apollo 11 climbs toward orbit on July 16, 1969. On board were astronauts Armstrong, Collins, and Aldrin.
BELOW: Buzz Aldrin was photographed on the moon by Neil Armstrong.

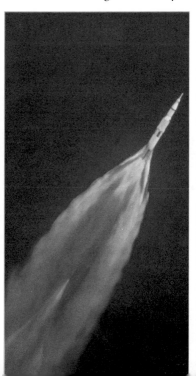

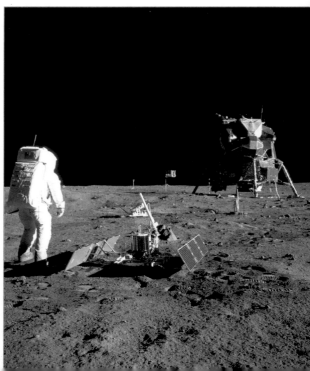

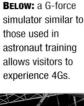

The Astronaut Hall of Fame pays tribute to the men and women of the US space program.

BELOW: a G-force simulator similar to those used in astronaut training allows visitors to experience 4Gs.

If you're coming to the space center specifically to view a launch, it's a good idea to plan on staying a few extra days in case there's a delay. There are no guarantees; launches are sometimes postponed for weeks. Call 321-449-4444 for information or buy launch tickets online at www.ksctickets.com.

Space tourism

Even before the final shuttle flight, the legacy of NASA's first voyages grew to new proportions with the development of private ventures designed to send anyone into the void – for a fee, of course. Virgin Galactic is testing a space

plane that will take tourists into the upper atmosphere, but has little practical application for scientific research. Space-X, founded by Elon Musk (the Internet entrepreneur behind PayPal), is one of several independent companies bidding for a contract with the US government to provide services for the International Space Station.

Astronaut Hall of Fame

"[T]he surface was beautiful, beautiful … Magnificent desolation." So wrote Buzz Aldrin in a 1972 letter describing how it felt to walk on the moon. The document, on exhibit at the **Astronaut Hall of Fame ❷** (6225 Vectorspace Blvd, Titusville; tel: 321-269-6100; daily 10am–6.30pm) about 6 miles (10km) west of the Kennedy Space Center, is just one artifact among thousands that are gathered here to tell the story of the American experience in space.

There's a lot more here, including a Mercury trainee capsule, the command module from Apollo 14, and wheels from the moon rover. One of the highlights is the state-of-the-art **Simulator Station** interactive

area, where visitors can experience firsthand a variety of astronaut-training devices. Among them is a G-force centrifuge that creates the sensation of gravity four times that on Earth, and a shuttle simulator that allows visitors to test their piloting skills.

Back to nature

In contrast to all this high-tech adventure are two nearby nature preserves. At the 140,000 acre (57,000 hectare) **Merritt Island National Wildlife Refuge ❸** (PO Box 6504, Titusville; tel: 321-861-0667; www.fws.gov/merrittisland; daily dawn–dusk, closed several days before launches), adjacent to Kennedy Space Center, endangered West Indian manatees loll peacefully in brackish lagoons, sea turtles waddle ashore to lay eggs on pristine beaches, and alligators bask in the sun on creek banks. The refuge lies along a migratory flyway, and the sky is filled in early spring with warblers and shorebirds while, on the ground, egrets and herons are in breeding plumage, wood storks and ospreys build nests, and bald eaglets test their wings.

The mild climate and varied environment of marshes, hardwood hammocks, pine forest, scrub, and coastal dunes sustain more than 500 species of wildlife, including more than 20 on the Endangered or Threatened Species List. This is one of the most important nesting areas in the country for loggerhead, green, and leatherback turtles. Much of the wildlife can be spotted along the 7 mile (11km), one-way **Black Point Wildlife Drive ❹**, a self-guided driving tour through salt- and freshwater marshes. The entrance is on SR 406, a mile east of the intersection with SR 402. Manatees, most prevalent in the spring and fall, can best be viewed from the observation area near Haulover Canal Bridge on SR 3.

The best time to visit the refuge is during the off-season, when wildlife populations are at their highest and mosquitoes, high temperatures, and thunderstorms are least likely to present a problem. The Visitor Information Center, 5 miles (8km) east of US 1 in Titusville on SR 402, has wildlife displays, educational resources, fishing information, and trail maps. Nearby

TIP

Canaveral National Seashore is also home to the Eldora Statehouse, a reminder of the challenges faced by early settlers along the "Mosquito Lagoon." Tel: 386-428-3384 for more information.

BELOW LEFT: more than 300 bird species inhabit Merritt Island, including great blue herons. **BELOW:** a leatherback hatchling swims out to sea.

Turtle Walks

It's one of the most riveting beachside spectacles served up by nature: a 600-pound (270kg) loggerhead sea turtle trudges ashore in the moonlight and, in a grueling act of devotion that can last as long as two hours, digs a sandy nest in which she deposits as many as 100 eggs. Rear flippers working counterpoint to cover up her handiwork, then carving out a shallow, false nest to trick yolk-hungry predators, the turtle finally crawls back to the ocean.

To see this or the hatchlings emerge two months later, there's no better place than Canaveral National Seashore. While it is a violation of federal law to harm a sea turtle or disturb its nest – the beach is zealously patrolled during nesting season to make sure the curious keep their distance – the park sponsors permit occasional evening turtle walks. After locating a female that has already begun laying eggs and is not likely to be spooked, rangers escort small groups to witness the ritual.

Tours start around 8pm and last until midnight. Reservations can be made in May or June by calling 386-428-3384, ext. 18.

An osprey nests within sight of Kennedy Space Center.

BELOW: a dolphin surfs the wake of a research boat on the Banana River.

Pelican Island National Wildlife Refuge is accessible via a boardwalk over the ocean which offers stunning views of the island (tel: 772-562-3909; www.fws.gov/pelican island; daily 7.30am–sunset). This bird rookery – the nation's first National Wildlife Refuge – was established in 1903.

Beauty and the beach

Adjacent to the wildlife refuge is the 57,000 acre (23,000 hectare) **Canaveral National Seashore ❺** (212 S. Washington Ave, Titusville; tel: 386-428-3384; daily 6am–6pm winter, to 8pm in summer; visitor center daily 9am–5pm), whose miles of barrier dunes and sea-swept beaches are a haven for beachcombers and nature-lovers. Two of the beaches, **Apollo** and **Playalinda**, at the northern and southern tips of the park, have restrooms, boardwalks and, from May 30 to September 1, lifeguards. In between, the landscape remains untouched. Portions of the seashore may be closed before shuttle launches or when parking lots are full.

A word of note: Canaveral is the destination of choice for Florida's nude sunbathers, who are constantly at odds with local authorities. The legal wrangle over whether Florida's laws against public nudity can be enforced on federal land has been going on for years. If you want to chuck your clothes, you'll have plenty of company. But there's no guarantee that a deputy sheriff won't slink out of a palmetto thicket and slap you with a citation.

Those who prefer beaches in a more developed setting will find **Cocoa Beach ❻** to their liking – an old-time seaside town with chain motels, restaurants, and souvenir shops, as well as first-rate beaches.

The biggest attraction in Cocoa Beach is the **Ron Jon Surf Shop** (4151 N. Atlantic Ave, Cocoa Beach; tel: 321-799-8888; daily 24 hours), a neon-lit palace devoted to bikinis, boogie boards, surfboards, and scuba gear. Famous surfers occasionally drop in for autograph sessions; scuba-diving and surfing lessons are also available. ❑

RESTAURANTS

Cocoa Beach

Cocoa Beach Pier
401 Meade Avenue, ½ mile north of SR 520, off A1A
Tel: 321-783-7549
$–$$$
You could do a lot worse than end your trip to the Space Coast on the pier at Cocoa Beach. Walk to the end of the structure and you can see the launch pads at Kennedy Space Center with your naked eye. It's no secret that this is prime launch-viewing real estate. On the pier itself are three places to eat: the Atlantic Grille is the fanciest option, the Boardwalk is a cheap and cheerful bar serving fish sandwiches and burgers, and Marlin's Good Times Bar and Grill splits the difference. Any of the choices affords a great view of the Atlantic and the surfers trying to ride it. The Tiki Bar at the end of the pier is a great place to enjoy an ice-cold beer or frozen daiquiri while the sun is setting.

The Fat Snook
2464 S. Atlantic Ave
Tel: 321-784-1190
$$$
This tastefully airy and arty restaurant does something others in Cocoa Beach dare not: feature locally caught seafood. It is amazing that most other seafood restaurants on this stretch of coast seem obsessed with telling you how far the seafood has come. But not at the Fat Snook. Local produce is featured in every course.

Gregory's Steak and Seafood Grille
900 N. Atlantic Ave
Tel: 321-799-2557
$$$
This family-run restaurant's signature 12oz baseball-cut steak is the best bit of beef on the beach. If you have room for appetizers or dessert, there is a fine selection of seafood nibbles, salads, and sweets. Vegetarians are given little solace here, but those who eat fish will have plenty of dishes to choose from so long as they don't dwell on the ironies of indulging in North Atlantic fish while on the South Florida coast. Groucho's comedy club is just upstairs to provide a laugh.

Mango Tree Restaurant
118 N. Atlantic Ave
Tel: 407-799-0513
$$$
A romantic, tropical setting of fresh flowers, wicker furniture, and white linen sets the tone for this quirky little restaurant. Inside, a tropical aquarium, extensive butterfly collection, and pianist provide a relaxing backdrop. The menu features fine Italian-American cuisine and several fresh seafood specialties. The Indian River crabcakes should be celebrated as they are one of the few indigenous seafood dishes on any Cocoa Beach menu.

Punjab
White Rose Shopping Center, 285 W. Cocoa Beach Cswy
Tel: 321-799-4696
$$
Unfortunately located in a characterless shopping center, Punjab is still worth a visit for its fine Indian cuisine. Budget travelers take note: the lunch menu featuring soups and curries is an absolute bargain. The evening menu is more extensive and features Tandoori and seafood and lamb specialties.

Silvestros Italian Restaurant
Banana River Square, 2039 N. Atlantic Ave
Tel: 321-783-4853
$$$
It would be very easy to miss Silvestros; the nondescript storefront does not exactly scream out "fine Italian dining" to passers-by. But they've done a great job of turning this corner of Banana River Square into a continental welcome. The menu is what you'd expect from any trattoria – carpaccio, saltimbocca, veal scaloppini, and an array of pasta dishes – but the extensive list of Italian wines makes Silvestros worth the time during your Cocoa Beach visit.

RIGHT: a burger joint in Cocoa Beach.

DAYTONA BEACH TO JACKSONVILLE

From America's premier auto race to its oldest
continuously inhabited city, Florida's northeast
coast encompasses high-speed thrills, big-city
attractions, and miles of beautiful beaches

In 1903 automakers Alexander
Winton and Ransom E. Olds, the
father of the Oldsmobile, raced along
the sands just north of **Daytona ❶** in
the first official time trial in motorsports history. In the 30-odd years that
followed, 15 land-speed records were
set on Daytona's 23 miles (37km) of
hard-packed quartz sand, culminating
with a 1935 run by English racer Sir
Malcolm Campbell that clocked in at
a stunning 276.82mph (445.49kmh).
The National Association of Stock Car
Auto Racing (NASCAR) was founded
here in 1947. In 1959 NASCAR president William "Big Bill" Henry Getty
France, once a beach stock-car driver,
opened the Daytona International
Speedway.

Motor city

These days NASCAR fans converge
on Daytona in early February for a
marathon of racing that culminates in
the annual **Daytona 500**. Motorcycles
take over several weeks later during
Bike Week, which – along with
Biketoberfest in October – is one of
the world's largest motorcycle events.
But Daytona offers plenty to entertain
racing enthusiasts any time of year.

Come into the city from I-95 along
International Speedway Boulevard and
the storied raceway looms large to the
right. At the adjacent visitor center, the

Daytona 500 Experience ❷ (1801 W.
International Speedway Blvd; tel: 386-
947-6800; www.daytona500experience.
com; daily 9am–7pm; charge) is an
interactive, multimedia attraction that
includes historical exhibits, simulation
rides, a pit-stop challenge, an IMAX
movie, and a trolley tour around the
speedway's steep banks.

Those with a low NASCAR toler-
ance will probably be satiated with a
walk around the extensive welcome
center and gift shop, but for a significant extra fee diehard fans can take

Main attractions
DAYTONA 500 EXPERIENCE
MAIN STREET PIER
MUSEUM OF ARTS AND SCIENCES
BULOW PLANTATION RUINS
  HISTORIC STATE PARK
ST AUGUSTINE
CASTILLO DE SAN MARCOS
FLAGLER COLLEGE
LIGHTNER MUSEUM
MUSEUM OF CONTEMPORARY ART
  JACKSONVILLE
NEPTUNE BEACH
AMELIA ISLAND

LEFT: Lightner Museum.
RIGHT: at the Colonial Spanish Quarter.

The Daytona 500 Experience features a 45 minute, 3-D IMAX movie about the race, cars, and drivers.

BELOW: originally powered by a kerosene lamp, the Ponce de León light could be seen 20 miles (32km) out to sea.

three laps around the track riding shotgun with a professional driver. If you haven't had enough, head over to the **Living Legends of Auto Racing Museum** Ⓑ (2400 S. Ridgewood Ave; tel: 386-763-4483; www.livinglegendsof autoracing.com; Mon–Sat 10am–5pm; free) for more racing memorabilia, vintage autos, and photos.

Spring Break, USA

Separated from the mainland by the Halifax River and reached via a series of high bridges, Daytona's famous beachfront is anchored by the historic **Main Street Pier** Ⓒ. At 1,000ft (305 meters), it's the longest pier on the East Coast, and while it's seen better days, it does boast fantastic panoramic views of the beachfront strip and the bright blue ocean from its observation tower and sky lift. Also at Main Street is the **Salute to Speed** exhibit of more than 30 granite plaques documenting the beach's racing heritage.

Nowadays the scene on the sands is less rowdy than its heyday as a spring-break destination for thousands of college students – many of whom have

moved on to places like Panama City and South Beach – but it's still festive, crammed with hot dog vendors and boogie-board rentals. Private cars are also allowed on certain strips of the beach, accessible (for a $3 fee) from designated ramps. But go easy on the gas pedal – the 10mph (16kph) speed limit is strictly enforced.

Beyond the beach

Daytona wasn't always full of fast cars and drunken students. Glimpses of quieter days can be found at the city's excellent **Museum of Arts and Sciences** Ⓓ (352 S. Nova Rd, State Route 5A; tel: 386-255-0285; www.moas. org; Mon–Sat 9am–5pm, Sun 11am–5pm; charge). Inside, the Center for Florida History tracks the story of the state's development from prehistory to modernity. The star of the exhibit – and a big hit with kids – is the 13ft (4 meter) -tall skeleton of a giant ground sloth. The largest and most complete ever discovered in North America, it was excavated in 1975 from a site known as the Daytona Bone Bed by a pair of amateur paleontologists.

Ponce Inlet

LIGHTHOUSE museum

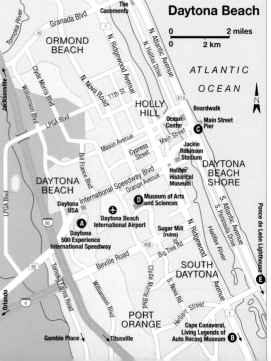

Daytona Beach

0   2 miles
0   2 km

Outside, an interpretive nature walk winds through the dense hardwood forest of pretty **Tuskawilla Park**.

A few miles south of the Daytona strip sits the meticulously restored **Ponce de León Lighthouse ❸** (4931 S. Peninsula Dr; tel: 386-761-1821; www.ponceinlet.org; daily 10am–6pm; charge). Completed in 1887, it is, at 175ft (53 meters), the tallest lighthouse in Florida, not to mention one of the best maintained in the country. The lighthouse keeper's residence and other outbuildings are full of exhibits on Daytona's maritime history and the development of lighthouse technology through the years.

Ormond Beach

As Route A1A North winds along the shore toward St Augustine it'll take you through the former "Millionaire's Colony" of **Ormond Beach ❷**, site of that legendary first time trial in 1903. Originally home to Timucuan Indians, the area was colonized by the British in the 18th century. Settlers established vast indigo and rice plantations such as the 20,000 acre (8,000 hectare) Mount

Oswald plantation, run by Scotsman Richard Oswald and now the site of **Tomoka State Park ❸**.

When Spain took control of Florida in the early 19th century, King Ferdinand offered land grants to planters living in the Bahamas. Ormond Beach is named for British sea captain James Ormond, who received a grant of 2,000 acres (800 hectares) to develop his plantation on the Halifax River. Other early settlers included Charles Bulow; the ruins of his vast plantation – destroyed in the Second Seminole Indian War – are preserved at **Bulow**

Packed sand at Daytona Beach is ideal for automobiles; driving on the beach (in designated areas only) is a long tradition.

BELOW: the Daytona 500 Experience captures the thrill of the race.

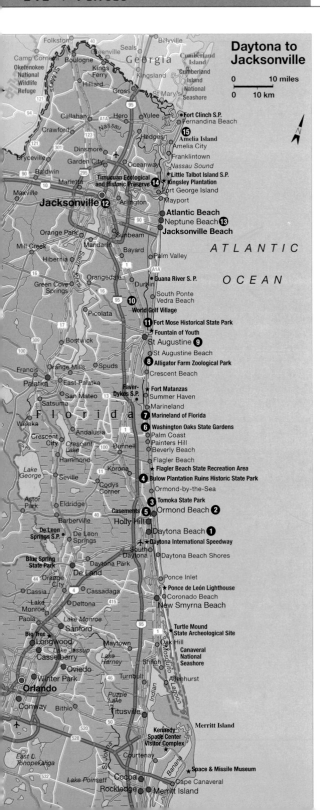

Daytona to Jacksonville

0   10 miles

0   10 km

Plantation Ruins Historic State Park
❹ (CR 2001; www.floridastateparks.org/
bulowplantation; Thur–Mon 9am–5pm;
charge) about 3 miles (5km) west of
Flagler Beach.

Henry Flagler extended the Florida
East Coast Railroad to Ormond Beach
in the late 1800s, and by the turn of the
last century the area was the summer
playground for wealthy society folk
with names like Astor and Vanderbilt,
who stayed at the posh Ormond Hotel.
Wealthy industrialists such as John D.
Rockefeller made Florida their winter
home. Rockefeller wintered for more
than 20 years in Ormond Beach, where
he was famous for his golf game and
passing out dimes to his neighbors.
When he died in 1937, at age 97, *The
New York Times* noted that "his spare
figure was a familiar sight" in the community. His home, the **Casements** ❺,
named for its many casement windows,
is now a museum and cultural center
(25 Riverside Dr; tel: 386-677-7005;
www.obht.org/casements.htm; guided tours
Mon–Sat, call for hours; charge).

Up the coast road

If you've got time en route to St
Augustine, take a detour just north
of Ormond Beach to drive **The Loop**
– a scenic 23 mile (37km) stretch
of road shaded by ancient live oaks
and curtains of Spanish moss. Take
Highbridge Road west from A1A, past
tranquil salt marshes full of herons
and egrets, to Walter Boardman Road,
then head south on the Old Dixie
Highway, which passes both Bulow
Plantation Ruins State Park and
Bulow Creek State Park – home of
the towering, 400-year-old Fairchild
Oak – before curving back toward
Ormond Beach.

Back on the road to St Augustine,
A1A passes through the quiet communities of **Flagler Beach**, **Painters Hill**,
and **Palm Coast**, home of **Washington
Oaks State Gardens** ❻ (6400 N.
Oceanshore Blvd; tel: 386-446-6780;
www.floridastateparks.org/washingtonoaks;
daily 8am–sunset; charge), notable for

its acres of formal gardens showcasing both indigenous and exotic flora.

Two miles (3km) north is **Marineland of Florida** ❼ (9600 Oceanshore Blvd; tel: 904-471-1111; www.marineland.net; daily 8.30am–4.30pm; charge), the world's first oceanarium. Originally built as an underwater film stage and research center, the aging facility has reopened as the home of a **Dolphin Conservation Center**, where kids and adults alike can interact and swim with 11 Atlantic bottlenose dolphins.

For yet another close encounter with Florida wildlife, stop just outside of St Augustine at the **Alligator Farm Zoological Park** ❽ (999 Anastasia Blvd; tel: 904-824-3337; www.alligator farm.com; daily 9am–5pm, extended summer hours; charge). Opened in 1893, it's home to scores of alligators and crocodiles and claims to have one of the largest bird rookeries in Florida.

St Augustine

Though Pensacola and Jacksonville can lay claim to European settlers before **St Augustine** ❾ was established in 1565, both earlier colonies quickly fell victim

to famine, plague, and war – making this pretty, historic city on Matanzas Bay the oldest continuously occupied settlement in the United States. First founded by the Spanish 42 years before the British staked a claim to Virginia's Jamestown, St Augustine endured thanks to a series of forts that helped the settlers defend against repeated attacks by Seminoles, pirates, and the British.

The last of these fortresses, **Castillo de San Marcos** ❻ (1 S. Castillo Dr; tel: 904-829-6506; www.nps.gov/casa; daily 8.45am–5.15pm; charge) still looms at

Castillo de San Marcos has stood guard over Matanzas Bay for more than three centuries.

BELOW: historic re-enactors prepare to fire a cannon from Castillo de San Marcos.

The Oldest Wooden Schoolhouse is one of dozens of historic structures in St Augustine's colonial district.

BELOW: a stained-glass panel in the Cathedral-Basilica of St Augustine depicts scenes from the life of the city's patron saint.

the edge of the bay. Built of coquina, a limestone made from bits of shell and coral that's indigenous to northern Florida, the Castillo withstood repeated bombardments thanks to the soft rock's unique ability to absorb cannon blasts. It was ceded to the British in 1763, returned to the Spanish in 1784, then turned over to the newly formed United States in 1821. It served as a Union prison (under the name Fort Marion) during the Civil War and was retired from active duty in 1901. Along with a reconstructed section of the defensive earthwork, the Castillo is now a national monument, the only extant 17th-century fort in the country.

St Augustine proudly celebrates its tempestuous history, noting that five flags have flown over the city: Spanish, British, Spanish again (under a new flag), Confederate, and US. Though there are many ways to explore the

town – including trolley, horse-drawn carriage, and a plethora of ghost-themed excursions – a walk through downtown may give the best sense of the scope of its heritage.

The old city

A short walk from the **Visitor Center** **G** at 10 S. Castillo Drive (www.ci.st-augustine.fl.us; daily 9am–5.30pm) takes you past the crumbling Huguenot Cemetery to the gate of the colonial district, a pedestrian-friendly strip of historically significant buildings and exhibits interspersed with shops selling everything from Spanish-inspired pottery to Thomas Kinkade paintings.

Just past the gate is the **Oldest Wooden Schoolhouse** **H** (14 St George St; tel: 888-653-7245; www.oldestwoodenschoolhouse.com; daily; charge), built in the early 18th century. Originally a bachelor's home, it was converted to a one-room school in 1788. Nearby is the **Colonial Spanish Quarter** **I** (53 St George St; tel: 904-825-6830; www.historicstaugustine.com/csq/history.html; daily 9am–5.30pm; charge), a living-history museum

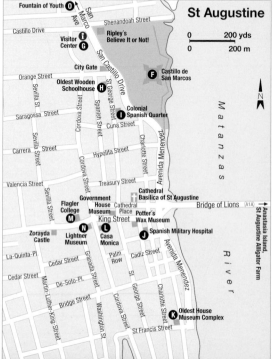

where costumed guides lead visitors through the daily life of a typical 18th-century Spanish colonial village. Down this street, the reconstructed **Spanish Military Hospital ❶** (3 Aviles St; tel: 904-827-0807; www.spanishmilitary hospital.com; Mon–Sat 10am–5pm, Sun noon–5pm; charge) gives a glimpse of the grimmer side of colonial life.

At the south end of the district, the **Oldest House Museum Complex ❶** (271 Charlotte St; tel: 904-824-2874; www.staugustinehistoricalsociety.org; daily 9am–5pm; charge), operated by the St Augustine Historical Society, includes Florida's oldest surviving dwelling from the Spanish colonial period. The site has been occupied since the 1600s, but the current structure dates to the early 1700s. It combines British, Spanish, and American architectural influences, with thick coquina walls on the first floor and a second floor made of wood. Inside are antique furnishings and exhibits detailing the workings of a colonial household. The complex includes several other buildings full of exhibits on the cultural and military history of St Augustine and the state of Florida, plus a traditional garden, an 18th-century detached kitchen, and a museum shop.

Henry Flagler's heyday

Head west up King Street to a trio of buildings built by railroad man Henry Flagler, a figure arguably as pivotal in Florida's development as the Spanish. All three were formerly luxury hotels, though only the crenellated **Casa Monica ❶** (95 Cordova St; tel: 904-827-1888; www.casa-monica.com), built in 1888, still serves in that capacity. The 400-room **Hotel Ponce de León**, a sparkling example of Spanish Renaissance architecture, is now the main residence hall for private **Flagler College ❶** (74 King St; tel: 904-829-6481; www.flagler.edu; charge for tour), a four-year liberal arts school with a student body of about 2,500. Only part of the building is open to the public.

St George Street leads through the heart of the historic district in St Augustine.

BELOW: Flagler College was formerly the Hotel Ponce de León.

Tiffany glass at the Lightner Museum.

Across the street, what was once the Hotel Alcazar is now the **Lightner Museum** ⓝ (75 King St; tel: 904-824-2874; www.lightnermuseum.org; daily 9am–5pm; charge). Chicago publisher Otto Lightner bought the building in 1946 to house his impressive and eclectic collection of Gilded Age ephemera, which includes everything from Tiffany glass and Art Nouveau furniture to mechanical musical instruments, needlework, buttons, and curiosities like a mummy and shrunken head. Be sure to check out the ceramic statuette of a newsboy in the stairs to the third-floor gallery: he's holding a copy of *Hobbies*, the magazine that made Lightner's fortune.

Heading north

On the edge of town, San Marco Avenue, the road leading back to I-95, is lined with antique shops and trolley-tour outfits. A garish sign points the way to the **Fountain of Youth** ⓞ (11 Magnolia Ave; tel: 904-829-3168; www.fountainofyouthflorida.com; daily 9am–5pm; charge) a 15 acre (6 hectare) archeological park on the site of the Timucuan village where Ponce de León first claimed Florida for the Spanish Crown. It's free to drink from the titular natural spring.

There's not a lot on the interstate between St Augustine and Jacksonville save for outlet malls and the **World Golf Village** ⓾, a golf resort encompassing two courses, the **World Golf Hall of Fame** (Mon–Sat 10am–6pm, Sun noon–6pm; charge), and an IMAX theater.

Back on Route A1A, about 2 miles (3km) north of the city lies the site of Gracia Real de Santa Theresa de Mose, better known as **Fort Mose** (pronounced *mo-say*), the first free community of former slaves in the United States. A century before the Emancipation Proclamation, enslaved African-Americans fleeing South Carolina plantations journeyed to this sanctuary where, if they pledged allegiance to the Spanish king and converted to Catholicism, they were guaranteed freedom. The fort had its own militia and served as the northernmost defense of St Augustine during the Revolutionary War. It was abandoned in 1763 and is now contained within **Fort Mose Historical State Park** ⓫ (15 Saratoga Blvd; tel: 904-823-2232; www.floridastateparks.org/fortmose; daily 8am–sunset).

Jacksonville

Sprawling across the St John's River, **Jacksonville** ⓬ is an odd hybrid. Neither a big tourist draw nor a center of industry, it is nonetheless Florida's most populous city and, thanks to its consolidated city-county government, the largest city in terms of sheer landmass in the United States. Founded in 1791 as Cowford – after the shallow, narrow part of the St John's across which farmers led cattle – it was later

BELOW: live oaks and Spanish moss form a canopy over a street near the Fountain of Youth.

renamed for Old Hickory himself, Andrew Jackson, then governor of the Florida territory.

An important port for both Union and Confederate forces during the Civil War, the little city emerged relatively unscathed from that conflict, only to be essentially destroyed on May 3, 1901. The Great Fire of that year started in a mattress factory and razed more than 2,000 buildings over 146 city blocks, as devastating in scope as the Great Chicago Fire 30 years earlier. Legend has it that the glow from the inferno could be seen from as far away as Savannah, Georgia. Still, the city rebuilt quickly, as architects and designers flocked to town to make their mark.

Ten years later it was a major naval and shipping hub, while the extension of rail lines to the area made it, like St Augustine and Ormond Beach, a popular resort destination for moneyed Northerners. Drawn by the mild climate, the nascent movie industry moved in as well; by 1916 Jacksonville had more than 30 studios, making it the winter film capital of

the world. It was also, perhaps most notably, a vital player in the development of an African-American film industry, thanks to directors like Richard Norman, whose Jacksonville-based Norman Studios produced a series of feature films depicting black characters as heroes and romantic leads at a time when parts for black actors were limited.

Like many American cities, Jacksonville suffered in the latter part of the 20th century as sprawl decentralized the civic core and investment

Colonial cannon are on display at the Fountain of Youth.

BELOW: World Golf Village.

Andrew Jackson was the first US governor of Florida and Jacksonville's namesake.

moved out of town. But today traffic over Jacksonville's magnificent bridges testifies to its continued vitality. The port remains a busy shipping center; a few miles north, at the mouth of the St John's, massive aircraft carriers and other vessels dock at the **Mayport Naval Station**, outside the fishing village of Mayport. Thanks to some aggressive urban planning, parts of a once-distressed downtown have been successfully refashioned as a tourist-friendly entertainment zone.

The rebirth of downtown

Jacksonville Landing, a pedestrian marketplace of shops, nightclubs, and restaurants on the north bank of the St John's, anchors the revitalized downtown. Nearby, at 128 Forsyth Street, is the lavish **Florida Theatre**. Designed in high Moorish style to resemble a starlit courtyard, it opened in 1927 as a luxury vaudeville and movie palace and is, perhaps most famously, the site of Elvis Presley's first-ever concert appearance. Extensively rehabbed in the 1980s, it's now a cornerstone of the downtown

arts renaissance; see www.floridatheatre. com for programming.

Also downtown are the **Museum of Science and History** (1025 Museum Circle; tel: 904-396-7062; www. themosh.org; Mon–Fri 10am–5pm, Sat 10am–6pm, Sun 1–6pm; charge), full of exhibits on Jacksonville's history and ecology, and the new **Museum of Contemporary Art Jacksonville** (333 N. Laura St; tel: 904-366-6911; www. mocajacksonville.org; Tue–Sat 10am–4pm, Wed until 9pm, Sun noon–4pm; charge). Originally founded in 1924, "MOCA Jax" moved to its new digs in the renovated Western Union Telegraph Building in 2003. Both the permanent collection and the changing exhibit galleries showcase a broad spectrum of work by contemporary artists.

The free "First Wednesday" art walk is another popular way to take the measure of the city's art scene. The self-guided gallery hop encompasses a range of venues in six downtown blocks and happens the first Wednesday of every month from 5pm to 9pm. You can pick up a map at Jacksonville Landing or MOCA Jax.

A few other attractions lie north of downtown. The **Jacksonville Zoo** (370 Zoo Pkwy; tel: 904-757-4463; www. jaxzoo.org; daily 9am–5pm; charge) reportedly has one of the largest exotic animal populations in the South, with everything from Florida box turtles to four massive African elephants. Nearby, the **Anheuser-Busch Brewery** (111 Busch Dr; tel: 904-696-8373, www. budweisertours.com; Mon–Sat 10am–4pm) offers free tours – and complimentary samples – to those interested in learning where their Budweiser comes from.

Into the neighborhoods

Across Main Street Bridge is the chic neighborhood of **San Marco**, whose business district was designed in the 1920s to mimic Venice's Piazza San Marco. At 1996 San Marco Boulevard, the Art Deco **San Marco Theatre** anchors an upscale commercial strip of boutiques, wine bars, cafés, and art galleries. Showing first-run movies and serving food and beer, it's a popular destination for young professionals and families.

Just southwest of downtown are genteel **Avondale** and **Riverside**, full of vintage 19th-century homes and soaring oaks and magnolias. One neighborhood landmark is the **Cummer Museum of Art and Gardens** (829 Riverside Ave; tel: 904-356-6857; www.cummer.org; Tue 10am–9pm, Wed–Sat 10am–5pm, Sun noon–5pm; charge). Inside, 13 galleries showcase traveling and permanent exhibits covering an 8,000-year span of art history. The Cummer is open late on Tuesdays, and admission is free from 4pm to 9pm. Behind the museum, beautiful formal gardens – one Italian, one English – slope down to the St John's River.

Tourists seeking more pop thrills may want to make a pilgrimage to Riverside's **Robert E. Lee High School**, whose strict former gym teacher, Leonard Skinner, unwittingly gave his name to Jacksonville's favorite

sons, the rock band Lynyrd Skynyrd, thanks to his habit of suspending the band members for having long hair. After the grave of front man Ronnie Van Zant was vandalized in 2000, his remains were moved and interred in the family plot in Riverside Memorial Park Cemetery.

Riverside's historic **Five Points** district offers a cluster of hip restaurants and funky shops around the intersection of Park, Lomax, and Margaret streets. The center of young, artsy

A marble archer takes aim in the gardens of the Cummer Museum of Art.

BELOW: the Cummer Museum of Art and its riverside gardens.

Cumberland Island

Just over the border in Georgia is
an island frozen in time, where
nature plays a dominant role and
wild horses roam the beach

Georgia's largest and southernmost barrier
island, Cumberland Island captures the
diversity of the coastal ecosystem in one
package. Sand dunes and an uninterrupted stretch
of beach line the eastern shore, where loggerhead
turtles creep ashore to lay their eggs. Inland are
quiet hardwood forests of oak and pine and freshwater ponds hospitable to gators; to the west, tidal
marshes, harbor fiddler crabs and myriad birds. It's
a peculiarly magical place, thanks to one simple
fact: though humans have inhabited the island
through the years, there have never been so many
as to significantly alter or endanger the natural
environment.

For centuries the island was a seasonal fishing
destination for Timucuan Indians. Later, Spanish
and then British settlers established military outposts. In the 18th century, Revolutionary War hero
General Nathanael Green bought land on the
island, and in time his widow and heirs built a mansion and named the estate Dungeness. By the mid-
19th century, the island supported 15 plantations
and small farms – and about 500 slaves.

Union troops held the island during the American
Civil War, but after emancipation, times were tough.
Farms failed and plantations shut down. Up on the
north end of the island, a small settlement was the
locus of a community of former slaves. The tiny,
rustic First African Baptist Church – best known as
the site of the 1996 wedding of John F. Kennedy,
Jr, and Carolyn Bessette – still stands today.

Then, in the late 19th century, industrialist Thomas
Carnegie, brother of Andrew, bought two defunct
plantations, including Dungeness, and built an
even grander home on the foundation of the old
mansion. Thomas died in 1886, but his wife, Lucy,
and their nine children remained on the vast estate,
eventually building several additional houses on
the island for the Carnegie daughters. With Vanderbilts and Duponts as their guests, they entertained
in high Gilded Age style.

When Lucy Carnegie died in 1916, her will dic-
tated that her horses be turned loose. Today about
200 wild horses, descendants of the Carnegie herd,
roam the island freely. Visitors probably won't get
close enough to see them, but they're often visible
by boat as they amble down a deserted beach.

In the 1970s, a Hilton Head developer endeav-
ored to turn land bought from the Carnegie heirs
into a resort, complete with marina and golf course.
Happily, those plans were abandoned, and most of
Cumberland Island is now preserved in perpetuity
as a National Seashore, though private citizens still
have rights to some tracts of land, which are held
in trust by the Park Service.

Island visitors are limited to 300 a day via a
$6-per-person twice-daily ferry from the village of
St Mary's, about an hour's drive from Jacksonville,
with an extra daily departure from the island
between March and October. Cars are forbidden to
all but Park Service personnel and permanent residents. The exclusive Greyfield Inn is the only lodging
on the island that doesn't require a tent. A day trip
allows for about four hours of sightseeing – enough
time to tour the otherworldly ruins of the Dungeness
estate and walk a loop through the salt marshes
and up the hard-packed beach of the Atlantic shore
before ducking back through the mossy forest to
the western shore and the ferry dock.   ❑

BELOW: a wild horse grazes at Dungeness.

Jacksonville, Five Points is a great area for a leisurely afternoon of window-shopping. Check out the eclectic offerings in the 1928 **Park Arcade Building**, one of Jacksonville's earliest commercial structures and once home to Florida's first indoor-outdoor miniature golf course.

Built in the 1920s as an exclusive subdivision, adjacent Avondale is a bit more upscale. On the central strip of St John's Avenue you'll find everything from Lilly Pulitzer boutiques to jazzy bistros. Side streets offer blocks of beautifully restored Mediterranean Revival homes and an array of welcoming parks. Much of Riverside/Avondale was designated a historic district in 1997.

Jacksonville's southernmost neighborhood of **Mandarin** has a fascinating history all its own thanks in large part to the influence of Harriet Beecher Stowe, who wintered in the small farming community from 1867 through 1884. Following the success of *Uncle Tom's Cabin*, Stowe owed her publisher another book. Rather than write a second novel, she lovingly documented the landscape and culture of northern Florida in *Palmetto-Leaves*. The collection of sketches about fishing on the St John's River and picnicking under live oaks laden with Spanish moss is considered some of the earliest (though unintentional) promotional writing about Florida and was instrumental in enticing tourists to the south. In 1872 Stowe helped found a racially integrated school in Mandarin; the building still stands today as home to the preservation-minded **Mandarin Community Club** at 12447 Mandarin Road. Across the street a plaque marks the site of the former Stowe cottage.

Powerboats and other pleasure craft are berthed at a Fernandina Beach marina.

BELOW LEFT: Fernandina Beach is a popular destination for charter fishing. **BELOW:** at American Beach.

A Beach of Their Own

In 1935, at the height of Jim Crow, African-Americans were forbidden to use Florida's beaches. So it was a monumental day when businessman Abraham Lincoln Lewis, president of the Afro-American Life Insurance Company, bought 200 acres (80 acres) of Amelia Island and founded American Beach, the country's first African-American resort.

In its heyday, middle-class black northerners traveled more than 1,000 miles (1,600km) through the segregated South to vacation on Amelia Island. Black families thronged to the beach on weekends, and jazz greats like Louis Armstrong and Cab Calloway drew packed crowds to the clubs. Ironically, the gains of the Civil Rights era took a toll on the community – black tourists finally had other options – but a determined core hung on and fought hard against encroaching development, refusing to sell to those who would turn the area into yet another golf course or gated community. Today only 120 acres (49 hectares) of the original 200 acres (80 hectares) remain, but its historic significance has finally been recognized. In 2002 American Beach was placed on the National Register of Historic Places.

A friendly tavern in Fernandina Beach.

BELOW: Amelia Island.

By the sea

The pretty shore communities of **Atlantic Beach** and **Neptune Beach** lie about 20 minutes due east of Jacksonville. While the white-sand beaches may not offer the hedonistic pleasures of Daytona, the sand iss softer, so no driving, and Jacksonville, lying north of Florida's tropical zone, actually has four seasons, so the water can be gray and choppy. But if all you want to do is soak in the sun, you should be fine most of the year.

Where Atlantic Avenue hits 1st Street and the beachfront, there's a strip of restaurants and shops. **Pete's Bar**, at 117 First Street, is a local landmark, popular for both the cheap beer and pool. Novelist John Grisham is a regular, and the watering hole features prominently in his novel *The Brethren*, set in and around Neptune Beach. A bit farther south, **Jacksonville Beach** offers a bikini-friendly strip of surf shops and bars popular with college students and others looking to party.

North to Amelia Island

Up A1A from Jacksonville's beaches are the resort communities of **Amelia Island** and **Fernandina Beach**. They're an easy day trip from downtown on the interstate or, if you're coming up the coast road, via the ferry from Mayport to Fort George Island. The brief crossing costs $5, and boats run every 30 minutes.

A half mile from the ferry dock is the **Kingsley Plantation** (11676 Palmetto Ave; tel: 904-251-3537; www.nps.gov/timu; daily 9am–5pm; charge) in the **Timucuan Ecological and Historic Preserve** ⓮, a 46,000 acre (18,600 hectare) expanse of woods and wetlands. Built in 1798, the plantation house is the oldest in the state. Merchant and planter Zephaniah Kingsley settled here in 1814 with his Senegalese wife, Anta Mdgingine Jia (or Anna, as she was known), whom he purchased as a slave in Cuba and consequently freed. Their vast estate produced cotton, indigo, and sugar

cane and was home to 80 enslaved Africans until 1837, when, faced with increasingly oppressive laws restricting the rights of persons of color, Kingsley moved his family and 50 freed slaves to Haiti. A self-guided tour of the restored grounds and buildings, which include both the large main house and the tiny slave quarters, offers a fascinating glimpse into an earlier way of life.

Seaside resorts

Just south of the Georgia border, A1A crosses the Intracoastal Waterway to beautiful **Amelia Island** ⓯, 32 miles (51km) northeast of Jacksonville. Amelia is famed as a posh escape for the wealthy, who congregate at the exclusive **Amelia Island Plantation Resort** and the lavish **Ritz-Carlton**. But the island has plenty to offer those outside the Forbes 500.

The quaint town of **Fernandina Beach**, on the island's northern tip, dates back to the 1850s. From the Victorian courthouse (now the post office) to the gracious frame homes bearing gingerbread balustrades, turrets, and gables, the town is a snapshot of another moment in time. In the late 19th century, Fernandina was a busy, affluent shipping port, and the state's first resort destination for the rich Yankees who later moved south to St Augustine, Ormond Beach, and beyond. A walking tour of the historic district's 40 blocks takes visitors past a fantastic array of Gothic, Queen Anne, and late Victorian architecture.

One building worth a particular look is the **Tabby House** at 27 S. Seventh Street. Made from a traditional cement mixture of crushed oyster shells called "tabby," the lacy, intricate Victorian home was designed by R.S. Schuyler and is now on the National Register of Historic Places.

The **Amelia Island Museum of History** (233 S. Third St; tel: 904-261-7378; www.ameliamuseum.org; Mon–Sat 10am–4pm, Sun 1–4pm; charge), housed in the former Nassau County jail, offers a quick and comprehensive overview of the area's evolution from Timucuan village to Spanish mission, Civil War port, and Victorian-era playground, and continues up to the modern day.

East of Fernandina Beach you'll find **Fort Clinch State Park** (2601 Atlantic Ave; tel: 904-277-7274; www.floridastateparks.org/fortclinch; daily 8am–sunset; charge). Construction of this fort at the mouth of the St Mary's River was begun in 1847 but was never completed. It served as a military post during the Civil War, the Spanish-American War, and World War I, and became one of the state's first parks in 1935.

Nowadays visitors can tour the remains of the barracks, preserved in their Civil War state, as well as hike, camp, and picnic on the dunes or along the freshwater ponds and salt marshes that provide a habitat for birds, turtles, alligators, and a multitude of other Florida wildlife. Across the sound you can see the heel of Georgia's Cumberland Island, a national seashore from top to toe. ❏

Leave room for a sumptuous dessert at the Amelia Island Plantation Resort.

BELOW: Segways are a fun and speedy way to explore Amelia Island Plantation.

RESTAURANTS

Restaurants

Prices for a three-course dinner per person, excluding tax, tip, and beverages:
$ = under $20
$$ = $20–45
$$$ = $45–60
$$$$ = over $60

Amelia Island

Ocean Grill
Amelia Island Plantation
6800 First Coast Hwy
Tel: 888-261-6161
$$$$
Expect high-end dining at Ocean Grill, an elegant resort restaurant with ocean views, an extensive wine list, and superior Continental cuisine. The shrimp and grits is served with chorizo and tetilla cheese, with stone-ground organic grits.

Atlantic Beach

Ragtime
207 Atlantic Blvd
Tel: 904-241-7877
$$
Finely crafted beers and Cajun-inspired seafood make this brewpub a busy – and relatively classy – spot on the beach strip. Gumbo and beignets are as good as you'll get in New Orleans; a children's menu features home-made root beer.

Fernandina Beach

La Bodega Courtyard Café
19 S. 3rd St
Tel: 904-321-1922
$$$
With wrought-iron fences and tinkling fountains, the romantic courtyard may be what draws you in, but the kitchen at this quaint Amelia Island spot delivers on the plate. The menu showcases contemporary Southern cuisine strong on fresh seafood and other local, seasonal ingredients. Reservations recommended.

Lulu's Bra and Grill
11B S. 7th St
Tel: 904-261-7123
$$
No, it's not a typo. This casual, Latin-inspired café tucked away off Centre Street works its whimsical theme to the hilt with walls decorated with ladies' undergarments. Pressed sandwiches, including a savory Cuban, and creative entrées like crab cakes with key lime mustard sauce make it a local fave.

Jacksonville

Al's Pizza
1620 Margaret St
Tel: 904-388-8384
$
With five locations in town and at the beach, this local minichain has a lock on ultra-casual dining. Pizzas are fresh and ample and available with "New York-style" thin- and Sicilian thick-crusts.

BB's
1019 Hendricks Ave
Tel: 904-306-0100
$$
Popular with both business lunchers and soccer moms, this casually modern sibling of Biscotti's (see below) offers a range of globally inspired bistro fare from fried calamari and wood-oven pizzas to prosciutto-wrapped pork chops.

Biscotti's
3556 St John's Ave
Tel: 904-387-2060
$$–$$$
A regular on "Best of Jacksonville" lists, this much-loved Avondale institution offers consistently excellent café fare and creative daily dinner specials, not to mention some of the city's best cheese grits. Ask for a tour of the cake case.

Bistro Aix
1440 San Marco Blvd
Tel: 904-398-1949
$$$
The night-out destination of choice for hip Jacksonville, this laid-back French-Mediterranean spot in chic San Marco dishes up sophisticated seasonal dishes like fork-tender organic short ribs and a devastating penne spiked with spicy sausage and goat cheese. The primo wine list has many pours available by the glass and half-bottle.

The Brick
3585 St John's Ave
Tel: 904-387-0606
$$–$$$
This spacious and airy eatery on Avondale's historic St John's Avenue is a reliable choice for Kobe beef burgers or a French dip, but it's even more popular as a nightspot. There's live jazz nightly and the bar is usually buzzing.

Clark's Fish Camp
12909 Hood Landing Rd
Tel: 904-268-3474
$$
A kitschy local institution, this ramshackle former bait shop is as famous for its amazing collection of taxidermy as for its epic

range of seafood. Daring diners go for the "Swamp Fest" platter, which includes fried bites of gator tail, soft shell crab, frog legs, conch, catfish, and squid.

The Fox
3580 St John's Ave
Tel: 904-387-2669
$
Hipster owned and operated, this vintage Avondale diner is wildly popular for weekend brunch. Waffles and French toast are some of the best in town; late risers can tuck into lunch specials like home-made meatloaf and chicken potpie.

Mossfire Grill
1537 Margaret St
Tel: 904-355-4434
$$
Named for the blaze that devastated the city in 1901, popular Mossfire offers a mash-up of contemporary American and Southwestern flavors – fish tacos, giant burritos, and an excellent shrimp quesadilla doused with red chili vinaigrette. Go off menu and try the gut-busting Texas Pete cheese fries if you dare.

Neptune Beach

Mezza Luna Ristorante
110 First St
Tel: 904-249-5573
$$$
No peel-and-eat-shrimp here: casually upscale Mezza Luna has been dishing up Mediterranean-inspired dishes like ahi tuna tartare and savory wood-fired pizzas for more than 20 years.

Pete's Bar
117 First St
Tel: 904-249-9158
A local landmark since 1933, Pete's lays claim to the first liquor license in Duval County. Rowdy and grimy, the beachfront dive features 25-cent pool and ice-cold Pabst and is a favorite haunt of novelist John Grisham.

Sliders Seafood Grille
218 First St
Tel: 904-246-0881
$$
Seafood fresh off the boat and prepared to order is the signature at this casual, dog- and kid-friendly spot near the beach. Thursday happy hour specials knock fresh shucked oysters even further down from an already ridiculously low price.

Ormond by the Sea

Betty's AIA Café
1900 Oceanshore Blvd
Tel: 386-441-8131
$
This friendly diner just north of Daytona on Route AIA offers all the standards, and has specials like meatloaf and gravy, and an unparalleled parking-lot view of the ocean.

St Augustine

Cap's on the Water
4325 Myrtle St
Tel: 904-824-8794
$$–$$$
With an award-winning wine list, a raw bar, and a menu of creative but classic seafood, Cap's is a textbook example of rustic Florida elegance. The deck, shaded by massive live oaks, offers sunset views of the Intracoastal Waterway. Kids, dogs, and boaters are welcome.

Columbia
98 St George St
Tel: 904-824-3341
$$$
In the heart of St Augustine's historic district, Columbia's gracious courtyard and dining rooms ooze old-world Spanish charm. The menu is laden with Iberian classics, from tapas and sherry to three takes on paella, the house specialty. Reservations recommended.

Mi Casa Café
69 St George St
Tel: 904-824-9317
$–$$
A laid-back spot in the historic district for beer and a bite. The menu has a few Spanish and vegetarian dishes. The shady patio is perfect for a mid-day break. There's live music Sat–Sun.

Mill Top Tavern and Listening Room
19½ St George St
Tel: 904-829-2329
$–$$
Head up above the working water wheel of this rustic former gristmill to the breezy deck overlooking the Castillo de San Marcos. The menu is basic coastal pub grub, but try the Mill Top Special: one pound of shrimp, 15 barbecued wings, and all the fixings. There's live folk music nightly.

Outback Crab Shack
8255 CR 13 North
Tel: 904-522-0500
$$
The sign says it all: "No shirt, no shoes, no problem." For $55 you can dine family-style from a heaping platter of boiled or fried sea critters; $40 nets you 5lbs (2kg) of crawfish boil. Boaters welcome.

Wilbur by the Sea

Boon Docks
3948 S. Peninsula Dr
Tel: 386-760-9001 **$**
This place is so casual they forgot the walls. The cabana-esque Boon Docks – perched above a marina on the Halifax River – is a local favorite for ultrafresh fish and seafood prepared simply and well.

LEFT: a bartender at Mi Casa pours a long tall beer.
RIGHT: a tasty entrée at the Ocean Grill, Amelia Island.

CENTRAL FLORIDA

Theme parks are the order of the day, but there are
also gardens, museums, and even a few nature
preserves where you can escape the crowds

The lake-studded, river-creased terrain of Central Florida
has long lured tourists seeking an escape from reality.
Initially they came to walk in gardens hung with
Spanish moss and brimming with flowers, gaze at tropical
fish through crystalline spring water, and encounter
birds, alligators, and other exotic wildlife. Then a famous
mouse set up shop in the neighborhood. The resulting
expansion of tourist attractions was unmatched in volume
and variety and, despite the stunning white sands and
aquamarine waters of the coast, visitors headed inland
in droves. They flocked to Central Florida to experience
self-contained pleasure domes that use technology
to tease and tantalize the senses. Simple pleasures
like fishing, swimming, and lazing in the sun have
been elbowed aside by hi-tech engineers who can
resurrect long-dead presidents and animal trainers
who teach killer whales to play basketball.

Inevitably, Walt Disney World Resort remains
king of Central Florida's theme parks and thus
merits a whole chapter to itself, beginning with
a little background information and progressing
through attraction-packed accounts of each of the
Disney theme lands. The other major theme parks –
Universal Orlando, SeaWorld, Wet 'n' Wild, Cypress
Gardens, and other more modest (though, in some
cases, no less endearing) attractions – are covered in their own chapter.

Orlando is a thriving modern city with more hotel rooms than Miami
Beach. Examples of Art Deco and Belle Epoque architecture survive among
the high-rises and shopping centers, and suburban, well-off Winter Park
is a pleasant place in which to touch base with reality. Art museums have
sprung up, too, which just goes to show that Orlando can appeal to those
interested in both high and low culture. ❑

PRECEDING PAGES: Dueling Dragons are twin roller-coasters at Universal's Islands
of Adventure. **LEFT:** at the Hard Rock Cafe. **TOP:** a SeaWorld orca show. **ABOVE**
RIGHT: Seuss Landing at Islands of Adventure is modeled after the colorful, lopsided
worlds imagined by beloved children's book author Theodor Seuss Geisel.

WALT DISNEY WORLD RESORT

Fantasy continues to thrive at this unique resort, just as Walt imagined. Disney World remains a magnet for millions of starry-eyed visitors, both young and old

I f you're under the impression that Walt Disney World Resort ❶ (www.disneyworld.com) is nothing but an overgrown amusement park, think again. Situated off Interstate 4 about 16 miles (26km) from downtown Orlando, Disney World is a city in its own right. Encompassed within its 47 sq miles (111 sq km) – an area twice the size of Manhattan – are four of the most elaborate theme parks ever constructed, as well as two water parks, two night-time entertainment districts, five golf courses, three spas, a sports complex, 16 hotels, and more than 100 restaurants.

Disney World has its own police force, fire and sanitation departments, power plant, and water treatment facility, and an average daily population of more than 110,000 people. It even has quasi-governmental status, thanks to a deal Walt Disney and brother Roy cut with the state of Florida creating the Reedy Creek Improvement District, a public corporation that gives the Disney company powers that are usually reserved to municipalities, such as issuing bonds, levying taxes, and establishing building codes. It can even build an airport or a nuclear reactor, if the need arises.

The motivation behind Disney World's expansiveness is to provide

an all-in-one vacation experience that induces visitors to stay longer and spend more. Indeed, many people find that one visit isn't nearly enough; they return year after year, with or without children, and never feel as if they've run out of things to do.

Survival strategies

For the uninitiated, visiting Disney World can be a bewildering experience; the happiest place on Earth takes on a very different aspect when you're waiting in line, sweat trickling down

Main attractions
MAIN STREET, USA
PIRATES OF THE CARIBBEAN
SPACE MOUNTAIN
MISSION: SPACE
WORLD SHOWCASE
HOLLYWOOD STUDIOS
KILIMANJARO SAFARIS
EXPEDITION EVEREST
BOARDWALK
TYPHOON LAGOON

LEFT: Epcot by night. **RIGHT:** Mickey and Minnie at the Magic Kingdom.

Walt Disney World

Universal Studios

Buena Vista Lake

HAWK'S LANDING GOLF CLUB ★

Marriott Orlando World Center ★

International Drive South

Central Florida Greeneway

535

Buena Vista Drive

Saratoga Springs Resort & Spa ★

Buena Vista Lagoon

DOWNTOWN DISNEY P 6

P

Buena Vista Drive

Disney's Typhoon Lagoon ★ 7

Bonnet Creek

Epcot Center Drive

536

Gaylord Palms Resort & Convention Center ★

4

Tampa

Lake Buena Vista

LAKE BUENA VISTA GOLF COURSE

Old Key West Resort ★

Port Orleans French Quarter ★

Port Orleans-Riverside ★

Vista Boulevard

Bonnet Creek Road

Epcot Center Drive

Caribbean Beach ★

Pop Century ★

Buena Vista Drive

Disney's Wide World of Sports

EAGLE PINES GOLF COURSE

Disney's Fort Wilderness Resort & Campground ★

Vista Boulevard

P

Epcot 3

World Showcase Lagoon

Epcot Main Entrance/ Toll Plaza

Walt Disney World 1

Disney's Hollywood Studios Main Entrance/ Toll Plaza

Osceola Parkway

Beach Club Villas ★

BoardWalk Resort & Villas ★

Yacht and Beach Club ★

Dolphin Hotel ★

Swan Hotel ★

Disney's Hollywood Studios 4

P

Magic Kingdom Main Entrance/ Toll Plaza

Monorail

World Drive

All-Star Music Resort, All-Star Movies Resort

West Buena Vista Drive

Coronado Springs Resort ★

P

Disney's Blizzard Beach 8

All-Star Sports Resort ★

Walt Disney World

Bay Lake

Discovery Island

Wilderness Lodge & Villas ★

Contemporary Resort ★

at same scale

Ticket and Transportation Center P

Magic Kingdom 2

Grand Floridian Resort & Spa ★

Seven Seas Lagoon

Polynesian Resort ★

Shades of Green ★

MAGNOLIA GOLF COURSE

World Drive

1 mile

1 km

0

0

Disney's Animal Kingdom 5

Animal Kingdom Main Entrance/ Toll Plaza P

Disney's Animal Kingdom Resort ★

US Highway 27

N

your back, and your kids – exhausted from a day of overly ambitious touring – are whining like police sirens.

How do you prevent your dream vacation from degenerating into a nightmare? The first thing you need to know is that Disney World is not the kind of place that rewards spontaneity. Planning is essential, and reservations – for hotels, rental cars, and restaurants – are a must.

Timing is equally important. The two biggest gripes tourists have about Disney World are the crowds and the prices. You can minimize both by traveling off-season, when the theme parks aren't quite so mobbed and hotels and airlines offer sizable discounts. Time of day is a consideration, too. In general, attendance at the theme parks peaks between the hours of 10am and 4pm. The best strategy, therefore, is to arrive as early as possible, take a break in the afternoon for shopping and a sit-down meal (or, if you're staying at an on-site resort, sneak back to your hotel for a snooze and a swim), then pick up the trail in the late afternoon or evening.

Keep in mind that the gates at Disney World sometimes open 30 to 60 minutes earlier than the scheduled times (for guests who stay at Disney hotels). Granted, dragging yourself out of bed at 7am to get to the parks by 8am is hardly appealing, but you can often do more in the first couple of hours, when lines are short, temperatures are milder, and you're feeling fresh, than in the remainder of the day.

Attitude is a key element, too. Resist the temptation to be too ambitious. The tendency among most visitors is to squeeze as much as possible into the shortest period of time. This seems like sound economics: you paid a bundle to get in and now you want your money's worth. But before committing yourself to an elaborate touring plan, consider the hazards of trying to do too much. Unrealistic expectations will lead only to disappointment and exhaustion. Don't try to do everything in one day, pick three or four attractions must-see each day and fill in with other experiences if time allows.

TIP

FastPass allows guests to avoid long lines at some of Disney World's most popular attractions. Insert your ticket in a FastPass turnstile, get a ride time, and return later with little or no waiting. Be aware the FastPass system may only allow you to have one FastPass ticket at a time. It also may not allow you to collect another FastPass ticket until the first one has been redeemed or the time frame has expired.

BELOW: costumed characters roam the park greeting guests.

Behind the Scenes

If you're curious about those secret corridors under the Magic Kingdom, want to learn about the art and history of Disney animation, or yearn to swim with the fish in Epcot's Living Seas aquarium, sign up for one of the resort's Behind the Scenes tours, which grants you special access.

There are over 20 tours guided by enthusiastic cast members or experts. Among the most popular are the five-hour Keys to the Kingdom tour, limited to the Magic Kingdom; Backstage Magic, a day-long excursion through the Magic Kingdom, Disney-MGM Studios, and Epcot; Wild by Design, which traces the planning and development of Animal Kingdom; Gardens of the World, which studies plants at Epcot's World Showcase; Disney's Architecture looks at how Disney "imagineers" design and construct the parks' whimsical buildings; and Backstage Safari, which includes a visit to a wildlife housing area and veterinary hospital at Animal Kingdom. Most tours require participants to be at least 16 years old; however, Disney's Family Magic, a two-hour interactive exploration of the Magic Kingdom, is open to all ages.

Tours vary in price, frequency, and duration. Some require the purchase of separate park admission, and those lasting more than four hours can include lunch. All require an advance reservation. For information, call 407-939-8687.

BELOW: a young visitor gets his face painted.

Magic Kingdom

The **Magic Kingdom ❷** (tel: 407-824-4321; daily, hours vary, see www. disneyworld.disney.go.com; charge) is Disney World's oldest park and the one closest to Walt's original vision of a "timeless land of enchantment." Over the years some attractions have changed or been updated, but this is, and always has been, a children's park. Painstaking detail, good humor, and whimsy with which Walt's vision is brought to life rarely disappoint even the most jaded traveler.

Main Street

Setting the stage at the entrance to the park is **Main Street, USA**, a picture-perfect evocation of an American town. Although there are no rides or shows here, there are more than a dozen shops and restaurants as well as a fleet of dou-ble-decker buses, horse-drawn trolleys, and old-fashioned fire trucks. The **City Hall** to the left has maps and informa-tion and can book meals. It also con-tains the park's Lost and Found office. At the top of Main Street, housed in a stately Victorian-style building near the

entrance, is the **Walt Disney World Railroad**, which takes passengers on a 20-minute circuit around the park in vintage steam engines. To the right of the main entrance is the tucked-away **Town Square Exposition Hall**. When not being used for conventions or presentations, the auditorium shows continuous reels of classic Disney films. This quiet and cool retreat on the fringes of the park is almost always less crowded than the main sights.

Otherwise, Main Street is meant to be explored. In addition to the highly decorated souvenir shops there are such gems as the barber's shop with a barbershop quartet and the **Main Street Watchmaker**, which sells time-pieces featuring Disney characters. Main Street leads to a roundabout known as the Hub, beyond which is **Cinderella's Castle**, the visual anchor of the park and a Disney icon second only to Mickey himself; the Forecourt Stage is home to **Dream Along with Mickey**, an energetic and entertaining live show. Pathways radiate from this central plaza into five distinct zones, starting on the left

(as you face Cinderella Castle) with **Adventureland**, a mélange of fantasy architecture and lush plantings meant to evoke exotic locales such as the South Seas and the Amazon. The attractions here are a mixed bag. **Pirates of the Caribbean** is the best of the lot – an audio-animatronic romp through the Spanish Main with rum-swilling buccaneers and lots of yo-ho-ho high spirits. This ride was recently updated to include Johnny Depp's character from the movie of the same name, which in a meta-twist was based on the original ride at Disney Land in California.

The other attractions in Adventureland serve to entertain kids with time to spare. These include the **Magic Carpets of Aladdin**, a basic hub-and-spoke ride; the **Swiss Family Treehouse**, a free play area based on the Robinsons' fictional home; **The Enchanted Tiki Room**, a short show featuring animatronic birds (which provides a chance to cool off); and **Jungle Cruise**, a 10-minute boat ride featuring animatronic animals and a hokey narration. Check them out if

lines are short; otherwise, stroll over to Frontierland, where the theme is the Old West and the rides are more interesting.

Naps are frequently needed after a busy day at the parks.

Frontier fantasy

The two biggies at **Frontierland** are **Splash Mountain** and **Big Thunder Mountain Railroad**. The first is a log flume ride with a *Song of the South* theme and a drenching, five-story finale – enough to elicit screams without inducing real terror. The other is a roller-coaster in an elaborate red-rock setting. Scenes of ramshackle mining camps whiz by as your runaway train

BELOW: Cinderella appears in Cinderellabration, a live stage show at the Magic Kingdom.

Arriving at the Magic Kingdom

If you are not staying at a Disney Resort, allow plenty of time to get to and from your car to the Magic Kingdom's entrance. Parking lot trams will drop you off at the Ticket and Transportation Center, where you can buy your ticket and then board a boat or the monorail to reach the main entrance. From here you must join the other people who have been directly deposited from their Disney Resort transportation. Other Disney parks operate similarly with trams delivering you from the parking lot, more or less, to the park's main entrance. Visitors staying with Disney enjoy an advantage as their transportation (monorail, bus, or boat) will bring them to the park's entrance from the front of their lodging.

careens through canyons and caverns and over rickety bridges. Though this is hardly a kiddie ride, it's a piece of cake compared to the big coasters at other Orlando parks.

Opposite Big Thunder Mountain you can hitch a ride on one of the rafts that crosses the so-called Rivers of America (actually a circular lagoon) to **Tom Sawyer Island**, a refreshingly low-tech attraction where kids explore caves, trails, and a pioneer fort under their own steam. Best of all, mom and dad can enjoy a cool glass of lemonade on the porch of **Aunt Polly's Dockside Inn**, an out-of-the-way spot for sandwiches, ice cream, and cold drinks.

Another big attraction in Frontierland is the **Country Bear Jamboree** – a 16-minute hillbilly revue starring a cast of animatronic bears. Though it's been a crowd-pleaser for nearly three decades, the cornball humor isn't everybody's cup of tea.

The Wild West melds into colonial America in **Liberty Square**. The most popular attraction here – and perhaps the best in the park – is the **Haunted Mansion**. Visitors board a "doom buggy" for a tour of the house, visiting a library full of "ghost writers," a haunted ballroom and, in a clever bit of "astral projection," an apparition that appears in your car. The holographic effects – cutting edge when the ride opened some 25 years ago – hold up pretty well. On the opposite side of Liberty Square, the **Hall of Presidents** is an animatronic show with a true-blue American theme. The high point is a roll call of all US presidents, followed by remarks by the current president and Abraham Lincoln. If you're looking for a quick way to rest your feet, head over to the Liberty Square Riverboat, a vintage Victorian steamboat that tours the Rivers of America.

For the youngest

Fantasyland is intended for the pre-school crowd. Kiddie rides such as **Dumbo the Flying Elephant** and **Cinderella's Golden Carousel** will be familiar to anyone who has been to a county fair, although Disney dresses them up beautifully. Dark rides like

BELOW: a crowd gathers for a parade down Main Street.

Snow White's Scary Adventures recap Disney's most memorable films and songs.

Notable, too, is the **Mad Tea Party** – what folks in the amusement-park biz call a "spin-and-barf" ride – which whirls you around in a teacup mounted on whirling discs. And then there's **It's a Small World**, the ride that Disney critics love to hate, featuring scores of animatronic dolls in folksy costumes singing a chirpy melody. Love it or hate it, you can't say you've experienced the Magic Kingdom without riding it at least once. Across from here are two of Fantasyland's finest children's attractions. **Peter Pan's Flight** is a fantastic dark ride over the streets of London to Neverland. Your pirate ship flies past key scenes from the classic Disney film before touching down. **Mickey's PhilharMagic** plays on vintage films, incorporating countless songs and characters into a so-called 4-D movie aimed at young children. Meanwhile, **The Many Adventures of Winnie the Pooh** is a ride that is worth no one's time, as it feels in every way a poor imitation of the slow, child-friendly rides Disney normally does so well. Quieter times are to be had at the **Fairytale Garden** between Cinderella's Castle and the entrance to Tomorrowland, where Belle from *Beauty and the Beast* tells stories; at **Ariel's Grotto**, home of the Little Mermaid; and at **Pooh's Playful Spot**, a playground for younger children.

Tomorrow's world

Wrap up your visit to the Magic Kingdom at **Tomorrowland**, a confection of chrome-and-neon architecture inspired by such disparate sources as H.G. Wells and Fritz Lang's *Metropolis*. **Space Mountain** is an indoor roller-coaster replete with whiz-bang visual effects, including scary stretches of inky darkness. The ride is bumpy enough to rattle your innards without the looping of the mega-coasters at other parks. **Buzz Lightyear's Space Ranger Spin** is fun, too – a cross between a dark ride and a shooting arcade that lets you zap aliens with a laser gun while being whisked around an indoor track. If you arrive at Tomorrowland from Fantasyland you will pass the noisy **Tomorrowland Indy Speedway**, a souped-up go-kart

TIP

The FastPasses for Space Mountain run out by midday, so get one early if you plan to ride it at all.

BELOW: Main Street was inspired by Walt Disney's boyhood hometown in Missouri.

How to Cut in Line, the Official Way

The biggest gripe people have about theme parks is the long lines. Both Disney and Universal have heard your grumbles and now offer programs that greatly reduce the amount of time you'll spend staring at the back of another person's head. The FastPass system allows you to collect a timed ticket for Disney's most popular attractions. As the day goes on, the time between ticket issue and your redemption window continues to grow. Some rides may run out of FastPass tickets before lunchtime.

You are allowed to hold two "waiting" FastPasses at any time so long as they are for different rides. For the big thrill rides, Single Rider lines offer a wait nearly as short as the FastPass system, but your party will be split up.

Walt Disney and his most famous creation are commemorated near Cinderella's Castle in the Magic Kingdom.

BELOW: small bronze statues of classic Disney characters are arranged around the Magic Kingdom's center.

track that takes many of the controls out of the drivers' hands.

At **Walt Disney's Carousel of Progress**, the audience sits in a rotating theater that chronicles the way technology has changed the lives of an animatronic family. Old folks seem to enjoy the show. Teens and young adults find it a snooze.

Hop aboard the **Astro Orbiter** and soar high above Tomorrowland. Afterward enjoy a relaxing ride on the **Tomorrowland Transit Authority People Mover**. This ten-minute eco-friendly tour guides you through Tomorrowland attractions including getting a look inside Space Mountain. **Stitch's Great Escape** features the mischievous alien getting loose and treating the audience to some special sights, sounds, and smells.

Parades and fireworks

No journey to the Magic Kingdom is complete without taking in one of the star-studded parades or seeing the night-time fireworks display. The **A Dream Come True Parade** (afternoons daily) is the lesser of the Magic Kingdom's two parades but still brings the park to a standstill and is a big hit with young children who can't get enough of waving at famous characters. This parade is not worth planning for; in fact, if you have teens this would be the perfect time to take advantage of short waiting times and take a couple of spins on Space Mountain. **SpectroMagic** (most evenings) is well worth planning for, especially as it is always followed by **Wishes**, the park's fireworks show. In addition to standard-issue characters and music, this show employs spectacular lighting technology on the floats – the Magic Kingdom is even plunged into darkness to heighten its effect. If you are planning to see Wishes afterwards, stay on the right side of the hub facing Cinderella's Castle before the parade starts. This provides excellent viewing for both the parade and the fireworks. Wishes (most evenings) is one of the most spectacular fireworks displays you are likely ever to see, and the choreography of live action, music, and explosions is flawless – even Disney cynics are likely to be converted by

Disney's Hometown

Epcot was originally conceived by Walt Disney as an experiment in urban planning – an Experimental Prototype Community Of Tomorrow inhabited by real citizens. His father had helped build an exhibit at the 1893 World Columbian Exposition in Chicago, and Disney himself had been a longtime advocate of inner urban planning and city beautification projects. The plan was abandoned after Walt's death in favor of an unimaginative "world's fair," but the dream wasn't permanently forgotten. It was resurrected in 1994 in the form of Celebration, a town designed from the ground up by Disney "imagineers."

Now with 11,000 residents, the town has the manicured, spotless look of a theme park, featuring houses designed by some of the world's most notable architects. Despite Celebration's commercial success, the experiment hasn't all been smooth sailing. Some residents chafed at the restrictive bylaws, and the school's progressive agenda provoked the wrath of parents and county supervisors.

So, is Disney's experiment in "new urbanism" a success? You can judge for yourself. Celebration is 5 miles (8km) south of Disney World near the intersection of US 192 and I-4. Special events include a Great American Pie Festival in February, a Beach and Seafood Festival in April, and vintage car shows in March and September. For information, call 407-566-1200.

the finale. To get the full effect you must have a clear view of the front of Cinderella's Castle. This makes the hub and the Plaza Restaurant very popular as showtime approaches.

Epcot

Opened in 1982, Disney World's second theme park, Epcot ❸ (daily, see www.disneyworld.com for details), is modeled loosely on a World's Fair. The park is laid out in two circular areas. The first, **Future World**, anchored by the monumental silver golf ball called **Spaceship Earth**, is devoted to science and technology. Its attractions are housed in pavilions that contain rides, shows, and exhibitions sponsored by big corporations. Inside Spaceship Earth, for example, is a dark ride sponsored by AT&T that transports passengers through a series of animatronic tableaux chronicling the history of communications from the Stone Age to the Space Age.

To the left of Spaceship Earth (in the outer ring of World Showcase) is **Universe of Energy**, sponsored by ExxonMobil. The main attraction here, a combination film and dark ride called **Ellen's Energy Adventure**, is a comedic take on the issue of energy use. Plodding and poorly scripted, the show isn't worth seeing on your first visit.

Another pavilion houses Epcot's most thrilling ride. Dubbed **Mission: SPACE**, it delivers an astronaut-like experience, simulating a rocket lift-off and the weightlessness of space. Disney hired NASA consultants to design the ride. It's so realistic that barf bags are available. A tamer version is available for those not wanting to experience the G-force of take-off.

Next is **Test Track**, by General Motors, featuring six-person vehicles that undergo a series of tests – acceleration, road handling, suspension, crash – that simulate the course at a GM proving ground. From Test Track, it's a short walk to **Innoventions**, a pair of low-slung buildings that bracket Future World's central plaza. This is an exposition of new products developed by companies like Motorola and IBM. A perennial favorite is a section devoted to Sega's latest video games. One problem: the coolest gizmos are

KIDS

Children can make masks and kites and other craft projects at Kidcot Fun Spots. There's one at each country in the World Showcase.

BELOW: Spaceship Earth looms over the entrance to Epcot.

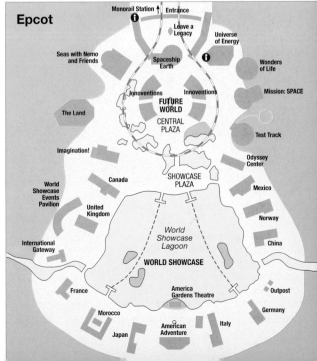

Epcot

Ice-cream stands and other food vendors are situated throughout the parks.

manatees have their own tanks, where visitors can get a close-up view.

Life and land

The strongest environmental message in the whole park is sponsored by Nestlé and found inside **The Land** pavilion. The **Circle of Life** features characters from *The Lion King* who are persuaded by Simba to stop the needless destruction of their native habitat for a useless holiday resort (a paradoxical sentiment for Disney to endorse by anyone's standards). **Living with the Land** is a slow boat ride through different exhibits about agricultural production. You will see many of the crops grown here on the menu at the Garden Grill.

One unqualified success in The Land is **Soarin'**, a hang-gliding simulator that takes you over various sights of outstanding beauty in California.

The big draw over at the **Imagination!** pavilion is a 3-D movie, **Captain EO**, which is an entertaining musical starring Michael Jackson and a cast of interstellar characters. The dark ride in this pavilion, called **Journey**

often monopolized by kids who have little patience for slow-moving adults.

On the opposite flank of Future World is a trio of pavilions, each worth a visit given enough time. **The Seas with Nemo & Friends** takes you down under in your ride vehicle – a clam mobile – and afterward you can join in **Turtle Talk with Crush**. The centerpiece is a saltwater aquarium containing an artificial coral reef with tropical fish, sharks, sea turtles, and an occasional scuba diver. Dolphins and

into Your Imagination with **Figment**, is one of Epcot's misfires; skip it.

World Showcase

Some children may consider World Showcase – a quick tour through 11 nations of the world – a bore, but most adults, at least those who like to shop, eat, or drink, will find it interesting. Each pavilion gives you the chance to experience a nation's consumables without actually visiting the country. As this half of Epcot usually stays open later than Future World, a couple could easily make a romantic, if early, night of it. In some ways it's better than Downtown Disney, as the food is more varied and the atmosphere, especially at night, is less hectic.

Top of the romantic destination list would be **Mexico's** dimly lit **San Angel Inn Restaurante**, set under a re-created Mayan temple. The only ride in Mexico is the **Gran Fiesta Tour Starring the Three Caballeros**, a poor dark ride featuring Donald Duck touring various Mexican landscapes. The land of the Vikings is retold in **Maelstrom**, a slow boat ride with unexpected turns

and drops that finishes with a short film about the Norwegian way of life. The main features of **Norway** are a re-created stave church and a Norwegian castle that houses the **Akershus Royal Banquet Hall**.

China features one of the best shops in World Showcase, a fine restaurant in the **Nine Dragons**, and an enjoyable Circle-Vision (the screen wraps completely around the audience) film called **Reflections of China**. Set in a re-created temple, it takes you from the Great Wall of China to Hong Kong and shows some of the most remarkable natural environments. There are no proper attractions at **Germany**, but with a year-round Oktoberfest atmosphere and several fine German beers on offer, no one ever really seems to notice. The **Biergarten Restaurant** is the main attraction, but shops in half-timber houses also sell some fine Christmas ornaments and wooden toys for younger children. Designer labels, wines, and even ashtrays are for sale in the **Italy** pavilion, which is a collage of Venetian architecture that includes the Doge's Palace and the Campanile from

TIP

IllumiNations is a spectacular fireworks show with lasers and fountains displayed in and above the World Showcase Lagoon.

BELOW: Mission: SPACE is an astronaut simulator ride and one of Disney's newest attractions.

TIP

A tip board at the corner of Hollywood and Sunset Boulevards lists the waiting times for all attractions at Hollywood Studios.

St Mark's Square. Italian cuisine is served up in **Tutto Italia Ristorante**.

Patriotic fervor

Portraying one's own country in a theme park full of sweeping generalizations was always going to make interesting viewing for outsiders. No one will be surprised by the patriotic nature of the attractions, but the **Spirit of America Fife and Drum Corps**, the **Voices of Liberty**, and even the **American Adventure** film do their best to explain this patriotism to foreign guests. The film, which features an animatronic Ben Franklin and Mark Twain among others, does its best to provide a balanced view of American history by including the destruction of Native American cultures and the horrors of slavery. By the end, though, emotive patriotism replaces historical accuracy. Even more disappointing is that with America's rich culinary scope, from Cajun cornbread to New England clam chowder, Disney chose for the **Liberty Inn** to serve burgers and fries.

Many people come to the **Japan** pavilion just to shop. There is a huge

selection of smartly designed sushi plates and knives, silk garments, eccentric toys, and other delicate trinkets. Though the quick-service restaurants here serve fine sushi, the **Mitsukoshi Dining Rooms** is the best place for a sit-down meal. The **Morocco** pavilion has some of the finest faux architecture in World Showcase. You can even have a go at getting lost in the warren of shops selling Middle Eastern art and dress, including fine rugs and bronzework. The country's cuisine is summed up at **Restaurant Marrakesh**.

It should be no surprise that you get two fine restaurants, **Les Chefs de France** and **Bistro de Paris**, and an accomplished patisserie in the France pavilion. There is also a fine wine shop and a delightful market selling soaps, cosmetics, and dinnerware.

Impressions de France is a panoramic film shown throughout the day that takes you on a sweeping journey over the French countryside. Get your gourmandizing done before you leave France – fish and chips are the main fare in the **UK**. This little Britain has everything from Blighty, including a

BELOW: a torii gate welcomes visitors to Epcot's Japan Pavilion.

Beatles cover band at the **Rose and Crown Pub**.

America's neighbor gets a more rugged display with mountainous terrain and the Circle-Vision Film, **O Canada!** The signature restaurant **Le Cellier Steakhouse** serves meals hearty enough for any lumberjack.

Disney's Hollywood Studios

Dedicated to the "Hollywood that never was and always will be," **Hollywood Studios ❹** (daily, see www.disneyworld.com for details) is, in many respects, Disney World's most satisfying park. An unabashed attempt to compete with Universal Studios, the park combines some of Disney's best rides with a behind-the-scenes look at movie making.

Upon entering the park, visitors are immediately transported back to the golden age of Hollywood. Lining either side of **Hollywood Boulevard** – the park's main staging area – are replicas of iconic Tinseltown buildings, most housing shops stocked with Disney merchandise. This is also the first place you'll encounter costumed

characters, including actors playing stock Hollywood types (a struggling actress, an imperious director, and so forth) who do street skits.

Towering over a plaza at the end of Hollywood Boulevard is a 12-story **Sorcerer's Hat** like the one worn by Mickey in *Fantasia*. Kiosks beneath the hat review highlights in Disney history – but it's not worth the time if you're on a schedule.

Behind the Sorcerer's Hat, in a replica of Graumann's Chinese Theater, is **The Great Movie Ride**, a Magic Kingdom-style dark ride through sets from classic film scenes, from the romantic ending of the famous *Casablanca* to scarier scenes from *Alien*.

Hollywood iconography continues on **Sunset Boulevard**, which veers off to the right of the plaza. About halfway down, in a roofed amphitheater modeled after the Hollywood Bowl, is **Beauty and the Beast Live on Stage**. This condensed version of the Disney film is a big hit with children. It lacks the *wow* factor and air conditioning of other live shows, but often fills up prior to showtimes.

Street performers at Disney's Hollywood Studios bring back the golden age of motion pictures.

BELOW: Johnny Weissmuller and Maureen O'Sullivan in *Tarzan*, an MGM classic featured on The Great Movie Ride.

ESPN Wide World of Sports Complex

Fans should make a point of checking the schedule of events hosted at this $100 million, 200 acre (80 hectare) complex. It features a baseball stadium, a 5,000 seat basketball fieldhouse, 12 tennis courts, and facilities for about 30 other sports.

The complex hosts scores of amateur and professional events including the Atlanta Braves' spring training. The Multi-Sports Experience features baseball, football, training programs for high school and college baseball, lacrosse, soccer, softball, and volleyball as well as tournaments ranging from Little League baseball and inline hockey for kids to the US Men's World Cup Soccer Team. The complex is on Victory Way near Hollywood Studios, just west of I-4. For a list of upcoming events, call 407-939-2040. Admission is charged for premium events.

For water sport fans, the Walt Disney World Resort has a web of waterways connecting its many lakes, large and small, and almost all the Disney resorts are on a lake or canal, with their own landing places or marinas. Dozens of different types of pleasure craft can be rented, even if you're not an experienced boat handler. For sailing, conditions are best at two big lakes – Seven Seas Lagoon and Bay Lake at the Magic Kingdom Resorts.

BELOW: Rod Serling welcomes visitors to the Twilight Zone at the Tower of Terror.

The big show

A few steps away is the entrance to a second open-air venue, the Hollywood Hills Amphitheater. This is the site of **Fantasmic**, Hollywood Studios' big finale, which plays nightly just before closing. The special-effects crew pulls out all the stops, dazzling the audience with lasers, fountains, and fireballs in a show that pits Mickey Mouse against Disney's nastiest villains.

The structure hulking over the end of Sunset Boulevard is the **Twilight Zone Tower of Terror**, housed in what appears to be an abandoned hotel. Inside, you're ushered into an elevator that hurtles through space – up, down, up, down – with a few pauses for creepy, heart-stopping views. This is decidedly not an experience for those with shaky stomachs or a fear of heights.

The excitement continues over at the **Rock 'n' Roller Coaster**, an indoor coaster with enough twists to satisfy hard-core thrill-seekers. The launch is especially riveting, achieving a speed of 60mph (97kph) in less than 3 seconds. A word of warning: This is not a ride

for lightweights. If you thought Space Mountain was a challenge, this one will knock you for a loop.

Around Echo Lake

Return to the Sorcerer's Hat and explore the area on the opposite side of the plaza around Echo Lake. The big draw here is the **Indiana Jones Epic Stunt Spectacular**, starring stuntmen who re-enact scenes from *Raiders of the Lost Ark*, and then explain how the tricks are done. There are gunfights, fistfights, and other feats of derring-do, not to mention a couple of searing explosions. Across the way is **Sounds Dangerous**, a comedy in which Drew Carey plays a reporter trailing a smuggler. Most of the action takes place in the dark, while the audience listens in with headphones. The script is inane, but the show illustrates how sound can advance a story.

An Imperial walker, one of those spacey war machines that sprang from the mind of George Lucas, stands in front of **Star Tours**, the park's only simulator ride. Here you're ushered into a starspeeder for a madcap journey through the cosmos. The ride isn't particularly frightening, but it does give passengers a good shake.

The atmosphere takes on an urban, brick-and-mortar quality as you drift into the area around New York Street. Here you'll find a statue of Miss Piggy standing in front of a theater showing Jim Henson's **Muppet Vision 3-D**, a raucous 25-minute romp with Kermit, Piggy, and the rest of the muppet crew.

Next, wander over to **New York Street**, a backlot rendition of the Big Apple. Take a few moments to appreciate the extraordinary detail that went into its construction. The subtle street sounds – a distant siren, car horns, a jackhammer – are a nice touch.

A side street leads to the **Honey, I Shrunk the Kids Movie Set Adventure**, a super-size playground designed from an insect's point of view. Kids zoom down slides on a blade of grass, explore tunnels in a giant

mushroom and get a good soaking around a leaky hose. A word to the wise: The playground is sweltering on a hot day, there's not much room for adults to sit, and once children disappear into the tunnels it takes a while to find them, much less convince them that it's time to leave. Nearby, **Lights, Motors, Action! Extreme Stunt Show** is a car-, motorcycle-, and JetSki-stunt show that will keep you on the edge of your seat. Fans of cars spinning around and making noise will love this type of thing, but for anyone else, this show is a waste of time. The Indiana Jones stunt show is much better.

Backlot tour

It's a quick stroll down **Commissary Lane** and across the central plaza to **Mickey Avenue**. To the far left is the **Backlot Tour**, a 35-minute tram ride with glimpses of the wardrobe department, scenery workshop, and what appears to be a quiet suburban street lined with trim little houses. The buildings are only shells, of course, used in television commercials and programs. Later, the tram pulls into Catastrophe

Canyon, which you're told is a movie set for a film currently under production. Within moments the earth begins to shake, an oil tanker explodes, and a flash flood comes barreling toward you. The tour ends with an exhibit of showbiz memorabilia at the American Film Institute Showcase.

At the end of Mickey Avenue in a little plaza called the Animation Courtyard is **The Magic of Disney Animation**, a tour of a working animation studio, including a presentation

Star Tours takes riders on a virtual adventure in space.

BELOW: 3-D rides provide an extra element of excitement to the traditional theme park ride.

by an artist and a couple of interesting films, one featuring the unlikely team of actor Robin Williams and newsman Walter Cronkite. The last two shows – **Voyage of the Little Mermaid** and **Disney Junior – Live on Stage!** – are sweet and schmaltzy, and intended for families with small children.

Animal Kingdom

Disney World's largest theme park, **Disney's Animal Kingdom** ❺ (daily, see www.disneyworld.com for details), is essentially a state-of-the-art zoo dressed up in extravagant style. You realize you're in for something special the moment you walk through the front gates into an area known as **The Oasis** – a tropical garden laced with trails that lead past alcoves containing river otters, anteaters, sloths, and other small animals.

Emerging from The Oasis, you're greeted by a view of the **Tree of Life**, an artificial banyan-like tree that rises 14 stories above **Discovery Island**, set in a large lagoon connected by bridges to the park's four main zones. What looks at first like the tree's gnarled

bark are actually carved animal figures – more than 300 in all – swirling around the trunk and limbs. Showing in a theater in the base of the tree is a 3-D film, **It's Tough to be a Bug!**, based loosely on the Disney-Pixar movie *A Bug's Life*. The story involves seeing the world from an insect's point of view. You experience what it's like being on the receiving end of a fly swatter and encounter several noxious members of the insect family, including an acid-spraying termite and a stinkbug with, shall we say, a bad case of gas.

Walking around Discovery Island in a clockwise direction, the first bridge on the left leads to **Camp Minnie-Mickey**, designed in Adirondack style and devoted to live shows. The big attraction here is **Festival of the Lion King**, an uplifting 30-minute pageant based loosely on the animated film, with song, dance, acrobatics, and flamboyant costumes. Children get a kick out of the four **Character Greeting Trails**, which lead back to pavilions housing costumed characters who spend a few minutes posing for pictures, signing

The Mouse at Sea

Since its inception in 1998, Disney Cruise Lines has upgraded to a full-service cruise line. Its ships travel to various ports of call in the Caribbean, Alaska, Mexico, and Europe, as well as making a biannual transatlantic voyage. Shipboard amenities range from lavish stage shows, first-run movies, fitness rooms, spas, and a choice of swimming pools. Passengers rotate among several theme restaurants. There are currently three Disney ships: Disney Magic, Disney Wonder, and Disney Dream. A fourth ship, Disney Fantasy, is scheduled to start service in 2012. In addition to the ships, Disney owns and operates its own island, Castaway Cay, which serves as a port of call for the cruise ships and is a unique Disney destination. Uniquely, the horns on Disney ships have been modified to play the first seven notes from When You Wish Upon a Star, in addition to the traditional horn.

Douglas Ward, author of the influential *Berlitz Complete Guide to Cruising and Cruise Ships*, describes the Disney ships as "a sea-going never-never land" providing "a highly programmed, strictly timed and regimented experience." Security, he adds, is very good, with children provided with ID bracelets and parents given pagers for emergencies.

For information, call 800-951-3532, visit disneycruise.disney.go.com, or contact a travel agent.

autographs, and joshing around with little ones and adults.

Out of Africa, into Asia

Return to Discovery Island and cross the first bridge on your left to **Africa**, where you immediately find yourself amid a clutch of shops and restaurants called **Harambe**, modeled loosely on a real-life Kenyan village. Next to an enormous, artificial baobab tree is the entrance to the park's most popular attraction, **Kilimanjaro Safaris**. Here visitors board safari vehicles for a 20-minute ride across a re-created patch of African veldt. This being Disney, merely seeing lions, giraffes, zebras, and other wildlife isn't enough. About halfway through the tour, your driver learns that poachers are threatening an elephant mother and calf, and off you go on a wild ride to rescue the threatened beasts and catch the bad guys.

It's only a few steps from the safari exit to the **Pangani Forest Exploration Trail**, a nature walk where you can view endangered species like black-and-white colobus monkeys, as well as hippos, gorillas, and meerkats. A research center harbors a colony of naked mole rats and a cleverly disguised aviary.

If you're looking for a break from the crowds, you might consider a side trip to **Rafiki's Planet Watch**, an area for environmental education. The journey starts with a ride on the Wildlife Express, a replica of a vintage steam locomotive that passes through the not-terribly-scenic backstage area. At the end of the line is the **Conservation Station**, a veterinary facility with exhibits on conservation and animal care. Skip both if pressed for time.

Next door to Africa is **Asia**, a pastiche of thatched huts, stone spires, and palace walls inspired by the traditional architecture of Thailand, Nepal, and India. Asia encompasses four main attractions. To your left as you enter is the Caravan Stage, presenting **Flights of Wonder**, a 20-minute show featuring hawks, falcons, parrots,

and more than a dozen other birds. Also here is **Kali River Rapids**, a whitewater ride with a jungle setting and an environmental message. The third stop in Asia is the **Maharajah Jungle Trek**, a nature walk with views of Bengal tigers, fruit bats, and exotic birds. Disney's thrill ride, **Expedition Everest**, feels like a decrepit mountain train scaling its way up the side of the world's tallest peak, and includes a steep backward drop when you come to the end of the track. As if that weren't enough to frighten you, there is always the chance that the Yeti might surprise you as well.

Return to Discovery Island and cross the first bridge on the left to **DinoLand, USA**. You'll notice a carnival-like atmosphere here, injecting a welcome dose of humor into the straight-faced approach elsewhere in the park. Just past an elaborate kids' play

A giraffe wanders the savanna at Animal Kingdom.

BELOW: King Louie from Disney's *Jungle Book.*

The Guitar Gallery is one of several shops at Downtown Disney.

BELOW: ferries cruise across the Seven Seas Lagoon near the Grand Floridian Hotel.

area called **The Boneyard** you'll find signs to **Dinosaur**, DinoLand's thrill ride. The concept here is that you're a visitor at the Dino Institute, a facility dedicated to "Exploration, Excavation and Exultation" and, you soon learn, the developer of a time machine that is about to transport you back to the Age of Dinosaurs. Your mission: Save the last surviving *Iguanodon* before an asteroid collides with Earth. What follows is a jolting ride through a misty Jurassic forest that's being pelted by a barrage of meteors. Dinosaurs abound, of course, not the least of which is a *Carnotaurus*, a ferocious predator with razor-sharp teeth and a sour disposition. The experience is quite intense, so exercise discretion when visiting with young children.

Next on the agenda is **Chester & Hester's Dino-Rama**, a mini-carnival, with midway games and a couple of amusement-park rides: **Primeval Whirl** and **TriceraTop Spin**. A large shop, **Chester & Hester's Dinosaur Treasures**, is packed to the rafters with dino-related toys and novelties – a good place to pick up gifts for the

folks back home. **Finding Nemo – the Musical** is the Animal Kingdom's production, and it's poor. The technique of using live actors carrying puppets is confusing, and at times this seems more of a college theater workshop than the highly accomplished production that is the standard for Disney.

Downtown Disney

Downtown Disney ❻ is an entertainment complex on Lake Buena Vista about a mile east of Epcot. It's divided into three sections – West Side, Pleasure Island, and Marketplace – and is intended mostly for an adult audience.

The **West Side** is the least defined of the three areas, a mixed bag of restaurants, shops, and showplaces anchored on one end by **Cirque du Soleil**, a wildly imaginative theater troupe combining circus art and stagecraft, and on the other by **Planet Hollywood**, the well-known theme restaurant. In between are a few more restaurants, including **Wolfgang Puck** and **House of Blues**. You'll also find a place called **DisneyQuest**, a sort of pinball arcade

on steroids, with cutting-edge video games and virtual-reality rides. Loud and crowded, it has limited appeal for the post-pubescent crowd. Nearby is a **Virgin Megastore**, with acres of floor space and dozens of listening stations. Several more specialty shops – ranging from cigars to guitars – are situated in a building next door, which also houses a 24-screen movie theater.

Sometimes called "Disney for adults," **Pleasure Island** was originally conceived as a nightclub district but is presently undergoing a complete overhaul. All of the nightclubs have closed in favor of family-friendly shops, restaurants, and attractions.

Among the venues that will remain open is the **Raglan Road Irish Pub and Restaurant**. They've successfully re-created the atmosphere of Dublin's Temple Bar during a tour-group party; in other words it looks much like any other Irish pub in America. Many shades of stout and ale are on offer alongside a fine selection of whiskey, and live Irish folk music takes you through the night. **Fuego by Sosa Cigars**, an upscale cigar bar, is one of the few remaining places

strictly targeting adults only. The cigar retailer offers a large variety of low- to high-end cigars.

Also in Pleasure Island is a **Harley-Davidson** shop. The merchandise here is dominated by leather jackets, T-shirts, hats, and assorted knick-knacks plastered wth the Harley logo, though actual motorcycles – most bristling with chrome and other custom adornments – are also on display.

If you're a surfer – or just want to look like one – make a point of checking out **Curl by Sammy Duval**, a high-end surf shop with an extensive selection of surfer-dude clothing, gear, and accessories. There are even a few surfboards.

Shopping zone

Marketplace occupies the eastern portion of Downtown Disney and is devoted to shopping and eating. In addition to the world's largest Disney store are shops carrying home furnishings, sporting gear, and toys. Far more interesting is the **Lego Imagination Center**, if only for the Lego sculptures displayed around the store. For eats, there's the Ghirardelli

TIP

You can sign up for a 150 minute surfing lesson at Typhoon Lagoon. Lessons are offered Tuesday and Friday at 6.30am. The fee is about $150.

Soda Fountain & Chocolate Shop, a giant McDonald's, and a Rainforest Cafe ensconced in what appears to be a smoldering volcano.

Disney's BoardWalk

You'll find a smaller entertainment complex at the **BoardWalk**. Diners have a couple of good choices: the Flying Fish Cafe serves seafood, and Kouzzina, by Cat Cora, specializes in Mediterranean cuisine, though sports fans may prefer the ESPN Club, a bar with more than 70 TV screens.

Drinkers can sample handcrafted suds at the Big River Grille & Brewing Works or join the singalong crowd at Jellyrolls, which features a raucous dueling pianos act. Dancers can boogie at the Atlantic Dancehall, modeled after the classic dancehalls of the 1930s and 40s.

Disney's water parks

If you're reasonably spry, don't mind hordes of teens, and aren't self-conscious about being seen in a swimsuit, you'll have a blast flying down the various chutes or bobbing peacefully on one of the gentle river trips.

Disney World has two excellent water parks to choose from when you're sticky with sweat and ready for a good dousing. A good fit for teenagers and young adults is **Typhoon Lagoon** ❼ (tel: 407-560-4141; 10am–5pm, extended hours summer and holidays; charge). Here you'll find a selection of high-speed slides as well as an enormous surf pool, a snorkeling trail where you can swim through the water with tropical fish and harmless sharks, and a relaxing 45-minute lazy-river raft trip that takes you through rainforest grottoes and waterfalls.

Blizzard Beach ❽ (tel: 407-560-3400; same hours as Typhoon Lagoon; charge) is Disney's largest water park and offers the scariest and hairiest rides, including Summit Plummet, which zips riders down a 350ft (107 meter) ramp at speeds close to 60mph (97kph). There are at least a dozen other slides, as well as the world's longest whitewater raft ride, in which five passengers bob through 1,200ft (360 meters) of standing waves and roaring cataracts. ❑

Shoppers, diners, and revelers crowd the streets of Downtown Disney at night.

BELOW: Planet Hollywood at Downtown Disney.

RESTAURANTS

Restaurants

Prices for a three-course dinner per person, excluding tax, tip, and beverages:
$ = under $20
$$ = $20–45
$$$ = $45–60
$$$$ = over $60

Reservations for any of Disney's restaurants can be made at any resort's reception desk, any park's information office, or by telephoning 407-939-3463.

Magic Kingdom

Cinderella's Royal Table
Cinderella's Castle $$$
Though the food at this restaurant is far below the standard you'd expect at this price, its setting at the heart of Cinderella's Castle can't be beaten. Children can have their picture taken with Cinderella before lunch, and other fairy-tale princesses visit while they are eating. In addition to the Fairytale Lunch, there is a Once Upon a Time Breakfast Buffet. Reservations must be made far in advance.

Tony's Town Square Restaurant
Main Street, USA $$
With decor inspired by the classic film *Lady and the Tramp*, this restaurant serves up Italian fare in a light and airy environment. Be warned of Disney's tomato sauce. This oregano-laden concoction is definitely not to everyone's taste but is served throughout the park, finding its way onto everything from the posh pasta here to kiddies' spaghetti meals in other restaurants.

Epcot

Akershus Royal Banquet Hall
Norway Pavilion $$–$$$
In addition to its character breakfast featuring Disney princesses in a castle setting, this restaurant offers a fine lunch and dinner menu, with a choice of good fish dishes and other Norwegian specialties. There's a smorgasbord of cheeses, pickled fish, and rustic breads.

Biergarten Restaurant
Germany Pavilion $$
This buffet-style restaurant set in a dimly lit mock-timber house serves uninspired German fare. There is, of course, a healthy selection of beers to wash it down with, and the accordion player will catch up with you eventually.

Bistro de Paris
France Pavilion $$–$$$
The signature restaurant for France is poorly appointed, with a dining area that feels not unlike a convention luncheon setting. The lengthy wine list and fine view could help you forget this, but you'd expect more from a Disney restaurant charging this much.

Chefs de France
France Pavilion $$
A faithful re-creation of a typical Parisian café. The cooking may not be up to Michelin-star status, but it is very good, and you can dine under a faux Eiffel Tower.

Coral Reef Restaurant
The Seas with Nemo and Friends $$–$$$
This seafood restaurant is situated alongside the aquarium at The Seas with Nemo and Friends, providing dreamy views into the largest inland saltwater environment ever built. The food is fine dining at Disney's best.

Garden Grill
The Land Pavilion $$
A revolving restaurant overlooking scenic ecosystems and a boat ride, its menu includes salads and vegetables grown in The Land greenhouses. The "Full Country Breakfast" stars Mickey, Minnie, and Chip 'n' Dale.

Le Cellier Steakhouse
Canada Pavilion $$–$$$
Americans like their steak as much as their northern neighbors do, and if you plan on having dinner here you must book in advance even during the slow periods. The wine cellar could make a romantic setting if you are lucky enough to get a table.

Tutto Italia
Italy Pavilion $$–$$$
After a day of walking through the park, what better way to recharge your batteries than with a plate of freshly made pasta? Tutto's offers traditional Italian cuisine with an Old World flare. The specialty is Antipasto Misto, but be sure to try the fresh, home-made mozzarella and the

RIGHT: a sushi chef at work at Wolfgang Puck Cafe.

Prices for a three-course dinner per person, excluding tax, tip, and beverages:
$ = under $20
$$ = $20–45
$$$ = $45–60
$$$$ = over $60

decadent gelato. All pastas are made fresh. Vegetarian options are available.

Restaurant Marrakesh
Morocco Pavilion **$$–$$$**
After experiencing the fantastic warren-like architecture of the Morocco pavilion, you can't help but be disappointed by the lack of authenticity at Restaurant Marrakesh. The interior beyond the guest services desk seems bare, and although some of the food excels, most of it is a poor Americanized version of Middle Eastern food. On a more positive note, the live music and belly dancing add a touch of Moroccan flare.

San Angel Inn Restaurante
Mexico Pavilion **$$**
Authentic Mexican food served in a faux environment – under the shadow of a Mayan temple and a smoldering volcano. The dim lighting makes a good option for couples hoping for a bit of romance.

Teppan Edo
Japan Pavilion **$$**
Reservations are usually necessary to get a seat in one of the teppanyaki dining rooms. Diners circle the chef as he creates stir-fry creations, which are shared around the table.

Animal Kingdom

Rainforest Café
Oasis
www.rainforestcafe.com **$$**
This is one of the most highly themed restaurants in Disney. Many will be familiar with this chain and its use of animatronic animals and faux decor to re-create a rainforest canopy. Unfortunately, the theme stops at the food. Instead of an iguana burger and plantains, expect large portions of typical American food. Waits of an hour or more are common without reservations.

Hollywood Studios

50s Prime Time Café
Echo Lake **$**
This reincarnation of mom's kitchen has a certain fetish appeal. Waiters discipline anyone who does not clean their plate or is caught with elbows on the table. And at times they behave like mom's children, too, becoming tattletales and pests just the same. The food is what you'd expect from mom and includes meatloaf, peas, and indulgent desserts you choose from a retro Viewmaster toy.

Hollywood Brown Derby
Hollywood Boulevard **$$$**
This re-creation of the legendary Hollywood restaurant features fine food at fine prices. Of course, the only celebrities you are likely to see here are in photos on the walls.

Sci-Fi Dine-In Theater
Commissary Lane **$$**
This is Hollywood Studio's best dining experience. Every party gets to take a seat in an old Chevy or other vintage car and watch classic sci-fi films on the drive-in screen. The food plays second fiddle to this theme and features burgers, sandwiches, and pasta dishes. Reservations are essential here, even during the slow seasons.

Downtown Disney

Bongos Cuban Café
Westside **$$**
The brainchild of pop star Gloria Estefan and her husband Emilio. A giant pineapple sprouting from the roof sets the tone, which throbs with Latin music and brilliant colors. Aficionados of Cuban cuisine may have better luck elsewhere.

Fulton's Crab House
Pleasure Island **$$–$$$**
Downtown Disney's lagoon provides a berth for this replica of a Mississippi riverboat. Inside is one of Disney's finer restaurants. The menu offers a bounty of seafood with a few beef, poultry, and pasta dishes to keep everyone in the party happy. The Alaskan king crab claws are huge, and there is a wine selector to help choose an appropriate vintage.

House of Blues
Westside **$$**
Founded by original Blues Brother Dan Aykroyd and done up like the kind of ramshackle wharfside warehouse you might find in the Mississippi Delta. The food is surprisingly good for a chain, with southern favorites like fried catfish, seafood gumbo, jambalaya, and bread pudding dribbled with brandy sauce. If you're traveling with kids, consider booking a table for the Sunday Gospel Brunch. You'll jump up for Jesus and chow down on all the southern vittles you can eat.

Wolfgang Puck
Westside **$$–$$$**
The cavernous rooms and chatty clientele aren't exactly conducive to an intimate conversation; the atmosphere is all color and energy, with open kitchens, video monitors showing chefs at work, and a bustling wait staff. The menu runs the gamut from sushi and gourmet pizza to lamb chops and seafood,

all prepared with the celebrity chef's Californian flair (except perhaps the Wiener schnitzel). The upstairs dining room is quite expensive. The downstairs café is cheaper and more casual.

Planet Hollywood
Westside **$$**
Every inch of the dome-shaped dining room is jammed with movie props, memorabilia, and other eye candy. The good news is that the food has improved since the company's brush with bankruptcy in 1999. The wait can be terribly long, especially when the theaters let out, so make reservations well in advance.

Portobello Yacht Club
Pleasure Island **$$–$$$**
First-rate northern Italian cuisine and seafood specialties fill the menu here, while diners cram the floor in a restaurant that could be a fine-dining experience if the spacing wasn't so similar to cafeteria seating.

Rainforest Café
Marketplace **$$**
The smoke you've been seeing billowing in the distance is from a smoldering volcano that sits atop the Rainforest Café, a cavernous restaurant with an extravagant jungle setting. Even with priority seating, you'll have a good long wait.

Disney Resort Dining
Magic Kingdom resorts
Artist's Point
Wilderness Lodge,
901 Timberline Dr,
Lake Buena Vista **$$$**
Inspired by national-park lodges, this hotel restau-

rant features salmon, rainbow trout, elk chops, venison, bison, and other hearty dishes associated with the American West. The wine list features labels from the Pacific northwest.

California Grill
Contemporary Resort, 4600 North World Dr **$$$$**
Views of the Magic Kingdom are spectacular from the 15th floor of the Contemporary Resort. The menu changes seasonally but usually includes entrées like oak-roasted chicken and pork tenderloin prepared with a light California touch. Don't pass up the appetizers, an eclectic mix of sushi, salads, and pasta. Ask to be seated in time for the fireworks.

Narcoossee's
Grand Floridian Resort and Spa, 4401 Grand Floridian Way, Lake Buena Vista **$$$–$$$$**
With a sweeping lakeside setting, this is the Grand Floridian's "casual" offering. Its inventive cuisine uses fresh ingredients and lots of seafood. Softshell crabs and Prince Edward Island mussels in white wine and garlic are signature dishes.

Victoria and Albert's
Grand Floridian Resort and Spa; 4401 Grand Floridian Way, Lake Buena Vista **$$$$**
Disney spins a Victorian fantasy at this prix-fixe restaurant. The seven-course meal is served by a white-gloved butler and maid (Albert and Victoria) in a romantic, domed dining room. The menu features some of the finest Continental cuisine in town. Very expensive but worth the money.

Epcot resorts
ESPN Sports Club
Disney's BoardWalk
$$–$$$
Jocks will love this theme restaurant crammed with all things sporty, including more than 70 television screens; there's even one in the restroom. Bring a big appetite. Entrées, including hamburgers, hot dogs, sirloin, and grilled chicken, are oversized.

Flying Fish Café
Disney's BoardWalk
$$$–$$$$
One of Disney's best restaurants, in a whimsical setting with a busy stage kitchen. It serves potato-wrapped yellowtail snapper and other creative dishes. There's chocolate lava cake for dessert.

Il Mulino New York Trattoria
Swan Hotel, 1200 Epcot Resorts Blvd **$$$–$$$$**
Is this the classiest restaurant at Disney World? The illuminated wine bar is tops for sure, and it has

a good selection of fine wines. The cuisine is based on classic Italian bistro recipes. The seafood dishes stand out the most.

Kimono's
Swan Hotel,
1200 Epcot Resorts Blvd **$$$**
The sushi chefs here are not shy and are happy to prepare their beautiful creations in front of your eyes. For those who prefer their fish cooked, there are hot dishes and tempura available as well. There's karaoke in the evening.

Todd English's bluezoo
Dolphin Hotel, 1200 Epcot Resorts Blvd **$$$–$$$$**
Presentation is king at this fine-dining restaurant, from the sleek backlit bar and minimalist design to the plates of seafood with a wedge of lemon. There is a kids' menu here, but do yourself a favor and leave the little ones behind so you can enjoy this very grown-up restaurant.

LEFT: movie memorabilia fills Planet Hollywood.
RIGHT: Rainforest Café is in Disney's Animal Kingdom.

ORLANDO AND ITS OTHER WORLDS

Beyond the gates of Disney is a wide array of destinations, ranging from elaborate theme parks and first-class museums to alligator farms and wilderness areas

Walt Disney World Resort's chief competitor is Universal Orlando (www.universalorlando. com), a complex of two theme parks, three hotels, and an entertainment district about 9 miles (15km) down I-4. Hipper than Mickey, with a knowing pop sensibility, Universal is especially appealing to teenagers and young adults who like big roller-coasters, loud music, and action movies.

Universal Studios

Universal's flagship property is **Universal Studios Florida ❶** (tel: 407-363-8000; daily, hours vary, see www. universalorlando.com; charge), a theme park inspired by the art and science of Hollywood movies. Sprawling across more than 400 acres (160 hectares), the park is laid out in six themed zones, each with its own rides and shows, arranged around a lagoon. As Universal likes to remind us, this is a working production facility: sections of the park double as movie sets.

Universal's newest thrill ride is **Rip Ride Rockit**, which is dubbed the most personalized roller-coaster experience in the world. Built with its own on-board sound system, guests are able to choose the music they want to listen to during their roller-coaster experience. This 3,800ft (1,160 meter) coaster is what's called an X-car, and

is the largest of its kind in the world. Each train has two cars with three rows, which hold six people in stadium-style seating. There's also **Revenge of the Mummy**, an indoor roller-coaster that takes you on a three minute ride through fireballs, with sharp twists and turns at high speed while trying to avoid capture by skeletal warriors. **Terminator 2 3-D** thrusts the audience into the action while resistance fighters John and Sarah Connor battle Skynet in an attempt to save the human race from annihilation. **Shrek 4-D** uses the

Main attractions
UNIVERSAL STUDIOS
ISLANDS OF ADVENTURE
WIZARDING WORLD OF
  HARRY POTTER
CITYWALK
SEAWORLD
AQUATICA
LOCH HAVEN PARK
CORNELL FINE ARTS MUSEUM
LEGOLAND

LEFT AND RIGHT: costumed characters greet visitors to Universal Orlando.

same cinema technology, but is suitable for small children. In this movie Lord Farquaad returns to kidnap Princess Fiona. Shrek and Donkey have to embark on a journey to save her.

Twister... Ride It Out gives audiences the chance to experience the awesome power of a tornado. If that encounter with Mother Nature wasn't enough, on **Disaster** you can experience a simulated San Francisco earthquake in the underground West Oakland Subway Station. If you take a gentle boat ride along the New England coast, be prepared to be violently disrupted by the notorious great white terror of the deep; you've just met **Jaws**. The top family ride is undoubtedly **ET Adventure**. This dark ride is a re-creation of the movie and is set in an area called **Woody Woodpecker's Kid Zone** devoted entirely to young children, which includes the **Woody's Nuthouse Coaster**, a kid-size roller-coaster that's fun for all ages. The water-soaked **Curious George Goes to Town** playground and ball factory is great for little ones. From there you can walk over to **Fievel's Playland** and see what the world looks like from a mouse's point of view. There are plenty of props for children to climb on. There are also two live shows: **A Day in the Park with Barney** and **Animal Actors on Location,** a terrifically entertaining show which features many animal shelter rescues. **Men in Black: Alien Attack** is like playing a live action video game where your job is to take out the aliens. Everyone will enjoy Universal's newest virtual attraction: **The Simpsons Ride**, a wild, virtual-reality journey through Krustyland, where the Simpson family tries to escape Sideshow Bob. **Jimmy Neutron's Nicktoon Blast** takes you on a cartoon simulation journey into outer space to the planet Yolkian to help save Earth.

The combination of humor and nostalgia is crucial to the success of shows like **Beetlejuice's Graveyard Revue** and **Blues Brothers**. In **Fear Factor Live**, which is based on the hit reality show, audience members are selected at random to try hair-raising (and sometimes harebrained) stunts. **Universal Horror Make-Up Show**

TIP

Universal's newest show is the acclaimed **Blue Man Group**. You do not have to buy a theme park ticket to see this show. Tickets start at $59 for adults and $49 for children.

BELOW: a cast member at Islands of Adventure poses with visitors after a show.

Universal's Express Expense

The Universal Express system allows visitors priority access to the most popular rides to avoid long lines. You have to pay for this privilege if you are not a guest at one of Universal Orlando's resorts. The cost ranges from $19.99 to $59.99 per person. Universal Studios website (www.universalorlando.com/Tickets) displays a color-coded pricing key and calendar. The pass is only valid for one day at one park. Though the cost can be steep, it's worth it. Guests do not need to wait for a time slot; just show up at the attraction and you'll be accommodated straight away, and you can do the same ride as many times as you like. The Express Pass is not currently available in conjunction with the park's most popular ride, Hollywood Rip Ride Rokit.

Shooting the rapids at Popeye & Bluto's Bilge-Rat Barges.

BELOW: nightlife on CityWalk's Plaza.
BELOW RIGHT: T. rex at the Jurassic Park River Adventure.

lets you get a behind-the-scenes look at how Hollywood's best make-up artists create the life-like creatures you see in the movies and on television.

Islands of Adventure

Universal's newest theme park, **Islands of Adventure** ❷ (daily, hours vary, see www.universalorlando. com; charge), isn't really made up of islands but rather of five elaborately themed zones. Children's books, cartoons, and comic strips provide themes for rides, shops, and restaurants, and costumed characters such as Popeye, Bullwinkle, and Spider-Man make appearances. **Seuss Landing** was inspired by the beloved children's books of Theodor Seuss Geisel, also known as Dr. Seuss. On **The Cat in the Hat**, hop aboard your couch and take a trip through the pages of this childhood classic with the most mischievous cat around. **If I Ran the Zoo** is an interactive playground filled with characters from a variety of Dr. Seuss classics. **The High in the Sky Seuss Trolley Train Ride** takes you on a journey high above the **Seuss Landing** attractions.

The **Lost Continent** is divided into two sections: The first is an Arabian marketplace; the second is styled after the mythical Atlantis. **Jurassic Park** is a dinosaur-themed area based on Spielberg's 1993 film. On the **Jurassic Park River Adventure** you dodge amazingly life-like dinosaurs before taking a stomach-flipping, 85ft (26 meter) plummet. Afterward walk over to the **Jurassic Park Discovery Center** where guests learn how dinosaurs lived through a variety of interactive exhibits and displays.

The **Wizarding World of Harry Potter** is Universal's newest attraction. Embark on an adventure in **Harry Potter and the Forbidden Journey** where you fly above Hogwarts, escape a dragon attack, and get pulled into the middle of a Quidditch game. Gather your courage and climb aboard the **Dragon Challenge** and choose between riding a Hungarian Horntail or a Chinese Fireball dragon. The two intertwine on the tracks and are devilishly engineered for several near misses at speeds in excess of 55mph (90kph). Before taking a training flight aboard **Flight of the Hippogriff**, visit the family-friendly roller-coaster **Care of Magical Creatures Grounds**. Next, pop in to **Olivanders** iconic wand shop and experience the magic of choosing the wand that's right for you. At the **Owl Post and Owlery Shop** guests can get an up-close look at a variety of owls, as well as mail letters to friends and family. **Zonko's** magic shop is filled with joke, magic, and novelty items. **Honeydukes** candy shop is the perfect place to try chocolate frogs and every flavor Bertie-Bott ever made.

What makes the park extra special are the high-tech thrill rides. **The Amazing Adventures of Spider-Man** combines simulator technology and 3-D visuals. Along the way you encounter a small army of evil-doers who send your tram into wild spins and lurches. The tour culminates in what feels like a headlong plunge into the city streets below, only to be saved at the last moment by Spider-Man.

If it's water action you're after, head to **Toon Lagoon** for **Dudley Do'Rights Ripsaw Falls**. Help Dudley save his love, Nell, before you take a jaw-dropping 75ft (23 meter) plunge. Embark on a white-water rapids adventure on **Popeye and Bluto's Bilge-Rat Barges**; be sure to bring a change of clothes. Kids will love exploring **Me Ship, the Olive**, where from a dry platform they can shoot water cannons on unsuspecting barge riders below.

The Incredible Hulk Coaster catapults you up a tunnel with the same force as a fighter jet, before turning upside down seven times and plummeting back toward the ground. **Dr.**

TIP

If viewing sharks through acrylic isn't thrilling enough, consider getting into the water with them. SeaWorld's new Sharks Deep Dive program ($150) puts guests into a diving cage for a swim in the shark tank.

BELOW:
an underwater viewing area gives visitors a unique perspective on one of SeaWorld's biggest stars.

A dolphin encounter is the highlight of the day at Discovery Cove.

Doom's FearFall rockets riders 150ft (45 meters) into the sky.

CityWalk

Before leaving Universal, drop in on **CityWalk**, where a dozen restaurants and nightclubs keep the party rolling long after the kids have gone to bed. **The Red Coconut Club** features signature Martinis, a happy hour, and live music daily, while at **Bob Marley: A Tribute to Freedom** reggae bands perform in an open-air courtyard that re-creates Marley's Jamaica home. Other nightspots include **Pat**

O'Brien's, with its dueling pianos and world-famous Hurricane drink; the sophisticated **Latin Quarter** features live music and Latin cuisine, and the world's largest **Hard Rock Cafe**, as well as the theme-laden **Jimmy Buffet's Margaritaville**, **NBA City**, and **NASCAR Sports Grille**.

SeaWorld, Discovery Cove, and Aquatica

The other don't-miss theme park in Orlando is **SeaWorld ❸** (tel: 407-351-3600; www.seaworld.com; daily, hours vary, see website; charge). The world's largest marine park is the home of dancing penguins, prancing seals, people who ski on the backs of dolphins, and more. The star of the show is Shamu the killer whale, who takes part in crowd-thrilling stunts. Other popular shows include bottlenose dolphins and pseudorcas (false killer whales) playing with their trainers and interacting with the audience; Clyde the otter and Seamore the sea lion cavort around a pirate ship. There are marine exhibits, including areas where you can touch the animals

and a tunnel that leads you through a pool of sharks.

SeaWorld has a couple of big thrill rides, too. The more benign is **Journey to Atlantis**, a cross between a log flume and a roller-coaster. There's a story behind the ride involving the emergence of Atlantis, but with two 60ft (18 meter) plunges, several smaller dips, and a nonstop barrage of laser lights, you won't have a chance to follow along. Only hard-core thrill-seekers should consider riding **Kraken**, a floorless roller-coaster with a drop of 144ft (44 meters), seven inversions, three subterranean passages, and a top speed of 65mph (105kph).

Roller-coaster enthusiasts will not want to miss **Manta**. With its 3,359ft (1,024 meters) of track, it's a coaster that simulates the experience of flying. It has a drop of 140ft (43 meters), reaches speeds of nearly 60mph (96kph), and is the second longest, tallest, and fastest coaster in the world.

Shamu Express is a junior-size coaster perfect for little ones. **The Sea Carousel** is a marine mammal themed merry-go-round ride. **The Flying Fiddler** is a free-fall children's ride. **Net Climb** is a great place to let the kids expend energy. It has a four-story climbing net, slides, and tire swings.

In recent years SeaWorld has revamped its shows. **Believe** is a visually stimulating show starring Shamu. It's not to be missed. **A'lure** is an amazing acrobatic production in a Cirque du Soleil style. **Blue Horizons** uses human acrobats and divers.

The animal exhibits are the best part of the park. **Wild Arctic** is an indoor exhibit where guests can see walruses, beluga whales, and polar bears. **The Penguin Encounter** is an indoor exhibit where you can get a close look at puffins and murres. At **Dolphin Nursery** you can see baby bottle-nosed dolphins. Have you ever wondered what it felt like to touch a sting-ray? Visit **Stingray Lagoon**, where you can reach out and touch the rays. Pacific Point Preserve houses the seals and sea lions and **Manatee Rescue** keeps injured and rescued manatees.

Adjacent to SeaWorld is a very different theme park. SeaWorld calls it **Discovery Cove**, and it's more akin

TIP

Public transportation along International Drive is provided by the I-Ride Trolley, which runs daily 8am–10.30pm. A single fare costs $1, whlie a one-day pass costs $3.

BELOW: Manta Dips a Wing will get your feet wet at SeaWorld.

With a little help, young children can interact with dolphins in shallow water quite easily.

BELOW: slide through the tanks at Aquatica.

to a tropical resort than an amusement park. For starters, admission is limited to 1,000 people per day, and guests pay a flat fee that includes just about everything they'll need – food, towels, snorkeling equipment, and more. What you get is the freedom to roam a beautifully landscaped 32 acre (13 hectare) property where you can snorkel around an artificial coral reef stocked with tropical fish, float down a tropical river, splash in waterfalls, or simply lounge beneath a palm tree on a perfect beach.

For most visitors, the highlight of Discovery Cove is an opportunity to swim with a dolphin. "Swim" may not be entirely accurate. What you do is interact with the animal under the watchful eye of a trainer, who teaches you hand signals that cue the dolphin to roll over, wave flippers, exchange kisses, and tow you along.

SeaWorld's latest addition is nearby **Aquatica** ❹. This new water park

leaves its Orlando rivals trailing in its wake by combining the traditional flume and tube rides with the sea life SeaWorld is famous for. **The Dolphin Plunge** is the most popular attraction. Its clear plastic slide dips through a pool inhabited by black and white Commerson's dolphins.

Taumata Racer is an eight-lane racing slide with open and enclosed sections. **Whanau Way** is a four-slide tower offering four different speed experiences. **Omaka Rocka** features high-speed tubes and funnels that send riders forward and backward. Aquatica features two wave pools: **Cut Back Cove** and **Surf Back Shores**. Then there's **Kata's Kookaburra Cove** and **Walkabout Waters**, which were designed with smaller children in mind. **Roa's Rapids** is a racing river action ride. **Wallhalla Wave** and **Hoo Roo Run** take you through a thrilling six-story maze of tunnels with twists and turns. For something quieter, take a nice leisurely journey down **Loggerhead Lane**, a lazy river adventure, which takes you through the beautiful **Fish Grotto**.

I-Drive

Running alongside I-4 for about 10 miles (16km) between Disney World and downtown Orlando is **International Drive**, a tourist strip with hotels, restaurants, shopping plazas, and, for lack of a better term, several "roadside attractions." Typical of this last category is **Ripley's Believe It or Not Odditorium** ❺ (8201 International Dr; daily 9am–1am; tel: 407-354-0501; www.ripleys.com; charge), a takeoff on Robert Ripley's books of oddities, with exhibits on such sideshow staples as two-headed calves and curiosities like a Rolls-Royce constructed of matchsticks.

Along the same lines is **WonderWorks** (9067 International Dr; tel: 407-351-8800; www.wonderworksonline.com; daily 9am–midnight; charge), although the emphasis here is on high-tech games and science-related exhibits. It's worth driving by just to see the extraordinary building, which looks like a neoclassical temple that's been turned upside-down. This is also home to the **Outta Control Magic and Comedy Dinnershow**. WonderWorks also runs the **Magical Midway** (7001 International Dr; tel: 407-370-5353; www.magicalmidway.com; Mon–Thur 2–10pm, Fri 2pm–midnight, Sat 10am–midnight, Sun 10am–10pm; charge). At **Pirate's Cove** (8501 International Dr; tel: 407-352-7378; www.piratescove.net; daily 9am–11.30pm; charge), miniature golf fans have two courses to get their licks on the links. Captain Kidd's course is good for beginners while the more difficult Blackbeard's Challenge is popular among the more serious duffers. There is another location at 12545 SR 535 in Lake Buena Vista near Disney World Resort (tel: 407-827-1242).

The **Marching Mallards** at the Peabody Orlando hotel (9801 International Dr; tel: 407-352-4000; www.peabodyorlando.com) is the best free show in town. You can see their grand entrance to John Philip Sousa's "King Cotton March" each morning and their return march each afternoon. **Wet 'n Wild** ❻ (6200 International Dr; tel: 407-351-1800; www.wetnwildorlando.com; daily, hours vary, see website for details; charge), yet another water park, is at the northern end of International Drive just across from (and owned by) Universal Orlando and has a reputation for some of the hairiest slides in Orlando.

International Drive is a prime area for shopping, too. **Pointe Orlando**

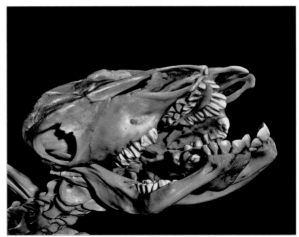

The skull of a two-headed calf at Ripley's Believe It or Not Odditorium.

BELOW: ducks enjoy the water wherever it can be found.

TIP

Special events at Leu
Gardens include a
summer concert series
featuring the Orlando
Philharmonic Orchestra.

(9101 International Dr; tel: 407-248-2838; www.pointeorlando.com; Mon–Sat 10am–10pm, Sun 11am–9pm, many restaurants and bars stay open later) is an attractive upscale retail complex, with live entertainment, lots of lively bars and cafes, a mix of restaurants, and a 21-screen Cineplex that has an IMAX theater.

ABOVE: Lake Eola
BELOW: paintings at
the Mennello
Museum.

Downtown Orlando

The downtown area of **Orlando** ❼ is a hub for business and the arts, with shops, galleries, and restaurants as well as gracious public spaces like **Lake Eola Park**, a 20 acre (8 hectare) oasis with an amphitheater, walking trails and paddleboats. **Church Street Station**, an entertainment complex in a restored 19th-century train depot, is in the midst of a slow revival.

Orange Avenue, named for the city's most famous export product, connects these Lake Eola and Church Street Station, and has become the main drag for downtown life. At its southern base is the **Westin Grand Bohemian** (325 S. Orange Ave, Orlando; tel: 407-313 9000; www.theboheme.com), a top-class hotel that includes the **Boheme**, one of the city's finest restaurants (*see page 276*), and the **Grand Bohemian Gallery** (Grand Bohemian Hotel, 325 S. Orange Ave., Orlando; tel: 407-581 4801; www.grandbohemiangallery.com; Mon 10am–5.30pm, Tue–Sat 10am–8pm, Sun 10am–3pm; free), which features a fine collection of European and American art.

From Church Street to Washington Street, there is a medley of bars that would seem more appropriate on a college campus than in a business center. But there is culture here, too. At 29 S. Orange Avenue is the **Cityartsfactory** (tel: 407-648 7060; www.cityartsfactory.com; gallery hours vary; free), now housed in the old Philips Theater. This is the center for the Downtown Arts District and features a large exhibition space and several art galleries.

North of Central Boulevard is **Wall Street Plaza**, a bar and restaurant complex with happy-hour specials to lure office workers. Most nights feature live music. Walk through Wall Street Plaza to Heritage Square. In the stately 1927 Orange County Courthouse is the **Orange County Regional History Center** (65 E. Central Blvd; tel: 407-836-8500; www.thehistorycenter.org; Mon–Sat 10am–5pm, Sun noon–5pm; charge). Here four floors of exhibits chronicle the history of central Florida. Changing exhibits focus on a variety of topics, ranging in recent years from the "rogues and rascals" of Florida's

pioneer period to the area's rock 'n' roll history.

Ella Fitzgerald and Duke Ellington are just two of the luminaries who stayed at the Wells Built Hotel, erected in 1929 by William Monroe Wells, Orlando's first African-American physician. Opened as the **Wells' Built Museum of African American History and Culture** (511 W. South St; tel: 407-245 7535; www.pastinc.org; Mon–Fri 9am–5pm; charge), it houses exhibitions on life in the segregated South.

African-American culture is also the subject of the tiny **Zora Neale Hurston National Museum of Fine Arts** (227 E. Kennedy Blvd; tel: 407-647-3307; www.zoranealehurston festival.com; Mon–Fri 9am–4pm; free) in nearby Eatonville, the first black township in the United States, founded in 1887. Raised in Eatonville, Hurston later became a prominent figure in the Harlem Renaissance, authoring books

The audience makes magic at Shazam.

BELOW: Zora Neale Hurston remembered her Florida birthplace in her autobiography, *Dust on the Tracks.*

Dinner Theater

A unique entertainment option in Orlando is a night at one of its many dinner theater shows. These often cheesy affairs focus on big productions accompanied by standard fare. Some are most definitely better than others. One of the best is **Arabian Nights** (3081 Arabian Nights Blvd, Kissimmee; tel: 407-239-9223; www.arabian-nights.com). This enchanting dinner show stars 50 Arabian, Lippizaner, palomino, and quarter horses that are put through their paces by skilled riders in an enormous arena. Equestrianism is also on display in the **Medieval Times Dinner and Tournament** (4510 W. Irlo Bronson Hwy, Kissimmee; tel: 866-543-9637; www.medievaltimes.com/orlando). Set in the 11th century, it features a well-executed jousting tournament.

Other theme dinners include **The Outta Control Magic Comedy Dinner Show** (9067 International Dr; tel: 407-351-8800; www.wonder worksonline.com), which offers hand-tossed pizza and unlimited beer, wine, and soda. Entertainment is a mixture of comedy, improv, and magic that promises to "tickle your funny bone every eight seconds." **Al Capone's Dinner and Show** (4740 W Hwy 192; tel: 800-220-8428; www.alcapones.com) is a mob-like affair where guests give a secret password to enter the restaurant. You can partake in the American-Italian buffet while enjoying a musical show.

A glass sculpture by artist Dale Chihuly.

BELOW: *Below the Dam* by Maurice Pendergast at the Orlando Museum of Art.
BELOW RIGHT: the Orlando Science Center.

such as *Their Eyes Were Watching God* and *Of Men and Mules*. The gallery features work by African-American artists; an annual festival is held in Hurston's honor.

Just northwest of downtown is Centroplex, home to the **Bob Carr Performing Arts Center** venue and **Amway Arena**. This is Orlando's main entertainment complex, hosting the Philharmonic Orchestra, theater productions, and the Orlando Magic basketball team.

Loch Haven Park

Just north of downtown in lovely **Loch Haven Park ❽** is a cluster of cultural institutions. The **Orlando Science Center** (777 E. Princeton St; tel: 407-514-2000; www. osc.org; daily 10am–6pm, Fri–Sat until 9pm; observatory Fri–Sat 6–9pm; charge) encompasses 10 halls filled with interactive exhibits that, among other things, lead visitors on a journey through the human body, back to the Age of Dinosaurs, and across the cosmos. An eight-story domed theater,

said to be the largest in the world, shows big-screen films, and sky shows are presented in the planetarium.

On the other side of the park is the **Orlando Museum of Art** (2416 N. Mills Ave; tel: 407-896-4231; www. omart.org; Tue–Fri 10am–4pm, Sat–Sun noon–4pm; charge), whose permanent collection of American and African art and works by American painters such as Maurice Prendergast and Georgia O'Keeffe is supplemented by visiting exhibitions. Special events are held on the first Thursday of every month.

So-called "outsider art" is the focus of the **Mennello Museum of American Folk Art** (900 E. Princeton St; tel: 407-246-4278; www.mennellomuseum.com; Tue–Sat 10.30am–4.30pm, Sun noon–4.30pm; charge), also in the park. In addition to visiting exhibitions, the museum shows works from its permanent collection, dedicated to the "primitive" paintings of Earl Cunningham, a self-taught artist, whose brightly colored canvases have been acquired by several major museums, including the Metropolitan Museum of Art and the Smithsonian Institution.

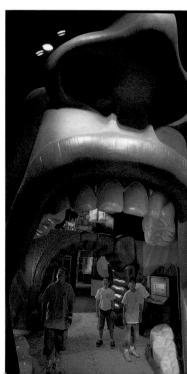

Center stage

The area's two best theaters are also in Loch Haven. The **Orlando Shakespeare Theater** (812 E. Rollins St; tel: 407-447-1700; www.orlandoshakes. org) began nearly 20 years ago as a month-long festival and has since grown into a year-round theater; it has now partnered with the University of Central Florida. The season is dominated by the Bard's works, but there is room for modern playwrights, too. **The Rep** (1001 E. Princeton St; tel: 407-896-7365; www.orlandorep.com) pays special attention to providing affordable productions suitable for a younger audience by transferring classic fairy tales and children's books to the stage.

It's a short drive from Loch Haven Park to the **Harry P. Leu Botanical Gardens and Historic House** ❾ (920 N. Forest Ave; tel: 407-246-2620; www. leugardens.org; daily 9am–5pm; charge), where paths meander through 49 acres (20 hectares) of specialty gardens, including one of the largest collections of roses and camellias and areas devoted to palms, herbs, tropical

plants, and wetlands. Short tours of the historic Leu House are offered throughout the day.

Winter Park

To the north of Orlando is **Winter Park** ❿, an upscale suburb with a gracious, old-money atmosphere. Park Avenue is a good place for strolling when the tourist trails lose their charm; there is not a themed restaurant in sight. At

A dinosaur perches precariously at the Orlando Science Center.

BELOW LEFT: Orlando's Shakespeare Theater. **BELOW:** Renaissance art at the Cornell Museum.

The Charles Hosmer Morse Museum.

BELOW: the Audubon Society of Florida's National Center for Birds of Prey.

the southern end of Park Avenue, on the trim Mediterranean-style campus of Rollins College, is the **Cornell Fine Arts Museum** (1000 Holt Ave; tel: 407-646-2526; www.rollins.edu/cfam; Tue–Sat 10am–5pm, Sun 1–5pm; charge). Though quite small, it is one of the finest and oldest art museums in the Southeast. Each year, the Cornell stages six to eight exhibitions drawn from its holdings of more than 6,000 European and American works of art. The collection encompasses paintings, drawings,

and sculpture from the 1450s to the 1990s. At the start of the school year, one gallery is dedicated to exhibiting work by contemporary local artists.

Also associated with Rollins College is the **Charles Hosmer Morse Museum of American Art** (445 N. Park Ave; tel: 407-645-5311; www.morse-museum.org; Tue–Sat 9.30am–4pm, Sun 1–4pm; charge), a few blocks away. Though the museum's holdings include paintings by such American artists as George Inness, John Singer Sargent, and Thomas Hart Benton, the star attraction is the collection of stained glass by Louis Comfort Tiffany. The highlight of the collection is a reconstruction of the Tiffany Chapel, designed for the 1893 World Columbian Exposition in Chicago.

Sculpture is the focus of the **Albin Polasek Museum and Sculpture Gardens** (633 Osceola Ave; tel: 407-647-6294; www.polasek.org; Tue–Sat 10am–4pm, Sun 1–4pm; charge), a short walk from Rollins College. The collection is dominated by the figurative sculpture of Albin Polasek, the Czech-American artist who lived and

Discount Shopping

Shopping in Orlando is dominated by enormous outlet malls. It's smart to plan for an entire day exploring these bargain retailers, and even smarter to purchase an additional suitcase for the trip back home. Many visitors can be found walking through the outlet malls towing rolling suitcases behind them. Some of the best options include **Orlando Premium Outlets** (4951 International Dr; tel: 407-352-9600) which currently houses designers such as Ralph Lauren, Banana Republic, Juicy Couture, Lacoste, Betsey Johnson, and Victoria's Secret. There are plenty of places to catch your breath and a bite to eat here as well, including **Tropical Sensations** (tel: 407-363-0899), **Vinto Ristorante** (tel: 407-354-0404), and **Kafe Kalik** (tel: 407-248-0889). **Florida Mall** (8001 S. Orange Blossom Trail; tel: 407-851-6255) is a destination in itself, with six department stores, 18 jewelry stores, 22 shoe stores, more than 53 clothing stores, and a hotel.

With so many supermalls in Orlando, it's easy to overlook the **Lake Buena Vista Factory Stores** (15657 State Road 535; tel: 407-238-9301) east of I-4, but its bargains are so good they stand out among the crowds. The Gap and Reebok outlets offer some of the best discounts in Orlando, while the IZOD store has unbelievable bargains for tailor-made suits, shirts, and pants for men.

worked here before his death in 1965. Works by Augustus Saint-Gaudens and others are also on display.

Maitland museums

The vision of a single artist is in evidence a few miles north at the **Maitland Art Center** (231 W. Packwood Ave; tel: 407-539-2181; www.maitlandartcenter.org; Tue–Sun 11am–4pm; charge) in suburban **Maitland ⓫** Founded as an art colony in the 1930s by visionary artist and architect André Smith, the museum is designed in an idiosyncratic Aztec style on 6 acres (2.5 hectares). Still an active center, it offers instruction, concerts, and exhibitions.

When William H. Waterhouse settled in Maitland at the end of the 19th century, he was a pioneer. By the time he completed his home here, he had become one of the area's most in-demand builders. The **Historic Waterhouse Residence and Carpentry Shop Museums** (820 Lake Lily Dr; tel: 407-644-2451; Thur–Sun noon–4pm; charge) have been fully restored to show how he

and his family would have lived on the shores of Lake Lily. Waterhouse built this entire house himself using basic tools like those found in the carpentry shop. The house is viewed by tour only. There is also a self-guided tour through a traditional Victorian herb garden.

Several hundred wounded eagles, hawks, ospreys, and other raptors are rescued and rehabilitated by the **Audubon of Florida's National**

The historic Waterhouse Residence and Carpentry Shop Museums.

BELOW: the Albin Polasek Museum.

The Dragon Coaster at Legoland is sure to be a treat for kids, both young and old.

Center for Birds of Prey (1101 Audubon Way; tel: 407-644-0190; Tue–Sun 10am–4pm; charge) on Lake Sybelia. Although recuperating birds are kept in an isolated facility to minimize human contact, visitors can view 32 animal species that are too severely injured to be returned to the wild.

A somber experience awaits visitors at the small **Holocaust Memorial Resource and Education Center of Central Florida** (851 N. Maitland Ave; tel: 407-628-0555; www.holocaustedu.org; Mon–Thur 9am–4pm, Fri 9am–1pm, Sun 1–4pm; free). One room tells the history of the Holocaust with multimedia displays, another offers changing exhibits on various aspects of the Nazi extermination campaign.

Kissimmee

South of Orlando, a short drive from Disney World, is **Kissimmee** ⑫, a small town chock-full of chain motels, fast-food joints, and second-string attractions, most clustered around US 192, also known as Irlo Bronson Memorial Highway.

Before Disney there was **Gatorland** ⑬ (14501 Orange Blossom Trail; tel: 800-393-5297; www.gatorland.com; daily 9am–5pm; charge), an old-fashioned tourist attraction that's managed to survive the development of modern theme parks by sticking with a simple formula: if one alligator is good, thousands are better. Visitors can view breeding pens and nurseries, stroll through a cypress swamp, see monkeys, snakes, and other exotic wildlife, and sample down-home delicacies like smoked gator ribs and deep-fried gator nuggets. Two shows keep visitors entertained: The Gator Jumparoo Show, in which alligators leap out of the water to snatch a chicken from a trainer's hand, and the Gator Wrestling Show, featuring a wrangler who manhandles one of the big reptiles.

Legoland

Polk County has found new life in **Legoland** ⑭ (One Legoland Way, Winter Haven; tel: 877-350-LEGO; www.florida.legoland.com; daily, hours

vary, see website; charge). Florida's newest theme park is also the biggest Legoland has ever built. The park is home to more than 50 rides, shows, and attractions and features an amazing array of Lego creations. In **Duplo Village** little ones can experience the thrill of driving a car or flying a plane. At **Castle Hill** take part in a **Royal Joust** while riding aboard Lego horses or take flight on **The Dragon**, an indoor/outdoor roller-coaster. **Imagination Zone** is all about letting your imagination and creativity take over. It is also home to the park's most impressive Lego statues, including a bust of Albert Einstein.

At the heart of the park is **Miniland USA** with six themed zones (Washington DC, New York, Las Vegas, Kennedy Space Center, Daytona and Florida). Pirates Cove features a live action pirate stunt show. Thrill seekers shouldn't despair, because **Xtreme** has **Lego Technic Test Track**, a powerful roller-coaster featuring life-size Lego Technic vehicles. In **Aqua Zone** ride wave racers while dodging water blasters. While inside

the **Land of Adventure** climb aboard the Coastersaurus, a junior coaster the little ones are sure to enjoy. **The Lost Kingdom Adventure** is a dark thrill ride, which means the ride is in the dark. Passengers fire lasers at targets while riding the all-terrain roller-coaster. **Pharaoh's Revenge** gives parents and children alike a chance to fire foam balls at their enemies. Afterwards see if you can find your way out of the maze and into the **Beetle Bounce**. In **Lego City** there's something for everyone. At **Fun Town Fire Academy**, families pile into a fire truck and race to put out a blaze. **Driving School** grants children ages 6 to 13 a real-life driving experience in a safe environment. **Junior Driving School** gives children ages 3 to 5 a chance to experience driving in a lesser capacity. **Flight School** is a steel, inverted coaster that lets children experience the feel of flight. Take some time and unwind with **The Big Test** an interactive, acrobatic show that playfully teaches about the responsibilities of fire safety in a fun and entertaining way. Wrap things up in the **Lego Clubhouse**, which houses the world's

EAT

Some Orlando area restaurants apply automatic gratuity to their bills. Be sure to check for this before adding an "additional" gratuity.

BELOW: Waldo Wright's Flying Service offers flying experiences.

Despite the quick pace of growth in the Orlando area, there are still some natural spaces.

BELOW: hiking among cypress trees in the Disney Wilderness.

first Massively Multi Online Game, or MMOG for short.

Polk County

Fantasy of Flight (1400 Broadway Blvd SE, Polk City; tel: 863-984-3500; www.fantasyofflight.com; daily 10am–5pm; charge) offers a trip down aviation's memory lane, beginning with the early years when pilots went skydiving because they had no other choice. In addition to a realistic flight simulator, the attraction has more than 40 rare and vintage aircrafts on display.

Wallaby Ranch Hang Gliding (1805 Deen Still Road; tel: 800-WAL-LABY; www.wallaby.com; daily; charge) is the perfect option if you're looking for something out of the ordinary. Wallaby Ranch will send you up on a tandem flight with an instructor using a technique they call aero-towing. This means the hang-glider is towed into the air with a specially designed ultra-light tow plane. Once you reach an altitude of 2,000ft (609 meters), the ultra light detaches the tow cable and the instructor takes over. After a few minutes of instruction, you'll be in control.

Gardeners should stop at **A World of Orchids** (2501 Old Lake Wilson Rd; tel: 407-396-1887; Tue–Sun 9.30am–4.30pm), a conservatory brimming with lush tropical plants, including thousands of orchids, some of them quite rare. There's also a nature walk that takes you out into the wetland area. Those who prefer nature in a, well, natural setting should visit the Nature Conservancy's **Disney Wilderness** (2700 Scrub Jay Trail; tel: 407-935-0002; Mon–Sat 9am–5pm; charge), a 12,000 acre (4,800 hectare) preserve with 7 miles (11km) of hiking trails through wetlands and pine flatwoods ecosystems. Guided walks and off-road tours are available.

Orange country

Citrus stands flourish along the backroads, and sweet-smelling orange blossoms saturate the air in spring. On a clear day, you can see 2.7 million orange trees, about a third of Florida's crop, from the top of the **Florida Citrus Tower** (141 N. Highway 27; tel: 352-394-4061; www.citrustower.com; Mon–Sat 8am–5pm; charge) on US 27

near **Clermont**, 20 miles (32km) west of Orlando.

South of Orlando

One hundred miles (160 km) south of Orlando, **Lake Wales** ⓯, at 250ft (76 meters) above sea level, is one of the highest places in the state and the southern anchor of Orlando's cultural corridor. The **Lake Wales Museum and Cultural Center** (325 S. Scenic Highway; tel: 863-678-4209; Mon–Fri 9am–5pm, Sat 10am–4pm; charge) in the railroad depot displays vintage railcars, antiques, and exhibits about the area's lumber, railroad and citrus industries. The downtown region is in the National Register of Historic Places. Even higher is the 205ft (62 meter) Singing Tower in **Bok Tower Gardens** (1151 Tower Blvd; tel: 863-676-1408; www.boktowergardens.org; daily 8am–6pm; charge), just north of town. The tower's 53-bell carillon rings daily.

Fifteen miles (24km) west of Lake Wales is **Bartow** ⓰, the center of an industry that has boosted the economy but taken a toll on the environment. SR 60 takes you past Bone Valley, heart of the phosphate mining industry. Florida produces 75 percent of the US's phosphate, a key ingredient in fertilizer. Draglines often dig up fossils of mammoths and giant sharks.

An unexpected gem

Lakeland ⓱ is another blue-collar city. But if you're a Frank Lloyd Wright enthusiast then you'll want to see the **Florida Southern College, where** students study within the world's largest collection of buildings designed by Frank Lloyd Wright (1869–1959). Maps available from the Visitor Center (Mon–Fri 10am–4pm) provide a self-guided tour of these functional works of art – the oldest of which is the **Annie Pfeiffer Chapel** (111 Lake Hollingsworth Dr; tel: 863-680-4111), built in 1938.

Explorations V Children's Museum (109 N. Kentucky Ave; tel: 863-687-3869; www.explorationsv.com; Mon–Fri 9am–5.30pm; charge) features three floors filled with kid-powered exhibits. This hands-on, fully interactive museum lets children create their own news report, become a news anchor, or take the stage like a Broadway star. ❑

Nearly 40 percent of the world's orange juice starts off growing on a tree in Florida.

BELOW:
Annie Pfeiffer
Chapel, Florida
Southern College.

RESTAURANTS

Celebration and Kissimmee

Azteca's Restaurant
809 N. Main St
Tel: 407-933-8155
www.aztecamex.com $$
There's nothing pretentious about this local favorite. The walls are decorated with eclectic hangings, and the menu includes Mexican standards such as burritos, enchiladas, and nachos for starters. All the typical Mexican

beers are available as the perfect accompaniment to the chimichangas.

Café D'Antonio Ristorante Celebration
691 Front St
Tel: 407-566-2233
www.antoniosonline.com
$$–$$$
This upscale Italian restaurant serves an extensive selection of pastas but an even wider selection of meat and chicken dishes, with several veal selections. Its wine list includes fine Italian wines and a healthy selection of vintages from California. There is also a location in Maitland that includes a deli and café.

Plantation Room
Celebration Hotel,
700 Bloom St.
Tel: 407-566-6002 $$–$$$

Affordable, gourmet, nouvelle Florida cuisine, including master dinners featuring everything from alligator to kangaroo. Breakfast is lovely and excellent value.

Sherlocks
715 Bloom St, Suite 130
Tel: 407-566-1866
www.sherlockgroup.com
$–$$
This little bit of England has nestled quietly into Disney's hometown. A combination teahouse, deli, and restaurant, it's open all day for a quick cup of Earl Grey. Or you can settle down and relax for the afternoon's Champagne Tea. Live music plays most weekend evenings.

Universal Studios

Finnegan's Bar and Grill
New York
Tel: 407-224-3613 $$
Meant to be a hometown Irish pub in New York City, Finnegan's Bar and Grill has a very friendly wait staff and serves the traditional fish and chips, corned beef, and, of course, an Irish stew you'll be dreaming about for weeks. The best bit is that the Guinness is fresh and on tap.

Lombard's Seafood Grille
San Francisco/Amity
Tel: 407-224-3613 $$
Lombard's serves the best food at Universal. The clam chowder pays homage to the East Coast, while the fresh seafood and tasty pastas have a more Californian feel. Either way, you're going to leave happy.

Islands of Adventure

Green Eggs & Ham Cafe
Seuss Landing $–$$
A dream come true for Seuss fans (if not for culinary critics), with burgers, fries, and the ubiquitous green-egg-and-ham sandwiches tinted with minced parsley.

Mythos
Lost Continent
Tel: 407-224-4012 $$–$$$
The park's best restaurant is ensconced in a regally appointed cavern with sculpted walls, purple upholstery, and lagoon views. Entrées include wood-roasted lobster with wild mushroom risotto, cedar-planked salmon with orange-horseradish mashed potatoes, and wood-fired pizza, plus child-friendly dishes.

CityWalk

Bob Marley: A Tribute to Freedom
Tel: 407-224-3663 $$
You can chow down on yucca chips, jerk chicken, and plenty of Red Stripe beer while jamming to the reggae beats. The exterior is modeled after Marley's home in Kingston, Jamaica. Inside, photos and other artifacts chronicle his life and career. Live bands perform nightly on the courtyard stage.

Emeril's Restaurant Orlando
Tel: 407-224-3663
$$$–$$$$
Featuring the creations of television chef Emeril Lagasse. Assertive Creole flavors bubble up through

artfully prepared specialties like grilled pork chop with caramelized sweet potatoes. Wine connoisseurs can choose from more than 10,000 bottles on offer. The desserts are equally glorious; homey favorites like root beer floats and banana cream pie become decadent masterpieces under Emeril's skillful hands.

Hard Rock Cafe Orlando
Tel: 407-224-3663 **$$**
When it comes to theme restaurants, the big daddy of 'em all is the Hard Rock Cafe. With seating for 600 in the restaurant and 3,000 in the concert hall, this is the largest Hard Rock Cafe in the world, and, like its humbler brethren, its walls are plastered with gold records, album covers, flashy costumes, and instruments that have been strummed and drummed by some of the rock world's biggest names. A pink Cadillac revolves over the bar; a Sistine Chapel-like mural featuring a heavenly host of dead rock stars adorns the ceiling; and stained-glass panels pay tribute to a trinity of rock legends – Elvis Presley, Chuck Berry, and Jerry Lee Lewis. It's a bit much to take in over a meal, which is why the Hard Rock offers free tours in the afternoon.

Jimmy Buffet's Margaritaville
Tel: 407-224-3663 **$$**
For a laid-back beach bum, Jimmy Buffet is quite the entrepreneur. Decked out in beachy, tropical style, this

restaurant leans toward Caribbean flavors – conch fritters, seafood chowder, grilled fish – with a sprinkling of American standards, including the inevitably named cheeseburger in paradise.

Latin Quarter
Tel: 407-224-3663 **$$**
Both the food and the music are spicy at the Latin Quarter, dedicated to the culture and cuisine of 21 Latin American nations. After dinner, an orchestra and dance troupe take the stage. Dance instructors initiate neophytes into the wonders of merengue, salsa, and the mambo. Don't be afraid to kick up your heels and join the fun.

Pat O'Brien's Orlando
Tel: 407-224-3663 **$$**
An older crowd inhabits Pat O'Brien's, a replica of a landmark New Orleans watering hole. The sing-along crowd loves the dueling pianos, and foodies enjoy jambalaya, muffeletta, and other Big Easy specialties. Wash it all down with a Hurricane, O'Brien's signature rum drink.

Universal Studios Resorts

Emeril's Tchoup Chop
Royal Pacific Resort,
6300 Hollywood Way
Tel: 407-503-3000
www.emerils.com
$$$–$$$$
Emeril Lagasse's second restaurant at Universal Orlando is dedicated to the delicate flavors of Asian and Polynesian cuisine. The restaurant's seductive decor is created using palm trees, bamboo, and waterfalls,

which enhances the flavorful food.

Mama Della's Ristorante
Portofino Bay Hotel,
5601 Universal Blvd
Tel: 407-503-3463
$$–$$$
As heavy on themes as on the stomach, Mama Della's is not just a restaurant, it's an experience. The Italian fare is accompanied by fine wines and strolling entertainment, including singers and guitarists. Mama herself usually makes an appearance, too, insisting that everyone eats up.

Palm Restaurant
Hard Rock Hotel,
5800 Universal Blvd
Tel: 407-503-7256
www.thepalm.com/orlando
$$–$$$$
Carnivores can slice into slabs of beef at this knock-off of the famous New York steakhouse – a favorite with the meat and Martini crowd. Like the original, there are

celebrity caricatures on the wall and a whiff of testosterone in the air.

International Drive and Lake Buena Vista

B-Line Diner
Peabody Hotel,
9801 International Dr
Tel: 407-345-4460
$$
A cozy, 1950s-style diner that's open 24 hours a day, B-Line Diner features thick sandwiches, griddle cakes, and a jukebox with vintage tunes. The corned-beef hash and eggs for breakfast is about as good as this kind of food can get.

Cala Bella
Rosen Shingle Creek,
9939 Universal Blvd
Tel: 407-996-3663
www.calabellarestaurant.com **$$–$$$**
Located at the out-of-the-way Rosen Shingle Creek Resort, this Italian restaurant has a reputation for well-presented basic Italian dishes like risotto, fresh

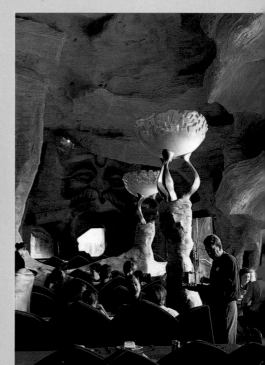

LEFT: the sound of New Orleans at Pat O'Brien's.
RIGHT: Mythos is set in a cavern-like dining room.

pasta, steak, seafood, and Tuscan bean soup. The vaulted ceilings are a nice atmospheric touch.

Capital Grille
Pointe Orlando,
9101 International Dr
Tel: 407-370-4392
www.thecapitalgrille.com/about/main.asp
$$$
Dry-aged steak is the centerpiece of the Capital Grille's menu, and while it is not kind to vegetarians, they do offer a few seafood options if you want to limit your red meat. The wine cellar has more than 5,000 bottles from vinyards around the world.

Ciao Italia Ristorante Italiano
6149 Westwood Blvd
Tel: 407-354-0770
www.ciaoitaliaonline.com
$$-$$$
This family-run restaurant has a warm, welcoming setting combined with fine food. The standard menu is basic, but evening specials offer

more adventurous entrées, and the wine list has a fine selection of Italian wines.

A Land Remembered
Rosen Shingle Creek,
9939 Universal Blvd
Tel: 866-996-9939
www.landremembered restaurant.com
$$$-$$$$
This steakhouse is named after a novel written by Patrick Smith, which focuses on Florida's history and landscapes. Therefore, it should be no surprise that alligator appears on the menu. Otherwise, the fine-dining menu is varied, with several seafood options available for those not wanting steak. The wine list will leave no one disappointed.

Ming Court
9188 International Dr
Tel: 407-351-9988
www.ming-court.com
$$-$$$
Interior koi ponds and gardens set the stage at

this fine Chinese restaurant. The chefs cook up specialties of several provinces and even produce fine sushi as well as a delectable dim sum menu. Ask for a table near the open kitchen.

Norman's
The Ritz-Carlton Grande Lakes, 4012 Central Florida Parkway
Tel: 407-393-4333
$$$-$$$$
Norman Van Aken's New World Cuisine is defined by dishes created when European tradition encounters the native cultures of the Caribbean, Central America, and Florida. Sommeliers offer advice on which vintages best accompany these dishes, and the setting is sheer elegance all the way.

The Oceanaire Seafood Room
Pointe Orlando,
9101 International Dr, Suite 1002
Tel: 407-363-4801
www.theoceanaire.com
$$$-$$$$
Decorated like a 1930s ocean liner, this sleek diner serves "ultra-fish" seafood, which means that it has arrived in the kitchen that day and was probably in the sea the day before. Such ideals deserve celebration, especially in a city where such sourcing of ingredients often plays second fiddle to grand themes. Hence the menu changes daily, but often includes oysters, simple and tasty fish entrées, and a fine wine list with stewards to guide your selection. Still, it's a pity that in the heart of Florida so much of the seafood is flown in from New England and Alaska instead of making the best of the nearby coasts.

Venetian Room
Caribe Royale,
8101 World Center Dr
Tel: 407-238-8060
www.thevenetianroom.com
$$$-$$$$
The Caribe Royale's flagship restaurant adds a touch of class to this corporate hotel. The fine-dining menu here features European favorites such as foie gras and cheese platters, with an extensive wine list containing some of California's most renowned winemakers.

SeaWorld
Seafire Inn Restaurant
$$
This sprawling restaurant serves Caribbean-style food during the daily Music Maestro lunch show. Reservations are required for the Makahiki Luau, a Polynesian-themed dinner theater that is especially popular with families.

Sharks Underwater Grill
Near Sharks Encounter
$$-$$$
Set beside the enormous Sharks Encounter aquarium, one entire wall of the Underwater Grill's dining room is exposed to the tank, letting you sit and dine in awe of the magnificent creatures swimming past. The food here, which is a touch ironic since it's mostly seafood, is simply exquisite. The restaurant can easily produce one of the best meals you'll have at any theme park.

Downtown and Loch Haven Park

The Boheme
Grand Bohemian Hotel,
325 S. Orange Ave
Tel: 407-313-9000
www.grandbohemianhotel.com/theboheme
$$$-$$$$

This is one of Orlando's best restaurants, and as each year passes it earns another award. The Bohemian Wine Room allows parties of up to 14 guests to enjoy a private dining room and exclusive service for the evening, which is ideal for a special party or private event.

Gargi's Lakeside Italian Ristorante
1414 N. Orange Ave
Tel: 407-894-7907
www.gargislakeside.com
$$–$$$
Located on Lake Ivanhoe in the heart of downtown Orlando, this family-run restaurant has grown over the years from a tiny bistro to the thriving restaurant it is today. The menu features veal, steaks, and seafood, all served with fresh pasta. In addition to a sturdy wine list, there is a wide selection of Martinis to choose from.

The Harp and Celt Irish Pub
25 S. Magnolia Ave
Tel: 407-481-2927
www.heartandcelt.com
$$$
Could this be Orlando's first gastropub? Perhaps. The attached Celt Irish Pub has a lively atmosphere, while The Harp serves meaty entrées from a limited menu in sedate surroundings. The prices are far too high for pub grub, but neither the atmosphere nor the food exceeds those standards.

Hue Restaurant
629 E. Central Blvd
Tel: 407-849-1800
www.huerestaurant.com
$$–$$$
Hue makes the most of local produce in creating

familiar American fare such as wood-grilled filet mignon. The designer interior has a cozy and Scandinavian vibe, with crisp lines accented by warm lighting and lit candles. The happy hour is very popular with locals on a night out.

Little Saigon
1106 E. Colonial Dr
Tel: 407-423-8539
www.littlesaigonrestaurant.com
$–$$
This no-nonsense, family-run restaurant is a much welcome addition to a town that tends to celebrate simulation and charade over authenticity. Traditional Vietnamese dishes range from delicate spring rolls and enriching rice noodles to big bowls of nourishing soup and fiery stir-fries, all of which are satisfying to even the most picky of taste buds.

White Wolf Café
1829 N. Orange Ave
Tel: 407-895-9911
www.whitewolfcafe.com
$–$$
This tiny slice of Bohemia is a breath of fresh air in theme-crazy Orlando. The service isn't exactly snappy, but the atmosphere is friendly enough. Luckily the menu – ranging from egg salad sandwiches to wild mushroom lasagna – has enough creative quirks to sustain your interest, especially after a day of information overload at the theme parks.

Winter Park

Brio Tuscan Grille
480 N. Orlando Ave,
Suite 108, Winter Park

Tel: 407-622-5611
www.brioitalian.com
$$
This dark-wood-lined Italian chain restaurant could make a good setting for a romantic evening, but one suspects business lunches are more common in this branch, which is part of the Winter Park Village shopping complex. The menu emphasis is on the heavier side with pork and steaks, but there are plenty of hand-tossed pizzas and other lighter touches available for vegetarians, children, and those who can't handle another burger.

Café de France
526 Park Ave,
South Winter Park
Tel: 407-647-1869
www.lecafedefrance.com
$$–$$$
Start your meal with foie gras, escargot, or the daily selection of pâté before enjoying a fine selection of soups and

salads and entrées that include lamb, pork, and a fish of the day. A fine wine list is available to accompany your meal. If you close your eyes, you might even think you're in Paris.

Luma on Park
290 S. Park Ave, Winter Park
Tel: 407-599-4111
www.lumaonpark.com
$$$
This is perhaps the finest dining experience in the buzzing Park Avenue restaurant scene. The menu features a lot of seafood, from scallops to barramundi, and there are steaks and chops, too. The wine list consists of boutique winemakers, mostly from California, and there is a flight available that provides samples of their bottles. Uniquely, half-glasses are available for those who would like to change wines for each course and yet remain upright for the journey home.

LEFT: Hard Rock Cafe. **RIGHT:** Luma on Park in Winter Park allows patrons to sample half-glasses of wine.

GULF COAST

Beautiful beaches lure travelers to the west coast, but you'll also find vibrant urban neighborhoods, fine museums, an elaborate theme park, and, in a few quiet corners, a slice of Florida as it used to be

The Gulf of Mexico caresses the fine, bleached sand of Florida's western shores. Its warm waters undulate gently or, sometimes, not at all, often flat as a sheet of glass on humid summer days. Shells of every color and shape are washed up on the sands to the endless delight of beach-combing vacationers.

Such tranquil scenes stand in sharp contrast to the clamor on the shores. Newcomers and developers have laid siege to this once placid part of Florida. From the metropolitan Tampa–St Petersburg nucleus, one of the fastest-growing conurbations in the US, north to New Port Richey and south to Fort Myers, the Gulf Coast has begun to resemble the waterfront wall of windows characteristic of the Miami-to-Palm-Beach strip on the Atlantic Coast. Here you'll find retirement farms, condos, and mansions. With them have come massive malls, traffic jams, and urban sprawl.

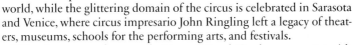

And like the rest of Florida, the Gulf Coast is a place for indulging the imagination. St Petersburg delves into the surreal at the Salvador Dalí Museum, containing one of the most comprehensive collections of Dalí's work in the world, while the glittering domain of the circus is celebrated in Sarasota and Venice, where circus impresario John Ringling left a legacy of theaters, museums, schools for the performing arts, and festivals.

When it comes to theme parks, Tampa's Busch Gardens competes with the best of Orlando's attractions. A great swath of land has been turned into a miniature Africa, complete with big game and a jungle cruise.

But the old Gulf Coast lingers in the fishing villages around Cedar Key and spots south of Naples, and Latino color still enlivens Tampa's Ybor City, founded by a wealthy Cuban tobacco merchant in the late 19th century and now, with its specialty shops, bars, and museum, a tribute to Florida's once thriving cigar industry. Art Deco, too, may still be encountered in downtown Tampa, proving this architectural renaissance is not confined to sunny Miami Beach. ❏

PRECEDING PAGES: a vintage train station is preserved at Heritage Village near Clearwater. **LEFT:** people and pelicans gather at Naples Pier. **TOP:** teeing off on Gasparilla Island near Fort Myers. **ABOVE RIGHT:** Ringling Museum, Sarasota.

TAMPA

The largest city on the Gulf Coast has numerous cultural attractions, a historic Cuban neighborhood, and one of Florida's best theme parks

Main attractions
HENRY PLANT MUSEUM
TAMPA MUSEUM OF ART
TAMPA BAY HISTORY CENTER
FLORIDA AQUARIUM
YBOR CITY
BUSCH GARDENS
MUSEUM OF SCIENCE AND INDUSTRY
LOWRY PARK ZOO

History, as well as archeology, tells us Tampa's coastline has been inhabited for several centuries. Native cultures once called this area home, living off the land and sea until European settlers arrived and began colonizing the region. Hernando De Soto came here in search of gold and other wealth, but it was Henry B. Plant who truly put Tampa on the map and brought the area into the modern age when his railroad arrived in 1884. Yankee-born Plant made his fortune by consolidating the bankrupt railroads of the South after the Civil War. A self-made man who got his start delivering express packages, Plant also helped spearhead winter tourism in Florida.

A love of travel and foreign locale inspired the Moorish design of the **Tampa Bay Hotel**, a national historic landmark. Constructed from reinforced concrete, the 6 acre (2 hectare) hotel building has six minarets, four cupolas, and three domes on the roof, totaling 13, the number of months in the Islamic calendar. One of six Florida hotels built by Plant, the 511-room Tampa Bay Hotel was the most modern resort of its day, with private baths, electric lighting, elevators, and telephones in every room. It had a beauty shop, barbershop, florist, grand salon, sanitarium, dining room,

solarium, and ballroom with orchestra. Landscaped grounds covering 150 acres (60 hectares) of waterfront included 21 buildings, an 18-hole golf course, tennis courts, croquet courts, a boathouse, stables, a racetrack, kennels, a bowling alley, a casino with a 1,500-seat auditorium, a swimming pool, even a zoo.

Another of Plant's triumphs is the Port of Tampa Bay (annexed to Tampa in 1961), on Old Tampa Bay. The swampy waterfront of 400 sq mile (1,000 sq km) Tampa Bay, whose name

LEFT: downtown Tampa.
RIGHT: *Immigrant Statue*, Ybor City.

Old-time cigar shops are part of Ybor City's Cuban heritage.

may derive from the Timucuan Indian word *Tampa*, meaning "sticks of fire," was one of the unlikely beneficiaries.

Set at the mouth of the Hillsborough River, this blue-collar port – the seventh largest in the US – is an industrial powerhouse, transporting more than 50 million tons of cargo annually, including phosphate from nearby mines, citrus, cattle, seafood, even yachts. Still, while Industrial Chic appeals to many – and it certainly is fascinating to visit the Twiggs Street docks and watch the banana boats unloading – it can be a headache for visitors navigating the sprawling city to visit attractions like Busch Gardens, the Lowry Park Zoo, the Museum of Science and Industry, Ybor City, and the Florida Aquarium.

Inspired by the grand vision of Plant, the City of Tampa is working to create new cohesion within the city. Distinct neighborhoods, such as the Cuban cigar capital of **Ybor City** and the historic upscale dining and shopping area of **Hyde Park/SoHo**, on either side of downtown, are now connected by an inexpensive streetcar and tram service. You'll still need to hop on I-275 to visit Busch Gardens, the Lowry Park Zoo, and the Museum of Science and Industry, but Tampa is beginning to feel like a manageable destination, worthy of more than a quick stop en route to the Gulf beaches.

Downtown Tampa

Symbolic of Tampa's ambitious revitalization project is the **Riverwalk** cultural corridor taking shape on the east bank of the Hillsborough River. The **Henry Plant Museum** ❶ (401 W. Kennedy Blvd; tel: 813-254-1891; Tue–Sat 10am–4pm, Sun noon–4pm; charge) lets you peer into 14 former guest rooms, each a cabinet of curiosities from around the world collected by railroad magnate Henry Plant and his wife, Margaret, and brought to the $3-million resort on Plant's railroad. At the north end, the five-theater **David A Straz Jr Center for the Performing Arts** ❷ (1010 North W.C. MacInnes Place; tel: 813-229-STAR; www.straz.org), the largest cultural center south of Washington, DC, is a major destination for theater productions, classical concerts, and the

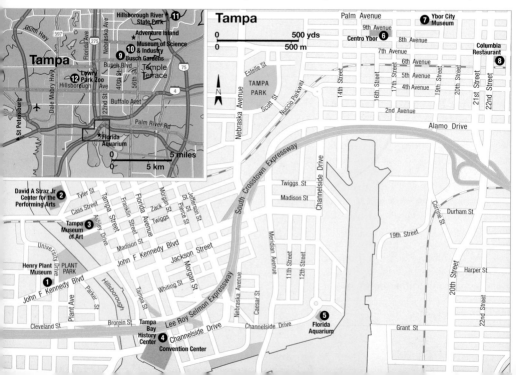

arts. Anchoring the southern end, the **Tampa Museum of Art** ❸ (120 W. Gasparilla Plaza; tel: 813-274-8130; www.tampamuseum.org; Tue–Sat 10am–4pm, Sun noon–4pm; charge) is emerging as a state-of-the-art facility. The museum has a two-story atrium, glass ceilings, stone floors, and a boxlike, cantilevered structure sheathed in a metal skin and programmable LED lighting that mirrors changes in the surrounding environment. TMA's wide-ranging art collection includes classical antiquities and regional contemporary art, such as a photo exhibit on Mexican artist Frida Kahlo and glass art displayed in a light-filled river terrace.

Days of yore

Tampa Bay History Center ❹ (801 Old Water St; tel: 813-228-0097; www.tampahistorycenter.org; daily 10am–5pm; charge), in the Tampa Convention Center Annex, is a small museum telling the story of Tampa from pre-historic times to the present. Tampa's strategic importance during a succession of wars is examined, starting with nearby Fort Brooke, the 1824

military outpost used by the US Army during the Second and Third Seminole Wars (1835–55) and occupied by the Confederate Army during the Civil War. Tampa's important national role as a major mobilization point for US troops during the Spanish-American War in 1898 was reprised in World War II, when 15,000 servicemen were stationed at McDill Air Force Base. In 1910, the Ybor and Sparkman channels, connecting the east side of Hillsborough Bay with the old channel running from the Hillsborough River

Moorish domes cap the Henry Plant Museum – formerly the Tampa Bay Hotel – at the University of Tampa.

BELOW LEFT: Ybor City.
BELOW: the annual Gasparilla Invasion.

Pirates of Gasparilla

Tampa's rites of spring occur every February when its businessmen and bigwigs exchange their suits and briefcases for puffed-sleeved shirts and buckled boots and board the *José Gasparilla*, which leads the annual Gasparilla Invasion. Pirates climb the three masts to the crow's nests, blast cannon, and set off for the mouth of the Hillsborough River flanked by hundreds of smaller craft with their own swashbuckling crews. Upon landing, pirates swarm the streets of downtown Tampa, where hundreds of thousands of spectators watch them lead a parade. The first Gasparilla Invasion was held in 1904. It grew out of the Gulf Coast's reputation as a haunt for blood-thirsty buccaneers, particularly a legendary character named José Gaspar, who was believed to have lived on Gasparilla Island near Charlotte Harbor and plundered his way along the Gulf Coast. History books sometimes refer to Gaspar, but no records prove his existence. One theory holds that Gaspar was the invention of a fisherman who, in the 1870s, claimed to have sailed with Gaspar in order to boost his business in treasure maps.

Decorative lights illuminate Seventh Avenue near Centro Ybor.

BELOW: a shark prowls the waters of the Florida Aquarium.

Florida water from its source to the sea, passing through different habitats. Allow plenty of time to enjoy the many interactive exhibits, which include the Bay and Beaches and the very popular Coral Reef, a simulated Key West dive site contained within a 500,000 gallon (2 million liter) tank filled with 1,500 tropical fish. Throughout the day, divers jump into the tank and answer visitor questions via intercom. This is the only aquarium in the country where, for a fee, kids six years old and over can don scuba gear and swim with the fishes in the coral reef. You can also board a boat outside the aquarium for a Wild Dolphin Ecotour, which allows you to look for some of the 400-plus dolphins that live in Tampa Bay.

to Tampa Harbor, were constructed, allowing Tampa to develop into a major port.

Water world

The biggest visitor attraction in the Port of Tampa is the soaring **Florida Aquarium** ❺ (701 Channelside Dr; tel: 813-273-4000; www.flaquarium. org; daily 9.30am–5pm; charge) in the Garrison Seaport Center on Channelside Drive. This attractive aquarium is one of the best in the country. A carefully crafted interpretive theme tying together exhibits on three floors lets you follow a drop of

Ybor City

About the time Plant was building his rail system, steamship lines, and hotels, Vicente Martinez Ybor was planning to move his cigar factory from Key West. Just northeast of downtown, near the train tracks, Ybor City (which grew to prominence as the Cigar Capital of the World) no longer pulsates with the color and excitement of its Cuban heyday when crowds gathered at cockfights and to hear Cuban freedom fighter José Martí make fiery speeches. Ybor City is now a popular New Orleans–style shopping and nightclub district, bustling with activity into the wee hours.

Of the building around which the enclave grew, Ybor's 1886 cigar factory is the centerpiece. Once upon a time, cigar workers sat in rows tediously rolling cigars while a reader, employed by the workers, entertained them with Spanish-language selections from poetry, books, and newspapers. Entrepreneurs rescued Martinez's handsome building, restored its iron grillwork and oak interiors, and cleaned its red-brick exterior. They have added restaurants and shops and now call it **Centro Ybor** ❻, where you can still buy a good cigar.

Start any visit by touring **Ybor City Museum** ❼ (1818 9th Ave; tel: 813-247-6323; www.ybormuseum.org; Mon–Sun 9am–5pm; charge). The museum complex includes three restored cigar workers' homes, historic photos, and artifacts of the cigar industry; guided tours of Ybor City are also available. The streetcar travels along **Seventh Avenue** (known as La Setima), the main strip, with shops selling cigars and lacy Spanish fabric. For lunch, sample a hot, pressed Cuban (a pork sandwich) at **La Tropicana**, considered the best in the city. Don't miss dinner at the landmark **Columbia Restaurant** ❽ on the corner of 22nd Street. The family-run Columbia, built in 1905, is the real deal. Sit back and enjoy the flamenco show, strolling musicians, and the gracious black-jacketed waiters serving classic Spanish dishes like paella and garbanzo bean soup. There are other branches in the city, but none as authentic as the original.

Wild kingdom

Started in 1959 as a family zoo of exotic animals and tropical gardens for visitors to the Anheuser-Busch Brewery, **Busch Gardens** ❾ (Busch Blvd and 40th St; tel: 813-987-5000; daily; charge) has matured into one of Florida's top three theme parks. It combines the best of everything: a superb conservation zoo; professional concerts and seasonal shows; landscaped grounds; and rides, from super-soaking water rides to state-of-the-art roller-coasters, featuring gravity-defying inversions, barrel rolls, and intertwining tracks.

The park's 335 acres (136 hectares) include 10 distinct areas: Morocco, Crown Colony, Edge of Africa, Serengeti Plain, Egypt, Nairobi, Timbuktu, Congo, Stanleyville, and Bird Gardens. Entering through Morocco, get an overview of the whole park by boarding the skyway ride, which begins at Crown Colony in the southeast and ends at Congo in the northwest. Or take a ride on the delightful miniature train, which puffs its way slowly around the 65 acre (26 hectare) Serengeti Plain on the

The birds in Busch Gardens' aviary are especially friendly.

BELOW: Ybor City Museum.

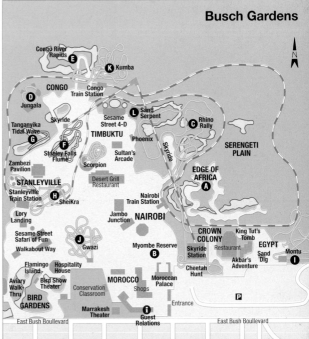

Busch Gardens

N

Congo River Rapids ❱E❰

❱K❰ Kumba

CONGO

Congo Train Station

❱D❰ Jungala

Sand Serpent ❱L❰

Rhino Rally ❱C❰

Tanganyika Tidal Wave

Skyride

Sesame Street 4-D

TIMBUKTU

Phoenix

SERENGETI PLAIN

❱G❰

Stanley Falls Flume

❱F❰

Sultan's Arcade

Skyride

EDGE OF AFRICA

❱A❰

Zambezi Pavilion

Scorpion

Desert Grill Restaurant

STANLEYVILLE

Stanleyville Train Station ❱H❰ SheiKra

Nairobi Train Station

Lory Landing

Jambo Junction **NAIROBI**

Sesame Street Safari of Fun ❱J❰

Gwazi

Myombe Reserve ❱B❰

CROWN COLONY King Tut's Tomb

Skyride Station Restaurant

EGYPT

Sand Dig Montu

Akbar's Adventure ❱I❰

Walkabout Way

Cheetah Hunt

Flamingo Island Hospitality House

Aviary Walk-Thru

Bird Show Theater

Conservation Classroom

MOROCCO Shops

Moroccan Palace

BIRD GARDENS

Entrance

❱P❰

Marrakesh Theater

East Bush Boulevard

Guest Relations ❱i❰

East Bush Boulevard

TIP

One day at Busch Gardens wasn't enough? Inquire about a free or discounted next-day ticket at Guest Relations before you leave the park.

park's east side, with stops at Nairobi, Congo, and Stanleyville. The southwest corner, the original roadside attraction of tropical gardens, with flamingos, snakes, and exotic animals, is more slow-paced. It has toddler rides, bird shows, walk-through aviaries, and pleasantly shaded pathways.

Plan your visit to this huge park carefully and pace yourself: there are few short cuts between attractions, so you'll be on your feet for the better part of the day. A two-day pass lets you dedicate one day to learning about the 2,700 animals that live in naturalized environments in the park and another to enjoy the rides. Busch Gardens' rides load very quickly, typically in half the time of the big Orlando parks. Note that wildlife is more active in the cooler morning hours and the animals sleep in the afternoon.

African safari

The park's hottest tickets for animal-lovers are five daily **Serengeti Safaris** (limit 20 people, first-come, first-served) that start at Crown Colony and trek out onto the Serengeti Plain to view rhinos, zebras and giraffes. If you're keen, head there first and sign up for a tour. If it's sold out, the next best thing is the **Edge of Africa** exhibit, which features nose-to-nose encounters with baboons, Nile crocs, hippos, a lion and lioness, hyenas, vultures, and meerkats. Rangers holding animal ambassadors, such as monkeys and snakes, stroll the park. They are trained wildlife biologists, and you'll learn a lot from them. Brass plaques have wildlife conservation messages that can be rubbed and collected in a free wildlife guide. Other displays mimic a biologist's field diary. Some of the best can be found in the entrancing **Myombe Reserve** gorilla exhibit in Nairobi, one of the most satisfying of Busch's animal exhibits.

Wild ride

It may seem odd to have rides in a wildlife park, but in the race for tourist dollars, Busch Gardens is determined to keep up with the other parks. Hot on the heels of Disney's Animal Kingdom, **Rhino Rally** ,

simulated Jeep ride, premiered at Busch in 2001. **Jungala** **D**, a new attraction in the revitalized Congo, has a zipline experience, a climbing area, a jungle village, and Bengal tigers, orang-utans, and other residents of the former Claw Island. Congo also has the popular **Congo River Rapids** **E**, which simulates a white-water ride, while next door, in Stanleyville, two other water rides – the **Stanley Falls** **F** flume ride and **Tanganyika Tidal Wave** **G** chute – guarantee a good drenching.

It is for its roller-coasters that Busch Gardens leads the pack. **ShieKra** **H**, North America's first dive coaster, is a floorless monster that climbs 200ft (60 meters) up, then rockets 90 degrees down in a simultaneous loop and roll. **Montu** **I**, one of the tallest and longest inverted roller-coasters in the world, reaches a G-force of 3.85 at 60mph (100kph). The deafening clatter of **Gwazi** **J**, an old-fashioned double wooden coaster that is the Southeast's fastest and largest, is half the reason this ride seems so scary. Terrifying **Kumba** **K** spirals 360 degrees through one of the world's largest vertical loops. For younger kids, there's **Sand Serpent** **L**, a five-story wild mouse style coaster. With a top speed of 22mph (35kmh), it's a perfect first coaster ride. The newly added **Sesame Street Safari of Fun** was designed just for the little tykes (under age five). It has play areas, junior rides, and shows. Busch Gardens unveiled its newest coaster, **Cheetah Hunt**, in May 2011. The 4,400ft (1,340 meter) -long coaster reaches speeds of 60mph (96kph) and runs through the new cheetah habitat.

Cooling off

After a steamy day in the jungle, refresh yourself in the body flumes, lagoons, and waterfalls of **Adventure Island** (10001 McKinley Dr; tel: 813-287-8844; www.adventureisland.com; open seasonally; charge). Another of Tampa's top attractions – the **Museum of Science and Industry** **10** (4801 E.

Fowler Ave; tel: 813-987-6100; www. mosi.org; daily 9am–5pm; charge) – is nearby. MOSI contains a vast array of lively science exhibits, a butterfly pavilion, Florida's first IMAX cinema, and hands-on contraptions that allow you to learn how your body works. One of the most popular attractions is Gulf Coast Hurricane, a re-created 75mph (120kmh) wind tunnel that pitches you right into the storm.

It's not all man-made hoopla. **Hillsborough River State Park** **11** (daily 8am–sunset; charge), 15 miles (24km) from downtown, has a large campground and hiking trails and is a prime spot for canoeing. **Lowry Park Zoo** **12** (1101 West Sligh Blvd; tel: 813-935-8552; www.lowryparkzoo.com; daily 9.30am–5pm; charge) has been named the top family-friendly zoo in the US. It has wooden walkways that wind through 56 acres (23 hectares) and seven exhibit areas, including Asian Gardens and Primate World, a petting park, and a free-flight aviary. One highlight is the manatee hospital, where you can watch recuperating manatees swimming from above and below. ❑

TIP

Canoe Escape (tel: (813-986-2067) organizes a variety of canoe trips through Hillsborough River State Park. Call for reservations.

BELOW: the so-called Mystic Sheiks of Morocco march through the Zagora Cafe.

RESTAURANTS

Restaurants

Prices for a three-course dinner per person, excluding tax, tip, and beverages:
$ = under $20
$$ = $20–45
$$$ = $45–60
$$$$ = over $60

Ashley Street Grille
200 N. Ashley Dr
Tel: 813-226-4400
$$–$$$
This quiet riverside restaurant allows fine ingredients to shine, using only the best seafood, heirloom vegetables, fine cheese, and a subtle, sure hand in the kitchen. It has tasting menus in addition to the standard fare. The homebaked breads are particularly good.

Bean There Traveler's Coffee House
3203 Bay-to-Bay Blvd
Tel: 813-837-7022 $
This South Tampa coffee shop serves all-day breakfast, strong coffee, and sandwiches. It's on the right side of the road, just past McDill Avenue.

Bern's Steak House
1208 S. Howard Ave
Tel: 813-251-2421
www.bernssteakhouse.com
$$$–$$$$
The Baroque decor has been likened to that of a funeral parlor, but the selection of beef and wines is what brings people to award-winning Bern's, one of Tampa's most famous restaurants. The menu gives the vital statistics of every cut of meat, up to a 60 ounce (2kg) sirloin that serves six. But vegetarians and pescatarians are well covered, too, with organic veggies pulled from the restaurant's own garden and a tank of live fish. Over one-half million bottles of wine, representing some 6,000 varieties, fill the cellars – thought to be the largest on-hand stock of wines kept by any restaurant in the world.

Byblos Café
2832 S. MacDill Ave
Tel: 813-805-7977
www.bybloscafe.com
$$–$$$
Authentic Lebanese food, including baba ghanoush, hummus, and tabouleh, anchors the menu of this family-owned Mediterranean café, named for a city in ancient Phoenicia.

Caffe Paradiso
4205 S. Macdill Ave, #D
Tel: 813-835-6622
$$–$$$
Italian classics win raves from native-born diners at this family-run storefront café. Try the delectable salmon-stuffed ravioli or the tender osso buco alla Milanese – just like your mother used to make.

Cephas
1701 E. 4th Ave
Tel: 813-247-9022
www.cephashotshop.com
$–$$
Jerk chicken and curried goat are on the menu at this sweet little West Indian restaurant run by Jamaica-born Cephas Gilbert. Portions are cheap and cheerful.

City's Gourmet Deli
514 N. Tampa St
Tel: 813-229-7400 $
They roast their own meats and use European chocolate in their brownies at this upmarket deli. Soups and sandwiches are all home-made.

Columbia Restaurant
2117 E. 7th Ave
Tel: 813-248-4961
www.columbiarestaurant.com $$–$$$$
Founded in 1905 as a corner café by Cuban immigrant Casimiro Hernandez, Sr, the block-long Columbia Restaurant in Ybor City is the oldest continuously operated restaurant in Florida and is still family owned. A perennial award winner for its Iberian meat and seafood cuisine, this landmark eatery features an old-fashioned cigar bar, two floors of majolica-tiled dining rooms, and excellent nightly flamenco dinner shows. Signature dishes, served by elegant waiters of the old school, include the house 1905 salad, tossed at your table; paella; Cuban black bean soup; shrimp al ajillo; red snapper Alicante; pompano en papillote; and the famous Cuban shredded beef dish, ropa vieja. There are sister branches in Celebration, Sarasota, Clearwater, St Augustine, and on the pier at St Petersburg.

The Dish
1600 E. 8th Ave
Tel: 813-241-8300 $–$$
The other not-to-be-missed Ybor City restaurant, Dish is located in Centro Ybor and offers grilling stations throughout the restaurant where you can make up your own plate.

Jackson's Bistro-Bar-Sushi

601 S. Harbour Island Blvd
Tel: 813-277-0112
www.jacksonsbistro.com
$$–$$$

The waterfront location is the big draw at this restaurant, which covers all the bases, offering sushi, bistro classics, and an extensive wine list. It can get busy when there are conventions in town.

Mise en Place

442 W. Kennedy Blvd
Tel: 813-254-5373
www.miseonline.com
$$–$$$$

Offering a fusion of fresh Florida seafood and Caribbean spices, this longtime chef-owned restaurant pleases both foodies and the style-conscious without being too full of itself or over-dressed. Eclectic dishes include mustard pecan-encrusted rack of lamb with bourbon shallot demi-glace. There's a full-blast tasting menu for the adventurous.

Oystercatchers

2900 Bayport Dr
Tel: 813-207-6815
www.hyatt.com/gallery/oystercatchers $$–$$$$

Fresh, line-caught, wild seafood, simply prepared on the grill, and organic produce highlight the menu of this restaurant in the Grand Hyatt Tampa Bay hotel, which is also one of the best places in Tampa for Sunday brunch. Newly remodeled in soothing pale woods, stone, and light tones, the restaurant is very relaxing, allowing signature dishes like fresh crab cakes to shine. Adjoining Armani's offers a fine-dining atmosphere for evening dinner. Both

restaurants are overseen by Tampa-born chef de cuisine Kenny Hunsberger, seen on the PBS program *Great Chefs of the South*.

Pelagia Trattoria

4200 Jim Walter Blvd
Tel: 813-313-3235
www.pelagiatrattoria.com
$$–$$$$

New Mediterranean cuisine, as envisioned by a talented Turin-born chef, makes this casual bistro a winner for breakfast, lunch, or dinner. Even the most health-conscious diner will be delighted by the creative menu, which has many low-carb and low-cholesterol options. Try the Mediterranean salad with warm pancetta and feta, roasted salmon with balsamic-green apple sauce, or broccoli rabe in sweet garlic. Finish with golden delicious apple tart, rosemary-almond cream, and caramel sauce for a treat. Everything is made from scratch and receives chef Fabrizio's creative touch.

Restaurant BT

2507 S. MacDill Ave
Tel: 813-258-1916
www.restaurantbt.com
$$–$$$$

In the mood for something different? This Vietnamese restaurant offers the fresh herb-sparked flavors of French-inspired Asian food with a personal touch. The green papaya salad or the bun noodle salad bowl are perfect lunchtime favorites, while the seared duck foie gras appetizer and the snapper à la Saigon dinner are excellent choices.

Side Berns

2208 W. Morrison Ave
Tel: 813-258-2233
www.sideberns.com
$$–$$$$

The sassy younger sibling of Bern's has achieved its well-deserved awards with a quite different take on cuisine from its famous parent. The fusion food runs heavily toward spiced seafood dishes and exotic game meats like ostrich. Desserts are works of art.

Vizcaya Restaurante and Tapas Bar

10905 N. Dale Mabry Hwy
Tel: 813-968-7400
www.vizcayarestaurante.com $$–$$$

Superb tapas win raves from locals at this family-run Basque restaurant. Try the sea bass, paella, and other mini-dishes with some of the excellent Spanish wine.

Wine Exchange

1609 W Snow Ave
Tel: 813-254-9463
www.wineexchangetampa.com $$–$$$$

Located in well-to-do Hyde Park, this hip location is all about the wine. Each entrée on the fairly straightforward menu of pizzas, pastas, and sandwiches, supplemented by attractive daily specials such as Dijon-encrusted salmon and grilled Delmonico steak, is paired with individual wine suggestions, by the bottle or glass. Patio dining is lovely.

Yacht StarShip

603 Channelside Dr
Tel: 813-223-7999
www.yachtstarship.com
$$$–$$$$

This well-reviewed dinner cruise aboard an $8-million yacht plies the waters of beautiful Tampa Bay. You'll strut about the deck in all your finery and enjoy the well-executed four-star Continental cuisine, dance to live music, and watch the sunset. A 25-percent discount for locals is a big draw.

LEFT: Columbia Restaurant specializes in Spanish and Cuban fare. **RIGHT:** a sidewalk café in Ybor City.

ST PETERSBURG TO CEDAR KEY

This city by the bay – home to the Dalí Museum
and other cultural attractions – is a gateway to
gorgeous beaches, unspoiled fishing villages, and
crystal-clear rivers where manatees swim

What makes the perfect beach? Florida geologist Dr Stephen Leatherman, also known as Dr Beach, thinks he can identify the best using criteria such as sand softness, number and size of waves, color and condition of water, presence of wildlife and pests, and human use and impacts.

When Dr Beach announces his annual list of Top Ten beaches, there are always a few Florida locations hovering near the top. **Fort De Soto Park ❶**, a huge county park, campground, and boat launch encompassing five barrier islands at the southern tip of the peninsula, was ranked America's Best Beach in 2005. In 2008, **Caladesi Island State Park ❷**, a boat-in-only beach on an island north of Clearwater, took first place. **Clearwater Beach ❸** is popular with many overseas visitors, and the Gulf of Mexico side of **St Petersburg** and the **Pinellas Peninsula** are perennial favorites.

Thousands of lodgings, from historic hotel resorts to vacation condos, along with neighborhood restaurants serving fresh grouper, stone crab, and other local seafood, crowd the seafront the length of Gulf Boulevard, the main thoroughfare. Each beach community is joined to the mainland by a causeway that crosses the tranquil Intracoastal Waterway. From here, you're just minutes from US 19, which links the 26 communities of the Pinellas Peninsula, and Interstate 275, linking Tampa and Sarasota via Tampa Bay bridges.

Gulf shore

With record sunshine and turquoise waters lapping 35 miles (56km) of shoreline, the gulf is mesmerizing. Walk for miles on these super-clean beaches, swim or kayak in shallow gulf waters, go fishing and scuba diving, watch seabirds and other wildlife, take boat

Main attractions
FORT DE SOTO PARK
CALADESI ISLAND STATE PARK
CLEARWATER MARINE AQUARIUM
WHEEDON ISLAND PRESERVE
CULTURAL AND NATURAL HISTORY
CENTER
MUSEUM OF FINE ARTS
SALVADOR DALÍ MUSEUM
TARPON SPRINGS
CEDAR KEY

LEFT: Don CeSar Beach Resort.
RIGHT: Clearwater canine.

A pedicab trawls for passengers on the Clearwater beachfront.

tours to undeveloped island refuges, or just soak up the sun. **Long Key**, at the south end, boasts **St Pete Beach ❹**, home to the bright pink historic Don CeSar Resort, and **Passe-a-Grill Beach**, with its low-rise historic district and quaint shops. On the quieter north end, the busy waterfront at **Clearwater ❺** has kid-flavored distractions, including **Captain Memo's Pirate Cruise** (25 Causeway Blvd, Dock 3; tel: 727-446-2587; daily), a two-hour cruise where parents relax while kids do educational activities.

Nestled in a residential waterfront neighborhood is **Clearwater Marine**

Aquarium (249 Windward Passage; tel: 727-441-1790; www.cmaquarium. org; Mon–Thur 9am–5pm, Fri–Sat 9am–7pm, Sun 10am–5pm; charge), which quietly carries out award-winning work as a marine rescue and release center. Enclosures hold recuperating sea turtles, otters, dolphins, and other sealife, all injured or impacted by human carelessness. CMA's star attraction is Winter, a bottlenose dolphin who lost her tail to a crab trap. Winter was fitted with a prosthetic tail in early 2011, and is now learning to swim properly again. There are regular enrichment exercises with resident dolphins in the main pool and reserved times to feed a dolphin and have your photo taken (additional fee; visitors provide the camera). Multimedia presentations about CMA's work take place in an attractive circular theater.

Suncoast Seabird Sanctuary (18328 Gulf Blvd; tel: 727-391-6211; www. seabirdsanctuary.com; daily; free) was founded by bird-lover Ralph Heath. Donations allow Heath to care for 500-plus injured and crippled cormorants, pelicans, sandpipers, white herons, and other seabirds.

Several miles inland, **Pinewood Cultural Park ❻** (Walsingham Rd and 125th St North, Largo) encompasses a trio of worthy attractions: the **Florida Botanical Gardens** (12520 Ulmerton Rd, tel: 727-582-2100; www. flbg.com; daily 7am–7pm), with 120 acres (48 hectares) of theme gardens and natural areas; the **Gulf Coast Museum of Art** (tel: 727-518-6833; Tue–Sat 10am–4pm, Sun noon–4pm), which shows contemporary art and fine craft objects by Southeastern artists; and **Heritage Village** (11909 125th St N, tel: 727-582-2123; Wed–Sat 10am–4pm, Sun 1–4pm), a compound with vintage structures from the 1850s to the early 1900s.

St Petersburg

St Petersburg ❼ is beginning to overcome its reputation as a retirement haven. A regenerated waterfront, top

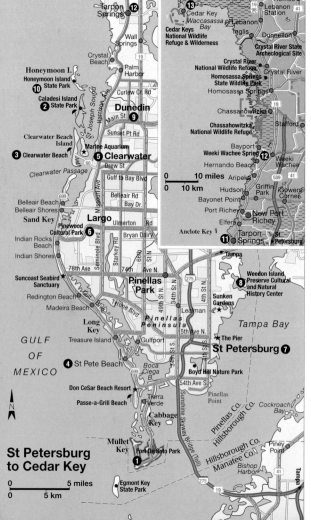

St Petersburg to Cedar Key

museums, a major-league baseball team, year-round festivals, and activities geared to an outdoor lifestyle are attracting a younger demographic. Shuffleboard is even becoming popular with the hipsters, thanks, in part, to a free St Pete Shuffle every Friday night at the historic courts.

Tampa Bay was once home to the Tocobaga, Timucua, and Manasota people. Villages, canoes, and shell mounds have been excavated at **Weedon Island Preserve Cultural and Natural History Center** ❽ (1800 Weedon Dr NE; tel: 727-453-6500; www.weedonislandcenter.org; Wed–Sun 10am–4pm; charge), a natural area of marshes crisscrossed by hiking trails on the Pinellas Peninsula. Spanish explorer Panfilo de Narvaez in 1528, followed by Hernando de Soto in 1539, named the peninsula Punta Pinal (or Point of Pines), which later became Pinellas. De Soto found the only mineral springs on the peninsula near a large Tocobaga village in Safety Harbor.

In 1875, 1,600 acres (650 hectares) of what would eventually become St Petersburg were purchased and settled by General John Williams of Detroit. Williams made a deal with exiled Russian nobleman Peter Demens to bring the railroad to Pinellas Peninsula. Demens overcame yellow fever and flooding to expand a short logging track on the peninsula into Henry Plant's Orange Belt Line, joining the gulf with citrus groves in Sanford in central Florida. The port prospered until the disastrous citrus freeze of 1894, when Plant bought the branch railroad for a song.

In 1914, St Petersburg again made transportation history when Tony Jannus piloted a flying airboat called the *Benoist* 21 miles (34km) over Tampa Bay, the world's first commercial flight.

Art and history

Folksy **St Petersburg Museum of History** ❶ (335 2nd Ave NE; tel: 727-894-1052; www.stpetemuseumofhistory.org; Wed–Sat 10am–5pm, Sun 1–5pm; charge), though at the foot of the commercial pier complex, has exhibits on local history, including a recreation of a Tocobaga dugout

A wildlife rehabilitator at the Suncoast Seabird Sanctuary introduces visitors to one of her patients – a double-crested cormorant.

BELOW: Fort De Soto Park is often ranked as one of America's best beaches.

One block west of Straub Park is the elegant **Museum of Fine Arts** Ⓒ (255 Beach Dr NE; tel: 727-96-2667; www.fine-arts.org; Mon–Sat 10am–5pm, Sun noon–5pm; charge). Founded by Margaret Acheson Stuart to house her private art collection, the museum has the atmosphere of a stately home showcasing family treasures, from masterpieces by Berthe Morisot, Claude Monet, Paul Cézanne, and other French Impressionists to pre-Columbian pottery and sacred Asian art. The Hazel Hough Wing doubles the size of this popular museum. The country's largest collection of glass-works by modern master Dale Chihuly can be seen at the nearby **Arts Center** Ⓓ (719 Central Ave; tel: 727-822-7872; www.theartscenter.org; Tue–Sat 10am–5pm). Artists can rent studio space and display their works in this complex, one of the largest glassblowing facilities in the Southeast.

Salvador Dalí's Nature Morte Vivante is on display at the Dalí Museum in St Petersburg.

canoe and a full-scale replica of the *Benoist* airboat. The stirring story of St Petersburg's historic African-American community is well told at this museum, as well as at the nearby **Dr Carter G. Woodson Museum of African American History** Ⓑ (2240 9th Ave South; tel: 727-323-1104; www.woodsonmuseum.org; Tue–Thur 11am–4pm, Fri 11am–3pm, Sat 11am–2pm; free).

By far the most famous cultural attraction here is the **Salvador Dalí Museum** Ⓔ (One Dali Blvd; tel: 727-823-3767; www.salvadordalimuseum.org; Mon–Wed 9.30am–5.30pm, Thur

BELOW: the Arts Center.

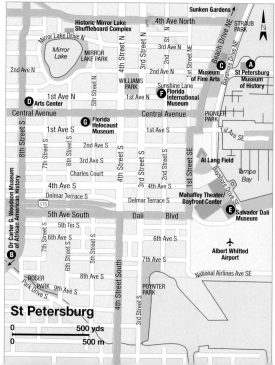

St Petersburg

0   500 yds
0   500 m

9.30am–8pm, Fri 9.30am–6.30pm, Sat 9.30am–5.30pm, Sun noon–5.30pm; charge), now in its new and much larger location, although this world-class institution may seem oddly out of place in this sun-loving vacationland. The gift of the Morse family, personal friends of Salvador and Gala Dalí, the collection features 1,300 diverse works. The core of the collection is not the six enormous masterworks, but rather the early Dalí landscapes of Spain, which are filled with lush Impressionist influences and are unexpectedly charming. Docent tours of the museum are highly recommended to understand the complex psychological references buried in Dalí's paintings. The gift shop is a must for Dalí fans.

Two other museums round out the cultural offerings. **Florida International Museum** ➊ (244 Second Ave North; tel: 727-341-7900; www.floridamuseum.org; Tue–Sat 10am–5pm, Sun noon–5pm; charge) is affiliated with the Smithsonian Institution and stages traveling exhibitions that attract thousands of visitors. Past topics have included Princess Diana and the Treasures of the Tsars. The Kennedy Gallery, a permanent exhibit, includes re-creations of the West Wing and Oval Office and more than 600 personal items once owned by the Kennedy family.

More somber is the **Florida Holocaust Museum** ➋ (55 5th St South; tel: 727-820-0100; www.flholocaust museum.org; Wed–Sun 10am–5pm, Thur 10am–8pm; charge), third largest in the country. Florida was the first state in the nation to mandate Holocaust education in schools. This museum's

A docent demonstrates old-fashioned kitchen utensils at Heritage Village in Pinewood Cultural Park.

BELOW LEFT: a Roman statue of Aphrodite at the Museum of Fine Arts. **BELOW:** a shuffleboard court.

The St Pete Shuffle

Shuffleboard is popular in Florida, where shuffleboard courts are found at many vintage motels. Players use cues to push weighted pucks down a narrow elongated court, with the aim of positioning them in a marked scoring area. The game, reputedly invented in England and played at the court of Henry VIII, is related to bowling, croquet, billiards, and shove ha'penny, a table-top pub version using coins. Organized in 1924,

the **Historic Mirror Lake Shuffleboard Complex** (559 Mirror Lake Dr North; tel: 727-822-2083) in downtown St Petersburg gained fame as the world's largest shuffleboard club in its postwar heyday, with a membership of 5,000 using 110 courts. Today, there are only 65 courts, but the historic shuffleboard complex is still going strong. It has a Shuffleboard Hall of Fame and tournaments, and attracts young families to free special events on Friday nights, dubbed the St Pete Shuffle. Themed events have included a Harry Potter night, an ice-cream social, a fashion show, a Hurricane Katrina fund-raiser, and an India night with yoga, bellydancers, a street bazaar, and music.

The collection at the Museum of Fine Arts ranges from Greek and Roman antiquities to 19th- and 20th-century European and American paintings.

BELOW:
Gulf Coast sunset.

central exhibit is a railroad car used for transportation to the camps.

Dunedin

The historic communities of Pinellas Peninsula are just a short drive away from St Petersburg. If you're feeling ambitious, you can bike, jog, or hike the popular **Pinellas Trail**, a paved north–south urban trail on the former railroad tracks that starts in St Petersburg and ends 37 miles (60km) away in the Greek fishing community of Tarpon Springs.

North of Clearwater, on US 19, **Dunedin** ❾, famous for its March Celtic Festival, owes its name to Scottish merchants who arrived with the railroad in 1889. This pretty waterfront town is a great place to stroll or bicycle and visit unique boutiques and homespun galleries. Time your visit to coincide with the Friday-morning **Green Market** and mingle with

residents buying fruits and vegetables, home-made bread, Caribbean foods, organic coffee, local honey, organic salsa, cheese, and other goodies. These make great gifts or picnic fixings if you decide to head over the causeway to **Honeymoon Island State Park** ❿ (1 Causeway Blvd; tel: 727-469-5942; daily 8am–sunset; charge), where rustic cabins became popular among honeymooners in the 1940s and '50s.

Tiny **Dunedin Museum of History** (349 Main St; tel: 727-736-1176; www.dunedinmuseum.org; Tue–Sat 10am–4pm; charge), in the former railroad station, offers historic walking tours and an exhibit of souvenirs from couples who vacationed on Honeymoon Island. To fulfill your own desert-island fantasies, hop aboard a ferry from Honeymoon Island, the only way to reach **Caladesi Island State Park** (tel: 727-460-5942; daily 8am–sunset; charge).

Tarpon Springs

Celtic influences give way to Greek ones in **Tarpon Springs** ⓫, which sprang up on the banks of the Anclote River with the railroad. Key West

The Sunken Gardens

Plumber George Turner, Sr, an avid gardener, created the 6 acre (2 hectare) **Sunken Gardens** (1825 4th Street North; tel: 727-551-3102; www.stpete.org/sunken) in St Petersburg in 1903 by draining a lake and using the resulting fertile muck as the foundation for waterfalls, lush tropical plantings, and hundreds of vibrant plants lining tranquil walkways. The gardens became so popular that Turner began charging admission. Three generations tended the gardens before they were sold in 1999 to the City of St Petersburg, which now offers daily admission, horticultural workshops, and a wedding venue. The children's science museum Great Explorations occupies the restored 1926 Mediterranean Revival building next door, making this a popular family destination.

"Conchs" cornered the sponge business in the late 1800s, but around 1900, with Key West's sponge beds dwindling, businessman John Corcoris summoned family and friends from the Aegean Islands to test the beds around Tarpon Springs. They found them rich in sponges, including grade A wool types and decorative finger sponges.

Corcoris pioneered the use of copper-helmeted diving suits for sponging in deeper waters, replacing the old-time "hookers" who rowed out to shallow waters, locating sponges by looking through a glass-bottomed bucket and hooking them with a hooked rod. Weighing up to 200 pounds (90 kg), diving suits were frequently death traps for the young Greeks who wore them, as they dived deeper and suffered the fatal effects of nitrous-oxide build-up, commonly known as the bends.

The multimillion-dollar sponge industry began to ebb in the 1940s, when a disastrous episode of red tide disease killed off the sponges. The introduction of inexpensive, synthetic sponges virtually shut down the

industry. The modern sponge market has since faded, but the epic story of Tarpon Springs' sponge divers lives on, kept alive by community pride, business know-how, and tourists eager to experience something real amid Florida's artifice.

In Tarpon Springs, you'll hear Greek spoken everywhere, see knots of older men passing the time on street corners, and enjoy moussaka, kebabs, baklava, and other Greek delicacies in family-run, Mediterranean-tiled cafés like **Mykonos** and **Hella's**. Tourism is concentrated along the sponge docks on whitewashed **Dodecanese Boulevard**, now sadly devoid of its piles of sponges and savvy buyers. Nearby are warehouses where sponges are still washed, dried, hand-trimmed, and sold to luxury bath stores and home improvement centers for use in faux paint effects.

Sponge divers

Numerous cruises to beaches on Anclote Key depart from the docks, but only a few old-time spongers like George Billiris of **St Nicholas Boat**

A sponge diver in Tarpon Springs shows off an old deep-water diving suit.

BELOW: though the sponge industry has declined, some sponges are still processed in Tarpon Springs and sold as luxury items.

A Cedar Key gallery features the work of local artists.

BELOW: snorkelers can get a close-up view of manatees in the Crystal River.

Lines (tel: 727-942-6425) still demonstrate sponge-diving on a real sponge boat. The 1907 **Sponge Exchange** is now a shopping arcade, where you can buy sponges in cool, dark shops smelling of the ocean. Tarpon's history is told on a plaque outside the Exchange and at **Spongearama** (tel: 727-942-3771; charge), which has items and photos from earlier sponging days. On the dock is a statue of a sponge diver – a heroic, Adonis-like figure gazing back to a glorious past, helmet in hand.

Greek youths in Tarpon still have their rites of passage. On the Feast of Epiphany in January, the Greek Orthodox archbishop blesses local waters and tosses a crucifix into **Spring Bayou**. Boys aged 16 to 18 dive into the chilly waters to retrieve it and earn extra blessings for themselves and their families. A white dove, symbolizing the Holy Spirit, is released to begin a glendi, or festival, with Greek food, music, and dance. **St Nicholas Greek Orthodox Cathedral** (36 N. Pinellas Ave), built in 1943 in downtown Tarpon, is a replica of St Sofia Cathedral in Constantinople. Its neo-Byzantine walls are full of icons. One – a statue of the Blessed Mother – is said to shed tears.

Mermaids and manatees

North of Tarpon Springs is another remnant of a glorious past: the 1940s roadside attraction known as **Weeki Wachee Spring** 12 (US 19/SR 50; tel: 352-596-2062; www.weekiwachee.com; daily in summer 10am–4pm, limited hours in other seasons; charge). Weeki Wachee had waters so clear that Navy frogman Newton Perry used them to stage underwater shows. He dressed young women in mermaid suits and taught then to breathe through hoses so they could remain below the surface for long periods of time. Today the mermaids perform strenuous acrobatics about 16ft (5 meters) underwater while visitors watch through plate-glass windows.

You can swim with manatees at the **Crystal River National Wildlife Refuge** (SE Kings Bay Dr; tel: 352-563-2088; www.fws.gov/crystalriver; daily;

charge) in nearby Crystal River, where more than 100 local springs feed into King's Bay.

Cedar Key

A 25 mile (40km) drive on SR 24 crosses several bridges to reach the quiet fishing resort of **Cedar Key** ⓭, known for bird rookeries on surrounding **Cedar Keys National Wildlife Refuge** (SR 24; tel: 352-493-0238; www.fws.gov/cedarkeys; charge) and as a weekend getaway for seafood-lovers. **Cedar Key State Museum Park** (12231 SW 166th Court; tel: 352-543-5350; Thur–Mon 10am–5pm; charge) documents the port's short-lived prominence and displays an incredible collection of seashells.

Cedar Key Historical Society Museum (609 2nd Street; tel: 352-543-5549; www.cedarkeymuseum.org; Sun–Fri 1–4pm, Sat 11am–5pm; charge) displays historical artifacts from the town, including the original heart-cedar Andrews Home and fiber brush factory. There is an exhibit on famed naturalist John Muir, who recuperated in Cedar Key in 1867, at the end of his

1,000 mile (1,600km) walk from Wisconsin.

Unique art galleries and boutiques occupy historic buildings on 2nd Street. Cedar Key's oldest and most famous building is the 1859 **Island Hotel** (372 2nd St; tel: 352-543-5111), a moody hostelry that has suitably creaky floorboards and is rumored to be haunted by spirits.

Local oysters, clams, and stone crab are reliably delicious when caught off the shores near Cedar Key. With the 1995 ban on gill nets, local fishermen began hatching clams and oysters in the shallow gulf waters around the salt marshes, aided by marine specialists from the University of Florida in Gainesville. This innovative thinking has invigorated the local fishing community. **Southern Cross Sea Farms** (12170 SR 24; tel: 352-543-5980) offers daily tours of a clam hatchery. The **Cedar Key Seafood Festival** attracts thousands of seafood-lovers each October. ❑

The historic Island Hotel has been feeding hungry visitors to remote Cedar Key for more than a century.

BELOW: in many parts of the Cedar Keys, boats are more common than cars.

RESTAURANTS

Restaurants

Prices for a three-course dinner per person, excluding tax, tip, and beverages:
$ = under $20
$$ = $20–45
$$$ = $45–60
$$$$ = over $60

Cedar Key

Blue Desert Café
12815 SR 24
Tel: 352-543-9111 **$–$$**
This funky little restaurant is near the bridge over the estuary into Cedar Key. There's no fried food here, and the wait can be long for the fresh Southwest and Mediterranean fare. Popular dishes include Greek pizzas, Italian calzones, Mexican burritos, and fresh local crab. Well worth the wait.

Island Hotel Restaurant
224 2nd St at B St
Tel: 352-543-5111
$$–$$$
The best fine dining in Cedar Key is at a pleasant corner restaurant in the gracious Island Hotel. Expect rich Continental cuisine, emphasizing fresh seafood done every which way but plain. Starters include the famous palm salad (combining hearts of palm, ice cream, and pistachio nuts), which was invented here. Breakfast and lunch are available, as well as dining in the Neptune Bar.

Tony's Seafood
597 2nd Street
Tel: 352-543-0022 **$–$$**
This restaurant is known for its world-famous clam chowder. Even a US senator has attested to how delectable it is. Other eats include fried green beans, oyster sandwiches, steamed clams, and the gilled seafood dinner.

Dunedin

Black Pearl of Dunedin
315 Main St
Tel: 727-734-3463
www.theblackpearl restaurant.com **$$–$$$**
For a fancy night out in Dunedin, this upscale New American restaurant is hard to beat. Elegant dishes like New Zealand rack of lamb, Maryland crab imperial, Long Island duck, and baked Florida oysters with spinach, pancetta, and Pernod are highlights.

Casa Tina
369 Main Street
Tel: 727-734-9226
$–$$
Here's something you don't find every day – a Mexican restaurant emphasizing healthy and authentic cuisine. But that's what this brilliant cantina in downtown Dunedin is all about. It wins raves from diners as far away as St Petersburg and Tampa. Recipes are authentic and made fresh daily. Sample a wide array of traditional moles, salsas, poblanos, and burritos, and hits like *pescado a la Vera-cruzana*, using the catch of the day, as well as amazing vegetarian entrées.

Walt's Seasonal Cuisine
1140 Main St
Tel: 727-733-1909
www.waltscuisine.com
$–$$$
There's lots of buzz over this unpretentious new bistro. Chef Walt, a Dunedin native with Cordon Bleu training, plans his menu around what's fresh, local, and seasonal each day. Look for pompano, grouper, sea scallops, and a surf and turf with crab cakes at dinner. Light and tasty items such as seafood chowder, poached shrimp and mango salad, and seared ahi tuna are available at weekday lunch for under $10 each.

Homosassa Springs

Riverside Crab House
5297 S. Cherokee Way
Tel: 352-621-5080 **$$**
The river views at this restaurant adjoining the Riverside Resort in Homosassa Springs are just lovely. The food is typical: lots of grouper, shrimp, and crab.

Clearwater Beach

Bob Heilman's Beachcomber
447 Mandalay Ave
Tel: 727-442-4144 **$–$$$**
For 60 years, this landmark restaurant has served reliable all-American favorites like dry-aged prime rib and steaks, fried chicken, and surf and turf. There's even fried chicken livers! Soups, salads, sandwiches, and burgers are on the lunch menu.

Caretta on the Gulf
500 Mandalay Ave
Tel: 727-674-4171
$$$–$$$$

LEFT: a tasty snapper dish at Caretta on the Gulf.

High-end, beachfront dining at the Sandpearl Resort features haute cuisine with Latin American and Caribbean influences, plus a sushi bar, wood-burning oven, and extensive wine list.

St Pete Beach

Crabby Bill's
5100 Gulf Blvd
Tel: 727-360-8858 $–$$
You can wear your sandy flip-flops to this fun, ultracasual, and very popular seafood shack, which serves the freshest and best-priced grouper, crab, and other seafood from its own boats daily. Seating is family style at picnic tables and booths. There are no reservations, so expect a line, but service is speedy.

The Hurricane
807 Gulf Way
Tel: 727-360-9558
www.thehurricane.com
$–$$
One of the most durably popular restaurants on the Gulf Coast, with multiple bars, commendable seafood, and the clincher – great sunset views.

St Petersburg

Bella Brava
515 Central Ave
Tel: 727-895-5515
$$–$$$
This upscale Italian-American hot spot is the place to be seen. The menu includes locally sourced and organic items such as grilled prosciutto-wrapped Florida grouper on a bed of charred corn kernels, asparagus, and pasta tossed with roasted pepper butter.

Café Alma
260 1st Ave South, #100
Tel: 727-502-5002
$$–$$$
Café Alma is the kind of chic, European-style, white-tablecloth eatery

that works just as well as an lunch bistro in the daytime and a casually elegant nightclub offering dinner, small plates, and a full bar until the wee hours. The international menu emphasizes healthy Mediterranean cuisine and includes many vegetarian and seasonal items. There's a patio, bar, and nightly DJ.

Central Café and Organic
243 Central Ave
Tel: 727-824-0881
www.centralcafeand organics.com $–$$
A local favorite, this downtown all-organic soup-salad-sandwich-dessert place has healthy and inexpensive takeout. Try the chicken salad and "cosmic cookies."

Ceviche Tapas Bar
10 Beach Dr
Tel: 727-209-2302
www.ceviche.com $$
Spanish-style small plates, or tapas, are the focus. They're the perfect food to share in this intimate, candlelit setting. Good for a light bite or full mix-and-match meal.

Marchand's Bar and Grill
501 5th Ave NE
Tel: 727-824-8072
www.marchandsbarandgrill.com $$–$$$
Specializing in Mediterranean-style seafood, the elegant Marchand's is located in the remodeled historic Renaissance Vinoy Resort overlooking Safety Harbor just north of downtown. Go for the creative antipasto plate and seared dayboat scallops on a bed of saffron couscous accompanied by baby bok choy and shallot truffle marmalade.

Moon Under Water
332 Beach Dr NE
Tel: 727-896-6160
www.themoonunderwater.com $–$$

Hot curry, enough to make you break into a sweat, is the specialty of this waterfront pub serving British-Indian food. On the menu are classics like shepherd's pie, cornish pasty, fish and chips (with traditional malt vinegar), burgers, a variety of lighter Mediterranean-inspired salads and sandwiches, and some very good British ale. There's live music on weekends. A great place for a swift pint and some nosh.

Parkshore Grill
300 Beach Dr NE
Tel: 727-896-9463
www.parkshoregrill.com $$–$$$
The location of this welcoming New American grill, opposite Straub Park in downtown St Petersburg, is unbeatable. And so is the food. The large menu has a selection of steaks, chops, light takes on seafood, and several vegetarian options. Sidewalk dining offers great people-watching.

Red Mesa
4912 4th St North
Tel: 727-527-8728
www.redmesarestaurant.com $–$$
Classic dishes from Mexico and the Southwest shine here. Look for *Divorciados* at breakfast (two fried eggs with separate sauces, chorizo-potato hash, and chipotle cactus salsa) and wild mushroom quesadillas and Southwest tuna sashimi at lunch and dinner along with elegant specials. Muy sabroso!

Savannah's Cafe
1113 Central Ave
Tel: 727-388-4371
www.savannahscafe.com $–$$
This family-run gem does Southern and Caribbean food right and has a loyal following. The menu

includes all the jambalaya, fried catfish, plantains, collard greens, and other Creole dishes of your dreams.

Steinhatchee

Roy's
100 1st Ave SW
Tel: 352-498-5000
www.roys-restaurant.com
$$–$$$
On the banks of the Steinhatchee estuary, Roy's has been pleasing diners since 1969. Fried food features heavily, including fried chicken, coconut shrimp, and catfish. You'll also find local Apalachicola oysters, soft shell crab, and grouper. A popular Sunday lunchtime place for day-trippers.

Tarpon Springs

Hella's
735 Dodecanese Blvd
Tel: 727-943-2400
www.hellas-restaurant.com
$–$$
Gaily painted Hella's offers dockside dining right across from the historic sponge docks in Tarpon Springs. The family-owned restaurant offers excellent spanakopita, gyros, moussaka, and other Greek delicacies. Save room for heavenly baklava and other honey-drenched sweets baked in the adjoining bakery.

Mykonos
628 Dodecanese Blvd
Tel: 727-934-4306 $–$$
One of the Greek fishing port's most popular restaurants, Mykonos is the real deal. Don't pass up its traditional specialties, including the signature Greek salad loaded with finely chopped parsley and dill as well as kalamata olives, tomatoes, onions, feta, and tangy dressing.

BEAUTIFUL BEACHES

Beaches account for more than 1,300 miles (2,080km) of Florida's Atlantic and Gulf coastlines and are among the best in the continental US

Broad ones, narrow ones, busy ones, quiet ones: beaches in Florida come in all shapes and sizes, and wherever you are in the state you should find one to suit your tastes. Even if you're not staying on the coast, the sea is never far away.

The Atlantic Coast has the best waves, while the water in the Gulf of Mexico is warmer and calmer. Many beaches lie on barrier islands, which ring much of the Florida peninsula, and an impressive number of beaches are protected as state or federal parks.

Florida's beaches, along with those of Hawaii, dominate lists of the top US beaches, which take into account everything from the softness of the sand to ease of access. Many of the best are on the Gulf Coast, where gorgeous sunsets are an added bonus. Everyone has his or her favorite beach, but below is a list of the beaches that are consistently praised. They are suitable for families and chosen from all areas. Even those within protected areas offer facilities.

- **Southeast:** Crandon Park, Bill Baggs, South Beach (Greater Miami); Bahia Honda State Park (Keys).
- **Atlantic Coast:** John Lloyd Beach State Recreation Area (Dania); Anastasia Beach (St Augustine).
- **Gulf Coast:** Caladesi Island State Park (Dunedin); Siesta Beach (Sarasota); Fort de Soto Park (St Petersburg).
- **Panhandle:** St George Island (Apalachicola); St Andrews (Panama City Beach); Grayton Beach; Port St Joe.

ABOVE: before hitting the beach, check the UV forecast which is often broadcast on local news programs and published in local papers. The general rule is: The higher the UV Index, the higher SPF needed in your sunscreen if you want to avoid a painful bur[n]

LEFT: Florida beaches can b[e] the best place [to] try your hand [at] flying a kite. There is almost always a breez[e] coming off the water, and ple[nty] of open space [to] avoid tangling the line.

LEFT: Florida has a number of rural trails that are suitable for inline skating, with compact or paved surfaces; there are also many beach boardwalks that are the perfect place to practice dodging the crowds.

SAFETY BY THE SEASIDE

Most people will enjoy a completely trouble-free time on the beach, but there are dangers to be aware of:

- **sunburn:** this tops the danger list; you should use plenty of sunscreen, wear a broad-brimmed hat, and stay out of the midday sun.
- **sea currents:** the waters off Florida are not generally dangerous, but you can encounter rough surf and strong currents, particularly along the Atlantic Coast. Most deaths occur when exhausted swimmers drown after trying to swim against a riptide or undertow. Riptides are the cause of 80 percent of lifeguard rescues in the US. If caught in either, do not panic! Swim across the current rather than against it.
- **marine life:** if you brush against a jellyfish in the water, you will receive only a short-lived sting; but stingrays, which move close to shore in August and September to mate, can deliver a very nasty sting. Seek medical help if the barb stays in the skin.

All popular beaches have lifeguards, who can advise on local conditions. There is also a warning system of color-coded flags:

- **green:** good swimming conditions
- **yellow:** caution
- **red:** danger from currents, winds, or lightning
- **blue:** hazardous marine life (eg jellyfish)

OVE: more than 50 percent of Florida's beaches are privately ned, but only above the high tide mark. According to the Florida nstitution, any beach below the high tide mark is publicly ned, although frequently these areas are out of reach because ate homes block the only access routes.

GOPHER TORTOISE XING

LEFT: tourists started coming to Florida in the late 1800s, but it was only after the 1920s that swimming in the sea and sunbathing became popular, and visitors today can't get enough.

SARASOTA TO NAPLES

Wonders abound on this stretch of the Gulf Coast,
ranging from the extravagant winter home
of circus magnate John Ringling to the
sugar sand beaches and abundant
bird-life on the barrier islands

Southwest Florida's natural beauty remains unrivaled in this corner of the United States. But don't look for a desert island atmosphere if you visit between January and May; instead you should expect high prices. Many hotels are sold out months in advance for the peak season. Anticipate narrow highways crammed with cars, traffic gridlock in the city centers, and beaches packed with sunbathers.

Consider vacationing here from May through June or October through December, when things are a little quieter. You could also stay on one of the islands that are accessible only by boat or floatplane, such as Cabbage Key or Cayo Costa Island. Boating is the most relaxed way to get an intimate look at this watery region, whether you're paddling a kayak on an estuary blue highway or steering a cabin cruiser on the famous Intracoastal Waterway.

Across the bridge

Drive south on I-275 over Tampa Bay, passing through St Petersburg, and continue south into Manatee County via the **Sunshine Skyway Bridge** ❶ ($1 toll). South of the bridge, I-275 joins I-75 and historic Tamiami Trail (US 41). Head west on SR 64 to the relaxed Gulf island of **Anna Maria Key** ❷, an ideal place for weary visitors to decompress.

Just beyond **Bradenton** ❸, at the mouth of the Manatee River, lovely Anna Maria Key is one of the least developed Gulf islands. The gorgeous white-sand beaches of Anna Maria, Holmes, Bradenton, and Coquina line the narrow Gulf Drive, which has a good choice of beachfront retreats. Fine dining is excellent on this island, but you'll also find seafood shacks and beach cafés serving fantastic food. Islanders are involved in conservation efforts to protect endangered sea turtles, which crawl ashore nightly

Main attractions
ANNA MARIA KEY
SOUTH FLORIDA MUSEUM
ST ARMAND'S CIRCLE
MOTE MARINE AQUARIUM AND
  LABORATORY
MARIE SELBY BOTANICAL GARDENS
JOHN AND MABLE RINGLING
  MUSEUM OF ART
MYAKKA RIVER STATE PARK
J.N. "DING" DARLING NATIONAL
  WILDLIFE REFUGE
NAPLES

LEFT: the beautiful estate of Cà d'Zan.
RIGHT: a Sanibel Island sunbather.

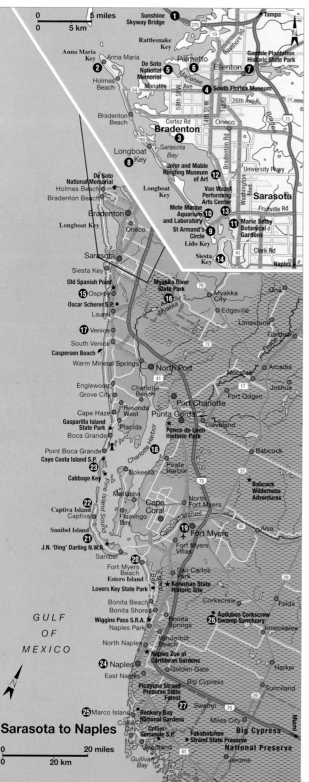

0 5 miles
0 5 km

Sunshine Skyway Bridge **1**
Tampa
Rattlesnake Key
Anna Maria Key
Anna Maria
De Soto National Memorial **2**
Palmetto **6**
Gamble Plantation Historic State Park
Ellenton **7**
Holmes Beach
Manatee Ave
South Florida Museum **4**
26th Ave E
Bradenton Beach
Cortez Rd
Oneco
Bradenton 3
Longboat Key **8**
Sarasota Bay
John and Mable Ringling Museum of Art **12**
University Pkwy
De Soto National Memorial
Holmes Beach
Bradenton Beach
Longboat Key
Van Wezel Performing Arts Center
Sarasota
Fruitville Rd
Bradenton
Mote Marine Aquarium and Laboratory **10**
13
Longboat Key
Oneco
St Armand's Circle **9**
Marie Selby Botanical Gardens **11**
Lido Key
Clark Rd
Sarasota
Siesta Key **14**
Naples
Siesta Key
Old Spanish Point
Myakka River State Park **16**
Ona
Osprey **15**
Myakka City
Oscar Scherer S.P.
Laurel
Edgeville
17 Venice
Limestone
South Venice
Gardner
Caspersen Beach
Warm Mineral Springs
North Port
Arcadia
Englewood
Nocatee
Joshua
Grove City
Charlotte Beach
Fort Ogden
Cape Haze
Rotonda West
Punta Gorda
Port Charlotte
Gasparilla Island State Park
Placida
Ponce de Leon Historic Park
Cleveland
Boca Grande
Point Boca Grande
Babcock
Cayo Costa Island S.P.
Charlotte Harbor
18
23
Pirate Harbor
Bokeelia
Cabbage Key
Babcock Wilderness Adventures
Matlacha
North Fort Myers
Captiva Island **22**
Cape Coral
Captiva
Flamingo Bay
Alva
Sanibel Island
Fort Myers **19**
J.N. 'Ding' Darling N.W.R. **21**
Fort Myers Villas
Sanibel
Fort Myers Beach **20**
San Carlos Park
Estero Island
Koreshan State Historic Site
Lovers Key State Park
Corkscrew
Felda
Bonita Beach
Bonita Shores
Wiggins Pass S.R.A.
Bonita Springs
Audubon Corkscrew Swamp Sanctuary **26**
Naples Park
Immokalee
GULF
North Naples
Vanderbilt Beach
OF
Naples Zoo at Caribbean Gardens
MEXICO
24 Naples
Golden Gate
Harker
East Naples
Big Cypress
Sunniland
Picayune Strand Preserve State Forest
25 Marco Island
Rookery Bay National Estuarine
27 Swamp
Big Cypress
Sarasota to Naples
Collier-Seminole S.P.
Fakahatchee Strand State Preserve
Miles City
National Preserve
0 20 miles
0 20 km
Goodland
Gullivan Bay
Jerome

from May through October to lay eggs on the beaches. Guided tours of nesting sites are available, call 941-778-5638 or visit www.islandturtles.com for detailed information.

The **South Florida Museum 4** (201 10th St W; tel: 941-746-4131; Mon–Sat 10am–5pm, Sun noon–5pm; closed Mon May–June and Aug–Dec; charge) in Bradenton is a well-interpreted museum that is renowned among aficionados for its Tallant Collection of more than 15,000 Native American artifacts that date from between AD 300 and 1725.

Snooty, the oldest manatee in captivity, shares living space with other injured manatees at the museum's **Parker Manatee Aquarium**. Daily shows about Snooty and his friends are a big draw for families and youngsters interested in ecology and the environment.

The **De Soto National Memorial 5** (3000 75th St NW; tel. 941-792-0458; www.nps.gov/deso; visitor center: daily 9am–5pm; free) commemorates the spot where Spanish conquistador Hernando de Soto came ashore in 1539. This site has a visitor center, exhibits, live re-creations and demonstrations, as well as a small beach, nature trail, and picnic area.

Another popular local hangout is **Emerson Point Preserve** (5801 17th St West) in nearby **Palmetto 6**. This bayfront archeological site preserves the area's largest shell mound. The **Gamble Plantation Historic State Park 7** (3708 Patten Ave; tel: 941-723-4536; daily 8am–sunset; free) in **Ellenton** preserves an antebellum home on a mid-1800s sugar plantation that was used as a refuge by Confederate official Judah P. Benjamin (he later escaped to England).

Sarasota's islands

Returning to the barrier islands west of Bradenton, Gulf Drive meanders through well-heeled **Longboat Key 8** to St Armand's Key. Laid out around a central plaza, **St Armand's**

Circle **❾** (300 Madison Dr; tel: 941-388-1554; www.starmandscircleassoc.com) offers a pleasant retail experience with boutiques specializing in fashion, footwear, and local art and sidewalk cafés offering everything from crab cakes to home-made ice cream and both hot and cold lattes.

A few minutes away, **Mote Marine Aquarium and Laboratory ❿** (1600 Ken Thompson Pkwy; www.mote.org) tel: 941-388-4441; daily 10am–5pm; charge) was founded in 1955 by shark researcher Dr Eugenie Clark. Mote is a 10 acre (4 hectare) aquarium and research center, displaying more than 100 marine species in exhibits showcasing the laboratory's cutting-edge research. Watch a device tracking sharks in the Gulf, see real sharks in an enormous tank, or experience a simulated shark attack. Touch tanks allow kids to pet rays, wriggly horseshoe crabs, and other sea life.

Nearby is the excellent **Marine Mammal Research and Rehabilitation Center**. Enclosures contain recuperating sea turtles and dolphins that play with each other and interact with keepers. You can get quite close to Hugh and Buffet, long-time resident manatees.

The adjoining **Dolphin and Whale Hospital** is the premier marine mammal rescue facility on the South Florida coast. Scientists and veterinarians have been rehabilitating animals here since 1992, with a dual goal of providing humane medical treatment while gaining scientific data and research information at the same time.

Folks gather on the pier at Anna Maria Key for a sunset view of the Gulf of Mexico.

The upper crust

Like Dunedin to the north, Sarasota was pioneered by a Scottish immigrant businessman in the 1880s. John Hamilton Gillespie, an aristocratic lawyer and businessman, built historic Desoto Hotel on Main Street and was named Sarasota's first mayor in 1902. Soon afterwards, wealthy Northerners started to settle in town.

Marie Selby Botanical Gardens ⓫ (811 S. Palm Ave; tel: 941-366-5731; www.selby.org; daily 10am–5pm; charge), south of downtown, was the home of Marie and Bill Selby. Voted one of Florida's top botanical gardens, it has

BELOW: a mastodon fossil at the South Florida Museum.

A roller rink lights up the night at St Armand's Circle.

a peaceful Zen theme, with plaques featuring Asian brush paintings and quotes, Buddha statues, and koi ponds amid peaceful pathways. There are native and seasonal plantings, Marie's beloved rose garden, spectacular banyan trees, a bamboo grove that Marie planted to screen out Sarasota's high-rises, and a popular gift shop and nursery. The greenhouse has many examples of the hothouse orchids and bromeliads (air plants) for which the gardens are known. The Selbys' former home is now a tranquil tea house.

Three-ring circus

Sarasota's star attraction is, of course, the **John and Mable Ringling Museum of Art** ⑫ (5401 Bayshore Rd; tel: 941-359-5700; daily 10am–5.30pm; charge), north of downtown. Devote a whole day to this attraction, as it's well worth the time. As well as the art museum, the estate includes historic Asolo Theater, the Ringling winter home, the circus museum, landscaped grounds, and a nice restaurant serving light Italian and American fare. Docent-led tours take place hourly.

BELOW: Mote Marine Aquarium and Laboratory.

Flush with profits from his Greatest Show on Earth and lucrative investments in oil, railroads, and real estate, John Ringling was a modest man with a grand vision. He brought artisans, red tile, stone, and artworks from around the world to create his estate. **Cà d'Zan** (House of John) was inspired by the Doge's Palace in Venice and was completed in 1926. You can tour the inside, where rooms feature tapestries and antiques, but it is the exterior, with its intricate terracotta decoration and boat landing, that makes this a unique American dream home.

John and Mable loved to travel and collect art. Their personal art museum, built in 1931 and now the state art museum, contains one of the most important collections of works by the Flemish painter Peter Paul Rubens (1577–1640). Along with exceptional Baroque art, the museum displays Asian and American works and a magnificent replica of Michelangelo's *David*, which dominates a formal courtyard of allées lined with topiaries.

The 18th-century **Asolo Theater** (tel: 941-360-7399), built in Italy, sits near Cà d'Zan. The interior was dismantled piece by piece at a castle in Asolo, then shipped to Sarasota in 1950 and reassembled. The theater is host to a year-round roster of events, including dance and theatrical performances, chamber music concerts, art lectures, and a film series.

A less imposing building houses the 1948 **Ringling Museum of the American Circus**. The collection includes memorabilia, including rare posters and props, from Ringling's three-ring circus extravaganza. Don't miss the 3,800 sq ft (350 sq meter) miniature replica of Ringling Circus. It took model-maker Howard Tibbals 50 years to complete.

Another venue for dance and music is the **Van Wezel Performing Arts Center** ⑬ (777 N. Tamiami Trail; tel: 800-826-9303; www.vanwezel.org), a shell-shaped building on the waterfront just south of Ringling Museum. Both the Asolo and Van Wezel theaters host classic and new films during the **Sarasota Film Festival** in April.

South of Sarasota, **Siesta Key** ⑭ is renowned for its pretty sandy beaches, low-rise development, and quiet, old-fashioned resorts. Just past Siesta Key, **Osprey** ⑮ is the location of the Blackburn Point Bridge, a one-lane bridge over the Intracoastal Waterway.

Myakka River State Park ⑯ 13208 SR 72; tel: 941-361-6511; www.myakkariver.org; daily 8am–sunset; charge) is Florida's largest state park and a good place to enjoy kayaking, hiking, and camping. The rustic cabins make a great alternative to busy beach hotels for those who love the outdoors and those on a restrictive budget. The park is used by local schools as an archeological and environmental education center. It has an interesting exhibit called *Window to the Past*, which allows you to look inside an excavated Indian shell midden.

From Venice to Fort Myers

Sarasota's circus legacy spilled over into **Venice** ⑰, a seaside community

Asian art is displayed throughout the Marie Selby Botanical Gardens.

BELOW: the Selby mansion houses exhibits botanical art and photography.

More than 20 large-scale artworks are on display along Sarasota's bayfront.

BELOW: the Renaissance-style gardens of the Ringling Museum of Art are filled with fountains and sculpture.

20 miles (32km) south along US 41, which served as home to the Ringling Clown College until the 1990s. Venice's main claim to fame is as the Sharktooth Capital of the World. Tiny fossilized sharks' teeth wash up on undeveloped **Caspersen Beach**, the longest beach in Sarasota County. The teeth lure fossil collectors to an annual festival every August, the highlight of which is a popular seafood contest among local restaurants.

Things are quieter in the retirement communities around **Charlotte Harbor ⑱**, where the Peace River opens into an enormous bay. Although they have little in the way of attractions, **Punta Gorda** and **Port Charlotte** provide a change of pace from the rapid growth to the north and south. Legends of pirates and explorers are rife along the coast, culminating on Gasparilla Island, the so-called kingdom of the colorful but imaginary José Gaspar, who is celebrated in Tampa's annual Gasparilla Festival. **Boca Grande**, mid-island, offers a peek at the lifestyles of the rich and famous at an historic resort.

One of the few things that draws people inland is **Crescent B Ranch**, the largest working ranch east of the Mississippi. Purchased from the Babcock family by a private company in 2006, 80 percent of this pristine western Everglades landscape is wilderness, and serves as an important wildlife corridor between Lake Okeechobee and the Gulf of Mexico. Nearly 20 percent of the land is scheduled to be developed as an environmentally sustainable community.

Babcock Wilderness Adventures (tel: 800-500-5583; reservations required) offers swamp-buggy tours of Babcock Ranch and Telegraph Cypress Swamp, where you might see cracker cattle, wild turkeys, alligators, and possibly panthers. The ranch is 40 miles (65km) northeast of Fort Myers on SR 331.

Paradise Coast

Farther south, in **Fort Myers ⑲**, the **Edison and Ford Winter Estates** (2350 McGregor Blvd; tel: 239-334-7419; www.efwefla.org; daily 9am–5.30pm; charge) spans both sides of McGregor Boulevard, the moneyed avenue leading into downtown. After moving here for his health at the age of 39, Thomas Edison lived to the age of 84. He produced some of his greatest inventions in his Florida laboratory, including phonographs and motion pictures. After his death, Edison's widow bequeathed the estate to the city, as a shrine to her husband and his accomplishments.

Overlooking the broad Caloosahatchee River, Edison's Seminole Lodge was among the first prefabricated buildings in the US, constructed in Maine and brought to Fort Myers by schooner. Tropical gardens engulf the homes. Native Florida palms, satin leaf figs, calabash trees from South America, cinnamon trees from India and Malaysia, and the largest banyan tree in Florida – some 6,000 species were collected by Edison at a cost of $100,000. In this idyllic

setting, he entertained famous friends such as President Herbert Hoover, Harvey Firestone, and automaker Henry Ford, whose modest vacation bungalow, **The Mangoes**, is part of the tour. Edison offered to light up his new town with electric installations, but the townspeople famously refused for fear the lights would keep their cattle awake at night.

Visitors peer through plexiglass into the furnished rooms of Edison's **Seminole Lodge**. You can also visit Edison's **Little Office**, the **Caretaker's House**, the **Moonlight Garden**, the **Rock Fountain**, and the **Swimming Pool Complex**. Edison's 1928 Botanic Research Corporation Laboratory, adjoining the visitor museum, gift store, café, and research garden across the street, is worth the wait to get in: it looks like the great man has just popped out for lunch, mid-experiment.

Fort Myers Beach ⓴, the lively resort town on **Estero Island**, attracts families in the high season. During the rest of the year, it reverts to being an attractive, old-fashioned, sleepy

island community, where locals can stroll at sunset in undeveloped **Lovers Key State Park**, on the south end of the island.

Sanibel and Captiva

Just west of Fort Myers Beach, a toll bridge leads to two exclusive island retreats – **Sanibel ⓴** and **Captiva ⓴** – where you can commune with nature and still buy a deli sandwich for lunch. The main attractions are the beaches and the millions of sea shells that turn up on the sands, luring thousands of collectors from all over the world.

Visitors take in the view from the top of Cà d'Zan.

Birdwatchers flock to the J.N. "Ding" Darling National Wildlife Refuge on Sanibel Island.

BELOW: Gasparilla Island golf course.

Just about everything related to mollusks – from classification to artistic illustrations to medicine – is covered in the **Bailey-Matthews Shell Museum** (3075 Sanibel-Captiva Rd; tel: 239-395-2233; www.shellmuseum.org; daily 10am–5pm; charge), a good place to spend an hour figuring out your *murexes* from your *junonias*.

In 1974, Sanibel seceded from Lee County, set up its own city government, and put a near halt to the runaway development threatening to ruin its beautiful environment. By law, buildings here may not rise higher than a palm tree and must blend with the scenery. Even though the island

is amply supplied with lovely homes, pricey hotels and restaurants, shopping centers, schools, and the like, natural beauty dominates the landscape.

Less regulated than Sanibel, the island of Captiva is undergoing a construction boom and, sad to say, minimansions are gradually creeping in, threatening the quiet island ambience. Gift shops, island-style cafés, and vacation rentals are crammed into a village on the far end, close to a popular public beach.

Sanibel has many protected areas, the most notable being the outstanding **J.N. "Ding" Darling National Wildlife Refuge** (off Sanibel-Captiva Rd; tel: 239-472-1100; www.fws.gov/ding darling; daily 7.30am–sunset, Wildlife Drive closed Fri; charge), named for the famous cartoonist and conservationist who made his home on Sanibel and helped develop the National Wildlife Refuge system.

These are some of the most productive wetlands for wildlife in Florida. The best birding is in winter, when early-morning low tides lure huge numbers of birds to the mudflats.

At the entrance to the 5 mile (8km) **Wildlife Drive**, look for roseate spoonbills (the only naturally pink-hued birds; flamingoes turn pink because of the crustaceans they eat); several species of herons, including little and great blues and tricoloreds; white and brown pelicans; curve-billed ibis; long-necked anhinga "snake" birds; and other wading birds. The most eco-friendly way to see the refuge is to take one of the excellent tram tours with a trained naturalist, ride a bicycle or walk through the refuge, or paddle a kayak with concessionaire **Tarpon Bay Explorers** (tel: 239-472-8900). Binoculars come in handy.

Cayo Costa Island State Park ㉓, north of Captiva, is one of Florida's most unspoiled barrier islands. It has terrific birding and 9 miles (14km) of dune-backed beaches, and you can spend the night in one of the island's rustic cabins or camp out beneath the stars. You'll need to come by boat and bring in your own supplies. Expect only basic facilities; there's no hot water or electricity.

Another option is to take a boat or floatplane to the **Cabbage Key Inn and Restaurant** (tel: 239-283-2278) from Captiva Island, Pine Island, or Punta Gorda. Historic Cabbage Key was built in the 1930s by the famous publishing family of author Mary Holt Rinehart. Today, it's a rustic island getaway, with cabins in the woods. Atop a shell mound perches an inn whose funky bar is papered with dollar bills. Things get lively when boaters tie up for hearty meals in the restaurant. Make your reservations well ahead.

Naples and environs

The pretty resort town of **Naples ㉔**, at the edge of the Everglades, is easy on the eyes but hard on the purse.

Naples revels in its outstanding natural beauty while, behind the beautiful facade, a long history of real estate speculation threatens the delicate balance of its fragile Everglades ecosystem. The infamous Golden Gate Estates boondoggle took place here in the 1960s, when crooked real-estate agents sold 29,000 lots to out-of-state

> *There is only one Fort Myers, and 90 million people are going to find it out.*
> — Thomas Edison, 1914

BELOW: the J. N. "Ding" Darling National Wildlife Refuge.

Fishing is excellent in the Gulf Coast's many bays and inlets.

BELOW: luxury condos overlook the Gordon River in Naples.

buyers who had no idea they were purchasing unusable swamp land. Progress has moved on, however, and today you'll find elegant seafront resorts, an emphasis on the arts and fine living, and abundant outdoor activities. These are a powerful lure for tourists and residents alike.

Unfortunately there are signs of trouble in paradise, as Naples becomes a haven of wealth and conspicuous consumption. It boasts the largest number of billionaires and golf courses in the country; over-scaled mega-resorts along the beaches of Naples and nearby **Marco Island** ㉕ continue to spring up; and every month new roads, strip malls, and residential areas are carved out of the swamp. In a sad irony, the names of these Las Vegas–style gated communities seek to celebrate the very threatened flora and fauna they are supplanting: Florida panthers, big cypress, and other disappearing Everglades species.

Excessive development is especially evident on Marco Island, which has little of the charm of the Gulf Coast's

other islands. The northernmost and largest of the Ten Thousand Islands, Marco became a popular tourist destination when Captain William Collier moved his family to the north end of the island in 1871 and offered guests rooms in his home for $2 a night. It's said that the enterprising Collier was responsible for the persistent rumors of pirates on the Gulf Coast.

Sadly, most of Marco Island was sold for development during the real-estate boom of the 1960s. Today, after you cross the bridge to the island via North Collier Boulevard from Naples, you run slap-bang into anonymous beachfront high-rise resorts, restaurants, condo complexes, and a few residential areas.

For casual visitors, Marco's attractions are all nature-oriented. **Rookery Bay National Estuarine Research Reserve** (300 Tower Rd; tel: 239-417-6310; daily), at the turn-off for southern Marco Island from US 41, interprets wildlife in Naples Bay and Ten Thousand Islands National Wildlife Refuge. It has a popular **Southwest Florida Birding and**

Wildlife Festival in January and offers guided birding tours to many locations, including **Tiger Tail Beach Park** (tel: 239-642-8414; parking fee) at the end of Hernando Drive on Marco Island, prime viewing for both shoreline and wetland birds.

For curiosity value alone, consider visiting **Goodland**, a funky little fishing village on the island's east side, where you'll find **Stan's Idle Hour Seafood Restaurant** (221 Goodland Dr West; tel: 239-394-304) on the waterfront. Every Sunday afternoon, Stan's is the site of a raucous outdoor dance party and features seafood, lots of alcohol, and a lively band.

Naples is much more sedate. The historic old town, a few blocks from the beach, has been thoughtfully preserved and is a wonderful place to linger. **Third Street South** has many historic Craftsman bungalows, more than 100 distinctive shops, galleries, and restaurants, and free entertainment on Thursdays. **Fifth Street South** is a pedestrian-friendly hangout with a dynamic mix of theater, boutique hotels, shops, and restaurants.

The popular **Naples National Art Show** takes place here in February, around the corner from the **Von Liebig Art Center** (585 Park St; tel: 239-262-6517). There is plenty of parking near beach access points. A small historic complex includes the 1895 **Palm Cottage** (137 12th St S.), which has exhibits on local history. It sits at the foot of **Naples Pier**, a small fishing pier that once served as Naples' only transportation access.

Zoo with a mission

For evidence of strong community spirit in Naples, look no farther than

Naples Pier was originally built in 1888 as a passenger dock and is now a popular gathering spot for viewing the sunset.

BELOW LEFT AND AND BELOW: Naples' Third Street shopping district.

Stan's Idle Hour is a tiny slice of Old Florida on Marco Island, now largely given over to condos and commercial development.

BELOW: a Marco Island marina.

Naples Zoo at Caribbean Gardens (1590 Goodlette-Frank Rd; tel: 239-262-5409; daily 9.30am–5.30pm; charge), set amid 45 acres (18 hectares) of historic botanical gardens. It started as a family operation in 1967, when "Jungle Larry" Tetzlaff moved his zoo from Ohio to these spectacular gardens, which had been planted in 1919 by conservationist Dr Henry Nehrling and restored in 1952 by Julius Fleischmann, heir to the vast yeast empire.

Parlaying a passion for wildlife into a job with animal collector Frank Buck, Tetzlaff and his wife, Nancy, offered more than merely another roadside attraction. They emphasized wildlife conservation by using live animal shows as teaching tools. In 2007, the City of Naples bought the zoo and gardens, but the Tetzlaffs still oversee daily operations.

Specializing in big carnivores, Naples Zoo is unique in Florida for exhibiting all of Africa's top predators, including leopards, lions, spotted hyenas, and wild dogs, as well as extremely rare Indonesian tigers. The zoo donates a portion of sales in its gift shop to various wildlife conservation organizations.

Among the ventures personally overseen by Conservation Director Tim Tetzlaff is a lemur project in Madagascar that involves local people in conserving the animal habitats around them. At Naples Zoo, lemurs live (alongside monkeys and apes) on an island in an alligator-filled lake. The animals can be viewed on daily boat tours.

Two of the cat exhibits at the Naples Zoo are memorable. With only a thick glass barrier as protection, the Leopard Rock exhibit allows you to sit inches from curious leopards. Look for the

gorgeous black leopard, which is commonly mistaken for a black panther. To see a real, endangered Florida panther, visit Panther Glade, a joint project with the National Wildlife Federation. They offer a look at an animal you may never see in the wild. The zoo's Black Bear exhibit houses Florida black bears in a replica of an Old Florida homestead.

Natural wonders

Nearly 80 percent of Collier County has been officially designated as protected land. Twelve sites are part of the south section of the Great Florida Birding Trail, where you can see some of the unique birdlife that calls Florida home. At the top of every birder's list is **Audubon Corkscrew Swamp Sanctuary** ❷⓺ (375 Sanctuary Rd West; tel: 239-348-9151; daily 7am–5.30pm, extended hours Apr–Sept), northeast of Naples. This sanctuary preserves the last of Florida's old-growth bald cypress forest and is the largest nesting site in the world for endangered wood storks.

Less well known is **Picayune Strand Preserve State Forest** ❷⓻ (tel: 239-348-

Relaxing on a Naples beach.

7557), where, directed by new laws to manage water for more natural, slow sheet flows for the Everglades wildlife and habitat, the South Florida Water Management District is removing decades-old canals, ditches, and roads, and is improving culverts through US 41 at the south end of the preserve. One of the first such projects, the Picayune Preserve is worth visiting for its environmental and educational value. The site is still a bit rough, and the only visitor services are a developed equestrian campground and a trail at the main entrance on the north side. Drive east from Naples and cross I-75 to enter the preserve.   ❏

BELOW LEFT AND BELOW: Naples Zoo at Caribbean Gardens.

RESTAURANTS

Anna Maria Key

Beach Bistro
6600 Gulf Dr, Holmes Beach
Tel: 941-778-6444
www.beachbistro.com
$$$–$$$$
Chef Sean Murphy's sumptuous but airy Beach Bistro, one of Florida's most lauded restaurants, is nestled in the bottom of a condo complex at the north end of Anna Maria Key, but the pilgrimage to reach it only sharpens the anticipation for diners. Murphy and his talented staff use fresh, local produce to create playful, French-influenced Floribbean cuisine. Try any dishes featuring tastebud-exploding local plum tomatoes and community farm veggies. Classics include three different sizes of Gulf bouillabaisse, a sinfully rich foie gras with brioche and Iowa lamb, tiny poached Nova Scotia lobster claws, beef tenderloin, island-style grouper, and an artisan cheese plate to finish.

Sun House Restaurant
111 Gulf Dr South, Bradenton Beach
Tel: 941-782-1122
www.thesunhouserestaurant.com
$$$–$$$$
Centrally located at Bradenton Beach, Sun House is popular for sunset dining on laid-back Anna Maria Key. The sunny, fruity Floribbean food is inspired by island living. At lunch, items like jerk chicken amp up sandwiches and salads. At dinner, try the catch of the day grilled, blackened, jerked, or fried, or crowd-pleasers like teriyaki ahi tuna and Key West chicken Oscar.

Captiva Island

Bubble Room
15001 Captiva Dr
Tel: 239-472-5558
www.bubbleroomrestaurant.com $–$$
If the idea of eating amid a brightly colored cornucopia of bric-a-brac from the 1930s appeals to you, then this unique restaurant is a must, if only for a drink and some appetizers.

Key Lime Bistro
11509 Andy Rosse Lane
Tel: 239-395-4000 $–$$$
This casual café in front of the Captiva Island Inn is a popular choice for a quick meal before or after the beach. The emphasis is on packing in a big crowd, so service tends to be perfunctory. But you'll find a large menu that will fuel you up for the day, including substantial egg dishes at breakfast, fried grouper sandwiches, burgers, and good salads.

Mucky Duck
11546 Andy Rosse Lane
Tel: 239-472-3434
www.muckyduck.com
$–$$
You can eat pub-style food right on the beach at this popular tavern, a fixture on Captiva since the 1970s.

Fort Myers

Cru
13499 S Cleveland Avenue #241
Tel: 239-466-3663 $$$$
A dead cert for the Martini crowd, Cru is a chic, urbane eatery that produces light, fresh Florida Fusion-style fare. A beguiling menu includes free-range chicken, Colorado bison, freshly caught pompano, tiger prawns, and organic veggies such as golden beets and heirloom tomatoes from the farmers' market in Centennial Park. There are small plates and an extensive wine list.

Prawnbroker Restaurant and Fish Market
13451-16 McGregor Boulevard
Tel: 239-489-2226
www.prawnbroker.com
$$–$$$
Catch of the day is the specialty at this casual restaurant and market. Patio dining is available. It gets busy, so make reservations.

The Veranda
2122 Second St
Tel: 239-332-2065
www.verandarestaurant.com
$$$–$$$$
Southern regional cuisine is the focus of this great little restaurant, which occupies two 1902 homes in downtown Fort Myers. The chef offers

LEFT: grilled scallops at the Naples Tomato.

gourmet versions of down-home specialties like grits, fried chicken, crab cakes, and fritters, the traditional accompaniments to grouper and other fresh seafood.

Longboat Key

Euphemia Haye
5540 Gulf of Mexico Dr
Tel: 941-383-3633
www.euphemiahaye.com
$$$–$$$$
Euphemia Haye doesn't have a long menu, but it's a perfectly chosen one, with duck taking center stage, along with imaginatively prepared fresh seafood, steak, poultry, pasta, and vegetarian options. The more casual upstairs Haye Loft has entertainment and longer hours. It serves an abbreviated version of the downstairs menu, along with thin-crust pizza, a daily sandwich special, and the killer pies for which the restaurant is known.

Marco Island

Olde Marco Restaurant
100 Palm St
Tel: 239-394-3131
www.oldmarcopub.com
$$$–$$$$
Bite into 124 years of history when you dine at this venerable restaurant. Continental dining at its finest includes fresh grouper, rack of lamb, and dramatically flambéed shrimp.

Naples

Bistro 821
821 5th Avenue South
Tel: 239-261-5821
www.bistro821.com
$$$–$$$$
Pacific Rim-influenced Floribbean cuisine with classic French styling soars at this sprightly restaurant in the heart of downtown Naples. Rock lobster is paired with a

satay sauce. Uptown macaroni and cheese includes shrimp and prosciutto. Sea bass is roasted in a miso-sake jus. There's even elk tenderloin for the adventurous. Desserts are outrageous and include profiteroles and crème caramel.

Naples Tomato
14700 Tamiami Trail North
Tel: 239-598-9800
www.naplestomato.com
$$–$$$$
This attractive Neapolitan-style restaurant is far out in Naples' north end in an unassuming strip mall. But that doesn't faze foodies: Naples Tomato is one of the most popular restaurants in the area. Pasta is made fresh daily, zucchini and eggplant are locally grown, and the menu includes wild salmon and the world's juiciest free-range chicken breast. The eponymous tomatoes are sourced locally in season; the tomatoes that provide the zing in the restaurant's signature tomato bisque and pasta and pizza dishes are San Marzanos from Naples, prized for their bright, rounded flavor. Help yourself to wines from the self-serve Enomatic system.

Shula's Steakhouse
5111 N. Tamiami Trail
Tel: 239-430-4999
www.shulas.com
$$$–$$$$
In the Hilton Naples, this steakhouse was started by the popular NFL coach and is highly rated for its Black Angus steaks.

Sanibel Island

Mad Hatter
6460 Sanibel-Captiva Rd
Tel: 239-472-0033
www.madhatterrestaurant.com $$$–$$$$
It may have only 12

tables, but this jewel on the Gulf is the best place on Sanibel for sunset dining. The New American cuisine rises to the challenge of its surroundings, with interesting variations on classics such as shrimp Wellington and sesame ahi tuna with Thai peanut satay sauce.

The Timbers Restaurant and Fish Market
703 Tarpon Bay Rd
Tel: 239-395-2722
$$$–$$$$
Set near the J.N. "Ding" Darling National Wildlife Refuge, the Timbers is a two-in-one: Sanibel Grill, a raw bar and grill with a sports bar atmosphere, and more formal service in the Timbers dining room.

Sarasota

Bijou Café
1287 First St
Tel: 941-366-8111
www.bijoucafe.net $$$–$$$$
This elegant European-style bistro has been winning kudos from diners for over 20 years. An engaging, internationally flavored menu created by the chef-owner, who is French-South African, includes local and organic produce and an array of homemade soups, salads, charcuterie, and artisan cheese plates, and Southern specials like jambalaya. Award-winning wine list.

Blue Dolphin Café
470 John Ringling Boulevard
Tel: 941-388-3566
www.bluedolphincafe.com
$–$$
A hands-down favorite for all-day breakfast, Blue Dolphin scores big by serving fabulous egg dishes made with local eggs. A good place for pre-shopping fortification in St Armand's Circle.

Michael's on East
1212 East Ave South
Tel: 941-366-0007
www.michaelsoneast.com
$$$$
Chic and always busy, Michael's has long been one of Sarasota's most lauded restaurants. The supper-club atmosphere is perfect for enjoying fine New American dining, with creative takes on steaks, seafood, and other classics.

Tommy Bahama's Tropical Café
300 John Ringling Boulevard
Tel: 941-388-2888
www.tommybahama.com
$$–$$$$
The eclectic but well-executed menu features tropically tinged seafood and meat entrées, such as Tortola chicken tortilla soup, coconut shrimp, mahi-mahi, and sea bass, which you can wash down with plenty of margaritas. There's even piña colada cake for dessert. A good place to wear a Hawaiian shirt and get your Jimmy Buffett on.

Siesta Key

Broken Egg
140 Avenida Messina
Tel: 941-346-2750
www.thebrokenegg.com $
A popular breakfast and lunch spot, whether you eat on the sunny patio or in the bright dining room. Healthy options include whole-wheat pancakes and turkey sausage.

Miguel's
6631 Midnight Pass Rd
Tel: 941-349-4024
www.miguelsrestaurant.net
$$$–$$$$
Its name to the contrary, Miguel's specializes in traditional French cuisine, served in a homey dining room. You'll find all kinds of Gallic faves here, including escargot, *crevette*, and *coquille St Jacques*.

SPRING TRAINING

The joys of summer come early in Florida, where baseball fans watch their favorite players and teams getting in shape for the upcoming season

Balmy temperatures and friendly crowds are two great reasons to travel to Florida in February, March, and April for a late winter vacation. Another is to get a preview of the upcoming major league baseball season during spring training. Spring training in Florida is now a century-old ritual that offers relaxed practice time for players, tryouts for new recruits, and professional-level games at a low cost. You might even see a game between big-league teams like the Boston Red Sox and Minnesota Twins.

Eighteen teams play in 17 venues throughout Florida in what's been dubbed the Grapefruit League. Most begin their workouts in mid-February, then play a series of games against other spring-training teams and minor league, college, and local teams in March and the first week of April. Games are held at popular venues like Legends Field in Tampa and Roger Dean Stadium in Jupiter, which also offer special events such as bat and T-shirt giveaways. The athletes often come over and meet fans after the games – an extra thrill for autograph-seeking kids. In 2008, a record-breaking 1.6 million fans attended 259 games in Florida stadiums, recording an average attendance of 6,478 fans per game. Tickets go on sale as early as December and range from $5 for bleacher tickets to $15 for reserved seats. Ticket information can be obtained by calling the team's Florida venue (*see Travel Tips, page 380*) or by calling TickCo Premium Seating (tel: 800-279-4444; www.tickco.com). For information about Florida's Grapefruit League, go to www.floridagrapefruitleague.com.

ABOVE: fans gather for autographs around Philadelphia Phillies pitcher Jamie Moyer at Bright House Networks Field in Clearwater

ABOVE: a trainer helps a ballplayer work out his winter kinks. Spring training gives veterans an opportunity to shape up for the regular season.

LEFT: the NY Mets do their spring training in Port Lucie, Florida.

RIGHT: a Phillies fan watches his favorite team take the field. Spring training is especially fun for kids, who often have a chance to meet their heroes up close.

THE BIRTH OF A TRADITION

Spring training in Florida traces its origins to 1913, when player-manager Johnny Evers brought the Chicago Cubs to Tampa for training, after the team slid to a disappointing third place in the league. In February, the Cubs played the first of a three-game series against the Havana Athletics, a team of Cuban hotshots, most of whom had played American college baseball. Some 6,000 fans packed Plant Field – many of them Cuban cigar factory workers from Ybor City and West Tampa whose employers let them out early from work to attend the games. The Chicago Cubs trounced the Athletics in all three matches, then played several intra-team games and even a local team on Egmont Key. Tampa fell in love with baseball.

By 1914, other Florida towns were working hard to attract major-league baseball teams. Among them was Jacksonville, which hosted the league champions, the Philadelphia Athletics, in 1914. Their manager was Connie Mack, grandfather of Florida Senator Connie Mack III, who had played for the Washington Senators in 1888 and had been the first to skipper the Athletics for an entire season in Jacksonville in 1903. Over the years, improved train and auto connections brought more players to the Sunshine State, and, with the exception of the World War II years, when trains were commandeered for troops, spring training has been an annual ritual in Florida ever since.

ABOVE: peanuts, popcorn, and Cracker Jacks are perennial favorites, though some stadiums offer more ambitious fare.

BELOW: the Grapefruit League encompasses 18 major league teams to play more than 30 games each. The spring training season usually lasts for six weeks, from mid-February to April.

ABOVE: Lou Gehrig (left) and Bob Shawkey with a mess of trout that Shawkey caught and brought to show his team-mates at the Yankees' training camp at St Petersburg in 1927.

NORTH FLORIDA

In this lightly traveled corner of the Sunshine State are historic cities, pristine beaches, colorful seaside villages, and a vast inland wilderness

I n the middle of a sprawling expanse of pine forest in North Florida, a billboard tells the story of this largely undeveloped region. "Florida's Last Frontier," proclaims the sign, put there by a real-estate agent eager to sell land to modern pioneers. If the billboard gives the impression that the northern reaches of the Sunshine State are a little old-fashioned and move at a slower pace than the rest of Florida, perhaps it is correct. And if the sign means that some of the state's hidden treasures – unsullied beaches, meandering rivers, and inland wilderness – still await discovery, that's true as well.

It is these piney woods that attracted Florida's first Spanish settlers, that resounded with gunfire during colonial and Indian conflicts and the American Civil War, and that helped some men amass fabulous wealth but seldom allowed them to keep it.

Pensacola is now a thriving metropolis, but the city over the years has been the possession of five different nations. There were places like Magnolia and Saint Joseph and New Port, once prosperous communities with fancy hotels and lavish mansions, now greatly diminished by disaster, disease, or economic downturns. Madison's Southern charm and Gainesville's air of academia have roots dating back before the Civil War. Indeed, the heritage of this entire region is written in overnight success – in booms of lumber, cotton, and citrus, followed by busts so total that little remains of the glory days.

And what of North Florida today? It is a land of contrasts, cosmopolitan in the cities of Pensacola and Tallahassee but overwhelmingly rural in the spaces that stretch between them. Like the rest of the state, it has vibrant seaside communities. But there are fewer of them here than elsewhere, and many more stretches of pristine beach – known collectively as the Forgotten Coast, white and powdery as sugar, without a hint of a high-rise building in sight. ❑

PRECEDING PAGES: Steinhatchee, on the Nature Coast. **LEFT:** a back-porch view of the Gulf of Mexico from a Seaside beach house. **TOP:** a docent in period costume at Historic Pensacola Village. **ABOVE RIGHT:** Saint Mark's National Wildlife Refuge.

GAINESVILLE AND NORTH CENTRAL FLORIDA

Miles of scenic horse country, several historic waterways, and the quiet Nature Coast make this one of Florida's best-kept secrets

For 50 years, zoology professor Archie Carr commuted from his home in Micanopy to the University of Florida campus in Gainesville via **Payne's Prairie**, a 50 sq mile (130 sq km) limestone sinkhole reminiscent of the Everglades, with its changing wetlands, luxuriant sea of grasses, and extraordinary wildlife. "To a taste not too dependent upon towns, there is always something," marveled Carr in his 1964 essay *The Bird and the Behemoth*. "If only a new set of shades in the grass and sky or a round-tail muskrat bouncing across the blacktop or a string of teal running low with the clouds in the twilight in front of a winter wind. The prairie is a solid thing to hold to in a world all broken out with man."

Green at heart

Thanks to the efforts of Carr and wife, Marjorie, Payne's Prairie (named after Seminole chief King Payne) was recognized in 1971 as Florida's first state preserve. Today, it's one of Florida's most important natural resources: A major recharge for the Floridian Aquifer, which provides drinking water for millions; a sanctuary for wildlife such as wild horses, bison, cattle, alligators, and Florida's largest population of sand hill cranes; and a beloved greenbelt for Gainesville residents, who flock to its six trails.

Naturalist William Bartram traveled here by steamboat in 1774 and wrote so inspiringly about Payne's Prairie that poet Samuel Taylor Coleridge used the descriptions in his poem *Kubla Khan*. In 1928, writer Marjorie Kinnan Rawlings moved to an old home amid the citrus groves on Orange Lake. Kinnan Rawlings' stories about life among the fish camps of Cross Creek brought worldwide attention to this Florida backwater and won her a Pulitzer Prize for the classic tale of a boy and his

Main attractions
FLORIDA MUSEUM OF NATURAL HISTORY
SAMUEL P HARN MUSEUM OF ART
PAYNE'S PRAIRIE PRESERVE STATE PARK
MICANOPY HISTORICAL SOCIETY CENTER
MARJORIE KINNAN RAWLINGS HISTORIC STATE PARK
OCALA
ICHETUCKNEE SPRINGS STATE PARK

LEFT: Gainesville's historic area.
RIGHT: Florida Museum of Natural History.

Exhibits at the Samuel P. Harn Museum of Art range from ancient to modern.

fawn, *The Yearling*. The sleepy homestead she restored, now a beautifully tended state park, is a symbol of Old Florida.

Gators in the swamp

North-central Florida is huge, encompassing Alachua and neighboring counties between the hill country around Ocala to the south; the spring-fed Santa Fe River to the north; the St John's River, Lake George, and Ocala National Forest to the east; and the Suwannee River to the west. Consider basing yourself in Gainesville and then make day or weekend trips to surrounding sights.

An interesting cultural mix of city and country, rich and poor, brainy and brawny, **Gainesville ❶** grew up around the citrus, turpentine, phosphate, and cattle industries in the mid-1800s, when the Cedar Key–Fernandina railroad opened East Coast markets. In 1906 a public university was founded in Gainesville, merging a seminary and agricultural college. A century later, 51,000 students attend the **University of Florida ❹**, the country's third largest. Famous for its Gators football team, which plays in a stadium dubbed the Swamp, this public university excels as a research institution, with regular breakthroughs in food

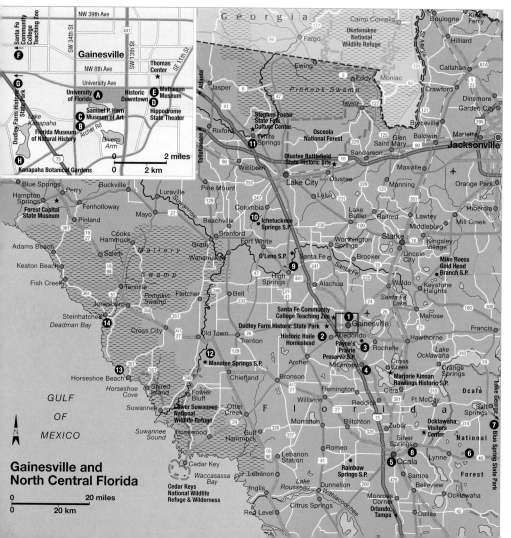

Gainesville and North Central Florida

0 _____ 20 miles
0 _____ 20 km

science (Gatorade and other commercial products were developed here), neurology, and agriculture. Archie Carr was one of UF's most popular professors until his death in 1987. To honour Carr's lifetime research and restoration work with endangered sea turtles, the Archie Carr Center for Sea Turtle Research was founded in 1986 to continue his conservation work.

Natural history

The best way to learn about Carr's passion for sea turtles is to read his many inspiring books and to visit the **Florida Museum of Natural History** ❸ (SW 34th St and Hull Rd; tel: 352-846-2000; www.flmnh.ufl.edu; Mon–Sat 10am–5pm, Sun 1–5pm; charge), housed in an airy modern building in the UF Cultural Plaza. Kid-friendly, intelligent exhibits include fossils from the last 65 million years and the role of water as it flows through a hardwood hammock, bog, limestone cave, and other habitats. Florida's first peoples are well interpreted, with walk-through exhibits that include a replica Calusa Indian hut.

The hottest ticket at the Museum is the **Butterfly Rainforest**, a 6,400 sq ft (600 sq meter) screened vivarium filled with tropical plants and living butterflies. A Wall of Wings displays thousands of stunningly beautiful butterfly specimens.

Crisp, flowing water and Zen-like tranquility greet visitors to the **Samuel P. Harn Museum of Art** ❻ (SW 34th St and Hull Rd; tel: 352-392-9826; www.harn.ufl.edu; Tue–Fri 11am–5pm, Sat 10am–5pm, Sun 1–5pm; free). This teaching museum contains more than 7,000 examples of world-class art, from traditional Asian and African crafts to a large collection of modern masterpieces, including works paintings by Claude Monet and photographs by Ansel Adams. Downstairs, the chic **Camelia Court Café** is a lunch spot offering light entrées, fresh roasted coffee, and free wireless Internet. It's open to 10pm on Thursdays for **Museum Night**, so if you're attending a performance at the **Phillips Center for the Performing Arts** (tel: 352-392-1900) across the plaza, you're in luck.

Century Tower rises 157ft (48 meters) above the University of Florida campus.

BELOW: an Asian butterfly alights on a flower in an indoor rainforest at the Florida Museum of Natural History.

Payne's Prairie Park

This park has the distinction of being Florida's first state preserve and was established in 1971. It is named for the eldest nephew of Seminole chief Ahaya (the Cowkeeper). In the past, the prairie has flooded to create a lake (Lake Alachua). The last occurrence was from 1871 through 1886, during which time steamboats would cruise the waters of the temporary lake. Today the park is home to some 270 species of birds. It's the gateway site for the Florida Bird Watching Trail. Within the preserve you can find American alligators and Florida cracker horses and cattle, which were once herded by Seminole Indians. In addition, the preserve is home to a herd of plains bison. Although it is rare to see the bison, the most frequent sightings usually occur at Cone's Dike Trail.

A boardwalk leads visitors into Payne's Prairie Preserve State Park.

BELOW AND BELOW RIGHT: Marjorie Kinnan Rawlings Historic State Park preserves the author's humble homestead.

On Wednesday afternoons, the **Gainesville Farmers' Market** is a good place to mingle with residents, listen to live music, and buy organic produce, dairy products, free-range meat, coffee beans, and European bakery items.

On the edge of Sweetwater Park, just east of downtown, is the **Matheson Museum ❺** (13 E. University Ave; tel: 352-378-2280; www.mathesonmuseum. org; Tue–Fri 9.30am–1.30pm; charge), where you can learn about Alachua County and tour the elegant 1863 **Matheson House**, the second-oldest home in Gainesville.

East of the university, the **Historic Downtown** is regenerating. Neighborhoods here are a mix of converted warehouses, turn-of-the-20th-century brick buildings, shotgun shacks, and Victorian mansions reviving as bed-and-breakfasts, restaurants, boutiques, and professional and government offices.

You can't miss the **Hippodrome State Theater ❹** (25 SE 2nd Pl; tel: 352-375-HIPP; http://thehipp.org) in the former Federal Building, a glorious 1911 Beaux Arts building with Corinthian columns. A local favorite, the Hippo has stage performances and movies every night of the week.

Among the family-friendly attractions on the rural outskirts of Gainesville are the **Santa Fe Community College Teaching Zoo ❻** (3000 NW 83rd St; tel: 352-395-5604; www.sfcollege.edu/zoo; daily 9am–2pm, call for appointment; charge), a unique and small zoo that teaches zookeeping skills; **The Thomas Center** (302 Northeast 6th Ave; tel: 352-334-5067; www.gvlcultur-alaffairs.org; Mon, Wed–Fri 8am–5pm, Tue 8am–7pm, Sat 1–4pm; free), listed

Cross Creek Memories

Born in Washington, DC, in 1896, Marjorie Kinnan Rawlings moved to the Cross Creek homestead in 1928, intending to write and live off the land. Along with a traditional Cracker home, she inherited an orange grove, two cows, two mules, 150 chicken coops, two chicken brooders, a planter, reaper, cultivators, and an old Ford truck. Her first husband didn't take to backwoods life, and the couple divorced in 1933, the year her first novel about Cross Creek appeared. Rawlings stayed on with her black maid, who later wrote a memoir about their relationship entitled *The Perfect Maid*. In 1941, Rawlings married Ocala hotelier Norton Baskin, and the couple split their time between Cross Creek and a home near St Augustine. Rawlings wrote nine books, including a cookbook (she was a passionate cook), the memoir *Cross Creek*, and *The Yearling*. Her publishing career was nurtured by legendary New York editor Maxwell Perkins, who was the first to suggest she write about her neighbors.

She died in St Augustine in 1953. Cross Creek was donated to UC Florida and became a state park in 1970.

n the National Register of Historic Places, is a restored Mediterranean Revival-style hotel. It features two art galleries which include 1920 period rooms, local artist exhibits, and beautiful gardens. A free historical cell phone tour about the property and the Thomas family is available. The **Dudley Farm Historic State Park** ● 18730 W. Newberry Rd; tel: 352-472-1142; Wed–Sun 9am–5pm; charge) is in Newberry, where costumed interpreters demonstrate pioneer life on a working family farm. Activities in the 18 historic buildings include tending heritage variety crops and livestock and cane grinding for a functioning cane syrup facility.

Kanapaha Botanical Gardens ● (4700 SW 58th Dr; tel: 352-372-4981; www.kanapaha.org; Mon–Wed, Fri 9am–5pm, Sat–Sun 9am–dusk; charge) is the second-largest botanical garden in Florida. Named for the adjoining Kanapaha Lake (*Kanapaha* is a Timucua Indian word meaning "palmetto leaf house"), this 62 acre (25 hectare) garden features 1.5 miles (2.5km) of trails that meander through 14 plant collections. Highlights include Florida's largest bamboo collection, the largest herb garden in the Southeast, and a water garden. There's also a terrific gift shop, which sells unique nature-themed items.

The **Historic Haile Homestead** ● (8500 Archer Rd; tel: 352-336-9096; www.hailehomestead.org; reserved tours on weekends only; charge) on the former Kanapa Plantation southwest of town, was a working farm of a different order. A cotton plantation and an antebellum home were built in 1854 by slaves who accompanied the Haile family from South Carolina. One feature of the homestead is its Talking Walls, unpainted surfaces where the Hailes recorded reflections on their lives.

Across the prairie

Sweetwater Branch Creek, on Gainesville's southeast side, drains into

Payne's Prairie Preserve State Park ● (tel: 352-466-3397; daily 8am–sunset; charge). Trails leave from the 15th Street preserve entrance. The 3 mile (5km) **La Chua Trail** begins at historic La Chua cattle ranch, passes Alachua Sink, where giant alligators loll menacingly below, and continues to an observation deck. Binoculars are helpful if you want to glimpse some of the 800 species of plants, 271 species of birds, and 430 species of vertebrates living in 25 diverse natural communities. To reach the main visitor center, drive south on US 441 and watch for signs. The center offers an interpretive film, exhibits, a bookstore, and ranger talks, and a trail leads to an observation tower. There's also a good observation platform on the east side of US 441.

Continue south to reach **Micanopy** ●, founded as a fort during the Seminole Wars and the oldest inland town in the state. Stop at the former warehouse that houses the **Micanopy Historical Society Center** (tel: 352-466-3200; www.hailehomestead.org; daily; charge) to view exhibits and pick up a historic walking-tour booklet for

BELOW: an old Micanopy inn.

Daphnis and Chloe
(1882) by Elizabeth
Jane Gardner at
Ocala's Appleton
Museum of Art.

BELOW: park
rangers in period
costume illustrate
life in the 1880s at
Dudley Farm
Historic State Park.

the quiet main street. Many buildings house bed-and-breakfasts, antique shops, cafés, and unique stores like Mosswood, a purveyor of back-to-the-land goods with a tiny farmers' market on Sundays.

Marjorie Kinnan Rawlings Historic State Park (18700 South County Road; tel: 352-466-3672; daily, no tours Mon–Wed or in Aug; charge) is southeast of US 441, off CR 325. You can self-tour the sleepy farmyard, where chickens peck around the barn, oranges ripen on trees, and a vintage car awaits its former owner under an awning. Female rangers, dressed in 1940s house dresses, give tours of the home, a classic dog-trot building designed to maximize breezes in the days before air conditioning. Bring a picnic – there's a pleasant park next door.

The great outdoors

Heading south to **Ocala ❺**, the landscape shifts to a pastoral scene of rolling hills, grazing horses, and picturesque barns. No surprise, then, that Ocala is the Horse Capital of the US, with more than 900 horse farms. A few stables offer tours, and there are horse-themed events throughout the year, including Horse Shows in the Sun in February and the Ocala Shrine Rodeo in August. Just east of the historic downtown is the **Appleton Museum of Art** (4333 NE Silver Springs Blvd; tel: 352-291-4455; www.appletonmuseum.org; Tue–Sat 10am–5pm, Sun noon–5pm; charge), a neoclassical building housing a wide-ranging collection and traveling exhibitions.

Ocala National Forest ❻ abounds with hiking trails and opportunities for camping, boating, and birdwatching on adjoining **Lake George**. The multi-agency **Ocklawaha Visitors Center** (3199 NE CR 315, Silver Springs; tel: 352-236-0288) has information on outdoor activities in Marion County. Lake George is fed by the **St John's River**, an important travel corridor for Florida's earliest canoe cultures and later steamboat travelers. The location of the St John's River, flowing north to meet the Atlantic at Jacksonville, led to the development of riverbank communities such as **Enterprise** and **Palatka**. Thriving tourist centers during the Victorian period, they are now mere shadows of their former selves.

Your best bets for canoeing or tubing are **Alexander and Juniper Springs**. It's better to come on weekdays when attendance is light. The largest recreation area in the forest is **Salt Springs** on SR 40 and 314, with a canoe path from **Lake George** to the St John's River.

Snorkeling in crystal springs at **Blue Spring State Park ❼** (2100 W. French Ave, Orange City; tel: 386-775-3663; daily 8am–dusk; charge) and **Lower Wekiva River Preserve State Park** (1800 Wekiwa Cir, Apopka; tel: 407-884-2008; daily 8am–dusk) is also popular. At the start of the paved **West Orange Trail**, you can rent bikes and rollerblades and cruise for 19 miles (30km) around Lake Apopka.

The state's oldest theme park, **Silver Springs ❽**, just east of Ocala, harkens back to the steamboat era on

the Ocklawaha River. It has wonderful old glass-bottom paddleboats that allow you to look down into Florida's deepest natural springs. The animals along these riverbanks live protected lives.

Springs eternal

"Springs are bowls of liquid light," wrote famed conservationist Marjorie Stoneman Douglas. That's certainly true of the hundreds of springs that percolate through Florida's underlying limestone. North of Gainesville, they feed the Santa Fe River and its tributaries, then merge with the Suwannee River. The farther north you drive toward the Georgia border on US 441, the more "southern" it gets. Historic towns like **Alachua** and **High Springs** ❾, which grew up with the railroad, have reinvented themselves as genteel rural villages, complete with historic bed-and-breakfasts, antique shops, and restaurants serving field-fresh greens. Canoeing and tubing are the preferred ways to beat hot summers in this neck of the woods, where almost every household has a boat in its yard.

At **Ichetucknee Springs State Park** ❿ (12087 SW US Hwy 27; tel: 386-497-4690; daily 8am–sunset; charge), 4 miles (6.5km) northwest of Fort White, rent a tube or canoe, park your car at the south entrance, board a tram to the north entrance, and float back down the crystalline Ichetucknee River to the parking lot at a leisurely pace (allow 2–3 hours). There are no alligators in the 72°F (22°C) water but plenty of basking turtles on logs (laughingly referred to as "shell stations" by

Pointy roots grow from the cypress trees in river wetlands.

BELOW: Silver Springs has an assortment of exotic wildlife.

The Nature Coast has a decidedly down-home and folksy atmosphere compared to the more developed parts of the state.

BELOW:
Steinhatchee is a remote fishing village at the mouth of the Steinhatchee River.

a ranger). Small fish among the eel grass form the main diet of the elegant snowy egrets and beady-eyed herons that stand motionless in the shallows, waiting to pounce. Park authorities protect water quality by banning water, food, and tobacco on the river, so eat a hearty meal and hydrate beforehand. Life doesn't get better than a canoe ride on the Ichetucknee in winter. Temperatures are pleasant and tubing is restricted to the south entrance, so you'll have the river to yourself.

The Santa Fe River joins the **Suwannee River** near Branford. The Suwannee rises in Georgia and meanders across northern Florida. Stephen Foster, composer of the 1851 song *Old Folks at Home*, never saw the Suwannee, but his lyrics evoked the way of life here so well that Florida adopted the tune as its state song in 1935. You can learn more at **Stephen Foster State Folk Culture Center** (US 41; tel: 386-397-2733; daily 9am–5pm; charge) in **White Springs ⑪**, north of Lake City. Among the attractions are rides on a riverboat and a carillon that rings out Foster favorites like *O Susannah* and *Camptown Races*. There's a **Florida Folk Festival** here every May, and you'll see baptisms in the river, eat black-eyed peas, and hear storytellers and folk singers perform.

Nature Coast

West of Chiefland, the Suwannee loses energy and meanders into Gulf waters in one of the largest undeveloped river delta-estuary systems. Protected as the 52,935 acre (21,422 hectare) **Lower Suwannee National Wildlife Refuge** (SR 347; tel: 352-493-0238), this area of scenic tidal marshes, coastal islands, and cypress groves is variously called the Big Bend, Hidden Coast, or Nature Coast. The refuge fronts 26 miles (42km) of Gulf coastline and protects 250 bird species. There are 40 miles (64km) of trails and 50 miles (80km) of forested back roads, but it's easiest to travel by boat. Kayakers can put in at **Shell Mound** and paddle the estuary or do three different river loops from the town of **Suwannee.**

Forgot your boat? **Lower Suwannee River Tours** in **Manatee Springs State Park ⑫** (SR 320; tel: 352-493-6072; daily 8am–sunset; charge) offers river rides. This park has a campground that makes a great base. Swim in the springs and walk a boardwalk to the observation point at the mouth of the spring run, a slam dunk for sighting manatees.

North of Suwannee is **Horseshoe Beach ⑬**, a retirement community so remote it feels like you're on an island. Most popular is **Steinhatchee ⑭**, a fishing village that attracts retirees and tourists. **Steinhatchee Landing Resort** offers activities for the whole family, and the pleasant waterfront has boat rentals, gift shops, and restaurants. Nearby **Keaton Beach** is one of the few settlements with a tiny patch of sand and slides for the kids.

The Nature Coast is Florida's most unspoiled region. Sunsets are extraordinary. For anyone looking to retreat from the modern world, a vacation cottage on stilts overlooking the Gulf may be your ticket to paradise. ❏

RESTAURANTS

Alachua

Conestoga's Restaurant
14920 Main St
Tel: 386-462-1294
www.conestogasrestaurant.com $$–$$$
This family-friendly restaurant is known for its hand-cut steaks, fresh seafood, and mouth-watering desserts. It's the perfect way to relax after spending the day floating down the Santa Fe River.

Cross Creek

The Yearling Restaurant
14531 E. County Rd 325
Tel: 352-466-3999
www.yearlingrestaurant.net $$
This no-frills backwoods restaurant is right on Cross Creek down the road from "Miz Rawlings'" former home. It is legendary for its down-home cuisine, the type local people hunted, fished, or trapped for themselves, then fried up for dinner. Look for frogs' legs, alligator, venison, quail, and land turtle, with hush puppies, collard greens, and grits.

Gainesville

Mildred's Big City Food
3445 W. University Ave

Tel: 352-371-1711
www.mildredsbigcityfood.com $$–$$$
Chef-owner Bert Gill buys organic produce from local farmers and seafood fresh off the boat in Cedar Key. The menu changes daily and includes imaginatively prepared specials like mushroom soup with truffle oil, sweetbreads with poached egg, and braised venison with Florida butter beans.

Booklover's Café
505 NW 13th St
Tel: 352-374-4241
Daily 10am–9pm $
This café inside an antiquarian bookstore serves cheap vegan food – bliss for thrifty bibliophiles with a health-conscious bent.

Paramount Grill
12 SW 1st Ave
Tel: 352-378-3398
www.paramountgrill.com $$–$$$$
All blond woods and white tablecloths, the lovely Paramount Grill is one of Gainesville's top fine-dining picks. Chef-owner Clif Nelson is devoted to local produce, and his New American cuisine combines elegance and freshness. Sunday brunch is popular.

Manuel's Vintage Room
6 S. Main St
Tel: 352-375-7372
www.manuelsvintageroom.com $$–$$$$
This intimate Italian restaurant offers classics such as pork Milanese, veal porcini, and make-your-own pasta dishes. Non-traditional signature dishes include snails as a starter, grouper in cognac sauce, and chicken breast sautéed with habanero peppers in a white wine butter sauce.

Dragonfly Sushi and Sake Company
201 SE 2nd Ave
Tel: 352-371-3359
http://dragonflysushi.com $$–$$$
This upscale sushi bar serves high-quality sushi in a hip atmosphere, complete with plasma TVs showing old Japanese movies and hypnotic techno music.

Emilano's Cafe
7 SE 1st Ave
Tel: 352-375-7381
www.emilianoscafe.com $$–$$$
This café is a local staple that has served up the finest Pan-Latin cuisine for more than 20 years. Popular dishes include the paella, guava barbecue pork ribs and churrasco. Diners can also enjoy items from the extensive tapas menu.

The Swamp Restaurant
1642 W. University Ave
Tel: 352-377-9267
www.swamprestaurant.com $$–$$$
Established in 1994, this popular smoke-free restaurant is rated the country's number one college establishment. House favorites include the spicy tuna bowl, the fried green BLT, the turkey artichoke panini, or the build-your-own-quesadillas. There is also a full bar.

High Springs

Floyd's Diner
615 NW Santa Fe Blvd
Tel: 386-454-5775 $
You can't miss this shiny vintage diner. The classic dishes on the large menu are very good, and there's even a separate menu for dogs who get to share food with their owners on the patio. A great local hangout. A full bar completes the package.

Newberry

Flour Pot Bakery
13005 SW 1st Rd #137
www.theflourpotbakery.com $
In the Tioga Town Center, just west of downtown Gainesville, this European-style bakery turns out authentic French baguettes and other breads, pastries, cakes, and cookies. You can order home-made sandwiches, salads, quiches, and savory croissants to eat in their café or take with you.

RIGHT: roadside stands sell locally grown pecans.

TALLAHASSEE AND THE PANHANDLE

The capital is a gateway to a "Forgotten Coast"
of gleaming white beaches, turquoise waters,
and sleepy seaside villages

In the early 19th century, most of Florida was a thick jungle. Settlement was concentrated in the northern tier, and Pensacola and St Augustine were the largest communities. Travel between these two territorial capitals was daunting and slow; trails through the interior were poorly marked, and pirates and storms plagued the ocean route. Each wanted to be the seat of territorial government, but the Territorial Legislative Council quickly realized that a more central location was necessary.

In 1823 two members of a site selection committee – one from Pensacola, the other from St Augustine – met at St Marks on Apalachee Bay to inspect the region selected by the council. This area was located between the Suwannee and Ochlockonee rivers and not far from a village that the Creek and Seminole Indians called "Tallahassee," meaning "old town" or "old fields." Both men were enamored with the hills and orchards of the area. One feature in particular seemed especially charming: a waterfall that graced a prominent hillside. The settlement that grew here kept the Indian name.

Government town

Tallahassee ❶ has undergone many changes since then, but it's still a government town. The skyline is dominated by the high-rise capitol soaring 22 stories above a steep hill, but high-rise residential condos are beginning to challenge the capitol's dominance.

Of those employed in the city, almost half work for local, state, or federal government. But don't let visions of boring bureaucrats frighten you. Tallahassee is one of the best-kept secrets in Florida. A friendly community, the city has done an excellent job of preserving its landmarks, its natural beauty, and

Main attractions
OLD CAPITOL
MUSEUM OF FLORIDA HISTORY
TALLAHASSEE MUSEUM
WAKULLA SPRINGS STATE PARK
APALACHICOLA NATIONAL FOREST
APALACHICOLA
PANAMA CITY BEACH
PENSACOLA
HISTORIC PENSACOLA VILLAGE

LEFT: a classic Panhandle beach.
RIGHT: Florida Supreme Court.

A satellite map gives visitors to Tallahassee a detailed overview of the state.

BELOW: an exhibit at the Museum of Florida History traces the development of the Spanish colony.

a small-town flavor that belies its burgeoning growth rate.

All this adds up to a metro-area population of about 181,000 who live amid a pleasing blend of old and new. It is a city rich in Old South town houses and plantation mansions that have been restored to their former grandeur. Oaks dripping with gray moss line picturesque streets, and dogwoods and azaleas bloom with vibrant spring color.

An elevator ride to the 22nd-floor observation deck of the **Florida State Capitol** Ⓐ (S. Monroe St and Apalachee Pkwy; tel: 850-488-6167; Mon–Fri 8am–5pm) will give you a bird's-eye view of the city, awash in a sea of trees. The **Old Capitol**, restored to its 1902 condition, is a museum piece that sits at the foot of its high-rise successor. The state legislature sits for just 60 days a year. If you visit in April or May, you can watch representatives and senators in action.

For some background, visit the **Museum of Florida History** Ⓑ (500 S. Bronough St, #G2; tel: 850-245-6400; Mon–Fri 9am–4.30pm, Sat 10am–4.30pm, Sun noon–4.30pm; free). This fine museum provides an overview of Florida's history, with exhibits ranging from a 12ft (4 meter)-tall mastodon to Spanish treasure and war relics.

In the beginning

In 1539, Spanish conquistador Hernando de Soto came to this area in search of the gold that he never found. While wintering here he celebrated the first Christmas in America.

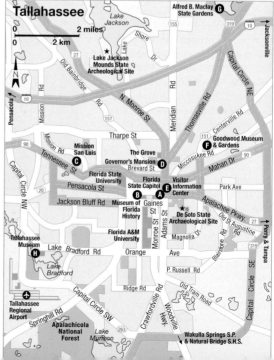

He explored the area around **Lake Jackson** north of town, but remains of his main camp were found at a site near downtown. Today, Lake Jackson is a favorite fishing spot, but it's known as the "disappearing lake" because of a sinkhole that periodically empties the lake in dramatic fashion.

In the 17th century, Tallahassee became the western capital of Spanish colonial Florida. A string of Franciscan missions ran between St Augustine and Tallahassee; the largest and most important of these was **Mission San Luis ©** (2100 West Tennessee St; tel: 850-245-6186; www.missionsanluis.org; tours Tue–Sun 10am–4pm; free), which today is re-created on the original site and is an archeological park.

Magnificent mansions

Wealth isn't new to the city, which has an array of restored homes built by prominent citizens in the years immediately before and after the Civil War. The most outstanding of these is **The Grove** (N. Adams Street), former home of territorial governor Richard Keith Call. Next door, at No. 700, is the more ornate **Governor's Mansion ◐** (tel: 850-488-4661; Mar–May, Mon, Wed, and Fri 10am–noon; free), which was modeled on General Andrew Jackson's plantation home in Tennessee. Access to the governor's house is limited, but tours are available by appointment. Other historic residences can be seen on guided tours arranged through local hotels or the city's **Visitor Information Center ◑** (106 E. Jefferson St; tel: 850-606-2305).

The real wealth, however, sparkles north of town in the form of 71 former plantations and 300,000 acres (120,000 hectares) that now serve as exclusive hunting preserves. In fact, the Tallahassee area boasts the largest concentration of plantations in America. Some of these estates are held by private owners, but there are a couple of exceptions. **Goodwood Museum and Gardens ◉** (1600 Miccosukee Rd; tel: 850-877-4202; main house: Mon–Fri

10am–2pm; free) is a replica of the plantation's 1911 Carriage House. You can explore the gardens and take tours inside the main house, which has original features such as marble fireplaces and a mahogany staircase.

You can also visit **Alfred B. Maclay State Gardens ©** (3540 Thomasville Rd; tel: 850-487-4556; daily 8am–sunset; charge). New York financier Alfred B. Maclay fashioned a garden of camellias, azaleas, palmettos, and

Tallahassee's Kleman Plaza serves as a civic hub near the state capitol.

BELOW: the Old Capitol.

The Panhandle has miles of undeveloped coastline and quiet fishing towns.

a wonderful working farm depicts Florida pioneer life in the late 19th century, and nature trails wind through the grounds, where bears, bobcats, and alligators reside. Other exhibits include the restored home of Napoleon's nephew, Prince Achille Murat; a one-room schoolhouse; and a grist mill. The museum is on the shores of Lake Bradford near Tallahassee Regional Airport, 4 miles (6km) southwest of downtown Tallahassee.

Memories of war

Although Florida's role in the Civil War was mainly to supply men and food for battles raging farther north, it did not completely miss the action. As the war entered its final month, Union troops landed near St Marks intending to take the fort there as well as Tallahassee itself. But attempts to cross the St Marks River were met with disaster at Natural Bridge, a spot southeast of Tallahassee where the river dips underground for 50 yards before resurfacing. Strongly entrenched Confederates – militia, old men, and teens – were ready for them. The Confederates inflicted heavy

other native and exotic plants around a tiny lake. Guided tours are available, and you can swim, fish, picnic, and go boating.

Tallahassee retained its rural Southern flavor longer than many other Florida communities of its size. The **Tallahassee Museum** ⓗ (3945 Museum Dr; tel: 850-576-1636; www. tallahasseemuseum.org; Mon–Sat 9am–5pm, Sun 12.30–5pm; charge) pays homage to its not-so-distant past. Here

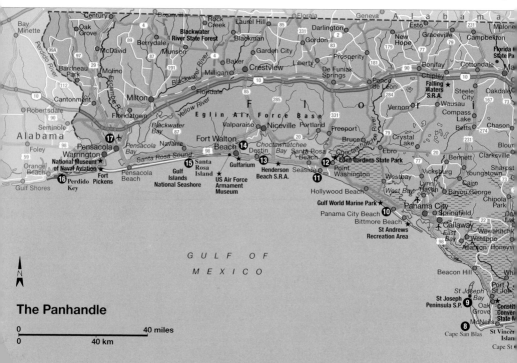

The Panhandle

0   40 miles
0   40 km

casualties on the Union soldiers and beat them back, making Tallahassee the only Confederate capital east of the Mississippi to resist capture.

The battlefield is preserved as the **Natural Bridge Battlefield State Historic Site** (7502 Natural Bridge Rd; tel: 850-922-6007; www.florida stateparks.org/naturalbridge; daily 8am–sunset; free), about 10 miles (16km) southeast of the city. There is an annual re-enactment of the famous battle on or about March 6.

The real Black Lagoon

From Natural Bridge, backtrack to Route 363 and head south to SR 267. Proceed west to **Wakulla Springs State Park** ❷ (550 Wakulla Park Dr; tel: 850-926-0700; daily 8am–sunset; charge). The park encompasses a large virgin hardwood and pine forest, but the main attraction is the spring for which the park is named, one of the largest in the world, pumping more than 687,000 gallons (2.6 million liters) of water a minute into a vast pool. You can swim in the clear spring waters or take a ride on a glass-bottomed boat.

There are boat trips upriver, where alligators laze on the shores and anhinga birds dry their wings on cypress branches. The classic 1954 horror movie *The Creature from the Black Lagoon* was filmed here.

If you want to dig in for a longer stay, consider booking a room at the gracious **Wakulla Springs Lodge** (U550 Wakulla Park Dr, Wakulla Springs; tel: 850-926-0700), with its rare Spanish tiles adorning the Moorish-style doorways. Note the ceiling beams in the lobby. They were etched with Aztec and Toltec Indian designs by a German immigrant reputed to have once painted castles for Kaiser Wilhelm.

The Panhandle

The Florida Panhandle is a world apart. In contrast to the theme parks, crowds, and craziness of the I-4 corridor in central Florida, the Panhandle is laid-back, shady, and more of what Old Florida used to be like.

Shoppers will find a mix of treasures and tchotchkes at antique shops and knick-knack stores throughout the region.

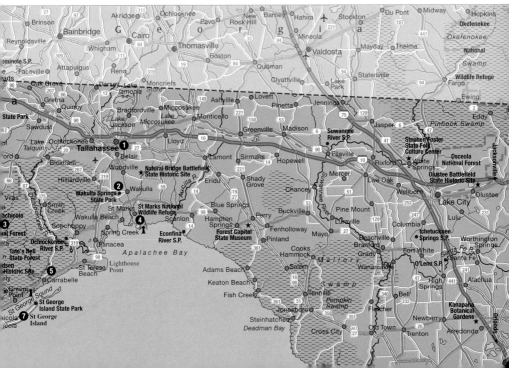

Ecotourism has taken root in this region, which is rich in opportunities for hiking, biking, fishing, kayaking, and canoeing. Birdwatching is especially popular. Birders come from far and wide to see the birdlife of **St Marks National Wildlife Refuge ❹** (1200 Lighthouse Rd, St Marks; tel: 850-925-6121; visitor center 8am–5pm, park 6am–8pm), a salt marsh that attracts some 300 bird species, including elegant, watchful hawks, noisy ducks, and numerous shorebirds.

Big Bend

There are a couple of ways to explore the Panhandle. If you are in a hurry to get to Pensacola, take I-10 west from Tallahassee. You'll get there in less than four hours but miss a scenic drive along the **Big Bend**, where the Panhandle dips into the peninsula. While it makes for a longer drive, US 98 and its side roads are the only way to experience the essence of the region. Several roads in Leon, Wakulla, and Franklin counties are part of what is called the **Big Bend Scenic Highway**, 200 miles (320km) of scenic roads that

Historic inns throughout the Big Bend region preserve the spirit of Florida.

BELOW: a lighthouse in St Marks National Wildlife Refuge guides ships in Apalachee Bay.

West of Tallahassee, the inland areas are covered in vast tracts of forest that hark back to the days when lumbermen and turpentine folks eked out a sparse living in the sandy woods. Wander through the **Apalachicola National Forest ❸** (tel: 850-643-2282) just west of Tallahassee and **Tate's Hell State Forest** (290 Airport Rd, Carrabelle; tel: 850-697-3734) near Carrabelle and you'll see how wild Old Florida used to be.

lead motorists around Apalachicola National Forest to St George Island State Park.

South of Tallahassee, US 98 leads past a string of small fishing towns. Among the most prominent is **Carrabelle ❺**. During the post-Civil War years it was a booming place, when lumber and turpentine were king, and stately schooners carried goods up north. The railroad also brought industry to Carrabelle and allowed salted mullet to be shipped north.

World War II brought another boom in the form of Camp Gordon Johnston, a gigantic training base for amphibious soldiers bound for Europe and the Pacific. Carrabelle later became a commercial fishing port, and, in recent years, a sportsman's paradise. What makes Carrabelle different from other coastal areas in this part of the Big Bend is its "true" beach – a rare commodity in a region noted more for its estuaries, tidal creeks, and rivers.

To hell and back

Carrabelle is set near Tate's Hell Swamp, which sprawls over most of Franklin County. The name is connected to the legend of Cebe Tate, a hunter who vanished into the swamp almost a century ago. According to local lore, he entered the wilderness in search of a panther that had been killing his livestock. It took him a week to find his way out, but not before suffering a snakebite that ultimately proved to be fatal.

Tate's Hell drains into another vast domain with remote nooks and crannies of its own, Apalachicola National Forest. Covering 557,000 acres (225,400 hectares), this is the largest of Florida's three national forests. It encompasses pine forest, swamps, and rivers, and has numerous recreational facilities.

The lower end of the Ochlockonee River meanders through Apalachicola National Forest, providing canoeists with pristine rowing through woodlands rife with wildlife. A canoe trail begins 20 miles (32km)

west of Tallahassee and continues downriver for 67 miles (108km) to **Ochlockonee River State Park**, south of **Sopchoppy**.

Florida's oyster capital

Twenty miles (32km) west of Carrabelle is the old cotton port of **Apalachicola ❻**. Oystermen from this area provide at least 90 percent of Florida's oysters, which are cultivated in the shallow waters of Apalachicola Bay.

Panhandle beaches are known for fine white sand and clear, blue water.

BELOW: nautical paraphernalia fill roadside shops near the Big Bend Scenic Highway.

TIP

Test your fish-flinging skills at the annual St George Island Mullet Toss in June; see page 347.

Oysters aren't Apalachicola's only claim to fame: the area is also well known for its rich estuaries. The Apalachicola River and Bay are home to the Gulf striped bass, a native fish which has been known to reach weights of more than 50 pounds (23kg). The Big Bend area offers some of Florida's best fishing, including the opportunity to catch tarpon and bull redfish. There are many charter fishing boats that will help you catch the fish of a lifetime. Offshore fishing offers the opportunity to land such big game fish as tarpon, cobia, and grouper. These giants can reach weights in excess of 200 pounds (90kg). For those who prefer to catch something a little more manageable, try inshore fishing, where fish such as Spanish mackerel, redfish, pompano, or speckled trout are likely to dangle from your hook. Many of these fish will be under 15 pounds (6.8kg).

During scallop season, which runs from July through early September, many charter companies offer scalloping trips. Catch them and cook them in the same afternoon. For a lovely evening on the water without the rod and reel, choose one of the local sunset cruises.

Apalachicola is famous as the birthplace of the world's favorite modern convenience, especially in places such as Florida. One of the city's early physicians made the world more bearable by inventing refrigeration and air conditioning. While trying to control malaria in the region in the late 1840s, Dr. John Gorrie succeeded in building an ice machine that kept his patients' rooms cool. Gorrie got a patent for the machine, but no credit for his work until long after his death in 1851. The **John Gorrie State Museum** (6th St and Ave D; tel: 850-653-9347; www.floridastateparks.org/johngorriemuseum; Thur–Mon 9am–5pm; charge) has a replica of the very first ice machine (the original machine is in the Smithsonian Institution in Washington, DC).

Calm before the storm

Connected by a toll bridge to US 98 is **St George Island** ❼, part of which is protected as **St George Island State Park** (1900 E. Gulf Beach Dr, St George Island; tel: 850-927-2111; daily

BELOW: the calm waters of the Gulf of Mexico are excellent for kayaking.

8am–sunset; charge), with 9 miles (14km) of undeveloped beach and woods that are a favorite nesting place for ospreys. The park was damaged during Hurricane Dennis in 2005, but all-new facilities have been built and the beach is open for business.

One of the most anticipated events here is the annual St George Mullet Toss, which is held at the Blue Parrot Ocean Front Café on West Gorie Drive. Visitors from miles around make pilgrimages to participate in this annual June event. There are events held for men, women, and children, and prizes are handed out to the winners in each category.

Next door, but accessible only by boat from Apalachicola, is St Vincent Island, a nirvana for wildlife enthusiasts, who come to see loggerhead turtles, wild turkeys, and non-native sambar deer, originally from India.

Back on the mainland, you can detour along SR 30E to sample the magnificence of **Cape San Blas ❽**. Sunset is a particularly moody time to sit on the sand dunes and gaze out over the Gulf of Mexico, but be sure

to take insect repellent. To the north is **St Joseph Peninsula State Park ❾** (8899 Cape San Blas Rd; tel: 850-227-1327; www.floridastateparks.org/stjoseph; daily 8am–sunset; charge), with miles of beautiful beaches and an excellent hiking trail, plus rental cabins and a basic campground.

Heading north on the mainland, you'll find **Port St Joe**, which burst into existence in the 1820s. In those days it was a major cotton-shipping

A recreational boat is equipped for a day of fishing on the Gulf.

BELOW: bikes at the beach.

BELOW: Seaside is a planned community modeled after a Victorian-era resort.

port replete with warehouses, casinos, and sprawling mansions. Yellow fever swept the town in the early 1840s, killing more than two-thirds of the population. The town boomed again in the early 20th century due to the expanding railroad and export lumber business.

Party town

To the northwest is **Panama City Beach ❿**. All the beaches in this area received a severe battering from hurricanes Erin and Opal in 1995 and hurricane Ivan in 2004; the scars left by Ivan are healing and the pristine white beaches still sparkle. In fact, this part of the Gulf Coast has some of the world's most beautiful beaches.

Panama City Beach – the "Spring Break Capital of the South" – is currently undergoing a sweeping revitalization. It's still a party town, but old buildings have been razed to make way for new museums, galleries, parks, homes, and shopping malls. **Pier Park** (Front Beach Rd at Pier Park Dr; tel: 850-236-9974; Mon–Sat 10am–9pm, Sun noon–6pm) is touted as the

premier shopping destination; and the new Panama City–Bay County International Airport, which opened in 2010, will undoubtedly boost visitation significantly.

While in Panama City Beach, stop at Zoo World (9008 Front Beach Rd; tel: 850-230-4839; www.zoo-world.us; daily; charge), which has more than 20 endangered species as well as one of Florida's better petting zoos; or catch the sea lion and dolphin shows at **Gulf World Marine Park** (15412 Front Beach Rd; tel: 850-234-5271; daily from 9am; charge), also on the seafront.

An architectural interlude

Between Seagrove Beach and Grayton Beach is **Seaside ⓫**, one of the state's most unusual communities. Built in the 1980s, this experiment in urban planning attempts to re-create a Victorian resort. It has tidy streets lined with quaint wooden cottages complete with gingerbread detailing and picket fences. Seaside is worth a peek (and there's a beach, of course), but, as with many modern planned communities, there is a sense of surreal conformity.

Little wonder that it was chosen as the setting for *The Truman Show*, the 1998 movie starring Jim Carrey.

You'll find rather more authentic grace inland at **Eden Gardens State Park** and the **Wesley House** (off US 98 and CR 295 in **Point Washington** ⑫; tel: 850-231-4214; www.floridastateparks.org/EdenGardens; tours hourly Thur–Mon 10am–3pm; charge), where a stately old Southern mansion is set in the ornamental gardens. The white-columned home was built of heart-pine and cypress in the late 1800s by a local lumber baron.

The Emerald Coast

Next on US 98 is **Destin** ⑬, a fishing town where marlin and sailfish test their strength and cunning against fishermen. While there aren't as many commercial fishing boats and shrimp boats as there used to be, the Gulf water is just as green and clear as the day it was created. That's why the area between Port St Joe and Pensacola is called the Emerald Coast. Here, dozens of charter boat captains begin their day at 5am loading barrels of

ice in anticipation of the day's catch. Closer to land, the "big game" fish is mullet – one of the most exciting of the inshore catches. Fishermen use long, narrow skiffs in their search, the better to pole shallow bayous favored by the fish. It's often the main course at local seafood joints and is usually served with coleslaw or baked beans, grits, and hush puppies.

Just across from Destin is **Fort Walton Beach** ⑭ and **Niceville**,

A dolphin trainer works with one of her pupils at Gulf World Marine Park in Panama City Beach.

BELOW:
Fort Walton Beach.

Architectural details add charm and character to Pensacola's historic downtown.

home to the vast **Eglin Air Force Base**. Eglin is the largest base of its kind in the US, encompassing some 724 sq miles (1,875 sq km) of land and more than 97,000 sq miles (250,000 sq km) of airspace. The base employs some 20,000 people who contribute considerably to the local economy. The **US Air Force Armament Museum** (100 Museum Dr; tel: 850-651-1808; Mon–Sat 9.30am–4.30pm; free), just outside Eglin near Valparaiso, will interest fans of military aviation. The gift shop is full of models and other curiosities.

Gulf Islands

There are numerous small beach communities west along US 98, but the best route is SR 399, which veers south at Navarre onto **Santa Rosa Island** ⓯. Here you can revel in miles of billowing dunes topped by miniature magnolias. The strip's promoters claim the sands are the whitest in the world.

This part of the coast is all part of **Gulf Islands National Seashore**, which protects 150 miles (240km) of pristine coastline that runs west as far as Gulfport in Mississippi. Visitors can stop at park sites and enjoy a day in the sun. There are campsites and nature trails as well as picnic areas and other facilities. Another gorgeous section of the National Seashore is on **Perdido Key** ⓰, a 30-minute drive southwest of Pensacola, with charming beaches and salt marshes rich in birdlife.

Pensacola

Finally, more than 200 miles (320km) from Tallahassee, is **Pensacola** ⓱, a coastal city that is a mixture of Old South charm, Spanish heritage, and Navy bravado. The city has taken steps

to preserve its 400-year-old heritage in two historic districts near downtown as well as in museums, battle sites, and forts. And it isn't just in museum pieces that the city's history lives. It's in streets with names such as Intendencia, Zaragoza, and Cervantes, and it moves in the wind at St Michael's Cemetery, where tombstones bearing Spanish inscriptions date back to the 1700s. The area also has beautiful beaches – miles and miles of undeveloped coast where sand dunes (not condominiums) rise high above blue seas.

Contested territory

Don Tristan de Luna was the first to attempt establishing a settlement in the area in 1559, six years before St Augustine. But de Luna and the 1,500 colonists who came with him abandoned the settlement two years later. It wasn't until 1752 that a permanent settlement was established at Pensacola, though the Spaniards had tried again in 1698 and 1722. Since its founding, Pensacola has flown the flags of five countries in Plaza Ferdinand VII. The city celebrates its proud history each spring with the **Fiesta of Five Flags**. There are parades, art shows, and a re-enactment of de Luna's landing in 1559.

The British occupied Pensacola during the Revolutionary War but lost the city to the Spanish in 1781 after a month-long siege. The victory cut off British access to the fledgling American states and buoyed the hopes of colonists fighting for independence.

Four decades later, Andrew Jackson marched into Pensacola to claim Florida for the United States. Jackson, the first territorial governor of Florida, tried to convince the Spaniards to clean up streets he found "filthy and disgusting." Fed up, he packed up and went home after two months.

Historic Pensacola Village

Today, the original town square near Pensacola Bay is the centerpiece of the **Seville District**, a 37-block section of restored homes, shops, and old-time eateries that is Pensacola's crowning achievement in historic preservation. The square and nearby streets are a pleasant place to spend an afternoon strolling around. Several museums and some lovely restored homes in this district have been gathered together under the name Historic Pensacola Village. **Tivoli House** (205 E. Zaragoza St; tel: 850-595-5985; www.historicpensacola.org), dispenses tickets and information and organizes guided tours.

One of the most notable restored houses in the neighborhood is "the Oldest House" on Church Street, known as the **Lavalle House**. The exact construction date of Lavalle House is unknown, but historians consider it typical of the French Creole cottages of the 18th century. Other fine houses are the nearby **Dorr House**, at the corner of Church and Adams streets, and the so-called **Steamboat House**, on Government Street.

There are several good museums. On Zaragoza Street is the **Museum of Commerce** and **Museum of Industry** (201 E. Zaragoza St; tel: 850-

Pensacola is a sizable city, with a metropolitan population of 402,000, seven colleges and universities, a fine airport, a distinctive downtown, an educated workforce, fine hospitals, and centers of research and technology.

BELOW: historic Pensacola Village.

Vacation houses – many available to rent – have views of the Gulf and direct beach access.

BELOW: cypress swamp.
BELOW RIGHT: Fort Barrancas.

595-5985; Mon–Sat 10am–4pm). The nearby **T.T. Wentworth Jr. Museum** (330 S. Jefferson St; tel: 850-595-5990; Mon–Sat 10am–4pm) is a fine Spanish Renaissance Revival building with a fascinating collection of Florida memorabilia. Other old houses have been turned into antique stores and restaurants serving deli sandwiches, wine and cheese, and gourmet ice cream. Here too is the **Pensacola Museum of Art** (407 S. Jefferson St; tel: 850-432-6247;

www.pensacolamuseumofart.org; Tue–Fri 10am–5pm, Sat–Sun noon–5pm; charge), which has an eclectic array of artworks ranging from pre-Columbian pottery to modern painting.

Seville Quarter, billed as Pensacola's premier entertainment and dining complex, is in a restored 19th-century building on Government Street, on the fringe of Seville Square. It's a good place for a night out, with a wide range of bars and restaurants.

Pensacola's other districts

For background on Pensacola's role in the Civil War, the **Civil War Soldiers Museum** is worth a visit (108 S. Palafox Pl; tel: 850-469-1900; Tue–Sat 10am–4pm; charge) in the **Palafox District** – a cluster of early 20th-century residences at the southern end of Palafox Street.

The city's third historic district takes you back to the days of Pensacola's lumber boom. Residents built big houses and made big money. Today, dozens of houses from the era still stand in a 50-block area called the **North Hill Preservation District**, north of

The Inland Empire

Most tourists in the Panhandle focus on the coastal region, but lovers of nature will find the interior equally enticing. For example, in an isolated spot on the Apalachicola River just south of I-10 is Torreya State Park (2576 NW Torreya Park Road; tel: 850-643-2674). The park encompasses more than 13,000 acres (5,200 hectares) of the state's most diverse geography and is home to a rare species of the Torreya tree. To the west, 3 miles (5km) north of Marianna off SR 167, is Florida Caverns State Park (3345 Caverns Rd; tel: 850-482-9598), one of a few parks with air-filled caves, replete with spellbinding limestone formations. On the surface are trails for hiking and horseback riding. A canoe trail runs 52 miles (84km) south to Dead Lakes, north of Wewahitchka on SR 71, where a forest of cypress, oak, and pine is drowned by the natural overflow of the Chipola River.

Closer to Pensacola, I-10 skims the edge of Blackwater River State Forest (11650 Munson Hwy; tel: 850-957-6140), a vast woodland with hiking and camping. The tannin-stained Blackwater River winds through the forest and is excellent for canoeing.

Wright Street. Thanks to preservationists who set out to save the decaying neighborhood, many of the handsome homes have been restored. Visitors must content themselves with a view from outside, as most are private residences.

Defending Pensacola

Across the bay, **Fort Pickens** (tel: 850-934-2635; daily; charge), a pentagonal stronghold with a bastion at each corner, took five years to build and accommodated as many as 600 men.

In the early days of the Civil War, Union soldiers at Fort Pickens on the western tip of Santa Rosa Island engaged Confederate troops at **Fort Barrancas** (Pensacola Naval Air Station; tel: 850-455-5167) on the mainland. Pickens guarded the harbor entrance and prevented the Confederates from using the shipyard and adjacent railyard. Some historians believe the first shots of the tragic conflict may have actually been fired here, not at Fort Sumter in South Carolina. In the end, the Yankee invasion of Tennessee in 1862 forced Confederate leaders to move their manpower north, and Pensacola was abandoned. The town stayed in Union hands for the rest of the war. In the 1880s the fortress was famous for its imprisonment of Apache chief Geronimo. Both forts can be toured; Fort Pickens has a campground.

High flying

The panhandle is also home to the **Pensacola Naval Air Station**, the nation's largest, founded in 1914. All Navy training for land and sea is headquartered at the base, and it is the center for advanced training for Naval flight officers. According to the Pensacola Chamber of Commerce, the Department of Defense is a powerful economic engine here.

The **National Museum of Naval Aviation** (1750 Radford Blvd; tel: 850-452-3604; www.naval-air.org; daily 9am–5pm; free) exhibits more than 150 restored aircraft, ranging from a World War II airship to four former Blue Angels Skyhawks. There is also an IMAX theater and flight simulators for those who need a little more speed and excitement in their entertainment. ❏

Docents in period costume interpret 19th-century life at the Historic Pensacola Village.

BELOW: the Blue Angels exhibit at the National Museum of Naval Aviation.

RESTAURANTS

Restaurants

Prices for a three-course dinner per person, excluding tax, tip, and beverages:

$ = under $20
$$ = $20–45
$$$ = $45–60
$$$$ = over $60

Apalachicola

Boss Oyster
123 Water St
Tel: 850-653-8139
www.apalachicolainn.com/boss $$–$$$
Here's where to find the world-famous Apalachicola Bay oysters, shrimp, and crayfish. Dine inside, or outside on the open-air porch.

Destin

Graffiti and the Funky Blues Shack

Village of Baytowne Wharf, 707 Harbor Blvd #D
www.grafitibs.com
Tel: 850-654-2764 $$
An expansive menu filled with gourmet pasta and pizza is served in a casual setting decorated with folk art. The Funky Blues Shack bar is open to 2am.

Rutherfords 465 at Regatta Bay
465 Regatta Bay Blvd
Tel: 850-337-8888 or 800-254-6065
www.rutherfords465.com
$$–$$$
Set at a country club, Rutherfords offers a variety of salads and sandwiches. There's also a full bar.

Eastpoint

That Place on 98
17 Avenue East

Tel: 850-653-9898
$$–$$$
A colorful waterfront eatery right on US 98 in a sleepy oyster village. You can accompany your meal of crab cakes, Panhandle chowder, crab claws, and smoked fish dip with a splendid view of Apalachicola Bay.

Grayton Beach

Criolla's
170 E. Scenic Hwy 30-A
Tel: 850-267-1267
www.criollas.com
$$$–$$$$
Criolla's features an Australian chef who specializes in dishing up plates of Down Under fare, from lemon myrtle-infused sorbet to kangaroo served mid-rare. Plank grilling is a house specialty that produces a smoke-enhanced flavor.

Panacea

Angelo & Son's Seafood Restaurant
US 98
Tel: 850-984-5168
www.panaceaseafood.com
$$–$$$
Commonly called Angelo's, this popular family-owned restaurant was all but destroyed during Hurricane Dennis in 2005 but has since been rebuilt high up on stilts. Angelo's – which benefits from having its own fishing fleet – features house specialties such as bull-dozer lobster, grouper, and escargot. There are always creative, daily chalkboard specials.

Panama City Beach

Another Broken Egg
11535 Hutchison Blvd,

Suite 100
Tel: 850-249-2007
www.anotherbrokenegg.com
$–$$
Another Broken Egg is a great place to take the family. It has something for everyone, all in a cozy French country atmosphere. Tasty omelets, crisp salads, and delicious sandwiches. The perfect spot for a nice Sunday brunch or a quick bite before hitting the beach.

Montego Bay Seafood House
473 Richard Jackson Blvd
Tel: 850-233-6033
$$–$$$
Craving raw oysters or a great seafood platter? Head over to this beach-side seafood house and raw bar. There's something on the extensive menu for all taste buds, including award-winning seafood gumbo, appetizers, large salads, juicy ribs and burgers, perfectly seasoned chicken, and fresh fried seafood.

Pensacola

Dharma Blue
300 S. Alcaniz St
Tel: 850-433-1275
www.dharamblue.com
$$–$$$
Set in a "vibrant coastal atmosphere," Dharma Blue offers the finest sushi bar in Florida, a cocktail bar, indoor and outdoor seating, and savory lunch favorites such as fried grouper sandwiches, seared crab cake sandwiches, and fried green tomato clubs.

Jackson's Restaurant
400 S. Palafox St
Tel: 850-469-9898

www.jacksons.goodgrits. com $$$–$$$$
Jackson's is an award-winning, upscale treat. It's housed in a 19th-century building, with a sophisticated but not stuffy atmosphere and an efficient wait staff. The kitchen is often best when it does the least, allowing the natural flavors of fresh seafood to play the dominant role. Elsewhere on the menu, Southern standards are given gourmet treatment. Be sure to leave room for the sumptuous desserts.

McGuire's Irish Pub
600 E. Gregory St
Tel: 850-433-6789
www.mcguiresirishpub.com
$$–$$$
Located in Pensacola's 1927 Old Firehouse, McGuire's is famous for its fine corned beef and cabbage, shepherd's pie, rosemary-scented Irish lamb stew, and mushroom pie, along with great local seafood and steaks.

The Melting Pot of Pensacola
418 E. Gregory St #500
Tel: 850-438-4030
www.meltingpot.com
$$$–$$$$
For a change of pace from the coastal surf 'n' turf eateries, try the Melting Pot, a fondue restaurant that won the Wine Spectator Award of Excellence for four years in a row.

Seville Quarter
130 E. Government St
Tel: 850-434-6211
www.sevillequarter.com
$–$$
Pensacola's premier dining and entertainment complex started in 1967 as the dream of Bob Snow, a multitalented

entrepreneur who fell in love with Pensacola while in the Navy. Today there are four themed restaurants gathered here in historical surroundings: Rosie O'Grady's, Apple Annie's, Lili Marlene's World War I Aviator's Pub, and the Palace Oyster Bar.

St George Island

Blue Parrot Oceanfront Café
68 W. Gorrie Dr
Tel: 850-927-2987
www.blueparrotcafe.net
$$–$$$
Situated right on the beach, the Blue Parrot features generous indoor and outdoor seating – and for those chilly evenings, the patio even has heaters. There's a well-rounded, surf 'n' turf menu that includes items such as conch fritters, seafood gumbo, burgers, salads, and Apalachicola Bay oysters raw, baked, or Rockefeller style.

Tallahassee

Andrew's Capital Grill and Bar
228 S. Adams St
Tel: 850-222-3444
www.andrewsdowntown. com $$
Andrew's is a local landmark, located downtown near the seat of Florida's political power. Andrew's was noted as "Best Outdoor Dining" by Tallahassee magazine and offers burgers, sandwiches, salads, and more ambitious entrées.

Café Huston Oven & Grille
3197 Merchants Row Blvd #110
Tel: 850-877-7833 $$
This is a quick-serve restaurant with an

upscale atmosphere, and a great place to socialize and catch a game on TV. American cuisine is made from scratch, including home-made pizza, gourmet salads, and char-grilled burgers, chicken, and grouper.

Harry's Seafood Bar & Grille
301 S. Bronough St
Tel: 850-222-3976
www.hookedonharrys.com
$$–$$$
Harry's will remind diners of the Big Easy. It serves a wide variety of New Orleans-style cuisine including fresh seafood, salads, sandwiches, desserts, and more.

La Lanterna
2766 Capital Circle NE
Tel: 850-878-9738
$$–$$$
This is an authentic Italian restaurant and a family-owned market and deli, featuring a wide array of Italian grocery items, meats, and cheeses. The food is freshly prepared for

takeout, including bread, pasta, lasagna, cannoli, gelato, sandwiches, and salads.

Mellow Mushroom
1641 Pensacola St
Tel: 850-575-0050
www.mellowmushroom. com/tallahassee
$–$$
This Italian-American restaurant features a variety of specialty pizzas, like the mega-veggie, the mighty meat, and the Hawaiian. Hoagies, calzones, salads, garlic and stone-baked pretzels, cookies, hummus, and seasonal soups round out the tasty menu.

Morelia Mexican Dining
1400-35 Village Square Blvd
Tel: 850-907-9173
$$
This casual and award-winning Mexican-style restaurant serves up classic dishes from south of the border such as tacos, tostadas, fajitas, burritos, and enchiladas, perfect for a tasty meal.

LEFT: the ambience at Dharma Blue is casual and arty.
RIGHT: Boss Oyster specializes in a local delicacy.

INSIGHT GUIDE — TRAVEL TIPS
FLORIDA

T RANSPORTATION

GETTING THERE
AND GETTING AROUND

By Air

Most major US and international carriers serve Florida. Shop around before buying a ticket; it's usually cheaper to travel midweek, and a variety of discount fares and "package deals," which can significantly cut round-trip rates to and from Florida, are also available. Special Internet-only deals can be found easily online.

Florida has 14 international airports, but the state's major hubs are Miami, Orlando, Fort Lauderdale, and Tampa. Miami International Airport is the state's largest. It is also a major jumping-off point for flights into the Caribbean and Latin America. In addition, there are connections to regional airports, such as Daytona Beach, Fort Myers, Jacksonville, Key West, Marathon, Melbourne, Naples, Palm Beach, Panama City, Pensacola, St Petersburg-Clearwater, Sarasota-Bradenton, and Tallahassee.

Scheduled services are supplemented by charter flights. Many of these land at Orlando-Sanford Airport, 30 miles (48km) north of Orlando. In summer, this small airport is jammed with tourists, and lines at immigration can be long. Furthermore, the extra distance can be costly, especially if you plan to use public transportation to reach Orlando. A rental car is essential if you arrive at a distant airport.

Special Note: Expect delays departing US airports due to Homeland Security anti-terrorism rules. These are apt to change, so check before flying. Pack items in both carry-on and checked luggage

in clear bags, leave gifts unwrapped, and take laptops out of bags for inspection. Consider wearing slip-on shoes as all footwear must be removed and scanned by x-ray machines. Travelers are allowed *one* carry-on resealable 1-quart (1-liter) clear plastic bag, which can contain liquids, gels, and aerosols in containers of 3 ounces (85 ml) or less. The contents in the plastic bag must be sealed and may be subjected to x-ray inspection.

The telephone numbers of the main airports are:
Miami International Airport (MIA), tel: 305-876-7000
Fort Lauderdale/Hollywood International Airport (FLL), tel: 954-359-1200
Orlando International Airport (MCO), tel: 407-825-2001
Orlando-Sanford Airport, tel: 407-322-7771
Tampa International Airport (TPA), tel: 813-870-8700

International and Domestic Airlines

Airlines serving Florida include:
America West: tel: 800-235-9292; www.americawest.com
American: tel: 800-433-7300; www.aa.com
British Airways: tel: 800-47-9297; www.british-airways.com
Continental: tel: 800-525-0280; www.continental.com
Delta: tel: 800-221-1212; www.delta.com
Frontier: tel: 800-432-1359; www.fly frontier.com
JetBlue: tel: 800-538-2583; www.jet blue.com
Northwest-KLM: tel: 800-225-2525; www.nwa.com
Southwest: tel: 800-435-9792; www.southwest.com

Spirit: tel: 800-772-7117; www.spirit.com
TED: tel: 800-225-5833; www.flyted.com
United Airlines: tel: 800-864-8331; www.ual.com
US Air: tel: 800-428-4322; www.us airways.com
Virgin Atlantic: tel: 800-862-8621; www.virginatlantic.com

By Boat

Surrounded by water, Florida is easy to travel to or from by sea, and cruises into the Atlantic, Gulf of Mexico, and Caribbean depart year-round. Packages vary, with cruises lasting from a few hours or a day to over two weeks. Three-day jaunts to the Bahamas are popular. So, too, are the one-day or one-night coast-hugging trips, which, for some people, are just an opportunity to gamble. Casinos are illegal in Florida, except on the Seminole reservation, but the law does not apply in international waters.

For a complete overview, ask a travel agent, check the travel ads in any Sunday newspaper, or check online at sites like www.cruise.com.

By Rail

Amtrak (tel: 800-872-7245; www. amtrak.com) offers leisurely service from the Midwest, Northeast, and South – and connecting service from points west – to 13 Florida cities. The Silver Service routes between New York City and Florida have major stops in Jacksonville, Orlando, Tampa, and Miami. For those who want to take their car, the Auto Train from Lorton, Virginia, near Washington DC, to Sanford, north of Orlando, is an option.

By Bus

Greyhound (tel: 800-231-2222; www.greyhound.com) provides bus services all over the state. Intercity service includes many out-of-the-way stops en route and can be slow; try to use "Express" buses, which stop in fewer places. Bus terminals are often in run-down areas of town, so take care when traveling to or from stations.

GETTING AROUND

Public Transportation

Cities with walkable historic downtowns, such as Tampa, Key West, St Augustine, and St Petersburg, encourage visitors and residents to use inexpensive trams and light rail to get around. Florida's abandoned railway beds have found new life as trails linking historic communities under the Rails-to-Trails program. For a list of public transportation in Florida, log onto www.apta.com/links/state_local/fl.cfm.

By Bus

Greyhound bus service links cities throughout Florida. Once there, city bus lines can be an excellent and inexpensive way of getting around.

By Rail

Amtrak serves 13 cities in Florida. The commuter **Tri-Rail** service (tel: 800-874-7245; www.tri-rail.com) links Miami and West Palm Beach and can be useful for reaching places like Fort Lauderdale and Boca Raton. Trains run hourly, with reduced weekend service. Several cities, including Tampa, have light rail service throughout the downtown and adjoining tourist areas.

By Taxi

Taxis are available in all the main tourist centers. They tend to be expensive, and you usually have to telephone for pick-up. Your hotel can call for you, otherwise numbers are listed in the Yellow Pages. Don't stand by the side of the road, even in Miami, and expect to hail a passing cab. Water taxis – a fun way to sightsee – are available on the Intracoastal Waterway in Fort Lauderdale.

Private Transportation

Boat Rental

Floridians have an intimate relationship with water and many can park a boat right next to their house;
in some places such as the Keys, a boat is almost a necessity, Guided sightseeing, fishing, and diving cruises are available in many areas, along with boat rentals. Don't leave Florida without getting out on its sparkling waters at least once.

Car Rental

Most rental agencies require you to be at least 21 years old and have a valid driver's license and a major credit card. Many take debit cards, too, and some will take cash in lieu of a credit card, but this might be as high as $500. Foreign travelers will need to produce a driver's license from their own country.

You will find rental car companies in most cities and airports; vehicles range from modest economy cars to luxury convertibles, vans, and 4WD vehicles. Rates are cheap both by US and international standards, but you should still shop around, preferably online, for the best rates and features. Smaller local rental firms outside the airports are often less expensive than the large national companies because they don't charge high airport fees. When choosing a vehicle, take into account gas prices, which, although cheap by European standards, add up on long-distance drives.

It's cheaper to arrange car rental in advance. Check with your airline, bus, or rental agent, travel agent, or the Internet for special package deals that include a car: rental rates can be reduced by up to 50 percent if you buy a so-called "fly-drive" deal. Be wary of offers of "free" car rental: such cars do not include extras like tax and insurance.

Go over the insurance coverage provisions carefully with the agent before signing the rental agreement. Loss Damage Waiver (LDW), or Collision Damage Waiver (CDW), is essential. Without it, you'll be liable for any damage done to your vehicle in the event of an accident, regardless of whether or not you are to blame. You are advised to pay for supplementary liability insurance on top of standard third-party insurance. Insurance and tax charges can add a lot to an otherwise inexpensive rental, so take it into account in your budgeting. Also, be sure to check your rental car carefully for existing damage, and make a careful note of any dents or dings before leaving the lot.

Driving

More than 20 million visitors enter the Sunshine State by car every year – about twice as many as those entering

Safety Tips for Motorists

Get advice from the car rental agent about the best route from the airport to your hotel. Better still, arrange to pick up your rental car from an agency near your hotel on the morning after you arrive, rather than tackle unfamiliar routes when very tired. Many car rental agencies will deliver your car to your hotel at no (or only a small) extra charge.

Use a map to plot your route before you begin any journey.

Ignore pedestrians or motorists who try to stop you. If you develop engine trouble, call the local police or state polic for assistance.

Always keep your car doors locked, windows closed, and valuables out of sight.

Avoid taking short cuts in urban areas. If you get lost, drive to a well-lit and preferably busy area before stopping to look at your map.

by plane. Bus, train, and taxi services within Florida are irregular, unreliable, and slow to cover the state's vast distances. A car is the most convenient way to travel around Florida.

Traffic has grown exceptionally dense on Florida's highways, reflecting the large numbers of new residents and growing tourism. Speed limits are strictly enforced. Drive with care and allow plenty of time to get to your destination. Avoid rush hour while traveling in metro areas. It's quickest to drive on interstates, the largest and fastest of the highways.

I-75 connects northern Florida with Gulf of Mexico cities and Miami; I-95 is the main east-coast route. I-10 is an east-west route across the Panhandle, and I-4 links Tampa to Daytona Beach. Toll roads include the Florida Turnpike across central Florida between the I-75 near Wildwood and Florida City, and the Bee Line Expressway between Orlando and the Space Coast. Carry plenty of quarters and dollar bills; some highways do not have manned toll booths to give change.

US highways are not fast through-routes; they are heavily trafficked and often lined with stores and interrupted by traffic lights. State routes are usually the same size as US highways. County roads are secondary roads that are better for enjoying the scenery.

Blue signs on the side of the road say "in case of emergency dial FHP" on your cell phone. It is just another way to call 911, Florida's Highway Patrol or Emergency Services.

TRANSPORTATION

ACCOMMODATIONS

ACTIVITIES

A – Z

ACCOMMODATIONS

HOTELS, YOUTH HOSTELS, BED & BREAKFAST

Choosing Lodgings

Accommodations in Florida range from luxury resorts, which cater to your every last need, to modest mom-and-pop motels; cozy, antiques-filled bed-and-breakfasts and small historic inns; and budget lodgings in youth hostels and campgrounds beside the ocean or in the forest.

Although rather anonymous, chain motels and hotels are usually reliable and in some places, such as Gainesville, are your main option if you don't want to go the bed-and-breakfast route. Family-owned motels, many built close to popular roadside attractions of the 1940s and 1950s, are usually acceptable if you're on a budget; a quick check online for photos and reader reviews can sometimes head off problems. In major tourist areas like Orlando, Kissimmee, and Miami Beach, the quality and variety of tourist accommodations is particularly good. Bedrooms are often large and normally come with two double or queen-sized beds.

Florida's beach communities and theme-park destinations like Orlando and Kissimmee also have a huge selection of self-catering vacation rentals, an often overlooked option. Most are either in modern housing estates called "subdivisions," or in self-catering complexes, consisting of privately owned individual properties, or condominiums. The former, though usually in residential areas, are generally the best choice: homes are often large and have a pool and excellent facilities. Major tour operators offer self-catering accommodations. If you don't want to go completely self-catering, consider staying in one of the

excellent new all-suites hotel chains or in a motel room with a kitchenette, known as an efficiency.

Beachfront vacation rentals offer the best of both worlds. Many are right on the beach within small resort complexes that have swimming pools, laundry, barbecue grills, and gear for beach activities. In remote undeveloped areas along the Gulf, vacation rentals predominate.

Reservations and Prices

Reservations are generally required in advance. If you are traveling in the high season, book several months in advance if you have your heart set on a particular hotel – or if you want to stay inside Walt Disney World. Room rates vary enormously between the high tourist season in the winter months and the off-season months of January through mid-February and September through December (except Christmas week); the cost can rise by 30 percent or more during peak tourist months. Ask for a discount if you are staying for a week or more, or if you are visiting during the off season, which for many hotel proprietors is an extremely lean time. Florida imposes a resort tax in addition to the usual sales tax, which is added to the price of the rooms. It varies from county to county and ranges from 2 to 5 percent.

Chain Hotels and Motels

These are ubiquitous throughout the United States. Some people dislike chains because they offer no variety, lack a personal touch, and are often located in the most commercial, nondescript areas of town next to

busy highways. The advantage is that once you've been to a hotel run by a particular chain, even though these are usually a franchise, you can bank on certain facilities and a standard of service wherever you are in the US. For travelers wanting to focus on their vacation, this can be a boon.

Bed and Breakfasts

Bed-and-breakfasts vary greatly in terms of price and quality, but the one thing they have in common is that they are almost invariably in a private and/or historic home. Old towns such as Key West, St Augustine, and Gainesville are known for their historic bed-and-breakfast accommodations; in outlying rural areas, bed-and-breakfast might be offered in a modern private home on several acres. Few have restaurants, and facilities will not be as extensive as in a regular hotel. Privacy can be an issue in older inns, but some have separate cottages with self-catering facilities, allowing you to come and go as you please. Hosts are usually a mine of information about local sights, and this can be a great way to make lifelong friends. For those travelers who enjoy the personal ambience – not to mention the afternoon teas, wine and cheese happy hours, and wonderful home-cooked breakfasts found in such places – bed-and-breakfasts are a great choice.

Camping

Over 100,000 campsites at some 700 campgrounds all over Florida offer ample choice of outdoors accommodations – from simple areas for tents and sleeping bags to elaborate villages with utility hook-ups for recreational vehicles (RVs), restaurants, pools, mini-golf courses, and planned activities.

Private Campgrounds

These have blossomed around popular tourist attractions, with the majority in Central Florida to accommodate the droves of Disney tourists. Walt Disney World is southwest of Orlando, in Kissimmee, an area that is surprisingly rural and densely forested. If you avoid the main commercial strip, which is noisy and heavily trafficked, camping can be a good option.

A nationwide network of private campgrounds, called Kampgrounds of America (KOA), has around 30 members in Florida. They offer good-quality facilities, including swimming pool, restaurant, laundry, etc. Most accept reservations. Contact KOA at PO Box 30558, Billings, MT 59114-0558; tel: 888-562-0000; www.koa.com.

To obtain information about private campgrounds in Florida, contact Florida Association of RV Parks and Campgrounds, 1340 Vickers Drive, Tallahassee, FL 32303; tel: 850-562-7151; www.floridacamping.com. The association will send you the Florida

Camping Directory, which lists hundreds of campgrounds representing nearly 50,000 campsites in Florida divided by region and with details of amenities. You can make reservations using toll-free numbers listed in the brochure.

Camping in State Parks

Florida's state parks are blessed with incredibly scenic settings such as barrier-island beaches, natural springs, and inland forests. Many have campgrounds where campsites can be rented for up to 14 days and excellent, clean facilities, including showers, laundry, etc. They are hugely popular, especially among Florida residents, so book well in advance to avoid disappointment. Reservations are accepted up to 60 days in advance of check-in: call the park where you plan to camp. In addition, parks normally hold back some spaces for people who arrive on the day.

Arrive early morning in the most popular areas to get a site. The base fee, usually $16–25, depending on location, covers up to four people; up to eight people may stay at any site. At least one person, 18 years or older, must be in each group. There is a small charge for extra cars and

electricity. Only pets on handheld leashes are allowed in state park picnic areas; no pets are allowed in the campgrounds or on public beaches. Fees tend to be higher in the Florida Keys, and only Florida residents may obtain an annual camping permit. Most state park campsites are booked solid in the busy late winter and early spring seasons.

For more information, contact Florida Department of Natural Resources, 3900 Commonwealth Boulevard, Tallahassee, FL 32399-3000; tel: 850-245-2157; www.floridastateparks.org.

Camping with Mickey

Walt Disney World's Fort Wilderness Resort, located amid 650 acres (263 hectares) of woods and streams on Bay Lake, east of the Magic Kingdom, has more than 800 campsites. You can also rent trailers, which have air conditioning, color TV, radio, cookware, and linens, and sleep up to six people.

For information and reservations, contact Walt Disney World Central Reservations, PO Box 10,000, Lake Buena Vista, FL 32830; tel: 407-934-7639; http://bookwdw.reservations.disney.go.com.

SOUTH FLORIDA

Miami

Biltmore Hotel
1200 Anastasia Avenue
Tel: 800-727-1926
www.biltmorehotel.com $$$$
This 1926 *grande dame* flaunts her Mediterranean style with the largest pool in the US and 150 acres (60 hectares) of tropical landscaping. The 276 rooms and suites have stone floors, European bedding, and lovely views. There are nine restaurants, a golf course, and tennis courts, too.

Hotel Inter-Continental
100 Chopin Plaza
Tel: 800-327-3005
www.interconti.com $$$
A soaring, high-rise hotel with 639 rooms, several gourmet restaurants, a pool, skyline views, a fitness center, and a jogging track in the center of downtown Miami.

Hotel Place St Michel
162 Alcazar Avenue
Tel: 800-848-HOTEL
www.hotelstmichel.com $$$
This historic hotel in downtown Coral Gables has 27 rooms with antiques galore and an elegant French restaurant.

Miami River Inn
118 SW South River Drive
Tel: 800-HOTEL-89 $$
www.miamiriverinn.com
The Miami River Inn is a beautifully restored 40-room inn by the Miami River in Little Havana with pool and whirlpool tubs.

Omni Colonnade Hotel
180 Aragon Avenue, Coral Gables
Tel: 800-533-1337
www.omnihotels.com $$$
A prestigious hotel in downtown Coral Gables with 157 rooms, pool, shopping complex, Jacuzzi, lounge, and small gym.

Miami Beach

Cardozo on the Beach
1300 Ocean Drive
Tel: 800-782-6500
www.cardozohotel.com $$–$$$
An oceanfront Art Deco hotel in the heart of the historic district of South Beach, with 44 beautifully decorated rooms.

Clay Hotel and Miami Beach International Hostel
1438 Washington Avenue
Tel: 800-379-CLAY $
www.clayhotel.com
A very popular, 200-bed youth hostel with dormitory rooms and kitchen facilities in the Art Deco district of South Beach.

Fontainebleau Hilton Resort and Towers
4441 Collins Avenue
Tel: 800-548-8886
www.fontainebleau.com $$$

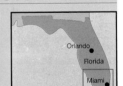

This is an opulent and extensively renovated 1,206-room hotel built in the 1950s. Facilities include a pool with waterfalls, tennis courts, a health club, restaurants, nightclubs (with famous Latin floorshow), shopping,

PRICE CATEGORIES

Price categories are for a double room for one night in high season (Jan–Apr):
$ = less than $75
$$ = $75–150
$$$ = $150–200
$$$$ = more than $200

ABOVE: the Hotel St Augustine.

and activities for children of all ages.

Hotel Chelsea
944 Washington Avenue
Tel: 305-534-4069
www.thehotelchelsea.com
$$–$$$
A hip hotel for the budget challenged, rooms here have stripped-down elegance, with futon-style beds. A DJ plays in the lobby on weekends; the front patio overlooks the avenue. A nightly cocktail is free.

Hotel St Augustine
347 Washington Avenue
Tel: 800-310-7717
www.hotelstaugustine.com **$$$$**
European chic pervades this new hotel in an Art Deco building in SoFi (South of Fifth). Spare rooms are cozied up with quilts on the beds, which is a nice detail.

National Hotel
www.nationalhotel.com
1677 Collins Avenue
Tel: 800-327-8370
$$–$$$
The National Hotel is an elegant, landmark, Art Deco masterpiece with all the amenities. It's beautifully renovated, and on the ocean. The long, narrow pool is unique.

Bay Harbor

Daddy O Hotel
9660 E. Bay Harbor Drive
Tel: 305-868-4141
www.daddyohotel.com **$$$**
Formerly the Bay Harbor Inn, this chic waterfront boutique hotel offers in-room iPod docks and flat-screen TVs, as well as designer furniture.

The Everglades

Note: Due to hurricane damage, Flamingo Lodge, the only overnight lodging in Everglades National Park, is closed. The closest accommodations are in Florida City and Everglades.

Best Western Florida City/ Homestead Gateway to the Keys
411 S. Krome Avenue, Florida City
Tel: 800-937-8376
www.bestwestern.com **$$**
This national chain motel has a pool, and some of the 114 rooms have microwaves and fridges.

Everglades International Hostel
20 SW 2nd Avenue, Florida City
Tel: 800-372-3874
www.evergladeshostel.com **$**
A friendly hostel located in a 1930s boarding house with

six-bed dorms and private double rooms with baths. The hostel has a kitchen and laundry room.

Everglades Spa & Lodge
201 W. Broadway, Everglades City
Tel: 239-695-3151 **$$–$$$$**
This unusual inn occupies the 1923 building of the former Bank of the Everglades. Some of the six one-bed rooms, suites, and efficiencies have kitchens. Amenities include Wi-fi, spa services, and daily continental breakfast.

Glades Haven Cozy Cabins
801 S. Copeland Avenue, Everglades City
Tel: 888-956-6251
www.gladeshaven.com **$$$**
A resort with 24 rustic but comfy cabins that will appeal to outdoor-lovers. Duplex cabins (some with screened porches) sleep four; full-size cabins have kitchens. All have a/c, heat, and TVs. Amenities include a lounge, pool, boat ramp, marina, and gear rentals.

Ivey House Bed and Breakfast
107 Camellia Street, Everglades City
Tel: 877-567-0679
www.iveyhouse.com **$–$$$$**
This historic landmark inn was built in 1928 to accommodate workers constructing the Tamiami Trail. It offers bed-and-breakfast accommodations in 18 luxurious poolside rooms in the inn; 11 rustic but air-conditioned rooms with shared baths in the original lodge; and two bedrooms in a cute cottage. Buffet breakfast is served daily. The inn is well known for its excellent naturalist-guided kayak tours into the Ten Thousand Islands.

Ramada Inn Florida City Hotel
124 E. Palm Drive, Florida City
Tel: 305-247-8833 **$$–$$$**
This chain lodging is superior to any other in Florida City. It is super-clean, has crisp white duvets on king-size beds, and some of its 123 rooms have fridges and sleeper sofas. The hot breakfast and pool are popular amenities.

River Wilderness Waterfront Villas
210 Collier Boulevard, Everglades City
Tel: 239-695-4499
www.river-wilderness.com **$–$$$**
Built on stilts, the 14 one- and two-bed villas and apartments at this resort on the river in Everglades City are perfect for independent travelers. All have kitchens, microwaves, fridges, and screened porches. On-site amenities include a pool, barbecue grill, dock, canoes, and continental breakfast.

Rod & Gun Lodge
Highway 29, Everglades City
Tel: 239-695-2101
www.evergladesrodandgun.com **$$**
Founded with Everglades City on the Barron River in 1864, the historic Rod & Gun Lodge has hosted presidents, famous musicians, and film stars. It has its own marina, and there are 17 cottages as well as a cocktail lounge, restaurant, and covered patio.

Florida Keys

Cheeca Lodge
8101 Overseas Highway (MM 82), Islamorada
Tel: 800-327-2888
www.cheeca.com **$$$**
Cheeca Lodge is one of the most popular resorts in the Keys, with 203 rooms, tennis, golf, pools, fishing pier, private beach, diving, and snorkeling.

Curry Mansion Inn
511 Caroline Street, Key West
Tel: 800-253-3466
www.currymansion.com **$$$**
A grand Victorian-style mansion turned into a charming 28-room inn with pool and lush gardens.

Cypress House
601 Caroline Street, Key West
Tel: 800-525-2488
www.cypresshousekw.com
$$$–$$$$
This elegant but unpretentious 1895 B&B is a fine example of Bahamian architecture. Rooms in the inn and two nearby historic buildings are well appointed, with TVs and a/c; two on the

first floor share a bath. There is an expanded continental breakfast buffet and afternoon cocktails are served by the secluded pool.

Dove Creek Lodge
147 Seaside Avenue (MM 94.5), Key Largo
Tel: 305-852-6200
www.dovecreeklodge.com **$$$$**
The emphasis at this refined waterfront lodge is on service. Rooms are large, with balconies, DVD players, large-screen TVs, and Internet. Staff can arrange a variety of activities, including deep-sea fishing.

Hawk's Cay Resort
61 Hawks Cay Boulevard, Duck Key
Tel: 800-395-5539
www.hawkscay.com **$$$**
A rambling, Caribbean-style resort that pampers guests, with 176 rooms, swimming pool, tennis courts, restaurants, bars, boat rental, and scuba lessons; a marina offers opportunities to get out on the water.

Holiday Inn Sunspree Key Largo Resort
Overseas Highway (MM 100), Key Largo
Tel: 305-451-2121
www.holidayinnkeylargo.com **$$$**
The Holiday Inn Sunspree is a modern, tropical resort with 132 rooms and a swimming pool; there is a marina, several bars, and spectacular ocean views.

Holiday Isle Resort
84001 Overseas Highway (MM 84), Islamorada
Tel: 800-327-7070
www.holidayisle.com **$$-$$$**
A holiday hotel resort with a choice of four hotels and five restaurants, pools, beach, and water sports. The hotel is pet-friendly.

Island City House Hotel
411 William Street, Key West
Tel: 800-634-8230
www.islandcityhouse.com **$$$**
Off the main strip, the Island City House Hotel has a tropical garden with 24 suites, most have kitchens and whirlpool tubs. There is a swimming pool, as well.

Jules Undersea Lodge
51 Shoreland Drive (MM 103.2), Key Largo
Tel: 305-451-2353
www.jul.com **$$$**
Experience underwater living in this extraordinary subaquatic hotel.

Pier House Resort & Caribbean Spa
1 Duval Street, Key West
Tel: 800-723-2791
www.pierhouse.com **$$$**

A luxury 142 room resort that feels like it's on its own island, with pools, private beach, bars, and cabanas.

Pines and Palms Resort
80401 Old Highway, Islamorada
Tel: 800-624-0964
www.pinesandpalms.com **$$-$$$$**
This is classic, family-friendly, Keys lodgings. Oceanfront and oceanview cottages and suites have one, two, or three bedrooms, full kitchens, living areas, and patios or balconies. The resort is fully air-conditioned.

Southernmost Motel
1319 Duval Street, Key West
Tel: 888-449-0633
www.southernmostresorts.com **$$-$$$**
A comfortable motel with 127 rooms, pool, and full-service concierge.

ATLANTIC COAST

Boca Raton

Boca Raton Resort and Club
501 E. Camino Real
Tel: 800-543-1277
www.bocaresort.com **$$$**
A plush and historic hotel with golf course, pools, tennis courts, and health spa, among other amenities.

Boynton Beach

Golden Sands Inn
520 SE 21st Avenue
Tel: 561-732-6075 **$**
The Golden Sands has 24 rooms in the downtown area and is not far from the beach. The restaurant has takeout service only.

Cocoa Beach

Comfort Inn and Suite Resort
3901 N. Atlantic Avenue,
Tel: 800-247-2221 **$-$$**
The Comfort Inn has 94 rooms on the beach with restaurant, lounge, pool.

La Quinta Cocoa Beach
1 Hendry Avenue
Tel: 800-874-7958
www.laquintacocoabeach.com

$$-$$$
Formerly the popular Oceanside Inn, this hotel has 40 rooms on the beach, with fishing, a pool, and restaurant.

Ron Jon Resort
1000 Shorewood Drive, Cape Canaveral
Tel: 888-933-3030
www.ronjonresort.com **$$**
Ron Jon is the closest oceanfront resort to Orlando and is the nearest place outside the Kennedy Space Center to watch a launch. Kids love the pools, lazy river, and water slide. The suites aren't big, but are comfortable enough for a night or two.

Daytona Beach

Hilton Daytona Beach
100 N. Atlantic Avenue
Tel: 800-444-2326 **$$-$$$**
Formerly the Adam's Mark, this hotel's distinctive architecture and oceanfront site make it perennially popular. There are multiple restaurants and lounges, as well as a health club, spa, and 437 rooms.

Beach Quarters Resort
3711 S. Atlantic Avenue

Tel: 386-767-3119
www.daytonabeachquarters.com **$$**
A mid-rise hotel with antique furniture in 26 suites, plus kitchens, a pool, and a cozy restaurant.

The Shores Resort and Spa
2637 S. Atlantic Avenue
Tel: 386-767-7350
www.shoresresort.com **$$-$$$**
A towering hotel with 214 rooms overlooking the beach, plus swimming pool, Jacuzzi, sauna, fitness center, and kids' playground.

Plaza Resort and Spa
600 N. Atlantic Avenue
Tel: 386-255-4471
www.plazaresortandspa.com **$$**
This oceanfront property offers family-oriented amenities, including in-room fridges.

Deerfield Beach

Carriage House Resort Motel
250 S. Ocean Drive
Tel: 800-303-6009
www.carriagehouseresort.com **$$**
The Carriage House is a tidy and friendly beach motel with 30 rooms, a pool, and shuffleboard court.

Fort Lauderdale

Howard Johnson Oceans Edge Resort
700 N. Atlantic
Tel: 800-663-2561 **$$$**
This chain hotel has more than 100 beachfront rooms with pool, lounge, 24-hour food, and shuttle service.

Marriott's Harbor Beach Resort
3030 Holiday Drive
Tel: 800-222-6543 **$$$**
www.marriottharborbeach.com
A high-rise, seafront resort with 624 comfortable rooms, pool, cabanas,

PRICE CATEGORIES

Price categories are for a double room for one night in high season (Jan–Apr):
$ = less than $75
$$ = $75–150
$$$ = $150–200
$$$$ = more than $200

Above: the gracious lobby of The Breakers.

tennis courts, and a health club.

Jacksonville

Riverside Hotel
620 E. Las Olas Boulevard
Tel: 800-325-3280
www.riversidehotel.com **$$$**
Located in the downtown shopping district, The Riverside Hotel is a historic place with 117 antique-furnished rooms, a swimming pool, restaurants, and lounge.

Tropic Seas Resort
4616 El Mar Drive
Tel: 800-952-9581
www.tropicseasresort.com **$$**
A 1950s motel on the beach just north of Fort Lauderdale with 16 rooms, swimming pool, shuffleboard court, and barbecue.

Comfort Suites Baymeadows
8277 Western Way Circle
Tel: 904-737-4477
www.comfortsuites.com **$–$$**
In the heart of the shopping and restaurant district, the 112 room Comfort Suites has free Wi-fi, a pool, and exercise room.

House on Cherry Street
1844 Cherry Street
Tel: 904 384-1999
www.geocities.com/houseoncherryst **$**
The House on Cherry Street is an antiques-filled riverside inn with four cozy rooms and hearty, homemade breakfasts. Most rooms overlook the river.

New Smyrna Beach

Ocean Air Motel
1161 N. Dixie Freeway
Tel: 386-428-5748
www.ocean-airmotel.com **$**
The Ocean Air Motel is a modest but pleasant, pet-friendly motel located five minutes from the beach with 14 rooms, a pool, and convenient picnic tables.

Riverview Hotel
103 Flagler Avenue
Tel: 800-945-7416
www.riverviewhotel.com **$$**
A landmark hotel overlooking the Intracoastal Waterway with 18 beautifully furnished rooms, pool, and restaurant.

Palm Beach

Brazilian Court
301 Australian Avenue
Tel: 800-552-0335
www.thebraziliancourt.com **$$$**
The Brazilian Court is an old tropical hotel with 103 rooms and suites, lush gardens, pool, restaurant, bar, and afternoon tea, if you're feeling a bit run down from the day's activities.

The Breakers
1 S. Country Road
Tel: 888-BREAKERS
www.thebreakers.com **$$$**
One of the grand old hotels of the 1920s, The Breakers is an oceanfront landmark with 572 luxurious rooms, pools, beach, croquet, tennis courts, golf course, health club, and restaurants.

St Augustine

Casa Monica
95 Cordova Street
Tel: 800-213-8903
www.casamonica.com
$$$–$$$$
This historic landmark was built in 1888 and beautifully restored in 1999. The property has a huge lobby, pool, fountains, art galleries, high-end shops, four-star restaurants, and luxurious rooms with fine linens and amenities.

La Fiesta Oceanside Inn
810 Beach Boulevard (Hwy A1A)
Tel: 800-370-6036
www.lafiestainn.com **$$–$$$$**
This beachfront inn sits on a private boardwalk and has a variety of rooms and suites, with fridges, microwaves, as well as balconies and/or patios.

Pirate Haus
32 Treasury Street
Tel: 904-808-1999
www.piratehaus.com **$**
Known for its "pirate pancake breakfast," this European-style budget hostel in downtown boasts clean rooms, a large kitchen, rooftop barbecue, laundry, bike rentals, and Internet access.

St Francis Inn
279 St George Street
Tel: 800-824-6062
www.stfrancisinn.com **$$**
This is an 18th-century historic home has been reborn as a B&B. There are 11 rooms and suites with old-fashioned decorative fans, plus a pool.

CENTRAL FLORIDA

Lake Wales

Chalet Suzanne Country Inn
3800 Chalet Suzanne Drive
Tel: 800-433-6011
www.chaletsuzanne.com **$$$$**
Chalet Suzanne has been owned by the Hinshaw family since 1931. Thirty classic guest rooms surround the chateau-style inn, decorated in sunny

yellows and creams and furnished with antiques, lace, quilts, and rockers. The inn overlooks tiny Lake Suzanne, and has a renowned restaurant serving rich continental cuisine, a private airstrip, pool, and gift shop selling Chalet Suzanne's famous cream soups.

The Green Gables Inn
21380 Highway 27

Tel: 877-747-8713
www.greengablesfl.com **$–$$**
This inn is located just minutes from Disney World and Kissimmee State Park and offers a free continental breakfast and Wi-fi.

Maitland

Thurston House Bed and Breakfast
851 Lake Avenue

Tel: 800-843-2721
www.thurstonhouse.com **$$$**
Set on the shores of Lake Eucalia, this Victorian

farmhouse is a reminder of days long gone in central Florida. You can still sit in a rocking chair on the veranda and watch the osprey dive for fish in the lake. The rooms have all the modern amenities you'd expect in a small hotel and some special touches you wouldn't, such as original fireplaces filled with candles.

Lake of the Woods Resort
8875 South Highway 17-92
Tel: 407-834-7637
www.lakeofthewoodsresort.net **$–$$**
This resort, close to Orlando, offers large, affordable lakefront rooms that feature refrigerators and microwaves.

Sebring

Kenilworth Lodge
1610 Lakeview Drive
Tel: 800-423-5939
www.kenilworthlodge.com
$$–$$$$
A historic landmark with modern amenities overlooking Lake Jackson. Guests receive a free deluxe continental breakfast, free Wi-fi, and in-room movie channels. There's an indoor heated Olympic-size swimming pool, billiards and foosball tables; pet friendly rooms are available.

La Quinta Inn and Suites
4115 US 27 South
Tel: 800-753-3757
www.laquintasebring.com **$–$$$**
The inn is close to the Sebring International Speedway, and features 77 guest rooms and a complimentary breakfast buffet.

Santa Rosa Inn
509 N. Ridgewood Drive
Tel: 941-385-0641
$–$$
This is a well-run, friendly, historic hotel with 25 beautifully furnished rooms and suites, and wonderful home-cooked meals.

Winter Park

Park Plaza Hotel
307 S. Park Avenue
Tel: 800-228-7220
www.parkplazahotel.com **$$–$$$**

A quiet and intimate bed-and-breakfast hotel built in the 1920s, with 27 beautiful rooms and lots of southern charm.

Winter Park Sweet Lodge
271 South Orlando Avenue
Tel: 407-644-6099 **$–$$**
A small, older hotel with a friendly staff that is just a short drive to all the area theme parks.

Magic Kingdom

Contemporary Resort
4600 N. World Drive
Tel: 407-824-1000
http://disneyworld.disney.go.com/resorts/contemporary-resort
$$$–$$$$
The monorail passes through the middle of this 15-story A-frame built over a quarter-century ago. Most rooms have two queen-size beds and a daybed. Tower rooms have private balconies overlooking the Magic Kingdom or Bay Lake; those in the Garden Wings have nice views but are somewhat distant from the central property. There are several bars and restaurants, including the elegant California Grill – a popular spot for watching the Magic Kingdom's fireworks. Amenities include a supervised evening children's program, salon, a health club and tennis center, several swimming pools, and a video arcade.

Grand Floridian Resort & Spa
4401 Grand Floridian Way
Tel: 407-824-3000
http://disneyworld.disney.go.com/resorts/grand-floridian-resort-and-spa
$$$–$$$$
The Victorian era in all its splendor is re-created at Disney's flagship property, an elegant confection of glistening white, wooden buildings with red shingled roofs, gracious verandas, and turrets. Open-cage elevators in the plant-filled, five-story, chandeliered lobby serve second-floor shops and restaurants. Most rooms in the four- and five-story lodge buildings have two queen-size beds and a

daybed; many overlook the Seven Seas Lagoon. Amenities include some of Disney's finest dining experiences at Victoria and Albert's and Citricos, and a fine waterside restaurant, Narcoossee's; several bars, a supervised evening children's program, the Grand Floridian Health Club and Spa, and several swimming pools.

Polynesian Resort
1600 Seven Seas Drive
Tel: 407-824-2000
http://disneyworld.disney.go.com/resorts/polynesian-resort
$$$–$$$$
One of Disney's most authentic theme hotels re-creates a Pacific Island retreat. Rooms (in 11 two- and three-story "longhouses") vary in size, but most have two queen-size beds, a daybed, and balconies. Those overlooking the Seven Seas Lagoon afford front-row seats for Magic Kingdom fireworks. There are several restaurants and bars, two pools, a playground, supervised evening children's programs, and water activities.

Wilderness Lodge and Villas
901 W. Timberline Drive
Tel: 407-824-3200
http://disneyworld.disney.go.com/resorts/villas-at-wilderness-lodge
$$$–$$$$
A skillful blending of wood and stone replicates the rustic architecture associated with early national park lodges. The eight-story lakefront dwelling appears rustic but its 728 rooms are large and comfortable, with two queen-sized beds, sitting areas, and balconies. The 181 villas, in a five-story adjoining tower, range from efficiencies to two-bedroom units with kitchens, dining areas, whirlpool tubs, and DVD players. Shuttle boats sail to the Magic Kingdom.

Epcot

Caribbean Beach
900 Cayman Way

Tel: 407-934-3400
http://disneyworld.disney.go.com/resorts/caribbean-beach-resort
$$–$$$
Each of the five areas at this vibrant, 2,112 room resort that circles Barefoot Bay re-creates a Caribbean Island and has its own pool, beach, and laundry. A food court and several restaurants offer casual dining. Family-friendly activities include water sports, bicycle rentals, video arcade, and playgrounds. There is easy access to Epcot and Disney's Hollywood Studios.

Disney's Boardwalk and Villas
2101 N. Epcot Resorts Boulevard
Tel: 407-939-5100
http://disneyworld.disney.go.com/resorts/board-walk-villas
$$$–$$$$
Elaborately detailed buildings with brightly colored facades and twinkling lights re-create an East Coast boardwalk circa 1920. The 372 rooms are spacious, with two queen-size beds, daybeds, and ceiling fans. Nightclubs, restaurants, games, and shops line the boardwalk. Ferry boats and buses serve the parks.

Dolphin Hotel
1500 Epcot Resorts Boulevard
Tel: 407-934-4000
http://disneyworld.disney.go.com/resorts/dolphin-resort **$$$–$$$$**
Two 56ft (17 meter) -high dolphins and hundreds of seven-story banana leaves festoon the facade of this 27 story, triangular, turquoise hotel with four nine-story wings. The lobby has a circus theme, and the rooms have two queen-size beds, desks, and chairs. Some have balconies. There is a supervised evening children's program. In addition to the pool there

PRICE CATEGORIES

Price categories are for a double room for one night in high season (Jan–Apr):
$ = less than $75
$$ = $75–150
$$$ = $150–200
$$$$ = more than $200

are several restaurants and lounges on the property, which is within walking distance of Epcot and the BoardWalk.

Old Key West Resort
1510 N. Cove Road
Tel: 407-827-7700
http://disneyworld.disney.go.com/resorts/old-key-west-resort
$$$–$$$$
This hotel's color scheme and architecture bear an uncanny resemblance to buildings in the seaside resort towns to the south. Options range from studios with two queen-size beds, tables and chairs, small refrigerators, microwaves, and coffeemakers to three-bedroom villas, with king-size beds in the bedrooms and queen-size sleeper sofas in the living room, full kitchens, and porches or balconies. All units except studios have private whirlpool tubs. There are grills and picnic tables, restaurants, a health club, pools, shopping, tennis courts, a video arcade, and playgrounds.

Port Orleans-French Quarter
2201 Orleans Drive
Tel: 407-934-5000
http://disneyworld.disney.go.com/resorts/port-orleans-resort-french-quarter
$$–$$$
This moderate hotel is reminiscent of New Orleans, and its landscaping makes it suitable for couples wanting to get away, as there are many quiet, romantic spots in which to linger. On the other hand, kids will love the Doubloon Lagoon pool with its colorfully themed attractions that include alligator and dragon slides.

Port Orleans-Riverside
1251 Riverside Drive
Tel: 407-934-6000
http://disneyworld.disney.go.com/resorts/port-orleans-resort-riverside
$$–$$$
The former Dixie Landings has been renamed but retains the feel of the Old South. Accommodations are in two- and three-story buildings divided into "parishes." All rooms are

the same size, and most have two double beds. Mansion rooms are in antebellum-style "estates," while Bayou rooms are in rustic-style buildings surrounding Man Island, a sprawling water complex. Only the mansion rooms have elevators. Amenities include six swimming pools, a restaurant and food court, shops, bars, and bike and boat rentals.

Swan Hotel
1200 Epcot Resorts Boulevard
Tel: 407-934-3000
http://disneyworld.disney.go.com/resorts/swan-resort
$$$–$$$$
Just across the road from the Dolphin is this Westin property, topped by two 47ft (14 meter) -tall swans. Rooms in the 12 story main building and two seven-story towers are a bit smaller in size than those in the Dolphin, but similar in amenities. There's a pool as well as several restaurants and bars, including the fine Il Mulino's and Kimono sushi bar, and a supervised evening children's program.

Yacht and Beach Club and Beach Club Villas
1800 Epcot Boulevard
Tel: 407-934-7000 (Yacht Club) and 407-934-8000 (Beach Club)
http://disneyworld.disney.go.com/resorts/beach-club-villas
$$$–$$$$
Each of the three properties overlooking a 25 acre (10 hectare) lake has a distinct theme, but they share many facilities. Yacht Club rooms are finished in a nautical motif; those in the Beach Club are reminiscent of a private seaside retreat. The resort's highlight is Stormalong Bay, an elaborate swimming area with whirlpools, water slides, and a private beach. In addition, there are several pools, a miniature golf course, a health club, restaurants and bars, a supervised evening children's program, a salon, tennis courts, a video arcade, and shops.

Animal Kingdom

All-Star Movies, Music, and Sports
1991 W. Buena Vista Drive
Tel: 407-939-7000 (All-Star Movies), 407-939-6000 (All-Star Music), 407-939-5000 (All-Star Sports)
$$
This was Disney's only budget complex until the Pop Century opened. It has 30 three-story buildings divided by themes. Each has a distinctive facade, but aside from a few decorative touches, the size and decor of most rooms are identical: they're 260 sq ft (24 sq meters), have two double beds, small bureaus, a table with chairs, and bathrooms with separate vanity areas. Popular with families, the resort has a game room, playground, outdoor pool, shopping, and food court. Buses transport guests to the parks.

Disney's Animal Kingdom Lodge
2901 Osceola Parkway
Tel: 407-938-3000
http://disneyworld.disney.go.com/resorts/animal-kingdom-lodge
$$$–$$$$
A 1,293-room, Africa-themed resort on a 33-acre (13-hectare) savannah teeming with wildlife. A four-story observation window in the elaborate lobby overlooks the savannah, as do many of the rooms, which have balconies, handcrafted furniture, and traditional tapestries. Amenities include three restaurants, a health club, shops, playground, video arcade, and outdoor pool.

Hollywood Studios

Coronado Springs Resort
1000 W. Lake Buena Vista Drive
Tel: 407-939-1000
http://disneyworld.disney.go.com/resorts/coronado-springs-resort
$$–$$$
The American Southwest and Mexico are re-created at this 1,921 room lakefront complex with fountains, a Mayan pyramid, and the country's largest ballroom. Each of the three buildings

evokes a different setting – oceanfront, the city, the countryside – with rooms decorated accordingly. Standard rooms have two double beds. There are pools, a health club and spa, playground, video arcades, shops, restaurant, food court, bars, and water sports.

Pop Century
1050 Century Drive
Tel: 407-938-4000
http://disneyworld.disney.go.com/resorts/pop-century-resort $$
Encompassing 20 four-story buildings, this resort is divided into two sections: The Legendary Years, depicting the first 50 years of the 20th century, and the Classic Years, depicting the second 50 years. Statues representing various aspects of pop culture are used to develop the themes. Rooms, smaller than at other Disney properties at 260 sq ft (24 sq meters), have two double beds, bathrooms with a separate vanity area, and small dressers, tables, and chairs. Each section has a food court, swimming pool, playground, shopping area, and video arcade.

Other Disney Resorts

Buena Vista Palace
1900 Buena Vista Drive
Tel: 866-397-6516
www.buenavistapalace.com $$–$$$
Located across the lagoon from Downtown Disney, the Palace's rooms are all very well appointed with sleek modern furnishings and pillow-top beds. Most have outdoor balconies, and all have views. The Island Suites provide more space than the smaller rooms. The resort has a large spa and pool facilities and six restaurants from which to choose.

Hilton
1751 Hotel Plaza Boulevard
Tel: 407-827-4000
www.hilton-wdw.com $$–$$$
Within walking distance of Downtown Disney, this large hotel is set among 23 acres

(9 hectares) of tropical landscaping. Hotel guests receive similar benefits as Disney Resort guests, including Extra Magic Hours, an on-site Disney Character breakfast, free transportation to the parks, and access to five Disney golf courses. Several grades of suite are available for those who need more space. All rooms have Hilton Serenity Beds to provide extra comfort and an MP3 compatible clock radio.

Royal Plaza Hotel
1905 Hotel Plaza Boulevard
Tel: 407-828-2828
www.royalplaza.com **$$–$$$**
Located near Downtown Disney, the Royal Plaza's standard rooms are the largest in the Downtown Disney area. They are appointed with subtle contemporary decor and furnishings, and have all the modern amenities you'd expect. Suites are also available. The pool is nothing to shout about, but being this close to Disney, you may not find time to use it.

Wyndham Lake Buena Vista Resort,
Walt Disney World
1850 Hotel Plaza Boulevard
Tel: 407-828 4444
www.wyndhamlakebuenavista.com
$$–$$$
The Wyndham is a lakeside resort with conventional facilities and comfortable, if not lavish, rooms. A variety of recreational facilities and restaurants are available. There's an aquatic playground and bedtime stories with milk and cookies for the children. Free transportation to the parks is provided for all hotel guests.

Around Walt Disney World

Celebration Hotel
700 Bloom Street
Tel: 888-499-3800
www.celebrationhotel.com **$$$**
Located in downtown Celebration, this 115-room boutique hotel evokes Old

Florida. Hand-painted murals and hand-tinted historic photos of orange groves, wildlife, and other scenes decorate the quiet lobby. The terrace has rocking chairs and overlooks the pool, lake, and adjoining workout room. Rooms have pinstriped wallpaper, and reproduction antique furnishings. Each has a CD player, TV, and DSL. Guest privileges at Celebration's 18-hole golf course and the Fitness Center at the hospital are included. On-site restaurant.

Celebrity Resorts
2800 N. Pionciana Boulevard
Tel: 866-507-1429
www.celebrityresorts.com **$$–$$$**
This timeshare establishment has several different sizes of accommodations, from standard rooms to three-bedroom villas. All are quite affordable and available for short stays. The resort has tennis, basketball, and racquetball courts, a fitness center, three outdoor pools and one indoor pool, and a playground. The rooms and suites are well designed, making the most of their space.

Grand Cypress Resort
1 Grand Cypress Boulevard
Tel: 407-239-1234
www.grandcypress.hyatt.com
$$$–$$$$
This luxurious resort has a lush garden setting near Downtown Disney. Amenities include the famous Grand Cypress Golf Academy and four exclusive Jack Nicklaus-designed golf courses on the property, a racquet club, windsurfing on the lake, a kids' club, and an equestrian center, as well as convention facilities.

Holiday Inn Hotel and Suites-Maingate East
5678 W. Irlo Bronson Memorial Highway (US 192)
Tel: 800-366-5437 **$$**
This large, family-oriented hotel near the Magic Kingdom, with 614 rooms and suites, has pools, children's entertainment, and special kids' suites.

Hyatt Regency Grand Cypress Resort
One Grand Cypress Boulevard
Tel: 800-554-9288
www.grandcypress.hyatt.com
$$$–$$$$
This luxury resort of 750 rooms and suites has a lush garden setting near Downtown Disney. Amenities include golf, a racquetball club, windsurfing on a lake, a kids' club, and an equestrian center, as well as convention facilities.

Mystic Dunes Resort and Golf Club
7900 Mystic Dunes Lane, Celebration
Tel: 407-226-9501 or 877-747-4747
www.mystic-dunes-resort.com.
$$–$$$
Located on 600 acres (245 hectares) of meticulously landscaped grounds, this timeshare resort makes for a grand short-term retreat. The sleekly furnished, one- to three-bed villas all have a fully equipped kitchen, washer and dryer, and a whirlpool bath. Resort amenities include the Mystic Dunes Golf Club, four heated swimming pools, mini-golf, tennis, and basketball courts.

Omni Orlando Resort at ChampionsGate
1500 Masters Boulevard
Tel: 407-390-6664
www.omniorlandoresort.com
$$–$$$$
Southwest of Celebration along the I-4 corridor, this luxury resort is surrounded by 36 holes of golf designed by Greg Norman. It is also home to the David Leadbetter Golf Academy. No prizes for guessing what brings most guests here. For those not wanting to golf, there is a big pool with a water slide, a lazy river, and seven restaurants to keep you busy.

Orange Lake Resort and Country Club
8505 W. Irlo Bronson Memorial Highway (US 192)
Tel: 800-877-6522
www.orangelake.com **$$$**
This handsomely constructed lakeside resort complex has several pools

set in beautiful landscaped grounds. The two- and three-bedroom suites feel spacious and inviting and have all the amenities you'd require on holiday, even a kitchenette. There is also a small lazy river to float along, and the Splash Lagoon pool has a water slide to entertain children. For the adults there are four championship golf courses to choose from.

Palm Lakefront Hostel
4840 W. Irlo Bronson Highway (US 192)
Tel: 407-396-1759
www.orlandohostels.com **$**
The only place in Orlando that properly caters to the backpacking crowd: you can get a bed for less than $20 at certain off-peak times, and a public bus connects the property directly to Disney and the other theme parks. Of course, this isn't luxury lodging, but it's not bad. With a clean pool and a lakeside view, it is more than serviceable.

Ramada Resort Maingate
7491 West Highway 192
Tel: 800-669-6753
www.ramadamaingatewest.com
$–$$
The Ramada offers comfortable, family-friendly lodging near the Magic Kingdom, with swimming pools and tennis courts, and 278 rooms.

Seralago Hotel and Suites-Maingate East
5678 W. Irlo Bronson Memorial Highway (US 192), Kissimmee
Tel: 407-396-4488 or 800-366-5437
www.seralagohotel.com. **$–$$**
The concept behind this large, family-oriented hotel near the Magic Kingdom is a winner: "kidsuites" and two-room suites that cost less than $100 a night – ideal if you are on a budget and want to put the little ones to bed in a different

space. The quality of the hotel, though, is no better than you'd expect for these prices. The rooms are as dull and dreary as any chain, the kidsuites are only one room with a fort built around the children's bunk beds, and even the 2-room suites feel a bit cramped (though they are still the best bargain in the area). The pool not only lacks any unique design but is also missing the most essential quality for most families: shade. There is shuttle service to the theme park once a day.

Universal Orlando

Hard Rock Hotel
5800 Universal Boulevard
Tel: 407-503-7625
www.hardrockhotelorlando.com
l$$$$
The accommodations at this Mission-style hotel range from comfortable standard rooms to opulent suites worthy of a rock star. Eclectic rock 'n' roll memorabilia is displayed around the building. The huge pool has a beach, water slide, and underwater sound system. There are restaurants, bars, fitness rooms, an indoor play area, and Hard Rock store.

Portofino Bay Hotel
5601 Universal Boulevard
Tel: 407-503-1000
www.loewshotels.com/en/Portofino-Bay-Hotel $$$$
A beautiful re-creation of the seaside village of Portofino, Italy, this expensive resort is worth every penny. Rooms are sumptuous, and there are three elaborate pools, a spa, an indoor children's play area, and restaurants, including the elegant Delfino Riviera. Free water taxis transport guests between Universal's theme parks and the hotel.

Royal Pacific Resort
6300 Hollywood Way
Tel: 407-503-3000
www.loewshotels.com/en/Royal-Pacific-Resort $$$$
Attempting to re-create the South Pacific in central Florida, this resort is

centered around a lagoon-like pool fringed with palm trees, waterfalls, a sandy beach, and cabanas. It's less expensive than the other two Universal hotels, and the quality is just as good. There are six restaurants and bars, a children's activity room, a fitness room, and convention facilities.

I-Drive and SeaWorld

Caribe Royale
8101 World Center Drive
Tel: 800-823-8300
www.cariberoyale.com $$
This enormous resort has more than 1,200 suites and over 100 villas. Each suite has either two queen beds or one king, a wet bar, microwave, refrigerator, and coffeemaker. Each suite has a full kitchen, washer, and dryer. The main pool has a 75ft (23 meter) water slide. Other amenities include tennis courts, a video arcade, fitness center, basketball court, and free transportation to Disney World. Their flagship restaurant, The Venetian Room, offers Italian cuisine.

Castle DoubleTree Resort
8629 International Drive
Tel: 407-345-1511
www.doubletreecastle.com
$$–$$$$
Spires, mosaics, banners, and rich purple-and-gold drapes and bedspreads give this mid-range hotel a touch of medieval whimsy. Amenities include two restaurants, a fitness center, free shuttles to the theme parks, and a pleasant courtyard pool.

Clarion Hotel
7675 W. Irlo Bronson Memorial Highway (US 192)
Tel: 407-396-4000
www.clarionhotelmaingate.net $$
Popular with families, this five-story hotel is close to major theme parks.

Enclave Suites at Orlando
6165 Carrier Drive
Tel: 800-457-0077
www.enclavesuites.com $$

Just off International Drive, this all-suites hotel offers a lot more than the average chain. All rooms include a fully equipped kitchen, and the Kid Suites are decorated in theme-park style. There are two outdoor pools and one indoor pool, two kiddie pools, and a playground to keep everyone busy.

Four Points Hotel Sheraton by Lakeside
7769 W Irlo Bronson Memorial Highway (US 192)
Tel: 800-848-0801 $
A 651-room resort with a choice of eateries, a pool, miniature golf, tennis, and paddleboats.

International Plaza Resort and Spa
10100 International Drive
Tel: 800-327-0363
www.intlplazaresort.com
$$$–$$$$
This 17-story mock Spanish tower at the center of this sprawling hotel complex resembles an old Californian mission on growth hormones. Set on 28 acres (11 hectares) of tropical landscaping, it has three pools and two kiddie pools, plus 60,000 sq ft (5,600 sq meters) devoted to meeting spaces. It's within walking distance of SeaWorld; other amenities include three pools and miniature golf. A refrigerator and coffeemaker are in each room.

Peabody Orlando
9801 International Drive
Tel: 407-352-4000
www.peabodyorlando.com $$$$
An elegant, 27-story landmark hotel in the tourist corridor, with an Olympic-size pool and convention center. Known for its twice-daily "March of the Peabody Ducks" and afternoon tea Monday to Friday. There are 891 rooms and suites.

Renaissance Orlando Resort
6677 Sea Harbor Drive
Tel: 800-327-6677 $$$–$$$$
Across the street from SeaWorld and Discovery Cove, and 15 minutes from Disney World and Universal Orlando, this elegant,

10-story tower and convention complex will suit business travelers as well as families. Rooms are huge and well appointed; service is excellent. The lobby is a sunny atrium with glass elevators, marble floors, waterfalls, goldfish ponds, shops, and restaurants. Amenities include a pool, exercise room, spa, tennis courts, and more than 40 meeting rooms. This is a great value option.

Ritz Carlton Orlando Grande Lakes
4012 Central Florida Parkway
Tel: 407-206-2400
www.ritzcarlton.com $$$–$$$$
Located to the east of International Drive, this luxury resort is designed to resemble a grand Italian palazzo. The rooms feature marble baths, are generously sized, and are impeccably appointed. Amenities include a 40,000 sq ft (3,700 sq meter) spa and a Greg Norman-designed golf course.

Rosen Shingle Creek
9939 Universal Boulevard
Tel: 866-996-9939
www.shinglecreekresort.com
$$$–$$$$
This enormous resort seems to come out of nowhere. Though it is situated near I-Drive, it stands alone and requires transportation to reach anything else. The rooms here are very well appointed and generously oversized compared to the average Orlando hotel room. Two fine restaurants, Cala Bella and A Land Remembered, keep guests more than happy on site. Among the other amenities are four heated pools, including a child's wading pool and a lap pool, the award-winning Shingle Creek Golf Club, and the Shingle Creek Spa.

Sheraton Safari Hotel
12205 S. Apopka-Vineland Road
Tel: 800-235-3535
www.sheratonsafari.com $$–$$$
This African-themed hotel has elaborate decor inside

and out, with an over-the-top swimming pool that has a 79ft (24 meter) python water slide, a lobby filled with indigenous sculpture, and animal print fabrics decorating every room. It offers free transportation to all Disney parks.

Sheraton Studio City Resort
5905 International Drive
Tel: 407-351-2100 $$–$$$
Across from Universal Orlando, the Sheraton Studio City Resort is an economical, 21-story round hotel with 302 rooms that evoke the Hollywood of the 1940s and 1950s.

Wyndham Resort
8001 International Drive
Tel: 407-351-2420
www.wyndhamorlandoresort.com
$$$
One of the best of the many choices along International Drive, this is a vast, sprawling and at times confounding place, yet it's surprisingly quiet, with more than 1,000 spacious rooms and pleasant swimming pools.

Downtown Orlando

Courtyard at Lake Lucerne
211 N. Lucerne Circle East
Tel: 407-648-5188
www.orlandohistoricinn.com $$$
The Courtyard at Lake Lucerne is actually four B&Bs located alongside each other in downtown Orlando. Three are fully restored historic houses, including a sprawling old plantation home; the fourth house is Orlando's finest surviving Art Deco building. In all of the houses, the rooms are well appointed and have a welcoming ambiance that you will never find in a chain hotel. Breakfast is included in the price, as is a sophisticated evening cocktail.

Eö Inn
227 N. Eola Drive
Tel: 888-481-8488
www.eoinn.com $$$–$$$$
This historic inn was built in 1923 and overlooks Lake Eola in the prestigious Thornton Park area. It was converted into a fine

boutique hotel in 1999. With only 17 rooms, the service is always personable, and the decor is chic and spacious. With the Urban Spa on site, this hotel feels as much a retreat as a place to stay.

Palm Lake Front Resort and Hostel
4840 W. Irlo Bronson Memorial Parkway
Tel: 800-909-4776 $
Sitting across from downtown's Lake Eola, this hostel is in a beautiful old house with 40 private and shared rooms, kitchen facilities, and park. Kids are welcome.

Sheraton Orlando Downtown Hotel
400 W. Livingston Street
Tel: 800-574-3160 $$$
A 15-story downtown hotel with 290 rooms, across from the Orlando Arena and the Carr Performing Arts Center. The Sheraton offers casual dining, as well as a signature sports bar for when you want to kick back and watch the football game.

Veranda Bed and Breakfast
707 E. Washington Street
Tel: 800-420-6822
www.theverandabandb.com
$$–$$$
Five homes from the 1920s in downtown Orlando have been combined and turned into a delightful bed-and-breakfast, with authentic hardwood floors and period furnishings.

Westin Grand Bohemian Hotel
325 S. Orange Avenue
Tel: 888-213-9110
www.grandbohemianhotel.com
$$$–$$$$
This 250-room hotel displays more than 100 works by European artists like Gustav Klimt and Egon Schiele. Sumptuous rooms and suites are furnished in dark Javanese wood tones, rich red and purple velvet fabrics, shiny silver paint, Tiffany-style lamps, and luxury bed linens. The attached Boheme Restaurant is one of the best you'll find in downtown Orlando.

GULF COAST

Bradenton and Gulf Islands

Harrington House
5626 Gulf Drive
Tel: 888-826-5566
www.harringtonhouse.com
$$–$$$$
An attractive beachfront B&B. Four houses and two bungalows contain 17 large rooms, many of which have balconies, fireplaces, and whirlpool tubs. Amenities include full breakfast in the dining room, a lounge, pool, kayaks, bicycles, and all the typical beach gear.

Holiday Inn Riverfront
100 Riverfront Drive West
Tel: 800-HOLIDAY
www.bradentonholidayinn.com
$$–$$$
A Mediterranean-style motor inn near the Manatee River, with 153 rooms, pool, restaurant, and lounge.

Palm Tree Villas
207 66th Street, Anna Maria Island
Tel: 941-778-0910
www.palmtreevillas.com
$$–$$$
The perfect tropical beach getaway situated right on Florida's Gulf Coast. It features six environmentally-friendly beachside villas, each equipped with a full kitchen. All have access to the garden patios and heated pool. It's ideal for those escaping the crowds.

Tortuga Inn Beach Resort
1325 Gulf Drive North
Tel: 877-TORTUGA
www.tortugainn.com $$–$$$$
An airy six-building complex with one-, two-, and three-bedroom hotel rooms, suites, and apartments facing the Gulf or bay. Amenities include full kitchens, two pools, Wi-fi, laundry, barbecue grills,

private dock, and beach. The inn is pet-friendly.

Tradewinds Resort
1603 Gulf Drive North
Tel: 888-686-6716
www.tradewinds-resort.com
$$$–$$$$
Choose from 34 one-bed, one-bath pastel-hued cottages and a two-bed unit in this lovely palm-lined island resort. Amenities include full kitchens, pools/spas, barbecue grills, laundry, Wi-fi, private dock, and beach. Pet-friendly.

Charlotte Harbor and Gulf Islands

Banana Bay Waterfront Motel
23285 Bayshore Road
Tel: 941-743-4441
www.bananabaymotel.com $$
A cute motel with rooms, suites, and efficiences overlooking Charlotte Bay.

DSL, pool, shuffleboard court, and fishing pier, plus kayak rental. Pet-friendly.

Boca Grande Club
5000 Gasparilla Road, Boca Grande
Tel: 941-964-2211
www.bocagrandeclub.com $$–$$$$
Gorgeous beachfront resort on Gasparilla Island specializing in romantic

PRICE CATEGORIES

Price categories are for a double room for one night in high season (Jan–Apr):
$ = less than $75
$$ = $75–150
$$$ = $150–200
$$$$ = more than $200

getaways. One-, two-, and three-bedroom condos have all you need. There is an on-site restaurant, bar, pool, fitness club, and tarpon fishing and other activities can be arranged.

Captiva Island Inn
11509 Andy Rosse Lane, Captiva Island
Tel: 800-454-9898
www.captivaislandinn.com
$$–$$$$
Large and small restored cottages surround a tropical-style bed-and-breakfast inn in the heart of historic Captiva Island. Some cottages have kitchens and fireplaces; rooms, suites, and lofts are in main inn. Restaurants and shops are nearby.

Carousel Inn on the Beach
6230 Estero Boulevard, Fort Myers Beach
Tel: 800-613-9540
$$–$$$$
The 27 spacious one-bedroom suites and efficiences at this quiet beachfront inn on Estero Island have full kitchens and are popular with families. There is a pool, barbecue grills, and shuffleboard court.

Casa Ybel Resort
2255 W. Gulf Drive, Sanibel Island
Tel: 800-276-4753
www.casaybelresort.com
$$$$
A secluded 1890s resort on 23 acres (9 hectares) of undeveloped beachfront. The 114 one- and two-bedroom suites have Gulf views and sleeper sofas. Amenities include a pool, restaurant, spa services, golf, basketball/volleyball, and bicycle rentals.

Days Inn – Port Charlotte
1941 Tamiami Trail
Tel: 800-329-7466 **$$**
The highest-rated Days Inn in the system, this modern motel sits among moss-covered oak trees and is centrally located. All rooms have fridges and free Wi-Fi; business rooms also have microwaves. There is a free continental breakfast.

McCarthy's Inns on the Beach
2550 N. Beach Road, Englewood
Tel: 941-474-5019
www.mccarthysinns.com **$$**
These attractive one- and two-bedroom vacation rental homes are located on the beach on tranquil Manasota Key. Fishing, hiking, shops, and a restaurant are nearby. Fully equipped, including laundry.

West Wind Inn
3345 W. Gulf Boulevard, Sanibel Island
Tel: 800-824-0476
www.westwindinn.com **$$**
A casual resort on Sanibel Island with miles of clear, white sand where you can collect the island's famous shells. Rooms come with fridges or kitchens. It's the nearest motel to the wildlife refuge.

Clearwater/ Clearwater Beach

Belleview Biltmore Resort
25 Belleview Boulevard
Tel: 800-237-8947
www.belleviewbiltmore.com **$$$$**
The only one of railroad magnate Henry Plant's luxury hotels still operational in this area, this 350-room resort has golf, tennis courts, pools, boats, and fishing excursions.

Green Gables Bed and Breakfast
1040 Sunset Point Road
Tel: 727-442-8722 **$$–$$$**
Clearwater's only bed-and-breakfast, this romantic 1910 inn is set amid lush gardens on the waterfront and offers three rooms with private baths. Loated ten minutes from downtown Dunedin.

Best Western Clearwater Grand Hotel and Suites
20967 US Hwy 19
Tel: 800-238-0767 **$–$$**
This property is just a few miles from the beach and offers 148 rooms, a 24-hour fitness center, and a complimentary hot breakfast buffet.

Sheraton Sand Key Resort
1160 Gulf Boulevard
Tel: 800-456-7263
www.sheratonsandkey.com **$$$**
A huge resort on the beach with a pool, tennis, sailboats, umbrellas, and beach chairs. Many of the 390 rooms have Gulf views.

Clearwater Beach Hotel
500 Mandalay Avenue
Tel: 800-292-2295
www.clearwaterbeachhotel.com
$$–$$$$
A beachfront hotel with more than 150 rooms and efficiencies, as well as a pool and restaurant. Pet friendly.

Quality Beach Resort
655 South Gulfview Boulevard
Tel: 727-442-7171
www.qualitybeachresort.com
$–$$
A smaller resort with 91 rooms, white-sand beaches, easy shopping access, and room service.

Fort Myers

Ramada Inn
2500 Edwards Drive
Tel: 800-833-1620
$$–$$$
Modern, high-rise downtown hotel with 416 rooms, pool, tennis, boat docks, and exercise room.

Indian Rocks Beach

Holiday Inn Hotel and Suites Habourside Marina
401 Second Street
Tel: 800-726-0865
www.hiharbourside.com **$–$$$**
An Old Key West-style hotel with 164 rooms, two heated pools (one is specially for families), fitness center, restaurant, and lounge.

Sarah's Seaside
306 Gulf Boulevard
Tel: 800-597-8063
www.gulfsideresorts.com **$$$$**
The seven weekly vacation rentals in this tropical-themed complex on a quiet beach are charming. One-, two-, and three-bedroom villas and a studio cottage have many personal touches, and all have modern kitchens and appliances, sitting rooms with TV and DVD player, queen or king beds, and decks. Extras include a pool, laundry, barbecue grills, Wi-Fi, sea kayaks. Check in at 810 Gulfside, the sister property. No pets allowed.

Marco Island

Marco Island Lakeside Inn
155 First Avenue
Tel: 800-729-0216
www.marcoislandlakeside.com
$$$–$$$$
Zen-like tranquility pervades this peaceful inn near Marco Island beaches. The 19 one- and two-bedroom suites and studios include kitchen facilities, Wi-Fi, washer/dryer, and irons. On-site laundry, pool, sushi bar, and steakhouse.

Olde Marco Island Inn & Suites
100 Palm Avenue
Tel: 877-475-3466
www.oldemarcoinn.com **$$$$**
This 1883 inn is built on a Calusa Indian shell mound. It has 58 modern and very spacious one-, two-, and three-bedroom suites and penthouses, with full kitchens, sitting rooms with sleeper sofas, and screened lanais. There is a pool, fitness center, golf, fishing, and nature tours. An award-winning gourmet restaurant is also on-site.

Naples

Hotel Escalante
290 Fifth Avenue South
Tel: 877-485-3466
www.hotelescalante.com
$$$–$$$$
An intimate, Mediterranean-style hotel with 10 rooms on a garden estate in old Naples. One- and two-bed rooms and suites have Plantation-style mahogany armoires, king beds with creamy linens, irons, ceiling fans, and Molton Brown bath amenities. Facilities include a courtyard with pool and hot tub; a library with large-screen plasma TV, wines, and ports; and spa services. Breakfast and lunch are offered in the hotel restaurant on Thur-Sun.

Inn on Fifth
699 Fifth Avenue South
Tel: 888-403-8778
www.innonfifth.com **$$$$**
This Irish-owned boutique hotel in old Naples exudes European elegance.

Amenities in its 87 rooms, suites, and efficiencies include whirlpool tubs and Wi-fi. Roof-top pool, hot tub, fitness center, spa packages, golf privileges, two on-site restaurants (one featuring Irish food) and full breakfast.
Naples Courtyard Inn
2630 Tamiami Trail North
Tel: 800-432-3870
www.naplescourtyardinn.com
$$–$$$
This tropical-flavored inn a couple of miles from the beach is a fantastic deal. Serene rooms and suites have granite vanities, king or double beds, fridges, coffeemakers, and Wi-fi. There's a fitness center and pool, and breakfast in the Chickee Hut in the gardens.
Vanderbilt Beach Resort
9225 N. Gulfshore Drive
Tel: 800-243-9076
www.vanderbiltbeachresort.com $$
A pleasant motel right on the beach with 50 rooms and efficiencies and a pool.

St Pete Beach

Colonial Gateway Inn
6300 Gulf Boulevard
Tel: 727-360-4385 $$
This property overlooks the beach, with 200 tastefully decorated rooms and efficiencies. It's popular with families.
Don CeSar Beach Resort
3400 Gulf Boulevard
Tel: 800-282-1116 $$$$
This fuchsia-colored 1920s resort on the beach has 277 super-deluxe rooms and attract celebrities. There's a pool, private beach, tennis courts, fitness center, and restaurant, plus sailing, windsurfing, and scuba diving lessons.
Grand Plaza Beachfront Resort Hotel and Conference Center
5250 Gulf Boulevard
Tel: 800-238-0767
www.grandplazaflorida.com $–$$$
Located between the Gulf of Mexico and Boca Ciega Bay and surrounded with white-sand beaches, this 156-room resort is the tallest resort on the beach. There's a beachfront pool, fitness

center, restaurants, and free Wi-fi.
Island's End Resort
1 Pass-A-Grille Way
Tel: 727-360-5023
www.islandsend.com $$$–$$$$
Five one-bedroom fully equipped cottages and a three-bedroom home sit dockside near the historic Pass-a-Grille's shops and activities. Tropical foliage, gazebos, wooden walkways, and light breakfast complete the picture.

St Petersburg

Bayboro House Bed and Breakfast
1719 Beach Drive SE
Tel: 727-823-4955
$$–$$$
A charming Victorian inn overlooking Tampa Bay with three cozy rooms, generous breakfasts, and an airy veranda.
The Pier Hotel
253 Second Ave North
Tel: 800-735-6607
www.thepierhotel.com
$$–$$$$
The Pier is the oldest continuously running hotel in St Petersburg. This lavish 32 room hotel is located in the heart of downtown close to shopping, dining, and the beaches. There is a free breakfast buffet, and free beer and wine reception nightly.
Renaissance Vinoy Resort & Golf Club
501 Fifth Avenue NE
Tel: 888-303-4430 $$$$
When it opened in 1925, this was the first US hotel with steam heat in every room. Now it's a lush restored resort, with excellent restaurants, golf course, tennis courts, fitness center, and private marina. Be sure to take the guided tours of the haunted nooks and crannies.

Safety Harbor

Mar Bay Suites
3110 Phillippe Parkway
Tel: 877-7-MARBAY
www.marbaysuites.com $–$$$
A quaint, family-owned

destination with a relaxing atmosphere located just minutes from downtown Tampa and the airport.
Safety Harbor Resort & Spa
105 North Bayshore Drive
Tel: 888-237-8772
www.safetyharborspa.com $$$$
This spa resort has a unique Florida attraction: mineral springs prized by pre-historic Indians. Enclosed since 1944, the springs are part of a comprehensive health and wellness program. There's an Aveda Concept spa, complimentary Aveda toiletries in guest bathrooms, and light New American cuisine in the on-site restaurant. Many of the 175 upgraded guest rooms and suites overlook Tampa Bay.

Sarasota

The Cypress – A Bed and Breakfast
621 Gulfstream Avenue South
Tel: 941-955-4683
www.cypressbb.com $$–$$$$
This graceful, two-story inn is built entirely of cypress wood and has lovely architectural features as well as a terrific setting across from the bay. Amenities in the four guest rooms include air conditioning, TVs, oriental rugs, fresh flowers, and ceiling fans. There is a gourmet breakfast and afternoon hors d'œuvres.
Gulf Beach Resort Motel
930 Ben Franklin Drive
Tel: 800-232-2489
www.gulfbeachsarasota.com $$
The Gulf Beach Resort Motel is a casual place that attracts families who return every year. There are 48 rooms, private gardens, kitchens, shuffleboard, and fine Gulf views.
Hyatt Sarasota
1000 Boulevard of the Arts
Tel: 800-233-1234
www.sarasota.hyatt.com $$–$$$
Modern downtown hotel with views of Sarasota Bay, 297 rooms, pool, sauna, health club, sailing, restaurants, and bars.

Surf View Resort Motel
1121 Ben Franklin Drive
Tel: 800-833-1818 $–$$
A clean, comfortable motel right on the beach with 27 rooms, pool, and playground.

Tampa

Clarion Hotel and Conference Center
2701 E. Fowler Avenue
Tel: 877-424-6423 $–$$
Family-oriented motel with 255 guest rooms, free transport to nearby Busch Gardens, pool, sauna, and exercise room.
Don Vicente de Ybor Historic Inn
1915 Republica de Cuba
Tel: 866-206-4545
www.donvicenteinn.com
$$$–$$$$
A boutique hotel with 16 rooms in a building constructed in 1895 by the founder of Ybor City. The lobby features a dramatic staircase. Rooms have wrought-iron balconies and antiques.
Embassy Suites Hotel Tampa Downtown
513 S. Florida Avenue
Tel: 813-769-8300
$$$–$$$$
This downtown Tampa hotel offers two-room suites with views of Tampa Bay, along with very hearty cook-to-order breakfasts each morning, and a manager's welcome reception every evening.
Hilton Garden Inn
1700 E. 9th Avenue
Tel: 800-221-2424
$$–$$$
This 95-room hotel, the first new hotel to be built in historic Ybor City in 100 years, is a good place to stay while enjoying Ybor City's nightlife and has "cooked-to-order" breakfasts.

PRICE CATEGORIES

Price categories are for a double room for one night in high season (Jan–Apr):
$ = less than $75
$$ = $75–150
$$$ = $150–200
$$$$ = more than $200

Hyatt Regency Tampa
211 North Tampa Street
Tel: 800-233-1234
$$-$$$
A modern high-rise hotel in the heart of downtown Tampa's business district and close to area attractions. The hotel features 521 guest rooms, and a swimming pool.
Saddlebrook Resort
5700 Saddlebrook Way
Tel: 800-729-8383
www.saddlebrook.com
$$$-$$$$
A relaxing 480-acre (195-hectare) resort, 12 miles (19km) north of Tampa. Renowned for its Arnold Palmer Golf Academy, it has year-round golf clinics to help improve your swing. The 800 luxury guest rooms and one-, two-, and three-bedroom suites all have kitchens. Olympic pool, spa, wellness center, restaurants, and 45 tennis courts.
Tahitian Inn
601 S. Dale Mabry Highway
Tel: 800-876-1397

www.tahitianinn.com **$-$$**
A rare non-chain hotel in Tampa, this classic 1950s inn is good value. It has tropical decor throughout and 79 comfy rooms. Heated outdoor pool, spa, and workout room.
University Inn Tampa
830 W. Kennedy Boulevard
Tel: 866-337-9496
http://universityinntampa.com
Located near the Henry Plant Museum and the University of Tampa, this budget motel covers the basics. **$**

Tarpon Springs

Spring Bayou Inn
32 West Tarpon Avenue
Tel: 727-938-9333
www.springbayouinn.com **$$**
The five antique-filled rooms and one efficiency each have a private bath, Wi-fi, and other amenities in this lovely two-story 1900s home in downtown Tarpon Springs. Small fridges in some rooms. Home-cooked gourmet breakfast.

ABOVE: Tarpon Springs is known for its natural sponges.

NORTH FLORIDA

Alachua

Econo Lodge
15920 NW US Highway 441
Tel: 877-424-6423 **$**
Although it's a chain, the Econo Lodge is a modest, clean 60-room hotel with restaurant and lounge, and is located near the highway.
Quality Inn
15960 NW US Hwy 441
Tel: 386-462-2244 **$**
A clean and serviceable 90 room hotel inn with a complimentary continental breakfast.

Cedar Key

Dockside Motel
491 Dock Street
Tel: 352-543-5432 **$**
A quaint, centrally located, nine-room harbourside motel, with friendly staff and a deck out back.
Island Hotel
373 2nd Street

Tel: 352-543-5111
www.islandhotel-cedarkey.com **$$**
This is an 1859 hotel in the former General Store. Ten spotless rooms are styled in shabby chic, with quilts on four-poster beds, antiques, hand-cut wooden walls and floors, ceiling fans, air conditioning, and private bathrooms with showers (some have clawfoot tubs). Rooms access a wraparound second-floor balcony. There are no phones or TVs, but there is a full breakfast.
Old Fenimore Mill Condominiums
PO Box 805, 3rd Street
Tel: 352-543-9803
www.fenimoremill.com. **$$$$**
These one-, two-, and three-bed vacation rentals are built on stilts overlooking the tranquil bay and are on the east end of downtown. Amenities include private beach, fishing dock, pool,

hot tub, barbecue grills, picnic area, and laundry.

Gainesville

Hilton University of Florida Conference Center
1714 SW 34th Street
Tel: 800-HILTONS
www.ufhotel.com **$$$$**
Set on 9 acres (4 hectares) across from UF Cultural Plaza, this attractive seven-story Hilton has 248 deluxe rooms with two queen beds, ergonomic work stations, DSL, computer games, and Web TV. Amenities include a restaurant, pool, hot tub, fitness center, and buffet breakfast.
Magnolia Plantation Inn and Cottages
309 SE 7th Street
Tel: 800-201-2379
www.magnoliabnb.com **$$-$$$$**
This Victorian B&B is surrounded by landscaped grounds and has five

second-floor guest rooms with queen beds, gas fireplaces, private baths with clawfoot tubs. Sitting parlors and a dining room are on the ground floor. The seven one- to three-bedroom cottages have fireplaces, Jacuzzis, kitchens, and sitting rooms. There is a full breakfast.
Sweetwater Branch Inn
625 E. University Avenue
Tel: 800-595-7760
www.sweetwaterinn.com
$$-$$$$
A picture-perfect 1885 B&B in downtown with 12 guest rooms and five cottages, all with showers and clawfoot

tubs. The owner's family antiques, vintage teapots, and romantic furnishings grace rooms and public spaces. Hot breakfast and afternoon wine and cheese.

High Springs

Grady House
420 NW 1st Avenue
Tel: 386-454-2206
www.gradyhouse.com **$$–$$$$**
This lovely Arts and Crafts B&B on the main highway in High Springs was built in 1917 as a railroad boarding house. Its five color-themed rooms have period details, antiques, and artworks; a two-bedroom cottage sleeps four. Gardens, ponds, gourmet breakfast, and friendly dalmatians.

High Springs Country Inn
520 NW Santa Fe Boulevard
Tel: 386-454-1565
www.highsprings.com/cinns **$**
Located on US 441, near downtown, this clean budget motel has 16 renovated rooms with one or two beds, private baths, phones, cable TV, fridges, coffeemakers, and Wi-fi.

Rustic Ranch Inn
5529 NW State Road 45
Tel: 386-454-1223
www.rusticinn.net **$$–$$$**
Set on 9 acres (4 hectares), this six-room ranch-style inn is a great place to unwind. Nature-themed rooms are spacious and have king or queen beds with carved headboards, baths, fridges, microwaves, coffeemakers, private decks, and views. A nice feature is the delivered continental breakfast. Packages include lodging, canoe rental, and dinner in High Springs.

Keaton Beach

The Eagle's Nest at Dekle Beach
5960 Potts Still Road, Perry
Tel: 850-584-7666
www.eagles-nest-vacations.com
$$$$
These three attractive seafront stilted vacation rentals between Keaton Beach and Perry are great

getaways. They are fully equipped with kitchens, three bedrooms, a private deck, pier, boat ramp, fish-cleaning station, and laundry.

Micanopy

Herlong Mansion
402 NE Cholokka Boulevard
Tel: 800-437-5664
www.herlong.com **$$–$$$$**
This B&B in Micanopy originated as a pioneer home and became a colonial-style family home in 1910. It has 11 Arts and Crafts-style rooms, suites, and cottages with high ceilings, antique beds and dressers, gleaming wood floors, rugs, and private baths. Some rooms have fireplaces. A full breakfast and afternoon wine and cheese are included; dinner is optional.

Shady Oak Bed and Breakfast
203 Cholokka Boulevard
Tel: 352-466-3476
www.shadyoak.com **$$–$$$**
Nestled in the quiet, oak-shaded streets of historic Micanopy, this four-room bed and breakfast offers guests a beautiful, quiet getaway. Shady Oak has lovely panoramic views, porch swings, barbecue grills, and a pool table. Gourmet meals can be provided by local caterers.

BELOW: honeymoon cabins in Steinhatchee.

Ocala

Comfort Inn and Suites
3720 SW College Road
Tel: 352-237-0715
www.countryinns.com **$–$$**
Located in the heart of horse country, this inn is convenient to I-75 and Ocala International airport. It has 59 guest rooms, free hot breakfast and Internet access. There is also a heated pool and fitness center.

Heritage Country Inn
14343 W. Highway 40
Tel: 888-240-2233
www.heritagecountryinn.com
$$–$$$
Each of the six historic-themed rooms on this peaceful ranch has a private entrance, fireplace, TV, phone, Jacuzzi, and shower. There is a full breakfast.

Ritz Historic Inn
1205 E. Silver Springs Boulevard
Tel: 888-382-9390 **$$**
A romantic 1925 inn amid fountains, courtyards, and gardens. Suites have king or queen beds, sleeper sofa, cable TV, phone, fridge, microwave, coffeemaker, and DSL. Other amenities include a mosaic pool, Jacuzzi, business center, and continental breakfast.

Seven Sisters Inn
820 SE Fort King Street
Tel: 800-250-3496
www.7sistersinn.com **$$**

Two adjoining 1880s Victorian houses have been transformed into an exotic themed inn with 13 rooms, period antiques, private baths, full breakfast, and afternoon tea.

Palatka

Azalea House
220 Madison Street
Tel: 386-325-4547
www.theazaleahouse.com **$$**
This elegant 1880 Victorian gabled B&B in Palatka's regenerating historic district has many links to the St John's River's storied past. It has six charming guest rooms with central a/c and heat. The best bit is the home-made pastries at breakfast. There is a pool with gardens, decks, and parlor.

Steinhatchee

Steinhatchee Landing Resort
203 Ryland Circle
Tel: 800-584-1709
www.steinhatcheelandingresort.com
$$–$$$$
This 35 acre (14 hectare) resort features vacation rentals. The one- to four-bedroom cottages are fully equipped and have screened porches and barbecues. There is a pool, Jacuzzi, petting zoo, shuffleboard court, swings, bicycles, and other equipment rental. Pets up to 28 pounds allowed in some cottages.

Steinhatchee Riverside Inn
1111 Riverside Drive
Tel: 352-498-4049 **$–$$**
A 17 room inn set amongst beautiful oak trees, this lovely inn is just across the street from the Steinhatchee River. Pool, garden, Wi-fi and cable TV.

TRANSPORTATION
ACCOMMODATIONS
ACTIVITIES
A – Z

THE PANHANDLE

Apalachicola

Gibson Inn
51 Avenue C
Tel: 850-653-2191
www.gibsoninn.com **$$–$$$$**
This venerable 1907 B&B
occupies a Victorian
structure with a tin roof
and wraparound porches.
Thirty chintz-laden rooms
and suites have antique
beds, private baths with
clawfoot tub, Wi-fi.
Restaurant, lounge. Pet-
friendly.

Old Saltworks Cabins
PO Box 526, Port St Joe
Tel: 850-229-6097
www.oldsaltworks.com **$$–$$$$**
Looking for a cabin in the
woods? The 11 rustic one-
and two-bedroom family
vacation hideaways at this
old Civil War saltworks on St
Joseph Bay are just the
ticket. Fully equipped. Play
fort, mini museum, nature
trails. There is a two-night
minimum.

Witherspoon Inn
94 Fifth Street
Tel: 850-653-9186
www.witherspooninn.com **$$–$$$**
A tastefully renovated
former sea captain's
residence in the historic
district of Apalachicola, this
homey historic B&B has
four guest rooms with an
Old Florida feel. They also
have great home-baked
goodies for you.

Fort Walton Beach

**Aunt Martha's Bed and
Breakfast**
315 Shell Avenue SE
Tel: 850-243-6702
www.auntmarthasbedandbreakfast.com
$$–$$$
A beautiful faux-Victorian
B&B with comfortable
rooms, library and grand
piano, porch, and feng shui
gardens. The breakfasts are
bountiful.

**Best Western
Fort Walton Beach**
380 Santa Rosa Boulevard
Tel: 877-243-9444 **$$–$$$**
Not your grandmother's
Best Western chain lodging,
this place is a shrine to pop

art, with snazzy color
themes and retro details.

Panama City Beach

Casa Loma
13615 Front Beach Road
Tel: 888-460-9336
www.casalomapcb.com **$$–$$$$**
The emphasis is on Mexico
in this mid-rise hotel. The
100 spacious guest rooms
and two-room suites all
have tiled floors, tropical
furnishings, and a south-of-
the-border ambience. All
rooms overlook the beach
and have balconies; some
have kitchenettes.

Driftwood Lodge
15811 Front Beach Road
Tel: 800-442-6601
www.driftwoodpcb.com **$$–$$$$**
A family motel on the beach
with a selection of rooms,
suites, efficiencies, and
cabanas. There's lots to do,
from shuffleboard and
volleyball.

**Marriott's Bay Point
Resort**
4200 Marriott Drive
Tel: 800-874-4025
www.marriottbaypoint.com
$$–$$$$
This is an elegant resort
with antique furnishings,
Asian rugs, and beautiful
views. There are 355 rooms
and suites, restaurants,
bars, pools, golf, tennis, a
marina, and sailboat
rentals.

Pensacola

Hilton Garden Inn
12 Via de Luna Drive
Tel: 850-916-2999
$$$–$$$$
This is one of those new,
post–Hurricane Ivan
beachfront hotels, but it
also has that trademark
airy feel, large pool, and
luxurious rooms for which
the Hilton brand is known.

New World Landing
600 S. Palafox Street
Tel: 850-434-7736
www.newworldlanding.com
$$–$$$$
This newly remodeled
boutique hotel is located
halfway between downtown

Pensacola and the
waterfront. Its 15 period
rooms offer understated
elegance and amenities.
There's also a lovely
courtyard.

Pensacola Grand Hotel
200 E. Gregory Street
Tel: 877-2-CROWNE
www.pensacolagrandhotel.com
$$–$$$$
A historic train station
serves as the lobby of this
15-story hotel, with
restaurant and health club.
It's the perfect location for a
train buff.

**Pensacola Victorian
Bed and Breakfast**
203 W. Gregory Street
Tel: 800-370-8354
www.pensacolavictorian.com
$$–$$$$
A restored ship's captain's
home, this attractive B&B
has four comfy rooms with
private baths, phones, TV,
and Wi-fi. Gourmet
breakfast and treats.

St George Island

Buccaneer Inn
160 W. Gorrie Drive
Tel: 800-847-2091
www.buccinn.com **$$–$$$**
This Gulf-front motel has
100 spacious, light-filled
rooms, some with
kitchenettes.

St George Inn
135 Franklin Boulevard
Tel: 850-927-2903
www.stgeorgeinn.com **$$–$$$**
A lovely three-story inn with
pleasant rooms opening
onto wraparound porches.
Huge curving pool.

Tallahassee

**Doubletree Inn
Tallahassee**
101 S. Adams Street
Tel: 850-224-5000
$$–$$$
One of many chains in
Tallahassee, this Doubletree
is a 243-room high-rise
hotel that is clean,
convenient, and aimed at
business travelers.

Governors Inn
209 S. Adams Street
Tel: 800-342-7717

www.thegovinn.com
$$$–$$$$
This boutique hotel near the
state capitol has 41 rooms
and suites with private
baths, antiques, four-poster
beds, TV, Wi-fi. Continental
breakfast, afternoon
cocktails.

Little English Guesthouse
737 Timberlane Road
Tel: 850-907-9777
www.littleenglishguesthouse.com
$$–$$$
An authentic English B&B
with the London owner's
antiques and two twee
rooms. With several cups of
tea and English bath
goodies, you might just
think you're in the Old
World.

**McFarlin House Bed and
Breakfast**
305 E. King Street
Tel: 877-370-4701
www.mcfarlinhouse.com
$$$
A restored Victorian inn, 16
miles (28km) from
Tallahassee, with eight
antique rooms, private
baths with showers or
clawfoot tubs, TV, phone,
and DSL. Full breakfast is
included.

The Inn at Park Avenue
323 E. Park Avenue
Tel: 850-222-4024
$$–$$$
This B&B is near the state
capitol and has an old-
fashioned ambience, with
high ceilings, hardwood
floors, parlor, and four guest
rooms with baths and
showers.

ACTIVITIES

FESTIVALS, THE ARTS, NIGHTLIFE, SHOPPING, SPORTS, CHILDREN'S ACTIVITIES, AND TOURS

FESTIVALS

The following festivals and other events are listed chronologically. Sports events are listed separately.

Annual Events

January

Art Deco Weekend (Miami). A celebration of Miami Beach's famous Art Deco architecture. Events include a street fair, music, and an art show. Early January. Tel: 305-672-2014.
Zora Neale Hurston Festival (Eatonville). The 20th-century writer is celebrated annually in the nation's oldest incorporated African-American community, featuring public talks and a street festival. Late January. Tel: 407-358-8108.

February

Florida Renaissance Festival (Deerfield Beach). A medieval fair with jousting, classical music, and art. Early February. Tel: 954-776-1642.
Gasparilla Pirate Festival (Tampa). A pirate invasion takes over downtown with music, food, and entertainment. Early February. Tel: 813-353-8108.
Coconut Grove Arts Festival (Miami). The largest arts festival in the state. Mid-February. Tel: 305-447-0401.
Florida State Fair (Tampa). The big daddy of Florida fairs, with everything from livestock to crafts. Second week in February. Tel: 813-621-7821.
Riverwalk Blues Festival (Fort Lauderdale). Music festival with hot rhythms and even hotter Cajun dishes. Tel: 954-761-5985. Second week in February.

Greek Festival (Fort Myers). Florida's Greek Orthodox community celebrates. Late February. Tel: 941-481-2099.
Mardi Gras Parades (Pensacola). Not as big as in New Orleans but still fun. Late February. Tel: 850-932-1500.

March

Carnival Miami. A week-long Hispanic heritage festival in Little Havana. Early March. Tel: 305-644-8888.
Florida Strawberry Festival (Plant City). A tribute to strawberries with music, food, and entertainment, east of Tampa. First week in March. Tel: 813-752-9194.
Las Olas Art Festival (Fort Lauderdale). Street arts, crafts, music, and food. Early March. Tel: 954-472-3755.
Florida Film Festival (Maitland). Documentaries, animation, short films. Late March. Tel: 407-629-0054.

April

Jacksonville Landing Annual Folk Festival. Folk music, art, and crafts. Early April. Tel: 904-353-1188.
Apalachicola Walk and Wine Festival. An art show, along with musicians, chef demonstrations, and wine tastings. Late April. Tel: 850-653-9419.
Conch Republic Celebrations (Key West). Key West once again tries to secede from the state. Late April. Tel: 305-296-0213.

May

Sunfest West (Palm Beach). Florida's largest music, art, and water sports festival. Tel: 561-659-5980.

June

Billy Bowlegs Pirate Festival (Fort Walton Beach). A tribute to the Seminole chief. First week in June. Tel: 800-322-3319.
Fiesta of Five Flags (Pensacola). Street festival with food and music memorializing the Spanish explorer Tristan de Luna. First week of June. Tel: 850-433-6512.

July

Florida International Festival (Daytona Beach). Prestigious music festival featuring anything from jazz to classical. Late July through early August. Tel: 386-252-1511.
Hemingway Days (Key West). A rowdy tribute to Hemingway and his work, plus literary events. The look-alike competition is a particular favorite, drawing middle-aged men with beards from far and wide. Late July. Tel: 305-296-2388/0320.

August

Annual Wausau Possum Festival. A celebration in honor of the marsupial in the small town of Wausau near Panama City Beach. First Saturday in August.

Buying Tickets

The easiest way to reserve and pay for tickets is simply to call up the relevant box office or go to the venue's website and pay by credit card. Sometimes, however, you will be required to make reservations through Ticketmaster, a ticket agency that runs a pay-by-phone operation and also has outlets in certain music and discount stores. Be warned that Ticketmaster charges a convenience fee above the normal cost of a ticket.

September

St Augustine's Founding Anniversary. A re-enactment of the first landing of the Spanish conquistadors in St Augustine in 1565. Saturday nearest September 8. Tel: 904-825-1010.

October

Roy Hobbs Baseball World Series (Fort Myers). More than 100 teams vie for first place in this tournament named after a legendary baseball hero. Mid-October–mid-December. Tel: 888-484-7422.
Fantasy Fest (Key West). Wild and crazy Halloween celebrations that last all week. Late October. Tel: 305-296-1817.
Guavaween (Tampa). Latin-style Halloween celebration with a parade through Ybor City. Last Saturday in October. Tel: 813-621-7121.
Halloween Horror Nights (Orlando). Halloween fun on the grounds of Universal Studios. October 31st. Tel: 407-22-HORROR.

November

Fort Myers Beach Sandsculpting Contest. A three-day event drawing amateur and professional sculptors. Early November. Tel: 239-332-2930.
Miami Book Fair International. This international congress of authors, publishers, and agents fills the city. Also street vendors, entertainment. Third week in November. Tel: 305-237-3258.

December

St Petersburg Boat Show. One of the South's largest boat shows at Bayfront Center. Early December. Tel: 954-764-7642.
Walt Disney World's Very Merry Christmas Parade (Orlando). Disney does Christmas in typical over-the-top style. From mid-December. Tel: 407-824-4321.
Orange Bowl Parade (Miami). The nation's top marching bands accompany amazing floats before the football bowl game. December 31. Tel: 305-341-4700.

THE ARTS

Entertainment in Florida is not an unadulterated diet of kitsch and theme-park razzmatazz nor is it just laid-back Jimmy Buffett music on the beach and neighborhood arts and crafts shows. The state has a surprisingly vibrant cultural scene, with everything from Broadway shows and modern dance to

At the Movies

The most famous movie theater in Florida is the Tampa Theatre, which is a restored 1926 movie house in downtown Tampa with a superb interior that was once described as an "Andalusian bonbon." The theater puts on a mix of classic and foreign films as well as special events. Another delightful venue for movies, plays, and other events is the Hippodrome, or Hippo, in downtown Gainesville, occupying the grand Beaux Arts building that once housed the Post Office.

Florida has several annual film festivals. The best known is the Miami Film Festival in mid-February, with screenings of foreign, US, and Florida movies. Also look out for the South Florida Black Film Festival in April, and Sarasota's film festival in November.

high-quality performances of opera, classical, and rock music starring the most famous musicians and singers in the world. As far as the performing arts are concerned, the majority of top-quality shows are staged during Florida's popular winter high season, between October and April, although there is plenty to choose from year-round. The best performances tend to be focused in southern Florida and the Gulf, in cities like Miami, Fort Lauderdale, Tampa, Sarasota, and Naples along with Orlando in central Florida. Below is a list of some of the main venues by region.

Miami

Adrienne Arsht Center for the Performing Arts of Miami-Dade County, 1300 Biscayne Boulevard; tel: 305-949-6722; www.arshtcenter.org. A stunning new center that is host to national and international ballet, symphony, and opera companies.
American Airlines Arena, 601 Biscayne Boulevard; tel: 786-777-1000; www.aaarena.com. Miami's main entertainment venue for basketball games and major pop and Latin music concerts.
Florida Grand Opera, tel: 305-854-7890; www.fgo.org. Miami's resident opera company features internationally prominent and regional singers and performs in various venues in Dade and Broward counties.
Gusman Center of the Performing Arts, 174 E. Flagler Street; tel: 305-374-2444; www.gusmancenter.org. An

ornate and historic theater that offers drama, dance, and musical productions.
Jackie Gleason Theater of the Performing Arts, 1700 Washington Avenue, Miami Beach; tel: 305-673-7300. An ultra-modern 1,800-seat theater that stages Broadway plays.
Miami City Ballet, tel: 305-929-7000; www.miamicityballet.org. Latin-flavored classical ballet company with hints of jazz and modern dance. Various South Florida locations.
New World Symphony, tel: 305-673-3330; www.nws.edu. First-rate repertoire of classical music performed at various Miami area theaters, but mainly the Lincoln Theater in Miami Beach and the Gusman Center for the Performing Arts.
Teatro de Bellas Artes, 2173 S.W. 8th Street; tel: 305-325-0515. A Spanish-language theater in Little Havana that offers live drama, comedy, and musical events.

Atlantic Coast

Bankatlantic Center, 1 Panther Parkway, Sunrise; tel: 954-835-7000; www.bankatlanticcenter.com. A modern entertainment center near Fort Lauderdale that hosts major concerts.
Broward Center for the Performing Arts, 201 S.W. 5th Avenue, Fort Lauderdale; tel: 954-462-0222; www.browardcenter.org. This 2,700-seat waterfront theater is the top venue for cultural events in Fort Lauderdale.
Caldwell Theater Company, 7901 N. Federal Highway, Boca Raton; tel: 561-241-7432; www.caldwelltheatre.com. A professional regional theater.
Jacksonville Symphony Orchestra, tel: 904-354-5479; www.jaxsymphony.org. Variety of classical music performed throughout the Jacksonville area.
Kravis Center, 701 Okeechobee Boulevard, West Palm Beach; tel: 561-832-7469; www.kravis.org. A major performing arts center with theater, dance, and musical productions.
Parker Playhouse, 707 N.E. 8th Street, Fort Lauderdale; tel: 954-764-1441; www.parkerplayhouse.com. Broadway plays, musical events, and dance troupes.
Surfside Playhouse, 300 Ramp Road, Cocoa Beach; tel: 321-783-3127; www.surfsideplayers.com. A community theater with first-rate performances.

Central Florida

Amway Arena, 600 W. Amelia Street, Orlando; tel: 407-849-2000; www.

orlandovenues.net. One of Orlando's main venues for evening events, sports, and concerts.

Bob Carr Performing Arts Center, 401 Livingston Street, Orlando; tel: 407-849-2001. A year-round community auditorium that hosts regional and national music, theater, and dance.

Orlando Philharmonic Orchestra, tel: 407-770-0071; www.orlandophil.org. Orchestra musicians present classics at the Carr Center and also accompany the Orlando Ballet.

Gulf Coast

Asolo Center for the Performing Arts, 5555 N. Tamiami Trail, Sarasota; tel: 941-351-8000; www.asolo.org. Nationally prominent multi-purpose theater.

Mahaffey Theater, 400 First Street South, St Petersburg; tel: 727-892-5798; www.mahaffeytheater.com. Municipal venue for traveling road productions.

Philharmonic Center for the Arts, 5833 Pelican Bay Boulevard, Naples; tel: 239-597-1900; www.thephil.org. Two theaters in a complex offering classical music and plays.

Players of Sarasota, 838 N. Tamiami Trail, Sarasota; tel: 941-365-2494; www.theplayers.org. A community theater that hosts comedy acts, dramas, and thrillers.

Ruth Eckerd Hall, 1111 N. McMullen Booth Road, Clearwater; tel: 727-791-7400; www.rutheckerdhall.com. National pop, jazz, classical, ballet, and dramatic acts.

The Sarasota Ballet, 5555 N. Tamiami Trail, Sarasota; tel: 941-359-0099; www.sarasotaballet.org. A regional opera company that performs classic and contemporary works in its own historic theater.

St Pete Times Forum, 401 Channelside Drive, Tampa; tel: 813-301-6500; www.sptimesforum.com. This arena is home to the Tampa Bay Lightning professional hockey team and is the site for many pop music concerts and wrestling.

Tampa Bay Performing Arts Center, 1010 N. MacInnes Place, Tampa; tel: 813-229-7827 or 800-955-1045; www.tbpac.org. One of the largest performing arts centers in Florida, with both classical and popular entertainment on the schedule.

Venice Little Theater, 140 W. Tampa Avenue, Venice; tel: 941-488-1115; www.venicestage.com. Community theater showing musicals, dramas, and comedies.

North Florida

Northwest Florida Ballet, 310 Perry Avenue Southeast, Fort Walton Beach; tel: 850-664-7787; www.nfballet.org. Regional dance company performing across the Panhandle.

Pensacola Little Theatre, 400 Jefferson Street, Pensacola; tel: 850-432-2042; www.pensacolalittletheatre.com. Presents regional plays and musical performances.

Pensacola Symphony Orchestra, 205 E Zaragoza Street, Pensacola; tel: 850-435-2533; www.pensacolasymphony.org. A regional company that performs at several locations.

Tallahassee Symphony Orchestra, 1020 E Lafayette Street, Tallahassee; tel: 850-224-0461; www.tallahasseesymphony.org. A regional orchestra performing concerts at the university.

NIGHTLIFE

Gainesville

Common Grounds, 210 S.W. 2nd Avenue; tel: 352-372-7320; www.commongroundslive.com. Provides a venue for a large number of bands from every music genre imaginable.

The University Club, 18 E. University Avenue; tel: 352-378-6814; www.ucnightclub.com. This is hands down one of the most entertaining clubs in Gainesville. The club has DJs playing dance music nightly and hosts everything from drag shows to karaoke.

Orlando

Antigua, 46 W. Church Street; tel: 407-649-4270; www.churchstreetbars.com. A multi-level venue with four bars where partygoers dance to thumping music. The lighting is intense, as is the 20ft (6 meter) waterfall prominently featured in the club. This place is definitely not recommended for the faint of heart.

Hard Rock, 6050 Universal Boulevard; tel: 407-351-5483; www.hardrock.com. Located in Universal Orlando's CityWalk, this musical venue hosts some of today's hottest music stars as well as some music legends. It is a small venue, with a 3,000-seat capacity, so advance ticket purchase is strongly recommended.

House of Blues, 1490 E. Buena Vista Drive; tel: 407-934-2583; www.houseofblues.com. Located in downtown Disney's West Side, this venue hosts some of the biggest names in music.

Tickets can sell out quickly for bigger shows, so check online and buy your tickets early.

Tallahassee

The Engine Room, 809 Railroad Avenue; tel: 850-222-8090; www.engineroomsounds.com. An all-ages establishment featuring live musical acts. Be aware high-heeled shoes are prohibited here and there is a $2 surcharge for under-age patrons.

The Moon, 1105 E. Lafayette Street; tel: 850-878-6900; www.moonevents.com. This has consistently been one of the most popular nightclubs in Tallahassee for years. The live bands and DJs provide an eclectic mix of music that keeps the local college students coming back for more.

Tampa

Centro Cantina, 1600 E. 8th Avenue; tel: 813-241-8588. This spot is best known for its live music and tequila selection of more than 30 varieties.

Club Prana, 1619 E. 7th Avenue; tel: 813-241-4139; www.clubprana.com. It's billed as the "Crown Jewel of Tampa's Nightlife." This European high-energy lounge has five levels of dance floors and bars, including "the sky bar" located on the club's rooftop.

SHOPPING

What to Buy

If you're into kitsch – plastic flamingo ashtrays, canned sunshine, orange

BELOW: Florida's strawberries are sweet.

perfume, and the like – you will find Florida a veritable treasure house. From roadside shacks to massive futuristic malls, stores carry plenty of traditional souvenirs, including fascinating examples of Haitian art, Art Deco, and Old Florida antiques, American Indian crafts, shells that forever smell of the sea, and folk art crafted from found objects.

For necessity shopping, there are convenience stores, drugstores, and supermarkets such as the Publix chain, found throughout Florida. Other shopping outlets, like shopping malls, contain the usual mix of department stores, boutiques, chain stores, and one-of-a-kind stores. Just ask the staff in your hotel for details of the best malls in your area. Hours vary, but most are open seven days a week.

Despite the abundance of citrus fruits, beef, fish, and other foods grown in Florida, much of it is exported out of the state and really good fresh, local food can be hard to find. There are Whole Foods stores in Winter Park, Orlando, and Tampa, but in many places organic produce can only be found in small stores with high prices. Farmers' markets can be found throughout the state with significantly lower prices; in addition to selling locally grown, often organic produce, meat, dairy, flowers, honey, fair-trade coffee and tea are also usually available. It's particularly good if you're staying in an efficiency or vacation rental and want to feel part of the local scene.

Where to Shop

Here are just a few of Florida's most famous shopping spots.

Miami

Bal Harbor Shops, 9700 Collins Avenue, Bal Harbor; tel: 305-866-0311; Mon–Sat 10am–9pm, Sun noon–6pm. An elegant shopping center with dozens of upscale boutiques.
Bayside Marketplace, 401 Biscayne Boulevard; tel: 305-577-3344; Mon–Thur 10am–10pm, Fri–Sat 10am–11pm, Sun 11am–9pm. A waterfront shopping and entertainment complex in downtown Miami with more than 150 shops.
Loehmann's Fashion Island, 18711 Biscayne Boulevard; Mon–Sat 10am–9pm, Sun noon–6pm. Miami is a great place to buy clothing, whether you are after designer labels or bargains. Loehmann's Fashion Island specializes in cut-rate designer clothes.
Seybold Building, 36 N.E. 1st Street #1021 Miami; tel: 305-374-7922; Mon–Sat 9am–6pm. Downtown Miami is known for its discount jewelry and electronics, and the Seybold Building has one of the best selections of gold, diamonds, and watches.
Streets of Mayfair, 2911 Grand Avenue, Coconut Grove; tel: 305-448-1700; Mon–Thur 11am–10pm, Fri–Sat 11am–midnight, Sun 11am–10pm. A small, attractive mall in the heart of Coconut Grove, with mainly fashion boutiques.

Key West

Fast Buck Freddies, 500 Duval Street; tel: 305-294-2007; daily 10am–6pm, extended Sat hours. A Key West institution, Freddie's is an emporium that specializes in the bizarre: sequined bikinis, battery-operated alligators, and fish-shaped shoes.
Haitian Art Company, 1100–1102 Truman Avenue; tel: 305-296-8932; www.haitian-art-co.com; daily 10am–8pm. One of the largest collections of paintings, sculptures, and papier-mâché art from Haiti in the US.
Key West Hand Print Fabrics and Fashions, 201 Simonton Street; tel: 305-294-9535; daily 9am–6pm. Watch as workers make brightly colored, hand-printed cotton and silk fabrics that are sold by the yard and made into casual clothing.

Cocoa Beach

Ron Jon Surf Shop, 4151 N. Atlantic Avenue; tel: 321-799-8888; www.ronjonsurfshop.com; 24 hours. Huge billboards along highways in central Florida advertise this local institution and beach bum's dream. Ron Jon sells bathing suits, surfboards, scuba equipment, suntan lotion, and lots of water toys.

Fort Lauderdale

Sawgrass Mills Factory Outlet Mall, 12,801 W. Sunrise Boulevard; tel: 954-846-2300; Mon–Sat 10am–9.30pm, Sun 11am–8pm. This is the largest factory outlet mall in the US, with about 300 stores, attracting around 20 million people a year. Shuttle buses ferry people from several Miami and Miami Beach hotels.

BELOW: Third Street in Naples is known for chic boutiques.

Swap Shop of Fort Lauderdale, 3291 W. Sunrise Boulevard; tel: 954-791-7927; Mon, Wed, Fri 9am–6pm, Thur 7am–6pm, Sat–Sun 7.30am–6.30pm. Not far from Sawgrass Mills, this bargain-hunter's paradise has rows and rows of stalls selling jewelry, sunglasses, and much, much more at rock-bottom prices. The carnival and free circus is an added attraction.

Fort Myers

The Shell Factory, 2787 N. Tamiami Trail, N. Fort Myers, tel: 941-995-2141; www.shellfactory.com; daily 9am–6pm. The world's largest collection of shells and coral, both natural and fashioned into jewelry, lamps, and baskets.

Orlando

Orange World, 5395 W. Irlo Bronson Memorial Highway, Kissimmee; tel: 407-396-1306; daily 8am–10.45pm. You can't miss this building: it's shaped like a gigantic orange. Inside is an assortment of freshly picked fruits, citrus candles, and orange blossom honey.

Orlando Premium Outlets, 8200 Vineland; tel: 407-238-7787; www.premiumoutlets.com; Mon–Sat 10am–11pm, Sun 10am–9pm. Over 100 stores including Anne Klein, Burberry, Armani, Barney's, Dior, and many more.

Prime Outlets Orlando, 5401 W. Oak Ridge Boulevard; tel: 407-352-9600; www.premiumoutlets.com; Mon–Sat 10am–11pm, Sun 10am–9pm. Outlets are the biggest shopping attractions in Florida and this is a bargain bonanza. This large, open-air mall is one of the best places to find designer clothes – Juicy Couture, Victoria's Secret, Saks Off Fifth Avenue, Ralph Lauren, Betsey Johnson, and many others. Save up to 75 percent off retail on jeans, sneakers, casual, and more.

SPORTS

Participant Sports

Florida is a great place in which to enjoy the outdoors and be active. Its large number of state parks, recreation areas, and nature preserves provide plenty of scope for walking, as well as swimming, fishing, cycling, boating, and so on. Being surrounded by water and with its numerous rivers, lakes, and springs, Florida has lots of activities that involve water. You can swim, either in the sea or in lovely freshwater pools inland. While not as good as California, surfing opportunities

abound along the Atlantic coast. Windsurfing is popular, but not all resorts rent out equipment. Divers and snorkelers will have a wonderful time exploring the coral reef off the Florida Keys, and glass-bottom boat tours give those who don't want to get their feet wet a taste of the rich marine life. Horseback riding is not as popular as in other parts of the US, but some parks have horses for rent and special trails. One of the best places to ride is the Payne's Prairie State Preserve near Gainesville.

Boating

Florida's waterways are suitable for boats of every shape and size. For many people in Florida, having a boat is as normal as having a car. There are hundreds of marinas, from those on the coast that provide all amenities to more basic ones in the interior. They are listed in *Florida Boating*, which is available free from Florida Game and Fresh Water Fish Commission, 620 S. Meridian Street, Tallahassee, FL 32399-1600; tel: 850-488-6257. For salt water, you must contact Florida Marine Patrol, 3900 Commonwealth Boulevard, MS 650, Tallahassee, FL 32399; tel: 850-488-5600.

The Intracoastal Waterway, a natural but dredged channel that runs parallel to much of the east coast and parts of the west coast of Florida, is very popular among boaters – partly because in many places it is protected from the open water by barrier islands. Another popular route is the Okeechobee Waterway, which runs for 135 miles (217km) along the St Lucie Canal from Stuart, on the east coast, across Lake Okeechobee, and onto the west coast near Fort Myers via the Caloosahatchee River. Several marinas rent out houseboats for exploring inland waterways. These can be like mini-apartments, fully equipped with everything from microwave ovens to color TVs.

Canoeing and Kayaking

You can canoe or kayak virtually anywhere in Florida, whether you want to paddle the testing Wilderness Waterway through the Everglades, paddle along the Blackwater River in the Panhandle, or explore the Peace River as it opens into Charlotte Harbor. You can rent canoes and kayaks in most parks, and there are plenty of private concessionaires, too. "Tubing" – floating down rivers on an inflated inner tube – has become a popular (and cheaper) alternative to canoeing and kayaking. One of the premier

tubing spots is the Ichetucknee River in north-central Florida.

Fishing

Fishing is more than a hobby for many Floridians. It is a way of life. Thousands of anglers travel from outside the state to enjoy the state's rich waters. **Saltwater fishing** requires no license, and there is no closed season on game fish. Florida's 8,000 miles (12,875km) of tidal coastline support over 600 varieties of saltwater fish. To catch them you can try anything from deep-sea fishing to surf casting or pier fishing. Grouper, amberjack, sea trout, mackerel, red snapper, sailfish, bonefish, and kingfish lurk in the deepest waters. In the late spring and summer, tarpon challenge deep-sea anglers off Tampa Bay, Marathon, Boca Grande Pass, and Bahia Honda Channel. The Keys, the lower East Coast, and upper Gulf regions are home to blue marlin. **Freshwater fishing** is outstanding in Florida, with its 30,000 lakes and miles of rivers and streams; licenses are inexpensive. Lake Okeechobee attracts few casual visitors, but it is very popular among anglers after bass. The St John's River is also big fishing territory. Angling is permitted in state parks and other preserves.

Golf

Florida is one of the top golfing states in the country. It is said that one out of every 10 golf games in the US takes place in Florida, and few states have more courses. With over 1,000 golf courses spread across the state to choose from, you are never far from a tee. Many of the courses are private, but there are enough public courses for out-of-towners who don't have a friend at a local country club. And don't think that because Florida is flat its courses lack challenge and rolling beauty. Many courses were designed by experts who have created beautiful man-made undulations, ponds, and rolling hills amid the greens. Green fees vary from over $75 per person at the more exclusive private courses to less than $20 per person at the public courses. At many, the fees are higher in winter months, when Northerners flock to the state for the game. For information on locations of golf courses, fees, and regulations, call the Florida Sports Foundation, tel: 850-488-8347, for a free copy of the *Official Florida Golf Guide*.

Jogging/Running

Sweat-drenched and sunburned joggers and runners are very much a part of the Florida landscape. Hundreds of miles of designated pathways are dedicated to the sport, and the flat and regular roads lend themselves to those who are willing to brave the traffic. If you are from a colder climate, take it easy the first time you are out running in Florida; the humidity and heat can easily dehydrate a non-acclimatized runner. Be sure to wear a hat and sunscreen and carry water. A few major and minor races take place in Florida, most in winter. For information on clubs, races, and paths, write to the Florida Athletics Congress at 1330 N.W. 6th Street, Gainesville, FL 32601.

Hiking

If you like to hike, you'll find numerous trails in city, county, and state preserves and parks throughout Florida. Trails are usually flat and sandy tracks surrounded by forests, lakes, rivers, and springs and, for some people, get a bit monotonous. The key is to learn about the natural history of the area you are in and watch for wildlife. Birding is particularly good along the coastline, especially the northwest Nature Coast, where trails have wider views over marshes and mudflats in the estuary to the Gulf of Mexico. Florida also has primitive and wilderness areas for hiking, such as Lake Wales Ridge and Disney Wilderness Preserve in central Florida, both run by The Nature Conservancy. And, of course, there are miles and miles of pristine sandy beaches, just perfect for long walks at sunset.

Tennis

As a major sponsor of international tennis matches, Florida attracts players from the world over. Many hotels have their own courts, with tennis instructors who offer lessons. Several state, county, and city parks have courts available to the public for free or a small fee. For information on over 7,000 courts in the state, contact the Florida Sports Foundation, tel: 850-488-8347.

Spectator Sports

Baseball

Currently the official spring training grounds of 18 major league teams, from February through March, Florida is the place to watch your favorite players warm up for the regular season. Visiting teams also meet in friendly games in the so-called Grapefruit League, which

Fishing Information

For information about fishing licenses and about limits on fish or closed seasons on certain species, contact the Florida Marine Patrol (tel: 850-488-1960) or write for the *Florida Fishing Handbook*, available from the Florida Game and Fresh Water Fish Commission at 2590 Executive City Circle, Ste 200, Tallahassee, FL 32399. A seven-day freshwater license costs around $16.50.

draws big crowds. Florida's own major-league baseball teams are the successful Florida Marlins and the Tampa Bay Devil Rays. The season runs from April through August. For further information on games, contact the Florida Sports Foundation, 1319 Thomaswood Drive, Tallahassee, FL 32312, tel: 850-488-8347.

Football

Florida has three teams in the National Football League: The Miami Dolphins, the Tampa Bay Buccaneers, and the Jacksonville Jaguars. The Miami Dolphins have competed five times in the Super Bowl, although they haven't won since 1973. Tampa Bay, however, won the championship for the first time in 2003. The season runs from September through December. College games are also big news, and draw almost as many

(highly partisan) fans as NFL matches. The best Florida teams are the Hurricanes of Miami, the Seminoles of Tallahassee, and the Gators from Gainesville. Tim Tebow, former quarterback for the Florida Gators, won the 2007 Heisman Trophy, the first sophomore to win the prestigious college football award. The top college games take place around the new year, including the Orange Bowl in Miami, the Citrus Bowl in Orlando, and the Gator Bowl in Jacksonville.

Pari-mutuels

Certain sports in the US are within the pari-mutuel betting system, which differs to the fixed-odds betting system in that the final payout is not determined until the pool of money bet is closed.

Greyhound Racing

Daytona Beach Kennel Club, 2201 Volusa Avenue, Daytona Beach, tel: 386-252-6484.
Flagler Dog Track, 401 N.W. 38th Court, Miami, tel: 305-649-3000.
Jacksonville Greyhound Racing, Highway 17, Jacksonville, tel: 904-646-0001.
Palm Beach Kennel Club, 1111 N. Congress Avenue, West Palm Beach, tel: 561-683-2222.
Pensacola Greyhound Park, 951 Dogtrack Road, Pensacola, tel: 850-455-8595.
St Petersburg Kennel Club, 10490 Gandy Boulevard, St Petersburg, tel:

BELOW: baseball fans watch pre-season action at Spring Training.

Learn Tennis in Style

Bradenton on the west coast of Florida is home to the famous Nick Bollettieri Tennis Academy, where stars such as Pete Sampras began their careers. Mere mortals can also have a go at nurturing their talent. As well as full-time courses, the Academy offers one-day sessions and also weekly training programs (for around $1,000). For more information, write to the Academy at 5500 34th Street West, Bradenton, FL 34210, or call 941-755-1000.

727-576-1361.
Sarasota Kennel Club, 5400 Bradenton Road, Sarasota, tel: 941-355-7744.
Tampa Greyhound Track: 8300 Nebraska Avenue N., Tampa, tel: 813-932-4313.
Washington County Kennel Club, Highway 79, Ebro, tel: 904-234-3943.

Harness Racing
Pompano Park, 1800 SW 3rd Street, tel: 954-972-2000. Year-round.

Jai-Alai Frontons
Fort Pierce Jai-Alai, tel: 772-464-7500. January–April.
Orlando Jai-Alai, tel: 407-339-6221. Year-round.
Ocala Jai-Alai, tel: 352-591-2345. January–March and June–September.
Dania Jai-Alai, tel: 954-927-2841. Year-round.
Miami Jai-Alai, tel: 305-633-6400. Year-round.

Thoroughbred Horse Racing
Gulfstream Park, 901 S. Federal Highway, Hallandale, tel: 954-454-7000. January–March.
Hialeah Park, 2200 E. 4th Avenue, tel: 305-885-8000. March–May.
Calder Race Track, 21001 N.W. 27th Avenue, Miami, tel: 305-625-1311. May–June.
Tampa Bay Downs, 12505 Racetrack Road, Tampa, tel: 813-855-4401. December–April.

Polo
Horse racing is a popular activity all over Florida, but polo is particularly big in southeast Florida, along the Gold Coast. The most famous polo clubs are in West Palm Beach, Boca Raton, and Lake Worth. The most prestigious tournament is the Challenge Cup, which takes place in Palm Beach in January. The season runs from December through April.

Sporting Events

January
Orange Bowl (Miami). The final game between Florida's two best college football teams. Tel: 305-341-4700. New Year's Day.
Annual PGA Tour Golf Event (Naples). Tel: 941-353-7767. Early January.
Speed Weeks (Daytona Beach). Three weeks of racing that culminate in the Daytona 500.

February
Islamorada Sport Fishing Festival. Tel: 305-664-2321. Mid-February.

March
Classics Day Vintage Motorcycle

Races and Supersport AMA Road Races (Daytona Beach). Tel: 615-851-3674. Early March.
Grand Prix of Miami. Tel: 305-230-7223. Early March. NASDAQ 100 Open (Key Biscayne). Florida's top tennis tournament, tel: 305-446-2701. Usually takes place in mid-March.
Doral Ryder Open Golf Tournament (Miami). Tel: 305-223-7060. Late March.
Tampa Bay Classic Equestrian Festival (Tampa). Late March.

April
Key West Fishing Tournament. Tel: 800-970-9056. April–November.
Ron Jon/Duke Boyd Easter Surfing Festival (Cocoa Beach). Early April.
PGA Seniors Championship Golf (West Palm Beach). Tel: 561-627-1800. Mid-April.
Gulf Coast Offshore Powerboat Races (Daytona). Tel: 954-618-2852. Late April.

May
Flagler Beach Fishing Regatta. Late May.

June
Annual Firecracker Beach Run (Daytona Beach). Late June.
Annual Ladies Billfish Tournament (Pensacola). Tel: 800-453-4638. Late June.

July
International Billfish Tournament. Tel: 850-453-4638. Early July.
Central Florida Soap Box Derby (Sanford). Tel: 407-330-5600. Mid-July.
Port of the Islands Annual Shark Tournament (Naples). Tel: 239-672-3133. Late July.

August
King Mackerel Tournament (Destin). Tel: 850-837-2506. Early August.

September
Power Boat Racing (Sanford). Late September.
Triathlon (Sarasota). Tel: 941-362-7339. Late September.

October
Destin Shark Fishing Rodeo. Tel: 850-837-6734. Early October.
Airboat Races and Festival (Okeechobee). Tel: 941-763-6464. Mid-October.
Annual Bonefish Tournament (Marathon). Tel: 305-743-2821. Mid-October.
World Championship Swamp Buggy Races (Naples). Tel: 800-897-2701. Late October.

Spring Training: Where to See Your Favorite Team

Below are US baseball team spring training locations. They're subject to change.
Atlanta Braves, Walt Disney World, tel: 407-939-4263.
Baltimore Orioles, Fort Lauderdale Stadium, Fort Lauderdale, tel: 954-776-1921.
Boston Red Sox, City of Palms Park, Fort Myers, tel: 941-334-4700.
Detroit Tigers, Marchant Stadium, Lakeland, tel: 863-686-8075.
Florida Marlins, Roger Dean Stadium, Jupiter, tel: 561-775-1818.
Houston Astros, Osceola County Stadium, Kissimmee, tel: 407-839-3900.
Minnesota Twins, Lee County Sports Complex, Fort Myers, tel: 800-338-9467.

New York Mets, Port St Lucie Complex, Port St Lucie, tel: 772-871-2115.
New York Yankees, Legends Field, Tampa, tel: 813-879-2244.
Philadelphia Phillies, Jack Russell Stadium, Clearwater, tel: 727-442-8496.
Pittsburgh Pirates, McKechnie Field, Bradenton, tel: 941-748-4610.
St Louis Cardinals, Roger Dean Stadium, Jupiter, tel: 561-775-1818.
Tampa Bay Devil Rays, Al Lang Field, St Petersburg, tel: 727-894-4773.
Toronto Blue Jays, Dunedin Stadium, Dunedin, tel: 727-733-0429.
Washington Nationals, Space Coast Stadium, tel: 321-633-9200.

TRANSPORTATION

ACCOMMODATIONS

ACTIVITIES

A – Z

November

Marathon Sailfish Tournament.
Tel: 904-743-6139. Late November.

December

Central Florida Sailfest (Sanford).
Early December.

CHILDREN'S ACTIVITIES

Orlando

Fun Spot, 5551 Del Verde Way; tel:
407-363-3867; www.funspot.tuten
graphics.com; daily 10am–midnight. A
place where kids and parents can
have fun together. Take a spin on the
go-karts, see how you fare on the
bumper boats, or see Orlando from
high atop the Ferris wheel. After the
rides the kids will want to get their
video game fix inside. Some of the
games are free with the purchase of
an armband, others will cost you
extra. Note: there are no refunds if the
weather is bad.
Gatorland, 14501 S. Orange
Blossom Trail; tel: 407-855-5498;
www.gatorland.co. Guests are greeted
by a giant green gator head at the
entrance, but you can also get an
up-close-and-personal view of what
a real Florida gator looks like. Sign
up to become a "Trainer for a Day"
and learn what it's like to soothe the
savage beast, or just watch someone
else do it. Additional packages are
available at an additional price.
Orlando Science Center, 777 E.
Princeton Street; tel: 407-514-2230;
www.osc.org; Sun–Tue 10am–5pm,
Thur–Sat 10am–5pm. The Orlando
Science Center is an exciting,
hands-on attraction that's fun for all
ages. Children will enjoy exhibits such
as Dino-digs, Kids Town, Science
Park, and H2Now. It's a great
alternative to a day at the parks.

The Panhandle

Shipwreck Island Waterpark, 12201
Hutchinson Boulevard, Panama City
Beach; tel: 850-234-3333; www.
shipwreckisland.com; Mid-April to Mid-
August. Price $28 and up. Looking for
a break from the ever-present Florida
sun? Then this is the perfect place to
cool down. The park offers guests
flumes, slides, a wave pool, a lazy
river, and a kiddie area.

Tampa Area

Bayshore Boulevard Trail, Bayshore
Boulevard; tel: 727-549-6099; daily

dawn–dusk. The 8.6 mile (13.8km)
trail is centrally located in downtown
Tampa, making it easy to access. It's
a great way for kids and adults alike
to burn off some excess energy or
just to see Tampa at a more leisurely
pace.
Great Explorations, 1926 4th Street
North, Tampa; tel: 727-821-8992;
www.greatexplorations.org; Mon–Sat
10am–4.30pm, Sun noon–4.30pm.
This is a hands-on museum where
children are encouraged to reach out
and touch every exhibit. Interactive
play areas include the touch tunnel,
climbing wall, veterinarian's office,
and a market.

SIGHTSEEING TOURS AND EXCURSIONS

Clearwater

Clearwater Gliders Segway, 609
Gulfview Boulevard; tel: 321-557-
2817; www.clearwatergliders.com; daily. A
Segway is a great way to travel while
seeing Clearwater's sights. The
packages are offered in one or two
hour sessions, and can be arranged
for individuals or groups.

Orlando

Blue Water Balloons, 1618 Norfolk
Court, Clermont; tel: 407-894-5040;
www.bluewaterbaloons.com; daily. Flights
daily at sunrise (5.30–6.30am) and
last approximately two hours.
International Heli Tours, 12651
International Drive; tel: 407-237-
8687; www.internationalhelitours.com;
daily. See Orlando in a way most
people never will, from the air.
Various lengths of tours available,
along with nightly firework tours and
"cupid tours" for the romantics.
Florida EcoSafaris, 4755 N
Kenansville Road, St Cloud; tel: 407-
957-9794 or 877-85-4EVER; www.
floridaecosafaris.com; daily. Experience

Florida just as the forefathers did, on
horseback. Or skim along the
treetops on Florida's first zipline
tour. If you prefer something a little
tamer, the Coach Tour takes you on a
relaxing ride through the
conservation preserve. **Scenic Boat
Tour**, 312 East Morse Boulevard;
407-644-4056; www.scenicboattours.
com. A 12 mile (19km) voyage, which
takes you on an hour-long adventure
through history.

St Petersburg

Pier Dolphin Cruises, 300 2nd Ave
SE #80; tel: 727-647-1538; www.
pierdolphincruises.net; daily. A narrated
90-minute cruise with guaranteed
dolphin sightings. You'll likely see
pelicans, ospreys, cormorants, and
manatees.

Tallahassee

The Wilderness Way, 3152
Shadeville Road; tel: 850-877-7200;
www.thewildernessway.net; daily. Kayaking
and eco-tours available on the
Wakulla River and the Apalachee
River Point.
Tallahassee Helicopter Tours,
3240 Capital Circle SW; tel: 850-
841-1111; www.tallahassee-helicopters.
com; daily by appointment. Air tours
include flybys of Wakulla Springs,
the downtown stadiums, and the
Nature Tour, which flies you over St
Marks National Wildlife Refuge and
is one of the most memorable ways
to see the land.

Tampa

Flats and Bay Fishing, 10913 North
Edison Avenue; tel: 813-727-8843;
www.flatsandbay.com; daily. Captain Steve
Betz is an experienced fishing captain
with US Coast Guard certification.
Captain Betz provides specific
instructions on how to best catch the
various species available in the
region.

BELOW: at Florida's Eco Safari guests can SkyCycle through the air.

A – Z

A HANDY SUMMARY OF PRACTICAL INFORMATION, ARRANGED ALPHABETICALLY

A dmission Charges

Admission is usually charged at both private and public museums and attractions, and national and state parks. As a rule, entrance fees are $10 or under per person, although very popular sites and special traveling exhibits at nationally known museums may charge as much as $20. Museums often offer free or reduced entrance fees certain days or evenings.

Consider buying multi-site passes for attractions in Orlando and Miami, if available. Local visitor centers and state welcome centers can assist you with planning, and many also offer discount coupons, with excellent deals on local attractions, hotels, and dining.

B udgeting for Your Trip

Allow $90–110 a night for good-quality hotels for two people, although really memorable hotels and bed-and-breakfasts tend to run closer to $150 or more a night. At the other end of the spectrum, Florida has many gorgeous Oceanside and forested campgrounds with full facilities for about $18 and up a night, and hostels and barebones motel lodgings can be found for less than $50.

You can probably get away with $30 a day per person for basic meals if you stick to diners, cafés, markets, and inexpensive restaurants and don't drink alcohol. Meals in better restaurants cost a lot more, but if you're determined to visit that famous high-end establishment and don't have the cash, one insider trick is to eat lunch there: you'll find many of the items on the dinner menu at much lower prices and still get to say you've eaten at a hip eatery.

Budget at least $4 per gallon for fuel for your rental car; most economy vehicles get over 30 miles per gallon. Trams, light rail, buses, and other public transportation in cities like Tampa and Miami are just a few dollars per ride, allowing you to get around for much less.

C hildren

Two things about traveling with children: First, be prepared, and second, don't expect to cover too much ground. Take everything you need, along with a general first-aid kit and those wonderful all-purpose traveler's aids: wet wipes and Ziplock baggies. If you need baby formula, special foods, diapers or medication, carry them with you.

Although Florida is known for its theme parks (which are geared toward children), much of the rest of the state can be an exciting destination for children of all ages. The many coastal towns offer beach opportunities, and exploring the Everglades can be an adventurous excursion. Make sure you have the appropriate gear whatever your destination. An extra bottle of water is always a good idea in the heat, and a high-factor sunscreen is essential with Florida's sunny weather.

Climate

Hurricanes

The hurricane season in Florida usually runs from June 1 through November 30. The number of Atlantic hurricanes in a given year can range from 2 to 20; on average one strikes Florida every two years.

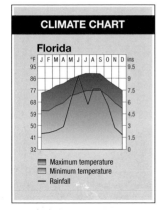

CLIMATE CHART

Florida

- ▨ Maximum temperature
- ☐ Minimum temperature
- — Rainfall

Still, the National Hurricane Center in Miami tracks each tropical storm very carefully, ready to issue evacuation orders if a hurricane is headed for the mainland.

Needless to say, tourists caught in Florida during an impending hurricane should immediately drop their plans and follow the National Weather Service bulletins on radio and television. A hurricane warning is usually issued 36 hours prior to predicted landfall; during this time high water and storm surges are highly possible. If warnings identify coastal areas where you are staying, be ready to evacuate to a designated shelter. Follow the blue road signs for your designated evacuation route.

Lightning

Florida is unofficially dubbed the "lightning capital of the country." The state records an average 10 deaths and 30 injuries annually. In just 1/1000th of a second, a bolt of lightning delivers a shock of 6,000–10,000 amps that can paralyze all body functions. If you see dark clouds and lightning nearby, take cover; many lightning victims are killed when getting in or out of cars. Boaters should head for the nearest place they can tie up and evacuate their vessel.

Rainfall

Florida's hottest months are also the rainiest. Thunderstorms occur with such regularity each day that you can set your watch by them. South Florida gets rain almost daily in June and July. The Everglades soak up nearly 9 inches (23cm) on average in June. In contrast with other parts of the US, there is little rain in November and December: only 2 inches (5cm) falls on average across the whole state.

Temperature

Average summer temperatures range from 86–91°F (30–33°C), with little variation from north to south. Due to the relatively mild winters, many South Florida homes do not have heating systems, and erratic winter weather in recent years (including occasional snow flurries in Miami) has caught residents unprepared. At night, temperatures "cool off" to between 70°F (21°C) and 80°F (26°C), which usually means you'll need to use air conditioning or a fan to sleep in comfort.

Sea breezes along the coast and daily thunderstorms can create more bearable temperatures in north Florida cities in summer. Having said that, Florida is equally well known for oppressive heat and humidity and extreme weather conditions, arising from its location in Hurricane Alley, the path of hurricanes forming in the Caribbean.

Crime and Safety

Florida doesn't have a squeaky-clean reputation when it comes to crime, and attacks committed against tourists ruin the state's idyllic vacation-in-the-sun image periodically. The authorities have come up with various safeguards designed to protect visitors. Many of these are aimed at motorists, particularly in Miami, where a number of violent assaults have occurred

when jet-lagged tourists disembarked long flights, missed the highway signs for Miami Beach, and found themselves in high-crime areas.

Car rental agencies have removed the special license plates that made rental cars an easy mark and have replaced them with standard-issue plates used by residents. In Miami, road signs have been improved and orange sunburst signs help guide visiting drivers along the main routes to and from the airport.

A little common sense goes a long way: Don't carry large sums of money or expensive video/camera equipment. Walk purposefully and don't make eye contact with unwelcome strangers or respond to come-ons. Don't travel alone at night. Ask the staff in your hotel for advice about areas that should be avoided.

Customs Regulations

You can bring into the US the following duty-free items: 1 liter of alcohol, if over 21 years of age; 200 cigarettes, 50 cigars (not Cuban) or 2kg of tobacco, if you're over 18; and gifts worth up to $100 ($800 for US citizens). Travelers with more than $10,000 in US or foreign currency, travelers checks, or money orders must declare these upon entry. Meats, fruits, vegetables, seeds, or plants (and many prepared foods made from them) can not be brought in to the country and must be disposed of in the bins provided

What to Do if a Hurricane Hits

During the storm

Stay indoors once the hurricane is buffeting your area. When the eye (the low-pressure area at the center of a hurricane) passes over, there will be a temporary lull in wind and rain for 30 minutes or more. Don't think it's over. When the eye has passed overhead, the storm will, in fact, resume – possibly with even greater force – from the opposite direction (hurricane weather systems rotate counterclockwise). Wait for word from the authorities before venturing out of your shelter.

If ordered to evacuate

Most coastal communities have detailed evacuation procedures in place. Evacuation route signs are permanently located along highways in many of these areas. Follow instructions and designated routes as quickly as possible. Take

blankets, flashlights, extra clothing, food, water, and medications. Leave behind pets (which are not allowed inside public shelters).

After the storm passes

Drive with caution when told to return home. Debris in streets can be a hazard. Roads in coastal areas may collapse if soil has been washed from beneath them. Steer clear of downed or dangling utility wires. Stay tuned to radio stations for news of emergency medical, food, housing, and other assistance. If you have been staying in a rented home, re-enter the building with caution and make temporary repairs to correct hazards and minimize further damage. Open windows and doors to air and dry the house. Be careful when dealing with matches or fires in case of gas leaks.

before entering. For more information, contact US Customs & Border Protection (tel: 877-227-5511; www. cbp.gov).

D isabled Travelers

Florida accommodations, attractions, restaurants, and parks welcome visitors with physical disabilities and impairments. From ADA-compliant hotels to on-loan beach chairs and even mobility-assisted snorkeling and hang-gliding, visitor services throughout Florida go to great lengths to make sure everyone enjoys barrier-free access to sun and fun.

Under the Americans with Disabilities Act (ADA), accommodations built after January 26, 1995, and containing more than five rooms must be usable by persons with disabilities. Older and smaller inns and lodges are often wheelchair-accessible. For the sight-impaired, many hotels provide special alarm clocks, captioned television services, and security measures. To comply with ADA hearing-impaired requirements, hotels have begun to follow special procedures; local agencies may provide TTY and interpretation services. Check with the front desk when you make reservations to ascertain to what degree the hotel complies with ADA guidelines. Ask specific questions regarding bathroom facilities, bed height, wheelchair space, and availability of services. To find more about accommodations in Florida, visit www. visitflorida.com/planning/prop_finder, where you can narrow your search to ADA-compliant properties.

Restaurants and attractions are required to build ramps for those with limited mobility. Many major attractions have wheelchairs for loan or rent. Some provide menus, visitor guides, and interpreters for hearing- and seeing-impaired guests. To search for ADA-compliant attractions, go to www.visitflorida.com/experience/attractions/listings.php.

For more information, read *Wheelchairs on the Go: Accessible Fun in Florida* by Michelle Stigleman and Deborah Van Brunt, www. wheelchairsonthego.com. For disability resources in Florida, contact the Clearinghouse on Disability (tel: 850-497-3423 or 877-232-4968). The Society for the Advancement of Travel for the Handicapped (tel: 212-447-7284; www.sath.org) publishes a quarterly magazine on travel for the disabled.

E lectricity

The United States uses 110–120 volts AC (60 cycles). If visiting from outside North America, you may require an electrical adapter for any electronics or appliances you want to bring.

Embassies and Consulates

Foreign embassies are located in Washington, DC. Phone numbers include Britain (tel: 202-462-1340); Germany (tel: 202-298-4000); France (tel: 202-944-6000); and Australia (tel: 202-797-3000).

Emergencies

Wherever you are in Florida, in case of emergency, dial 911 to contact the local police, fire, or ambulance service *(see also Driving p.359).*

G ay and Lesbian Travelers

Florida is in the conservative Bible Belt, and rural destinations away from the cities may be less welcoming of gay travelers. Keep a low profile in such areas to avoid any problems. Gay travelers receive a huge welcome in gay-friendly locales like South Beach (Miami), Fort Lauderdale, and Key West and to a slightly lesser extent in Orlando, where the annual Gay Day at Walt Disney World is very popular. For more information, contact South Beach Business Guild in Miami (tel: 305-534-3336), the Gay and Lesbian Community Centers in Fort Lauderdale (tel: 954-463-9005), Key West (tel: 305-292-3223), and Orlando (tel: 407-228-8722).

You'll find lots of information on GLBT activities in different parts of Florida at www.queeramerica.com. The Gay and Lesbian Yellow Pages (tel: 800-697-2812; www.glyp.com) offers regional information. Damron Company (tel: 415-255-0404 or 800-462-6654; www.damron.com) publishes guides aimed at lesbians and gay men and lists gay-owned and gay-friendly accommodations nationwide.

H ealth and Medical Care

Most visitors to Florida will encounter no health problems during their stay: sunburn and mosquito bites in summer are the main nuisance. If you need medical assistance, ask the reception staff at your hotel or consult the Yellow Pages for the physician or pharmacist nearest you (in large cities, there is usually a physician's referral service number listed). The larger hotels may have a resident doctor. If you need immediate attention, go to a hospital emergency room (ER).

There is nothing cheap about being sick in the US – whether it involves a simple visit to the doctor or a spell in a hospital. The initial fee charged by a good hospital might be $250, and that's before the additional cost of x-rays, medicines, examinations, and treatments have been added. Walk-in medical clinics are much cheaper than hospital emergency rooms for minor ailments. Foreign visitors are strongly advised to purchase travel insurance before leaving to avoid high urgent-care costs. Be sure you're covered for accidental death, emergency medical care, trip cancellation, and baggage or document loss.

Health Hazards
Insects
People aren't the only creatures attracted to Florida's sun and sand. The state has many different types of insect.
Cockroaches or Palmetto Bugs: These pests grow to sizes unheard of in colder climates and usually steer clear of people. Love bugs are another Florida nuisance, albeit a harmless one.
Fire ants: Another Florida nuisance, fire ants can deliver a painful bite feeling like a stinging sensation. Some people suffer allergic reactions (dizziness and/or nausea) from fire ant bites and should seek immediate medical attention.
Love Bugs (Bibinoid Flies): These insects are sometimes called "love bugs" because you usually find them "flying united" into your hair, face, or car's windshield. They don't bite and are considered harmless, although they can be annoying.
Mosquitoes and Sand Flies: Are notorious for ruining outdoor gatherings, especially at sunrise and sunset. The best combatant is repellent and a thick skin.

Sunburn
One of the most common sights in Florida is that of the over-baked tourist painfully trying to sit or walk without rubbing against anything. If you are determined to get a suntan, do so gradually. Always wear a broad-brimmed hat, good-quality sunglasses, and use a high-factor sunscreen (40 plus) to protect your skin. Even on overcast days the

sun's ultraviolet rays penetrate the clouds, giving you a false sense of safety. Dehydration and salt deficiency can lead to heat exhaustion, especially if taking medications or drinking alcohol or strong coffee. It's important to moderate these, drink plenty of water, and take time to acclimate to the heat and humidity if you aren't accustomed to it.

Heatstroke is a common problem for those from northern climates and is a potentially serious condition, so don't ignore the telltale signs. Long, uninterrupted periods of exposure to high temperatures can lead to heatstroke, which means that the body's core temperature rises to dangerous levels, and its normal cooling system – reddening and sweating – is overwhelmed. If you feel dizzy and fuzzy-brained, feel muscle weakness and start to stumble, and your skin has become pale and dry rather than red and sweaty, immediately begin spraying yourself with water or, better yet, pour it on. To head off problems, keep major arteries in your neck cool by wearing a wet bandanna or cotton shirt with a collar.

Internet

The modems of many foreign laptops and handheld computers won't work in the US. You may need to purchase a global modem before leaving home or a local PC-card modem once you arrive in the US. For more information, log on to www.teleadapt.com. There are now numerous cyber cafés and business centers, such as Kinko's, in the US, where you can pick up email. Most charge a fee for Internet access, either on their computer or your laptop. At Starbucks coffeehouses, for example, you must first purchase a T-Mobile Hot Spot pass (currently $9.95 day), before being able to log on; other coffeehouses and restaurants offer free Internet access as a customer incentive. You'll have fewer options in rural areas, but many lodgings offer dial-up high-speed (DSL) or wireless Internet (Wi-fi) hot spots. Public libraries often offer free Wi-fi.

Media

Newspapers

Daily newspapers roll off the presses in every large Florida city. The most widely read is the *Miami Herald*, but papers like the *Tampa Tribune* and

Orlando Sentinel also have a reasonably wide circulation. There are several Spanish-language newspapers, and the *Miami Herald* has a very popular Spanish language section, *El Nuevo Heraldo*. You can usually pick up *USA Today* from newspaper dispensers in the street or receive a free copy at certain hotel chains. Other national newspapers available in dispensers or good newsstands and bookstores include the *New York Times*, *Washington Post*, and *Wall Street Journal*. If you are planning on staying in a particular area, check out the local newspaper ahead of time for advance information. Most newspapers today have online equivalents.

Television

All major cities have stations affiliated with major networks, local stations, and a vast number of cable hookups and satellite dish offerings. Hotel rooms usually have cable television, but you often have to pay to watch movies (Pay Per View). Newspapers give daily and weekly information on TV and radio programs, and you can view an on-screen program guide for TV.

Money

American dollars come in bills of $1, $5, $10, $20, $50, and $100, all the same size. The dollar is divided into 100 cents. Coins come in 1 cent (penny), 5 cents (nickel), 10 cents (dime), 25 cents (quarter), 50 cents (half-dollar), and $1 denominations. There is no Value Added Tax (VAT) in the US, but cities charge a sales tax, usually around 7–8 percent of sale. Car rental companies charge both sales tax and service fees.

Foreign visitors are advised to take US dollar travelers checks to Florida since exchanging foreign currency – whether as cash or checks – can prove problematic. An increasing number of banks, including First Union National Bank, Nations Bank, and Sun Bank chains, offer foreign exchange facilities, but this practice is not universal. Some department store chains offer foreign currency exchange. Most shops, restaurants, and other establishments accept travelers checks in US dollars and will give change in cash. Alternatively, checks can be converted into cash at the bank.

Credit Cards are very much part of life in Florida, as in other parts of the US. They can be used to pay for just

about anything. It is very common for car rental firms and hotels to take an imprint of your card as a deposit. If you rent beach equipment or bicycles you man have to leave your card at the counter. Car rental companies may oblige you to pay a large deposit in cash if you do not have a credit card.

You can also use your credit card to withdraw cash from ATMs (Automated Teller Machines). Before you leave home, make sure you know your PIN and find out which ATM system will accept your card. The most widely accepted cards are Visa, American Express, MasterCard, Diners Club, Japanese Credit Bureau, and Discovery Card.

Opening Hours

Stores are often open seven days a week and tend to stay open into the evening, especially in tourist areas. Government offices are usually open only on weekdays from 8am or 9am to 4pm or 5pm. Post offices are usually open weekdays from 8am to 5pm and have limited hours on Saturday morning.

Postal Services

The opening hours of federal post offices vary between central, big-city branches, and those in smaller towns or suburbs, but all are open Monday to Friday and some are also open on Saturday mornings. Drugstores and hotels usually have a small selection of stamps. There are stamp-vending machines in the lobbies of most post offices as well as Automated Postal Centers that allow you to use a credit card to ship mail. As of April 17, 2011, first-class domestic rates are 44 cents for 1oz with 20 cents for each additional ounce. Postcards are 29 cents each. Postage for overseas letters is 98 cents for 1oz; 80 cents to Mexico and Canada. Postage for overseas postcards is currently 98 cents; 80 cents to Canada and Mexico.

Large envelopes over 13 ounces must now be sent by two- to three-day Priority Mail in the US, or Media Mail if the envelope contains printed materials. The fastest service offered by the post office is Express Mail, which guarantees next-day delivery to most destinations within the US, and delivery within two to three days to foreign destinations by Global Express Mail. Private courier services offering overnight and two-day delivery are usually the most

reliable, although more expensive than the US Post Office. Ground delivery, taking an average of five days, is very popular. Telephone numbers for the main courier services are:
FedEx: 800-238-5355
DHL: 800-345-2727
UPS: 800-742-5877

Public Holidays

Public holidays in the US include: New Year's Day (January 1), Martin Luther King's Birthday (January 15), President's Day (third Monday in February), Memorial Day (last Monday in May), Independence Day (July 4), Labor Day (first Monday in September), Columbus Day (second Monday in October), Veteran's Day (November 11), Thanksgiving (fourth Thursday in November), and Christmas Day (December 25).

T elephones

In this era of cell phones, you'll find fewer public telephones in hotel lobbies, restaurants, drugstores, garages, roadside kiosks, convenience stores, and other locations throughout the state. The cost of making a local call from a payphone for three minutes is 35–60 cents. To make a long-distance call from a payphone, use either a prepaid calling card, available in airports, post offices, and a few other outlets, or your credit card, which you can use at any phone: dial 1-800-CALLATT, key in your credit card number, and wait to be connected. In many areas, local calls have now changed to a 10-digit calling system, using the area code. Watch out for in-room connection charges in the more upscale hotels: it's cheaper to use a payphone in the lobby.

Cell phones
American cell phones use GSM 1900 or CDMA 800, a different frequency from other countries. Only foreign phones operating on GSM 1900 will work in the US. You may be able to take the SIM card from your home phone, install it in a rented (or consider buying a budget model after you have arrived) cell phone in the US, and use it as if it's your own cell phone. Ask your wireless provider about this before leaving. Cell phones can be rented for about $45 a week in the US. Also available are GSM 1900 compatible phones with prepaid calling time, such as those offered by T-Mobile

(www.t-mobile.com). Be aware that you probably won't be able to pick up a signal in remote rural areas, such as the Everglades and Keys in South Florida. Check the coverage before starting out.

Time Zone

The continental US is divided into four time zones. From east to west, later to earlier, they are Eastern Standard Time, Central Standard Time, Mountain Standard Time, and Pacific Standard Time, each separated by one hour. Florida is on Eastern Standard Time (EST), five hours behind Greenwich Mean Time. On the first Sunday in April, Floridians set the clock ahead one hour in observation of daylight saving time. On the last Sunday in October, the clock is moved back one hour to return to standard time.

Tipping

Service personnel expect tips in Florida. The accepted rate for baggage handlers is $1 per bag. For others, including taxi drivers and waiters, 15–20 percent is the going rate, depending on the level and quality of service. Sometimes tips are automatically included in restaurant bills when dining in groups of six or more. In high tourism areas 15–20 percent may be automatically added to any restaurant bill. In a hotel, count on around $1 per bag or suitcase handled by porters and bellboys, and 15–20 percent for room service. You should tip a doorman if he holds your car or performs other services. It is not necessary to tip chambermaids unless you stay several days, then budget about $1 a day. Some resorts include a mandatory "resort fee" that covers the service for the duration of your stay, regardless of your use of the various resort amenities.

Tourist Information

Information is available from various outlets in Florida. Most cities have a Convention and Visitors Bureau (CVB), while elsewhere you must rely on the local chamber of commerce. State and national parks normally have excellent visitor centers, which dispense information and maps and offer ranger-guided talks and walks.
Below is a list of tourist information offices in Florida:
Bradenton Convention and Visitors Bureau

PO Box 1000, Bradenton, FL 34206-1000
Tel: 941-729-9177
www.annamariaisland-longboatkey.com
Daytona Beach Convention and Visitors Bureau
126 E. Orange Avenue, Daytona Beach, FL 32114
Tel: 800-544-0415
www.daytonabeach.com
Everglades City Area Chamber of Commerce
PO Box 130, Everglades City, Tel: 239-695-3172
www.evergladeschamber.net
Everglades National Park Headquarters
40001 SR 9336, Homestead, Tel: 305-242-7700
www.nps.gov/ever
Big Cypress National Preserve Headquarters
33100 Tamiami Trail East, Ochopee
Tel: 239-695-1201
www.nps.gov/bicy
Greater Fort Lauderdale Convention and Visitors Bureau
100 East Broward Boulevard, Suite 200
Tel: 954-765-4466 or 800-227-8669
www.sunny.org
Lee County Convention and Visitors Bureau
12800 University Drive, Suite 550
Tel: 239-338-3500 or 800-237-6444
www.fortmyers-sanibel.com
Fort Myers Chamber of Commerce Visitor Center
2310 Edwards Drive, PO Box 9289
Tel: 239-332-3624 or 800-366-3622
www.fortmyers.org
Emerald Coast Convention and Visitors Bureau
1540 Miracle Strip Parkway Fort
Tel: 850-651-7131
www.emeraldcoastfl.com
Alachua County Visitors and Convention Bureau
30 E. University Avenue, Gainesville
Tel: 352-374-5260 or 866-778-5002
www.visitgainesville.com
Islamorada Chamber of Commerce
MM 83.2, PO Box 915, Islamorada
Tel: 305-664-4503
www.islamoradachamber.com
Jacksonville and Jacksonville Beach Convention and Visitors Bureau
200 N Laura Street, Suite 102
Tel: 904-798-9111 or 800-733-2668
www.jaxcvb.com
Key Largo Chamber of Commerce
106000 Overseas Highway
Tel: 305-451-4747 or 800-822-1088
www.keylargochamber.org
Florida Keys and Key West Tourism Development Council
PO Box 1146, Key West

TRANSPORTATION
ACCOMMODATIONS
ACTIVITIES
A – Z

ABOVE: a Miccosukee Indian family in the Everglades.

17001 Panama City Beach Parkway, Panama City
Tel: 850-233-5070 or 800-722-3224
www.visitpanamacitybeach.com
Pensacola Visitor Information Center
1401 E. Gregory Street, Pensacola=
Tel: 850-434-1234 or 800-874-1234
www.visitpensacola.com
St Augustine Chamber of Commerce
1 Riberia Street, St Augustine
Tel: 904-829-5681
www.stjohnscountychamber.com
St Petersburg/Clearwater Area Convention and Visitors Bureau
13805 58th Street North, Suite 2-200, Clearwater
Tel: 727-464-7200 or 877-352-3224
www.visitstpeteclearwater.com
Sanibel/Captiva Islands Chamber of Commerce
1159 Causeway Road, Sanibel Island
Tel: 239-472-1080
www.sanibel-captiva.org
Sarasota Convention and Visitors Bureau
701 N. Tamiami Trail, Sarasota
Tel: 941-957-1877 or 800-348-7250
www.sarasotafl.org
Stuart/Martin County Chamber of Commerce
1650 S Kanner Highway, Stuart
Tel: 772-287-1088
www.stuartmartinchamber.org
Tallahassee Convention and Visitors Bureau
106 E. Jefferson Street, Tallahassee
Tel: 850-413-9200 or 800-628-2866
www.visittallahassee.com
Tampa/Hillsborough Convention and Visitors Bureau
401 E Jackson Street, Suite 2100
Tel: 813-223-1111 or 800-44-TAMPA
www.visittampabay.com
Indian River County Tourist Council
1216 21st Street, Vero Beach
Tel: 772-567-3491
www.indianriverchamber.com

Tel: 305-296-1552 or 800-771-5397
www.fla-keys.com
Key West Chamber of Commerce
510 Greeme Street, First Floor, Key West
Tel: 305-294-2587
www.keywestchamber.org
Marathon Chamber of Commerce
MM 53, 12222 Overseas Highway, Marathon
Tel: 305-743-5417 or 800-262-7284
www.floridakeysmarathon.com
Greater Miami Convention and Visitors Bureau
701 Brickell Avenue, Suite 2700
Tel: 305-539-3000 or 800-933-8448
www.miamiandbeaches.com
Miami Beach Chamber of Commerce
1920 Meridian Avenue, Suite 1, Miami
Tel: 305-674-1300
www.miamibeach.com
Art Deco Welcome Center
1001 Ocean Drive, PO Box 190180, Miami Beach
Tel: 305-531-3484
Coral Gables Chamber of Commerce
224 Catalonia Avenue, Coral Gables

Tel: 305-446-1657
www.gableschamber.org
Naples Visitor and Information Center
900 Fifth Avenue South, Naples
Tel: 239-262-6141
www.napleschamber.org
Naples, Marco Island, Everglades CVB
3050 Horseshoe Drive North, Suite 218, Naples
Tel: 239-403-2384 or 800-688-3600
www.paradisecoast.com
Orlando/Orange County Convention and Visitors Bureau
6700 Forum Drive, Suite 100
Tel: 407-363-5800 or 800-972-3304
www.orlandoinfo.com
Walt Disney World Company
PO Box 10000, Lake Buena Vista
Tel: 407-939-6244
http://disneyworld.disney.go.com
Palm Beach/West Palm Beach Chamber of Commerce
1555 Palm Beach Lakes Boulevard, West Palm Beach
Tel: 800-554-7256
www.palmbeachfl.com
Panama City Convention and Visitors Bureau

V isas and Passports

Foreign travelers to the US (including those from Canada and Mexico) must carry a passport; a visa is required for visits of more than 90 days. A return ticket is also normally required, and you may be asked to show it at immigration control. For the most current information, contact the US Department of Homeland Security at www.dhs.gov.

W eights and Measures

Despite efforts to convert to metric, the US still uses the Imperial System of weights and measures.

FURTHER READING

Fiction

Carl Hiassen: a *Miami Herald* journalist, Hiassen writes excellent comic thrillers set in Florida. They include: *Native Tongue*, which pokes fun at theme parks, and *Lucky You*, a twisted, wacky look at lottery winners.
Ernest Hemingway: many of "Papa's" novels and short stories were written in the 10 years he lived in Key West, but *To Have and Have Not* is the only one set in the town.
James W. Hall: the author of excellent Florida-based thrillers, including *Tropical Freeze, Bones of Coral, Hard Aground*, and *Mean Tide*.
James Weldon Johnson: raised in Jacksonville, son of Florida's first black female teacher, Johnson was part of the Harlem Renaissance. His *Autobiography of an Ex-Colored Man*, a fictional account of a biracial man, was originally published anonymously.
John D. MacDonald: one of Florida's most prolific novelists, MacDonald wrote many color-themed yarns about his detective Travis McGee, including *The Deep Blue Goodbye, The Dreadful Lemon Sky*, and *Dress Her in Indigo*.
Marjorie Kinnan Rawlings: the former New Yorker's 1942 work *Cross Creek* celebrates her colorful neighbors in the eponymous backcountry hamlet. *The Yearling*, the story of a boy and his fawn, won her a Pulitzer Prize.
Frank Slaughter: *Storm Haven, East Side General*, and *In a Dark Garden* are all novels with a Florida backdrop from another of the state's tale-spinners.
Harriet Beecher Stowe: The famed author of the 1851 antislavery serial novel *Uncle Tom's Cabin* also wrote travel essays that boosted Florida tourism in the Victorian steamboat era.
Zora Neale Hurston: one of Florida's leading black authors, Hurston is best known for *Their Eyes were Watching God*, about the devastating 1928 hurricane.

Natural and Cultural History

Birds of Florida by Frances W. Hall. The definitive guide to Florida's feathered inhabitants.

Diving Guide to Underwater Florida by Ned DeLoach. An excellent guide to Florida's underwater world.
Dream State: Eight Generations of Swamp Lawyers, Conquistadors, Confederate Daughters, Banana Republicans, and other Florida Wildlife by Diane Roberts. The title of this engaging book by a Florida native says it all!
Everglades: River of Grass by Marjorie Stoneman Douglas. This seminal work describing the magic of the Everglades contributed to the creation of Everglades National Park.
The Florida Keys: A History and Guide by Joy Williams and Robert Carawan. This book provides a good introduction to the history of the islands.
Life on Mars: Gangsters, Runaways, Exiles, Drag Queens and Other Aliens in Florida by Alexander Stuart. An entertaining look at Florida, giving an insight into the motley bunch of people who live there.

The Magic Kingdom: Walt Disney and the American Way of Life by Steven Watt. A highly readable account of Walt's life and analysis of his huge influence on US – and world – culture.
Miami Then and Now by Carolyn Klepser and Arva Moore Parks. A look at the historical and contemporary development of Florida's famous city.
The Tropic of Cracker by Al Burt. An insightful and diverting look at past and future Florida.
Kerouac in Florida: Where the Road Ends by Bob Kealing, Arbiter Press (2004). A well-written account of the famed writer's secretive Florida life.
A Naturalist in Florida: A Celebration of Eden by Archie Carr. Poetic essays about Florida's extraordinary natural history by the famed UF professor.
The Hiking Trails of Florida's National Forests by Johnny Molloy. A vividly descriptive guide to Florida's hiking trails, filled with facts and tidbits.
Some Kind of Paradise: A Chronicle of Man and the Land in Florida by Mark Derr. A fascinating history, with an emphasis on the impact of human society on the environment.
Team Rodent by Carl Hiassen. A scathing rant against all things Disney.
Visiting Small-Town Florida by Bruce Hunt. An insightful and interesting look into small-town Florida.

Other Insight Guides

City Guide titles include *New York City, San Francisco*, and *Las Vegas*, which provide detailed and local insight into the vibrant cities of the USA. Laminated, easy-fold **Insight Flexi-Maps** contain useful travel details. Titles include *Florida, New York, San Francisco*, and *Orlando*.
Insight Step by Step Guides provide precise itineraries and recommendations from a local, expert writer for dining, lodgings, and sightseeing; titles include *Boston*, and *New England*.
Insight Smart Guides are packed with information, arranged in a unique A–Z format that helps you find what you want quickly and simply. Titles include *Orlando* and *San Francisco*.

ART AND PHOTO CREDITS

Dawn Ashley 111B
José Azel 83
Charles E. Bennett 28, 30, 35, 39
Bettmann/Corbis 46T
Courtesy The Breakers 364
Steven Brooke/Museum of
Contemporary Art, North Miami
105T
Busch Entertainment Corp. 54, 79
Ecosafaris 382Frederick Dau 36R
Court4esy Disney World 245,
245T, 246, 253
Discover Dominica Authority 71
Fairchild Tropical Botanic Garden
111T,
Courtesy Fantasy of Flight 271
Najlah Feanny/Corbis 50
Ricardo Ferro 190
Florida Division of Tourism 47
Tont Firriolo 267
BLRaymond Gehman/Corbis 55
Gaston de Cardenas 102
Courtesy Granfd Bohemian 264B
Greater Miami Convention &
Visitors Bureau 27T, 98, 102B
107BR, 114, 129
Clare Griffiths 207
APA/Alex Havret 115
Gavin Hellier/Robert Harding
World Imagery/Corbis 172
Henry Morrison Flagler Museum
48
Historical Museum of Southern
Florida/Tony Arruza 26B
Courtesy Hotel Victor
Istockphoto 220
Courtesy Legoland 270T
Library of Congress 31, 37, 38B,
40, 41, 42, 43L, 43R, 44, 45, 46B,
48-49, 51, 53B, 256B 273
Courtesy Maitland House 269T
Mennello Museum of American
Folk Art 266B
Miami Herald 106BL
MOca/Steven Brooke 105B
nasa/Kennedy Space Center 27B,
196, 197, 202, 203T, 203BL,
203BR, 204T, 204B, 206T, 206B
Courtesy National Centre for Birds
of Prey 268B
APA/Abraham Nowitz 2-3, 50,
56-57, 58, 84-85, 94, 96-97, 99,
100, 101, 104T, 104B, 106BR,
107BL, 107T, 108T, 108B, 109T,
109B, 110T, 110B, 112T, 112B,
113B, 118, 119, 121T, 121B, 122T,
122B, 123L, 123R, 124T, 124B,
125T, 125B, 126, 128, 182, 184,
186T, 186B, 187T, 188, 189T, 189B,
191B, 191T, 195
APA/Richard Nowitz 1, 2, 4T, 4B, 5,
8B, 9T, 10-11, 12-13, 14-15, 16,
17T, 17B, 18, 19, 20, 21, 22, 23,
24, 29, 32, 36L, 59, 60, 61, 62, 63,
66, 67, 68L, 68R, 69, 70, 73, 74,

75, 77R, 80, 81, 82, 86-87,
88-89, 90, 91T, 91B, 132, 133,
134, 135T, 135B, 136T, 136B, 137,
138, 139T, 139B, 140T, 140B, 141T,
141B, 142T, 142B, 143, 146, 147,
148, 150T, , 151, 152, 153T, 154,
155, 158, 159, 161T, 161BR,
161BL, 162T, 162B, 163, 164T,
164B, 165T, 165B, 166, 167, 168-
169, 170, 171T, 171B, 173, 175B,
177T, 177B, 178T, 178B, 179T,
179BL, 180, 193T, 193B, 198,
199T, 199BL, 199BR, 200T, 200B,
201L, 201R, 205L, 208, 209, 210T,
210B, 211T, 211B, 213T, 213B,
214T, 214B, 215T, 215B, 216T,
216B, 2197, 217B, 218T, 218B,
219T, 219BR, 221T, 221BL, 222T,
222B, 224T, 223B, 224, 225, 226-
227, 228, 229T, 229B, 230, 231,
234, 235T, 236, 239, 240T, 240BL,
240BR, 241, 242, 247T, 247B,
248T, 248-49, 250T, 250B, 251,
252, 254, 257, 258T, 258BL, 260T,
260B, 267TBL, 266BR, 268T, 269B,
269BL, 269BR, 272T, 272B, 273T,
274, 275, 276, 278-279, 280,
281T, 281B, 282, 283, 284, 285T,
285BL, 285BR, 286T, 286B, 287T,
287B, 288, 289, 290, 291, 292,
293, 294, 295T, 295B, 296B, 297T,
297BL, 298T, 298B, 299T, 299B,
300T, 300B, 301T, 301B, 302, 306,
307, 309T, 309B, 310T, 310B, 311T,
311B, 312T, 312B, 313T, 313B,
314T, 314B, 315, 316T, 316B, 317T,
317BL, 318T, 318B, 319T, 319B,
320, 324-325, 326, 327T, 327B,
328, 329, 330, 331T, 331B, 332T,
332BL, 332BR, 333, 334T, 334B,
335T, 335B, 336T, 336B, 337, 338,
339, 340T, 340B, 341T, 341BR,
342, 343, 344T, 344B, 345T, 345B,
346B, 347T, 347B, 348, 349T,
349B, 350T, 350B, 351, 352T,
352BL, 352BR, 353T, 353B, 354,
355, 356, 360, 372, 375, 378, 380,
381, 382, 388
Palm Beach County Convention &
Visitors Bureau 183, 187B, 194
Mike Parry/Tom Stack &
Associates 205R
Timothy O'Keefe 267BR
Orange County Regional History
Center 23T
Orlando Museum of Art 266B,
266T
Rubell Family Collection, Miami
59, 103T, 103B
Courtesy Peabody Hotel 263B
Salvador Dalí Museum 296T
Courtrsy Ripley's believe It Or Not
263T
Courtesy Seaworld 72, 76, 259,
261, 262T, 262B,

Courtesy St Augustine 262
State Library and Archives of
Florida 38L, 150BL, 179BR, 221BR,
297BR, 317BR
Steinhatchee Landing 373
Topfoto 35
Universal Orlando 8T, 9B, 10T, 77,
78, 257, 258BR, 277, 365
Gregory Wrona 153, 175T, 176,
181, 185T, 185B, 190T, 192, 192T,
192B, 264T, 358

PHOTO FEATURES

6-7: Clockwise from bottom left:
Richard Nowitz, Universal Orlando,
Richard Nowitz, Richard Nowitz,
nasa, Richard Bickel/Corbis,
Gregory Wrona, Salvador Dalí
Museum, AWL Images, George
Tiedemann/GT Images/Corbis

62-63: Clockwise from bottom left:
Mark Read, Robert Harding,
Photolibrary, Istockphoto, Mark
Read, Richard Nowitz, NASA

116-117: Clockwise from bottom
left: Abraham Nowitz, (statue)
Superstock, Abraham NowitzVisit
Florida, Robert Harding, Visit
Florida

130-131: Clockwise from bottom
left: TIPS Images, AWL Images,
Historical Association of Southern
Florida, Living Dreams, Inc, AWL
Images

144-145: Clockwise from bottom
left: Istockphoto, Richard Nowitz,
Istockphoto) Richard Nowitz

156-157: Clockwise from bottom
left: Istockphoto, Fotolia,
Istockphoto, Fotolia Istockphoto

304-305: Clockwise from bottom
left: Richard Nowitz, Mark Read,
Richard Nowitz

322-323: All photos Richard
Nowitz except 322BL Getty Images,
323TR Bettmann/Corbis

Map Production:
Original cartography Berndtson &
Berndtson, updated by Apa
Cartography Dept.

© 2011 Apa Publications (UK) Limited

Production: Tynan Dean, Linton
Donaldson, Rebeka Ellam

INDEX

Main references are in bold type

N

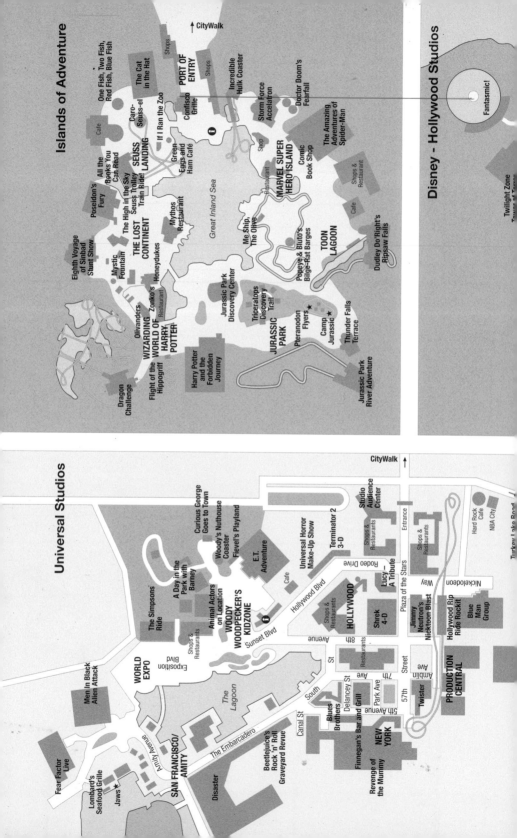

Islands of Adventure

↑ CityWalk

Shops

One Fish, Two Fish, Red Fish, Blue Fish

The Cat in the Hat

PORT OF ENTRY

Shops

Confisco Grille

Incredible Hulk Coaster

Cafe

Caro-Seuss-el

If I Ran the Zoo

Storm Force Accelatron

Doctor Doom's Fearfall

All the Books You Can Read

SEUSS LANDING

Green Eggs and Ham Cafe

Shop

Poseidon's Fury

The High in the Sky Seuss Trolley Train Ride

THE LOST CONTINENT

MARVEL SUPER HERO ISLAND

The Amazing Adventures of Spider-Man

Comic Book Shop

Eighth Voyage of Sinbad Stunt Show

Mythos Restaurant

Restaurant

Shops & Restaurant

Mystic Fountain

Honeydukes

Great Inland Sea

Me Ship, The Olive

Cafe

Olivanders

Zonko's

Restaurant

Popeye & Bluto's Bilge-Rat Barges

Dudley Do-Right's Ripsaw Falls

WIZARDING WORLD OF HARRY POTTER

Flight of the Hippogriff

Jurassic Park Discovery Center

Triceratops Discovery Trail

TOON LAGOON

Dragon Challenge

Harry Potter and the Forbidden Journey

Pteranodon Flyers ★

Camp ★ Jurassic

JURASSIC PARK

Thunder Falls Terrace

Jurassic Park River Adventure

Disney - Hollywood Studios

Twilight Zone Tower of Terror

Fantasmic!

Universal Studios

CityWalk ↑

Curious George Goes to Town

Woody's Nuthouse Coaster

Fievel's Playland

Universal Horror Make-Up Show

Terminator 2 3-D

Studio Audience Center

Shops & Restaurants

Entrance

Hard Rock Cafe

NBA City

The Simpsons Ride

A Day in the Park with Barney

Animal Actors on Location

E.T. Adventure

Cafe

Rodeo Drive

Shops & Restaurants

Way

Nickelodeon

Shops & Restaurants

WOODY WOODPECKER'S KIDZONE

Hollywood Blvd

HOLLYWOOD

Lucy – A Tribute

Plaza of the Stars

Jimmy Neutron's Nicktoon Blast

Hollywood Rip Ride Rockit

Blue Man Group

Men In Black Alien Attack

WORLD EXPO

Exposition Blvd

Sunset Blvd

Shops & Restaurants

Shrek 4-D

8th Avenue

Shops & Restaurants

St

Restaurants

7th Ave

Park Ave

Street

Amblin Ave

57th

Twister

PRODUCTION CENTRAL

The Lagoon

South

Avenue

Delancey St

5th Avenue

Canal St

Fear Factor Live

Men In Black Alien Attack

Lombard's Seafood Grille

Jaws ★

SAN FRANCISCO/ AMITY

Amity Avenue

The Embarcadero

Beetlejuice's Rock 'n' Roll Graveyard Revue

Disaster

Blues Brothers

Finnegan's Bar and Grill

NEW YORK

Revenge of the Mummy

Turkey Lake Road